PENGUIN BOOKS
BASEBALL BABYLON

DAN GUTMAN is the author of *It Ain't Cheatin' If You Don't Get Caught: Scuffing, Corking, Spitting, Gunking, Razzing, and Other Fundamentals of Our National Pastime* (1990), *I Didn't Know You Could Do* That *with a Computer!* (1986), and *The Greatest Games* (1984). He writes a syndicated column about technology, and his articles have appeared in *Newsweek*, *Success*, *USA Today*, the *Miami Herald*, the *Detroit Free Press*, the *Los Angeles Daily News*, and many other publications. He lives in Haddonfield, New Jersey, with his wife, Nina Wallace, and their son, Sam.

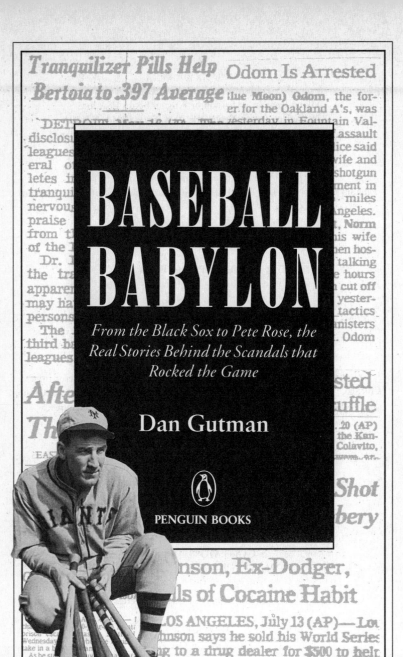

BASEBALL BABYLON

*From the Black Sox to Pete Rose, the
Real Stories Behind the Scandals that
Rocked the Game*

Dan Gutman

PENGUIN BOOKS

PENGUIN BOOKS
Published by the Penguin Group
Viking Penguin, a division of Penguin Books USA Inc.,
375 Hudson Street, New York, New York 10014, U.S.A.
Penguin Books Ltd, 27 Wrights Lane, London W8 5TZ, England
Penguin Books Australia Ltd, Ringwood, Victoria, Australia
Penguin Books Canada Ltd, 10 Alcorn Ave., Suite 300,
Toronto, Ontario, Canada M4V 3B2
Penguin Books (N.Z.) Ltd, 182–190 Wairau Road, Auckland 10, New Zealand

Penguin Books Ltd, Registered Offices:
Harmondsworth, Middlesex, England

First published in Penguin Books 1992

1 3 5 7 9 10 8 6 4 2

Grateful acknowledgment is made for permission to reprint an excerpt from
"Chicago," words and music by Fred Fisher. Copyright 1922, Fisher Music Group,
New York City. Copyright renewed. International copyright secured.

LIBRARY OF CONGRESS CATALOGING IN PUBLICATION DATA
Gutman, Dan.
Baseball Babylon: from the Black Sox to Pete Rose, the real
stories behind the scandals that rocked the game/by Dan Gutman.
p.   cm.
ISBN 0 14 01.6542 8
1. Baseball—United States—Corrupt practices—History.
I. Title.
GV863.A1G89   1992
796.357′0973—dc20   91–37312

Printed in the United States of America

Set in Sabon
Designed by Kingsley Parker

To Sam

ACKNOWLEDGMENTS

Many thanks to Roger Devine at Penguin, the constant guiding force behind this project; Mitch Rose, for selling the thing to Roger (and Craig Kubey for introducing me to Mitch); my wife, Nina, who typed, edited, did library research, relieved me of child care for six months, and read every word on these pages despite the fact that she doesn't even *like* baseball; and George White, whose valuable suggestions really improved the manuscript, despite his borderline psychotic insistence that all negative mentions of the Philadelphia Phillies be deleted.

At the Baseball Hall of Fame, thanks to Tom Heitz, Gretchen Curtis, Christy Zajack, and particularly Bill Deane for his help and for supplying all those morbid lists. For the great photos: Pat Kelly at the Hall of Fame, Nat Andriani at AP/Wide World, Catherine Koatz at *Penthouse*, Marcia Terrones at *Playboy*, and Mike Sowell of the *Tulsa Tribune* for raiding his personal collection.

Thanks to Michael Reingold, for sparking the idea in the first place; Boris Ginsburgs for saving me countless hours of microfilming; Dr. John Waterbor at the University of Alabama and Loren Coleman at the University of Southern Maine for sending information about their work; Ed Rouh for lending me his baseball books and his Rototiller; Ad and Harold Berlin for lending me their car and buying—what was it?—twenty copies of my last book; Mark Roman for letting me crash at his pad; "Beat It" Bob Guerra for digging up the Boston clippings; the librarians at the Haddonfield, Cherry Hill, Camden County, Haddon Heights, New York, and Philadelphia public libraries; Chris Michener at Cabbages & Kings in Haddonfield, who let me use her fine bookstore as if it was my personal public library.

Special thanks to Ron Sataloff, Elizabeth Law, Dan Janal, Alan Dawber, Bill "The Baseball Professor" Borst, Steve Bloom, Ray Dimetrosky, Herb Dunn, Justin Wallace, and Ralph Hammelbacher.

You know what you did. Now you'll have to live with it for the rest of your lives.

Finally, thanks to my friends who took *It Ain't Cheatin' If You Don't Get Caught* and put it in front of George Will's book in stores across the country. Now that I'm done with this book, I hope you'll forgive me for not calling last year, and do it all over again.

CONTENTS

3. DRUGS

INTRODUCTION
The Day I Shot George Steinbrenner

In 1989, while working on my first baseball book, I was lurking in the catacombs beneath Yankee Stadium, trying to find the clubhouse. A group of people stood in the distance. When I got closer I could see Yankee owner George Steinbrenner giving an impromptu interview to a small group of reporters.

I hovered at the periphery of the group. Never having written a word about baseball, I was too bashful to participate. But as I stood there listening to the writers ask Steinbrenner all the usual questions, one thought kept going through my mind: *RIGHT HERE, RIGHT NOW, I'M CLOSE ENOUGH TO KILL GEORGE STEINBRENNER.*

My mind raced. I was ten feet away from the most hated man in New York—the most hated man in *baseball*. It would be so simple to pull out a gun and blow him away. I could see the headlines:

BOSS KILLED   LUNATIC SHOOTS
BY INSANE WRITER!   STEINBRENNER!

Instantly, I would leap from total obscurity to world fame. The press was even right there to record the event for history. My book would sell like crazy, I couldn't help thinking.

However, being a pacifist and coward who had never even *held* a gun pretty much ruled out killing George Steinbrenner. And since I'm not a Yankees fan, I really couldn't have cared less whether Steinbrenner lived or died, though I'm certain a large number of New Yorkers would have hailed me as a hero and given me the key to the city.

It was at that moment, I realize now, that I became aware of my fascination with the dark side of baseball.

Like any other American boy growing up, I memorized the game's cherished numbers—Babe Ruth's sixty home runs in one season, Ty Cobb's .367 lifetime average, Joe DiMaggio's fifty-six-game hitting streak. The statistics and heroics were interesting, but what *really* intrigued me were the controversies and scandals that occurred off the field.

What about all those women Babe Ruth had, I wondered? What about the time Cobb charged into the stands and beat up a guy who only had one arm? And what happened the night DiMaggio and Frank Sinatra busted down some lady's apartment door thinking Marilyn Monroe was inside?

Now *that* was interesting stuff.

While others wondered if the 1927 Yankees were the best of all time, I wondered how Jimmy Piersall landed in a mental institution. Why did Willard Hershberger slash his throat in a Boston hotel room during a doubleheader? How come Cesar Cedeno was allowed to play again after being convicted of involuntary manslaughter?

Baseball history books ordinarily sum up these incidents in a sentence—"Leo Durocher was thrown out of the game in 1947 for conduct detrimental to baseball." Or, "Eddie Waitkus was shot by a deranged female admirer."

Whoa! Stop the presses! What did Durocher do? Who was Eddie Waitkus, and how did his shooting take place?

If I had been alive in 1941 I would have totally ignored the heroics of Ted Williams and Joe DiMaggio, focusing my attention on Brooklyn pitcher Van Lingle Mungo, who was chased around a Havana hotel that year by a jealous husband waving a carving knife.

It's an unfortunate fact of life that we find the private lives and personal misfortunes of famous people so interesting. We can see the ballgame on TV and watch the highlights on the news. But what we want to know is: Who's sleeping with whom? Who's getting arrested? Who's addicted? Who's in cahoots with the mob? Who's about to have a nervous breakdown?

Most fans probably think of baseball as a proud game with a great tradition that has been marred by two isolated scandals in seventy years—the Black Sox Scandal of 1919 and the recent downfall of Pete Rose. After reading this book, you may be left with the impression that everyone who ever pulled on a uniform was a murderer, junkie, alcoholic, womanizer, or car thief. The truth, of course, is somewhere in the middle. For one reason or another, baseball is just as likely to turn up on the front page of the newspaper as it is on the sports page.

The purpose of this book is not to burst any bubbles or destroy any heroes. If you've been following the game over the last two decades, your bubble has been burst for some time. The purpose of this book, like that of many other books about baseball, is to tell great stories—tragic and funny stories of players, managers, owners, and others caught up in circumstances that got out of control. Some people in these pages had their lives ruined by success, others by failure. Still others simply found themselves in a nasty situation, crawled out and got on with their lives.

When people found out I was writing this book, they asked a lot of questions: Is there something about baseball that lends itself to scandal? Are there more scandals in baseball than in other sports? What motivated these players to do the things they did?

I can pretty safely say that when Ty Cobb's mother blew her husband's brains out with a shotgun two weeks before Ty's first big-league game, it might have had some effect on his personal development. Beyond that, I'm not going to guess.

It's easy to trot out all the stock answers: Ballplayers are only human, and tempted by the same vices as the rest of us. They have a ridiculous amount of disposable income. They have too much free time. They've been coddled since the age of twelve by parents, teachers, wives, and fans, arresting their emotional development at that point.

You will find little psychologizing in this book. I studied psychology for six years thinking it would help me understand what makes people tick. I dropped out of graduate school when I became convinced that *nobody* knows what makes us tick. How could anybody explain why a man would murder his entire family with an ax and then kill himself (as Boston catcher Marty Bergen did on January 19, 1900)?

In doling out his fines and suspensions, the Commissioner of Baseball always announces that he is doing it "for the good of baseball."

Players are always being punished for committing acts that are "not in the best interests of baseball."

What the commissioners have failed to realize is that baseball is too perfect a game to be ruined by the moral character of the men who play it. The Black Sox Scandal didn't ruin baseball. The 1985 Pittsburgh drug trial didn't ruin baseball. Baseball wasn't ruined when fans found out that Mickey Mantle drank and slammed bus windows on kids begging for his autograph.

A long time ago, somebody—it *wasn't* Abner Doubleday—figured out the formula for a perfect game: A mound of dirt sixty feet and six inches away from a five-sided plate, surrounded by a diamond shape with three bases ninety feet apart. A cloth-covered sphere. A wooden club. Three outs. Three strikes. Nine innings. Hot dogs.

Perfect, like a soap bubble.

Baseball is the perfect game and we'll keep loving it even though the men who play it no longer serve as our personal heroes or role models. Charles Manson could be out there and we'd still come to watch if he could hit to the opposite field.

This book is not meant to trash baseball. On the contrary, if baseball has been able to survive everything described in these pages, it must be one helluva game.

Dan Gutman
September 1, 1991

Polonia Arrested in Sex-Assault Inquiry

RUTH OUT OF DANGER   RUTH FINED $5,000;
AFTER CO   BANNED
ON ARR   FF FIELD

ONE

SEX

Hurts Head in   of Yankees
    Escapes C   at St. Louis
        the   duct."

RED SOX PLAYER IS HELD
HAS AN A   ON RAPE OFFENDER ORDERED HOME
            CHARGE   Tyson's Mother-In-Law
                          Sues Winfield Over VD

BASEBALL STAR SHOT z seized Baseball Star and Wife Sue
BY GIRL FAN RALLIES g game— to Halt Newspaper Stories
                    ctim, 14

                    Mrs   Discusses   ,000
                           e of Famili

        f the Phillies, Lured
           m   000 Salary During
        N   definite Sus

> *"Why don't you blow out of here? You cramp my style."*
>
> —Babe Ruth to his wife, Helen

Sex, in the immortal words of would-be immortal Pete Rose, is one of the fringe benefits of being a major-league baseball player. Women who refuse to give most men the time of day will gladly debauch themselves with a total stranger whose face appears on a bubble gum card. Sophisticated women with impeccable taste seem only too happy to offer their charms for an hour in a hotel room with a utility infielder for the Cleveland Indians.

When Detroit's 1976 Rookie of the Year phenom Mark Fidrych went for a haircut, women would overrun the barbershop and fight each other over his clipped curls.

Experts say artificial turf, designated hitters, and free agency have destroyed the allure of baseball. Baloney. You'll know the magic is gone when supermodels and up-and-coming actresses stop showing up at Dodgers games. Baseball is alive and well, judging by its powerful attraction to members of the opposite sex.

Sex scandals in the National Pastime didn't begin the night Wade Boggs was introduced to Margo Adams. They've been around since the game began. Few of us are old enough to remember when newspapers were filled with stories of St. Louis Browns third baseman Arlie "The Freshest Man on Earth" Latham, whose wife filed for divorce on grounds of perversion. And Philadelphia infielder Sam Crane is forgotten long after he ran off with a Scranton fruit dealer's wife.

The most sensational early sex scandal occurred in 1894, when Baltimore pitcher Edgar McNabb had a year-long affair with actress Louise Kellogg. Kellogg was a good-looking blonde who happened to be married to Seattle ice merchant R. E. Rockwell.

On February 28, the pair checked into the Hotel Eiffel in Pittsburgh as "E. J. McNabb and wife." At eight o'clock that evening, screaming was heard coming from their room, followed by scuffling and finally four pistol shots. When the police kicked open the door, they found blood pouring from two holes in Mrs. Rockwell's neck. McNabb was in even worse shape. He had put the gun in his mouth and pulled the trigger, killing himself instantly.

Louise Kellogg survived (paralyzed from the waist down), but she never revealed what had driven McNabb to shoot both of them. Newspaper articles said she had wanted to break off their relationship.

Like peanuts and Cracker Jack, groupies have always been considered a tradition in professional baseball. Once called "Baseball Daisies," they are now known as "Baseball Annies" or "green flies." Tillie Shafer, a shortstop with the New York Giants from 1909 to 1913, was known as "The Perfumed Note Man" because he received so many invitations from secret admirers.

In the same era, a pair of groupies dubbed "The Two Little Girls in Blue" followed the Giants around the country year after year. They were so "loyal" that catcher Chief Meyers suggested they be voted a share of the team's World Series money.

Then there's the legend of "Chicago Shirley," a woman who supposedly went through an entire team (or vice versa) in one night.

"Sometimes a girl who has an eye for the bright lights is known as the 'fifth pitcher' of the club," hinted a 1928 article in *Collier's* magazine, "because she takes the hurlers of the visiting club out for a round of the cabarets at night, and they are not as effective as usual in the game the next day."

The same article described players known as "Dick Smiths" who would stay out all night and ask their roommates to muss up their beds so they would look as if they'd been slept in. "There probably was a fellow named Dick Smith once who was like that and he started the name," hypothesized *Collier's*.*

Yeah, and blacksmiths, silversmiths, and coppersmiths were named after real people too! Any major-league baseball player, if he wants to, can be a dicksmith.

---

* Don't bother looking it up. *The Baseball Encyclopedia* lists two Dick Smiths, but they played in the 1950s and 1960s.

BABE RUTH

*"He was continually with women, morning and
night. I don't know how he kept going."*
                    —former teammate

The story is told that Babe Ruth was sharing a hotel suite with
teammate Bob Meusel when Ruth brought a girl up to his room.
They had a session of noisy sex, and when they were finished Ruth
strolled into the living room of the suite to relax with a cigar. Then
he went back to his room and had sex with the girl again. Afterward
he came back out and smoked another cigar.

In the morning, Meusel asked Ruth, "How many times did you
lay that girl last night?" Both men instinctively glanced at the ashtray,
which held seven butts.

"Count the cigars," Ruth said.

The popular image of Babe Ruth is that of a jolly, lovable fun-
maker—a Santa Claus figure who could swing a bat. His enormous
appetite for everything has been well documented. Ty Cobb said he
witnessed Ruth going through six club sandwiches, a platter of pigs'
knuckles, and a pitcher of beer in one sitting. The Babe would
gamble—and lose—$25,000 on a single horse race. He not only
had to hit the most home runs; he also had to have the biggest car
and the highest salary, spend the most money, drink the most whiskey, and live life to its absolute fullest.

"The ladies were quite frank in their invitations," Claire Ruth
wrote in her autobiography, *The Babe and I*. "The Babe brought
out the beast in a lot of ladies the world over . . . but he was man
enough to fight off his wilder impulses toward wine, women, and
song."

If she only knew. The idealized portraits of Babe Ruth are usually
careful to omit his special weakness: an endless parade of women
and sex.

To put it bluntly, Babe Ruth was a sex machine. "Sex was a
constant part of his life," wrote Robert Creamer in the definitive
biography, *Babe: The Legend Comes to Life*. Creamer claimed that
Ruth was quite well endowed and quoted a former teammate who

said, "He was continually with women, morning and night. I don't know how he kept going."

Sportswriter Fred Lieb, who covered the Yankees in Ruth's prime, wrote, "One woman couldn't satisfy him. Frequently it took half a dozen."

Stories of the Bambino's sexual escapades are legendary—and usually accurate. After the Yankees clinched the 1928 pennant in Detroit, the team threw a wild party. Sometime during the evening, Ruth got up on a chair and announced, "Any girl who doesn't want to fuck can leave now." Very few left.

Babe once walked into a St. Louis whorehouse and announced that he was going to have sex with every girl there. He did, then sat down to a big breakfast.

During a barnstorming trip with Lou Gehrig, Babe came back to his room one evening with his arms around two women. In the middle of the night, one of them came out and said to Gehrig, "You better come and see if you can straighten out your friend." Lou went to see what the matter was and found the Babe sitting on his bed sobbing uncontrollably, tears running down his face. It turned out that he was upset because he hadn't been able to service both women.

Ruth, often taunted for resembling a baboon, could not walk into a restaurant or hotel lobby without being mobbed by women. His usual response to the question "How's it going?" was "Pussy good. Pussy good." He was constantly propositioned by mail. Because Babe rarely bothered opening fan letters, teammates would do the job for him and set up dates with the female admirers themselves.

Ruth only agreed to date women if they made it clear in advance that sex would be part of the evening. Rather than waste time courting, he preferred the company of prostitutes and knew the red-light district of every town.

Fred Lieb said that Ruth had something of a penis fixation. He would pepper his conversation with things like "I can knock the penis off any ball that ever was pitched." Seeing a large stack of mail, he would say it was "as big as my penis." When he had gotten old and fat, he claimed, "The worst of this is that I no longer can see my penis when I stand up."

Ruth's total disregard for the conventions of polite society got him into trouble on occasion. Fred Lieb recalled that he was playing cards on a train in 1921 when Ruth came sprinting through the car, pursued by a dark-haired woman waving a knife. It turned out that she was the wife of a Louisiana legislator. Later that season, the Babe was chased out of a Detroit hotel by an angry husband holding a revolver.

For all those sick kids he visited in hospitals, Ruth was startlingly insensitive to the feelings of the women he supposedly loved. The day he arrived in Boston in 1914, he met a sixteen-year-old waitress named Helen Woodford. Less than three months later they married, though that was clearly just a formality in Ruth's view.

He flaunted his adultery shamelessly. When Babe took Helen on road trips, he would sneak into teammates' rooms to have sex with other women. One time he left Helen home and brought another woman on a trip to Binghamton, where she accepted a gift as "Mrs. Babe Ruth." While he was married to Helen, a Long Island woman named Dolores Dixon filed a $50,000 paternity suit against him (one of several during his career), and there were open rumors in the press about Ruth seeing a woman named Claire Hodgson.

By 1925, the marriage was falling apart, and Helen suffered the first of several nervous breakdowns. Babe and Helen separated the following year, but as Catholics they felt they could never divorce. On January 11, 1929, Helen was burned to death in a fire at Watertown, Massachusetts. She had been living with a dentist named Edward Kinder for two years, and was addicted to alcohol and drugs.

Three months after Helen died, Babe married Claire Hodgson. Claire has been described as a model and actress, but Robert Creamer wrote, "She was simply a striking-looking girl who wore clothes well and knew the right people." Her first cousin was New York Giants first baseman Johnny Mize. Claire had been married previously—when she was fourteen years old. Over the next twenty-eight years she settled Babe down somewhat—as much as anyone could settle Babe Ruth down.

Despite his uninhibited behavior, the only Ruthian off-field adventure to make the papers was his celebrated "Bellyache Heard 'Round the World" in 1925.

The Yankees were playing a series of exhibition games across the

South. Ruth had been hitting over .400 but feeling lousy, and on April 7 he suddenly collapsed in the Asheville, North Carolina, train station. When the train missed its connection, rumors spread that the great Bambino was dead, a London paper going so far as to describe the death scene in vivid detail.

But Babe revived. When the train approached Washington, he went to the bathroom to wash up, sending Yankee scout Paul Kritchell to get a comb. When Kritchell returned, he found Ruth crumpled in a heap on the floor—he had passed out again and smashed his head against the sink.

Finally in New York, his unconscious body—all 270 pounds of it—was hoisted through the train's window and placed on a rolling stretcher. Before being delivered to St. Vincent's Hospital, Ruth awoke three times, delirious and convulsing—lashing out with his arms and legs and muttering incoherently. It took seven men and several sedatives to keep him on the stretcher.

A writer named W. O. McGeehan invented the story that most of the press picked up on—the Bambino had consumed too many hot dogs, peanuts, and soda pop. The *New York Times* called Ruth's illness an intestinal abscess ("Fried potatoes for breakfast yesterday morning are said to have contributed to his sudden relapse"). Claire, in an attempt to be candid years later, wrote that Babe had slid heavily into first base and suffered a groin injury.

"This was 1925, a long time ago in our mores," she wrote in 1959. "Perhaps the club felt that in the interests of delicacy the exact nature of the Babe's injury should not be publicly stated."

Perhaps. But the baseball writers, and some of Ruth's teammates, whispered that the "groin injury" was, in fact, a whopping dose of gonorrhea and syphilis.

After an operation on April 17, Babe healed quickly and promptly went back to boozing and whoring. When the Yankees arrived for a series in St. Louis, he didn't even go to the Buckingham, where the Yankees were staying.* Instead, he spent two days at his favorite whorehouse. The Yankees received a report from a private detective that Babe had slept with six women in one night.

---

* Ruth's first roommate, Ping "The Wonderful Wop" Bodie, will always be remembered for his classic response when asked what it was like to room with Babe Ruth. "I ain't rooming with Ruth," he replied. "I room with his *suitcase*."

When he walked into the clubhouse for the next game, Ruth whisked by manager Miller Huggins and said, "Sorry I'm late, Hug."

"Don't bother to suit up," Huggins responded. "You're suspended."

Ruth was also fined $5,000, an enormous sum in 1925. Huggins told the press that the penalty was for "misconduct off the field." When a reporter asked if that meant drinking, the little manager replied, "Of course it means drinking, and it means a lot of other things besides. There are various kinds of misconduct."*

It's hardly necessary to call in a psychologist to get at the root of Ruth's insatiable need to accumulate women, food, money, home runs, attention, and affection. When he was just seven and already drinking and stealing, his parents requested that Babe be put in St. Mary's Industrial School for Boys, a reform school in Baltimore (Al Jolson also went there). He was in and out of the institution five times, spending most of his youth there. When they finally let him out of St. Mary's for good, Babe wasn't just an overgrown kid turned loose on the world—he was more like a wild animal being released from its cage. Until cancer tore at his body when he was in his fifties, he was an uncontrollable force that no authority figure, including managers and team owners, could contain. Ruth was suspended five times—in 1922 alone.

That was the year he was invited to a dinner at the New York Elks Club. Senator James Walker, soon to be the famous mayor Jimmy Walker, gave a long talk about the dangers of drinking, going out on the town, and other forms of misbehavior. It was pretty much lost on Ruth, until Walker got to the part about letting down the little "dirty-faced kids in the street." With tears rolling down his cheeks, Ruth rose and offered a sincere apology, promising to be good. He was, too, for a few weeks.

At every step of the way during his twenty-two years in the majors, people around Ruth tried to get him to mend his ways. When Yankee co-owner Colonel Tillinghast Huston signed him to what at that time was a spectacular $50,000-a-year contract in 1922, he informed

---

* Ruth always denied the famous story in which he grabbed manager Miller Huggins and dangled him by his feet off the rear end of a speeding train. But in her book, his wife said the incident actually happened.

the slugger that part of the bargain was that Ruth would stop drinking, screwing, and staying out all night.

"Colonel," Ruth replied, "I'll promise to go easier on drinking and get to bed earlier. But not for you, fifty thousand dollars, or two hundred fifty thousand dollars will I give up women. They're too much fun."

Other Ruthian Adventures

• During a spring training game in Jacksonville, a man in the outfield bleachers shouted, "You're a big bunch of cheese!"—apparently a serious insult in those times. When the inning was over, Ruth argued with the heckler, who invited him to come into the stands and settle it man to man. Ruth did, and the guy pulled a knife on him. Pitcher Ernie Shore pulled Ruth away before any damage could be done.

• 1925: Shortly after Ruth got hit with his $5,000 fine, his English bull terrier, Dot, ran wild on his Sudbury, Massachusetts, farm and killed a pedigreed cow owned by a neighbor. The neighbor sued for the value of the animal.

"They come in bunches, like bananas," Ruth said. "Well, this luck can't last forever."

• 1926: Before a trip to St. Louis, Babe was arrested at Howell, Michigan, and charged with fishing out of season. His catch was described in the *New York Times* as "a few scrawny bluegills."

Ruth and Cars

Babe was an enthusiastically awful driver who was involved in perhaps a dozen accidents and very nearly killed himself several times. These are just a few of his adventures behind the wheel.

• 1918: He was driving a girl (not his wife) around Boston and the car got stuck between two trolleys. The girl was hospitalized, but Babe wasn't injured.

• 1920: Three months after joining the Yankees and three weeks after buying a new car, Ruth was driving from Philadelphia to Washington when he had his most serious accident. With him in the car was his wife, Helen, rookie outfielder Frank Gleich, second-string catcher Fred Hofmann, and coach Charley O'Leary.

The group was singing, laughing, and pulling over frequently for bootleg liquor. At 2:00 A.M. outside Wawa, Pennsylvania, Ruth skidded off the road into a ditch, the car flipping over several times. O'Leary was unconscious briefly, and Ruth suffered a twisted knee, but everyone else was fine. Ruth told a mechanic to sell the car and keep the money. When they were late getting to Washington, rumors of Ruth's death swept the nation.

Two months later, a private telegraph wire in Cincinnati received a "flash" that Ruth, Bob Meusel, and several other Yankees had been killed in an automobile accident. Later it was discovered that the phony story had been planted by gamblers hoping to influence the odds of the upcoming series against Cleveland.*

• 1921: After an argument in a New Jersey bar, a man followed Ruth in his car and cut him off on the side of the road. The argument continued, but this time the man held a gun to Ruth's head. Harry Harper, a friend of Ruth's, drove by and tried to run the man down. When the assailant dove out of the way, Ruth and Harper disarmed him.

BO BELINSKY
Baseball's Biggest Womanizer

It's one thing to attract women when you're the biggest drawing card in the history of the game. What's more remarkable is a pitcher with limited talent and twenty-eight career wins who has *hundreds* of women begging to sleep with him. The greatest womanizer in baseball history had to be Robert "Bo" Belinsky.

He was a dark-haired, good-looking, half Jewish–half Polish kid

---

* Rumors of Ruth's death appeared regularly. In 1933, word got around that he had perished in a plane crash.

from Trenton, New Jersey. More than looks, he had the attitude—
that confident, cool, don't-give-a-damn-about-anything demeanor
that men envy and women pretend to hate.

When the Brooklyn Dodgers and New York Giants moved to California in the late 1950s, baseball opened its doors to expansion.
The new teams, such as the New York Mets, were stocked with
mediocre players. The Los Angeles Angels (now the California Angels) were born in 1961 and brought up Belinsky the following year.

He had the audacity to hold out for more money in his rookie
season (the Angels offered $6,000 and Bo wanted $8,500), which
made him a celebrity in Tinseltown before he'd thrown his first pitch.
When he somehow won his first three games, Hollywood had discovered a new hero.

There was another Jewish kid in town named Sandy Koufax who
could pitch a little, but Koufax didn't drive a candy-apple-red Cad-
illac Eldorado. Koufax didn't stay out all night at the Whiskey-A-
Go-Go dancing with beautiful women. Koufax didn't say things like
"I think whores got a lot more class than some straight broads. You
know where you stand with them." Sandy could pitch, but Bo could
fill newspaper columns.

With each win, more women propositioned Belinsky at parties,
nightclubs, hotels, and restaurants—and right outside the Angels'
clubhouse. Gossip columnist Walter Winchell saw that Bo made
good copy, and took him under his wing. (Winchell became such a
nuisance that eventually he had to be asked to leave the Angels'
clubhouse.)

Thanks to Winchell, Bo became a fixture at Hollywood parties.
Agents and producers introduced him to their latest discoveries in
hopes that being seen with the sexy ballplayer would get a starlet's
picture in the paper. A male chauvinist pig before the term existed,
Belinsky truly considered women to be disposable, like used razor
blades.

"I had only one rule about these broads," Bo proclaimed. "They
had to come highly recommended."

In his fourth game in the big leagues—May 5, 1962—Belinsky
pitched the first no-hitter in California, beating Baltimore 2–0. If

he'd been doing well with women before, his services were really in demand after he got the last out in the ninth inning. That's when he switched from starlets to stars.

In quick procession, Bo romanced Tina Louise ("Great body, great legs . . . a hell of a broad"), Ann-Margret ("She wasn't quite as good-looking or sexy in person as she was on the screen"), Paulette Goddard ("She was such a beautiful woman, so elegant, so courtly"), Doris Duke ("She's an old broad but she's fun to be with"), and Connie Stevens ("Great girl, but I wound up dating her nineteen-year-old cousin"), as well as Juliet Prowse, paper-goods heiress Jane Weyerhauser, and DuPont family widow Ricky DuPont.

Bo got around so much, he even went out with the Shah of Iran's former wife, Queen Sorraya ("She was into all that mystical stuff, witchcraft, everything far out. . . . But really a nice broadie").

After throwing the no-hitter, Bo lost six of his next seven games, but Hollywood didn't care. He was hired to make appearances on the popular TV shows 77 *Sunset Strip*, *Dakota*, and *Surfside Six*.

Belinsky's most highly publicized relationship was with Mamie Van Doren ("She was great to look at and took real good care of that body of hers"), one of several blond bombshells who tried to fill the void left by the death of Marilyn Monroe.

Mamie (named after President Eisenhower's wife) had been married at sixteen and divorced three months later. Walter Winchell set her up on a blind date with Bo at the Peppermint West nightclub. It wasn't just another scoop for Winchell. Bo and Mamie really loved—or at least *liked*—one another. The romance blossomed, and on April 1, 1963, the *Los Angeles Times* put their engagement on page one.

But when reality set in and Mamie started talking about setting a date, Bo bolted. Mamie refused to give back his $2,000 engagement ring, so Bo hired a detective to get some dirt on her. The detective came back with some incriminating recordings of Mamie with a guy in her show. Bo got his ring back. Bo and Mamie were engaged and disengaged several times after that. In the end, he announced, "I needed her like Custer needed Indians."

(Mamie must have had a thing for baseball players. She later dated Red Sox phenom Tony Conigliaro and married Cubs pitcher Lee Meyers. She was thirty-five and he was nineteen. Meyers was killed in 1972 when his Porsche ran off a road in Huntington Beach, California.)

One woman actually did lure Belinsky to the altar: Jo Collins, *Playboy*'s Playmate of the Year in 1965 and background for such movie classics as *How to Stuff a Wild Bikini* and *Beach Blanket Bingo*. They were a pretty typical couple—Bo and Jo got married, Bo and Jo had a kid, Bo threatened Jo with a gun, Bo nearly killed both of them by smashing his car into a utility pole, and Bo and Jo were divorced.

Bo had more than an I-don't-give-a-damn attitude. He really *didn't* give a damn. He enjoyed partying more than pitching. At one point in his career, he was sent down to play in Hawaii and liked it so much he didn't want to go back to the majors. Hawaii was where he moved when he faded out of baseball in 1970. He had a lifetime record of 28–51 over eight seasons; perhaps no player has ever received more attention for accomplishing less.

Sportswriter Maury Allen wrote a book about Bo (titled, naturally enough, *Bo*) that revealed Belinsky's theory on why his career went downhill right after his no-hitter.

"The night before my no-hitter I banged into this secretary out on the Strip," he said. "She was tall and thin and black haired. We had a couple of drinks and I wound up making it with her at her pad. . . . I got home at four A.M. That night I pitched my no-hitter. I tried to find her and never did. She was my good luck charm. When I lost her I lost all my pitching luck."

WADE BOGGS AND MARGO ADAMS
Love and Extortion

It was a dull Monday evening in Crackers, an Anaheim, California, club that attracted ballplayers. Wade Boggs, the undisputed supreme hitter in baseball, was hanging around that night—April 2, 1984—with some teammates.

About three thousand miles away, his wife, Debbie, was home

with their two children, Meagann and Brett Anthony. Just ten feet away, a pretty brunette was giving him the eye.

Most baseball groupies are thrilled just to enjoy the company of a major-league ballplayer for an hour or so in a hotel room. They're supposed to be passive, grateful for any crumbs of affection that might be tossed their way. Margo Adams was not your typical baseball groupie.

She didn't bring Boggs home from Crackers that night, but they had dinner the next night and began seeing one another seriously. The affair snowballed until the two began traveling as a couple on Red Sox road trips. This arrangement continued for the next four years.

Eventually, of course, the shit hit the fan. Margo learned that Wade was seeing other women. Debbie Boggs got suspicious. Wade tired of living a double life.

When he told Margo the relationship was over, she asked him for $100,000 to compensate for the income she calculated she would have earned as a mortgage broker during their last year together. He said Margo also threatened to send Debbie Boggs photographs of herself and her past travel itinerary if he didn't pay up. (Debbie eventually found Adams's travel itinerary anyway, as well as her underwear, in Wade's suitcase.)

Boggs contacted friends at the FBI to investigate what he believed was extortion. When she found out, Adams contacted her attorney, who filed an $11.5-million suit.

That's when the Boggs-Adams affair became front-page news. Boggs said on national television that he was "addicted to sex" and that it was a *disease,* which caused howls in the press. Boston fans, always sympathetic, chanted "MAR-go! MAR-go!" when Boggs took the field. "According to *The Sporting News,*" quipped David Letterman, "over the last four years, Wade Boggs hit .800 with women in scoring position." Wade's wife, a paragon of tolerance, forgave him.

According to Adams's breach-of-contract suit, Wade and Margo had a "business relationship" in which she acted as Boggs's chauffeur, financial adviser, travel agent, autograph broker, clothier, valet, seamstress, and washerwoman.

Boggs said there was never an oral agreement about an amount Adams would be paid for her services. He refused to settle and got a lawyer of his own: Jennifer King, a self-proclaimed "bimbo buster."

"I'm not going to let this person destroy my world," Boggs told *Sports Illustrated*. In the end, he paid a small undisclosed sum to Margo to get her out of his life.

Adams *did* cash in with *Penthouse*—the last refuge for famous floozies—for the same $100,000 she had hoped to get from Boggs. She bared all in an interview and most in a photo layout that appeared in the April and May 1989 issues.

Penthouse described baseball as a world "where wins and losses finished second to infidelity and racial stereotypes, and where runs, hits, and errors became less prevalent than partying, groupies, and various childish pranks."

Adams hoped to win the public relations war in her interview, but never did. It was difficult to appreciate the seriousness of her argument while she was displaying her bare butt in a bathtub.

Anyway, these were the most startling revelations Margo made in *Penthouse*:

- Wade enjoyed having phone sex with Margo, and shaving her private parts.
- Wade had gotten venereal disease from one girl during a previous spring training and had made another pregnant. The latter had a miscarriage.
- Wade tried to make his wife look like Margo, with the same haircut and hairdo. Every year in the Red Sox yearbook, Debbie Boggs looked more like Margo Adams. "Wade was creating a clone of myself."
- Margo would go to Red Sox games and sit a few rows behind Debbie Boggs. During one game, she followed Debbie to the ladies' room and stood next to her as they brushed their hair together.
- Boggs was deeply resentful that the Red Sox had kept him in the minors for six years.
- Boggs played for himself, not the team. If Boston won and he didn't get any hits, he'd be in a terrible mood. "Winning or losing was never that important," Margo revealed. "All that was important was how many hits he got."

• Wade was deeply superstitious. Besides making sure to eat chicken before each game, he had to control which underwear Margo wore. When he went 4 for 5 one game and found out that she had not worn panties, he asked her not to wear any for the next couple of months.

• Wade and Margo consulted a psychic, and they determined that they had been together in a past life. She had been the man and he had been the woman.

• A friend calculated that Wade hit .341 when he was with Margo and .221 when he was with his wife. (Sabermeticians may want to investigate this area of statistics further. The season after Boggs and Adams split, he dropped to a career-low in batting average (.302), runs (89), and walks (87), while striking out a career high of 68 times.)

• Wade was a "connoisseur" of oral sex. He told Margo that players only perform this activity for their wives, not their girlfriends. Also that black men don't do it at all—because they have large penises, he said, they don't "have to."

• Pete Rose would tease Wade by saying, "Hey, I see what you're hitting, boy. You're getting that hitting pussy."

• Some self-proclaimed born-again Christian players did drugs and had extramarital affairs. No names were mentioned.

• A favorite trick among ballplayers was to bring a girl to a hotel room where a roommate was sleeping, telling her nothing would wake the guy up. Once sex had begun, the roommate got up and both players had sex with the girl at the same time.

• Boggs was intensely jealous of Don Mattingly, feared John Candelaria more than any other pitcher, and said of Dwight Gooden, "I don't want some fucking cokehead throwing a ball ninety miles an hour at me."

• All the players agreed that George Bell was the most hated man in baseball.

• The place where players got the most sex was Florida during spring training. Guys would have sex with groupies and girlfriends while their wives and children were down the hall. And during the last week of spring training, when the wives headed home, "everybody is getting laid continuously."

• Wade said that if he ever was hitting .400 near the end of the season, he would fake an injury.

• Boggs had lied when he said he injured his back taking off his boots in a hotel room several years ago. According to Adams, he got so drunk in a Toronto bar that he fell onto the arm of a couch. He was, however, taking off his boots at the time—so Ernie Whitt of the Blue Jays could try them on.

• To make Wade jealous, Margo had an affair with Steve Garvey. "As far as a lover, he's much better than Wade," she said.

• Ninety percent of the items sent to ballplayers to autograph were actually signed by batboys and clubhouse boys.

When the whole Margo Adams affair was over, Boggs said it had made his marriage stronger. "The best thing that ever happened to me was getting caught," he said. "Man, love is the strongest thing in the world."

Second strongest, maybe. In March 1991 Boggs fell out of a moving pickup truck driven by his wife. "I'm just glad to be alive," he said. "The back tire narrowly missed running over my head." He walked away with a few cuts and bruises.

FRITZ & SUSAN & MIKE & MARILYN
Baseball's Most Unusual Trade

At first, everyone on the 1973 Yankees thought it was just another one of Fritz Peterson's diabolical pranks. Then they thought he was crazy. Then they believed it.

During the off-season, Peterson and fellow Yankee hurler Mike Kekich had swapped wives. And kids. And station wagons. And dogs.

"It wasn't a sex thing," Peterson said. "It was not a cheap swap."

"It wasn't a wife swap," claimed Kekich. "It was a *life* swap."

And it may not have been *Bob & Carol & Ted & Alice*, but it was baseball's most titillating contribution to the Sexual Revolution.

Fritz had met Marilyn Monks in the cafeteria when they were both students at Northern Illinois University. He called her "Chip." They married in December 1964. Mike and Susan were high school sweethearts, marrying seven months after the Petersons. When Kekich joined the Yankees in 1969, the two couples became fast friends. Both lived in New Jersey at the time.

One night in the spring of 1972, the Petersons and Kekiches went to see *The Godfather*. Afterward they went out for a few beers.

"I don't remember who said it first," Susan told sportswriter Maury Allen. "I just remember the subject of wife swapping was discussed. All I remember doing about it that night was giggling."

Soon after, Allen switched from covering the Yankees to covering the New York Mets, so he invited Fritz, Mike, and their wives over for a farewell dinner. They kidded about swapping spouses all night, and when the party broke up at 4:00 A.M., Marilyn and Susan agreed to go home with each other's husband. The ballplayers, Allen revealed in an article for the *Ladies' Home Journal*, instigated the swap.

The next morning, Fritz, Marilyn, Mike, and Susan gathered at a diner in Fort Lee, New Jersey, to discuss the situation. Apparently, all parties enjoyed the experiment and decided to continue.

"Some nights I would go home with Fritz and some nights I would go home with Mike," Susan explained.

After baseball season was over Fritz moved into the Kekich home with Susan and her daughters, Kristen and Reagan. Mike moved into the Peterson home with Marilyn and her sons, Gregg and Eric. The children were all under six years old and accepted the new arrangement with varying degrees of understanding.

Baseball clubhouses are hotbeds of rumor, and when the Yankees gathered for spring training in Fort Lauderdale, the story got around to other players. On March 3, rookie pitcher Scott McGregor happened to ask a reporter, "Is it true about Peterson and Kekich?"

"Is *what* true about Peterson and Kekich?"

The story became a time bomb, so the Yankees scheduled an

emergency press conference to maintain *some* control over what reporters would be told.

The result, of course, was a media circus. Who cared about the Yanks' chances in '73 when you could write about the "Yankee Panky" going on in the bullpen? Every newspaper, TV, and radio sports reporter dropped their coverage for a snickering story on the swap. Marilyn fled to her parents' home near Chicago to avoid the press. A religious group canceled its block of seventy-five tickets for a Yankee game.

Baseball Commissioner Bowie Kuhn, who was never accused of letting it all hang out, made this statement: "I deplore what happened and am appalled at its effect on young people. It's a most regrettable situation that does no good for sports in general."

He took no disciplinary action against the pitchers, only because there's nothing in the rulebook that says you can't swap wives with a teammate.

Susan Kekich was relieved that the situation was finally out in the open, and somewhat surprised by all the fuss. "A lot of people get divorces," she said. "We didn't do anything sneaky or lecherous. There isn't anything smutty about this. We were all attracted to each other and we fell in love."

The love lasted, at least for Susan and Fritz. They married in 1974. Fritz retired from baseball in 1976, found God, sold real estate, and has recently been mentioned as a possible college baseball coach.

The Mike and Marilyn relationship wasn't as successful. A few weeks after the big swap hit the papers, they broke off their romance. Mike was traded to Cleveland later that season, and he also pitched in Texas, Mexico, Venezuela, Seattle, and the Dominican Republic and on Earl Weaver's Gold Coast Suns in the Senior League in 1990. He remarried in 1978 and runs a health examination company in Albuquerque.

STEVE GARVEY
One-Man Baby Boom

"The last time I was surrounded by this many beautiful women," Bob Hope quipped during the 1989 Oscars, "was when I spent Father's Day at Steve Garvey's house."

"The Surgeon General is stepping up his campaign about condom use," reported Jay Leno. "In fact, last night he even mentioned Steve Garvey by name."

"HONK IF YOU'RE CARRYING STEVE GARVEY'S BABY."

If any *other* ballplayer had fathered a child or two out of wedlock, he wouldn't have become a laughingstock or wound up on every bumper sticker in California. But because it was Steve Garvey—the Pat Boone of the big leagues—the story became a national joke in 1989.

Garvey, it was said, was so clean that he squeaked. His life was a living Norman Rockwell painting. When Steve was seven, his dad was the Dodgers' bus driver, so Steve became the team's batboy. Fourteen years later, kids handed *him* the bats—he was the Dodgers' third baseman. During his brilliant career, he played in 1,207 consecutive games (the National League record), 10 All-Star games, and 5 World Series, and won 4 straight Gold Glove Awards. Hall of Fame numbers.

Naturally, he had a gorgeous blond wife. Cyndy Garvey was a model who did commercials for Swanson, Geritol, and Chevrolet before becoming cohost of the popular TV show *AM Los Angeles*. She first set eyes on Steve when they were students at Michigan State University. She was dishing out meat in the dorm cafeteria and gave him an extra portion.

The college sweethearts married in 1971 and had two picture-perfect daughters. Steve shared the housework. He didn't drink or take drugs. His biggest vice was that he occasionally ate too much cake. He did charity work and went to church each week. The Jaycees named him one of the most outstanding young men in America. There was talk of running for the Senate. He was such a perfectly wholesome All-American boy next door, it was sickening.

"I'm trying to set an example for kids," Garvey said. "I picked up things from my heroes that made me what I am today."

If he ever *does* run for public office, that quote will come back to haunt him. The Garvey myth began to unravel on August 3, 1980, when *Inside Sports* magazine ran a cover story titled "Trouble in Paradise." Minor-league pitcher-turned-writer Pat Jordan interviewed Cyndy Garvey and probed into the problems and frustrations that go with being the wife of a professional ballplayer. Jordan focused on the Garveys' sexually troubled relationship.

"You can't even make love to your husband when you want to," Cyndy was quoted as whining. "You've got to wait for an off day."

In the article, Cyndy hinted that she would like to have an affair with somebody, and Jordan described a flirtatious lunch date Cyndy had in the Polo Lounge of the Beverly Hills Hotel with a "tall man in his 40s, with a salt and pepper beard."

The Garveys swiftly socked Newsweek Inc.—publisher of *Inside Sports*—with an $11.2-million lawsuit for libel, invasion of privacy, and breach of contract. The suit claimed that the article was filled with "falsehoods, inventions, gaps and opinions masquerading as facts." Obscene mail arrived at the Garvey household, along with flying eggs.

Ordinarily a case like this gets thrown out of court. However, when writer Jordan's taped interviews and notes were turned over to the court, it became obvious that he wasn't exactly an objective reporter—he had the hots for Cyndy. In fact, the man Jordan described Cyndy flirting with at the Polo Lounge turned out to be Pat Jordan himself.

Inside Sports decided to offer a settlement rather than sling mud with "Barbie and Ken" in court.

The joke was on *Inside Sports*. A year later the Garveys split up, for many of the reasons mentioned in Jordan's article. After the Garveys pocketed a reported $100,000 in damages from the magazine, revelations about Steve's *real* personal life made the libelous article look like a puff piece.

After their divorce was final in 1985, Cyndy did all she could to expose the real Steve Garvey. Through her and through various paternity suits, it came out that Steve had conducted at least three overlapping romances, and two of the women had become pregnant.

"The guy is a sociopath," Cyndy told *Esquire* in 1989. "He needs therapy. I know I've had a lot of therapy in my life because of Steve Garvey."

The chronology of Garvey's infidelities is complicated. In 1978, he took up with a mistress, Judith Ross of San Diego. They moved in together in 1982, while Steve was separated from Cyndy. The romance lasted until 1989, even though Ross discovered Garvey had been having an affair with *another* woman in Atlanta two years earlier.

This was Cable News Network assignment editor Rebecka Mendenhall. Garvey proposed to her in November 1988. The following January, hours after she told Garvey she was pregnant, he broke off the engagement. Mendenhall, in fact, claimed that Garvey once put her on a plane to visit him and then he slept with Judith Ross while waiting for her to arrive. Mendenhall filed a suit against Garvey for paternity and breach of promise.

Around the same time, Garvey courted a medical sales representative named Cheri Moulton, and *she* subsequently gave birth to a daughter. Finally, during the same period when he was seeing Mendenhall and Moulton, Garvey met former high-school cheerleader Candace Thomas. She became the second Mrs. Garvey in 1989.

In between all these activities, Steve found time to have a fling with Margo Adams—who later made national headlines by traveling with Boston Red Sox hitter extraordinaire Wade Boggs for four years while Boggs was married.

In his playing days, it should be noted, Steve Garvey's nickname was "Iron Man."

In all fairness, Garvey said he was *not* seeing all those women simultaneously, and claimed he did not find out about Rebecka Mendenhall's pregnancy until he had proposed to Candace Thomas. However, he said he would "step up to the plate" and take responsibility for any and all babies if tests proved they were his. (Both Moulton's and Mendenhall's children were determined to be Garvey's.)

Some guys have it, some guys don't. Something about Steve Garvey attracts women. When he left the Dodgers to play for the San Diego

Padres in 1983, a group of Girl Scouts picketed Dodger Stadium. For a boy next door, he certainly got around the neighborhood.

DAVE PALLONE
Baseball's First Open Homosexual

"REPORT LINKS UMP PALLONE TO
SEX SCANDAL"

The headline filled the back page of the *New York Post* on September 21, 1988. Within twenty-four hours the story was in every paper in the country and Dave Pallone's eighteen-year umpiring career was ruined, not to mention his life.

Surveys show that about 10 percent of the male population is homosexual, so it shouldn't have come as any great shock that there might be gay players, coaches, managers, or umpires. But it did. In the 150 or so years baseball has been played, Dave Pallone was the first man to come out and publicly declare that he is a homosexual.

After what Pallone endured as a result, it may be another 150 years before anyone dares try it again.

Pallone had his first gay encounter when he was twelve, he revealed in his book *Behind the Mask: My Double Life in Baseball* (perhaps the only baseball book to open with a quote from Bette Davis). He realized that he loved baseball long before he realized that he loved men. Lacking the skills to be a ballplayer, he chose umpiring as the next best thing. And like millions of other homosexuals, he hid his sexual orientation for fear that he would be drummed out of his profession.

"My toughest chore every day during the baseball season wasn't my umpiring," he wrote. "It was living a lie."

The idea of an umpire having *any* sex life is a little disconcerting, and Pallone told more than most fans really wanted to know ("When Scott and I first did it, not only didn't it feel unnatural, but it suddenly seemed like the most natural thing in the world").

He didn't name names, but Pallone said he had an affair with a top "straight" movie star ("late twenties, about six-two, slim, darkly handsome, with a sensual smile") and several major-league baseball players. One, whom he called "Wes," was a rising young star in 1984. During an appearance on *Donahue*, Pallone claimed there were enough gays in baseball to field a team—"including some of the best-known and most accomplished players in the game."

He also revealed that umpires always wear black underwear (in case they split their pants).

Controversy seemed to follow Pallone throughout his career. While he was in the minors, a rumor circulated that he had run up a $50,000 gambling debt. The day before he was to work the All-Star game in 1983, he was pulled over for drunken driving (he was found innocent). When Cincinnati shortstop Dave Concepcion disputed a call and spit in his face, Pallone went after him and would have started the first umpire-player brawl if he hadn't been held back. Before he came out of the closet, he was best known for the 1988 shoving match he had with Pete Rose that nearly erupted into a Riverfront Stadium riot. Pallone believes his explosive temper was an outgrowth of the emotional turmoil in his personal life.

Little by little, Pallone became more comfortable with his homosexuality, frequenting gay bars and confiding his secret to close straight friends. By 1985, the rumors began to circulate. Kevin Hallinan, head of security in the baseball commissioner's office, questioned Pallone about accusations that he had picked up men in bars in Cincinnati (false) and St. Louis (true).

Realizing that he needed to be open about his homosexuality and that baseball would never accept that, Pallone planned to fulfill his dream of working a World Series and then retire.

It didn't happen that way. The Pete Rose incident on April 30, 1988, made him too controversial. Two months later the commissioner's office began investigating the "Saratoga Springs sex scandal" and it was all over for Pallone.

The facts of the case, according to Pallone, are as follows: In October of 1987 a friend named Sam Gennaro introduced him to two acquaintances who lived in upstate New York, Larry Blodgett and Bill Desadora. The group had lunch in Manhattan and it was suggested that Pallone and Gennaro come up to visit sometime. They did in December, spending most of the day seeing the sights. Later they went to Blodgett's Saratoga Springs house for about half an hour.

Ten minutes after they walked in the door, a teenage boy came down the stairs and was introduced to Pallone. Several minutes later, Pallone and Gennaro went to lunch and never saw the others again.

Blodgett and Desadora, it turns out, were operating a sex ring involving teenage boys. The fourteen-year-old Pallone had met, for reasons unknown, signed a sworn affidavit that he had performed oral sex on Pallone, followed by mutual masturbation.

The case against Pallone fell apart when every adult present—including Blodgett and Desadora—testified that Pallone had nothing to do with the sex ring. The investigation of Pallone was dropped on November 1. Blodgett, Desadora, and several other men were charged, convicted, and sentenced to jail.

It's a fact of life that when a well-known figure is charged with a crime, the media trumpets it in big headlines. But when he or she is cleared, it may not be mentioned at all. When the story hit the papers, Pallone was forced by the baseball commissioner's office to take a leave of absence. After he was cleared, Pallone was fired by Commissioner Bart Giamatti.

"Baseball had really found me guilty," Pallone said, "of being gay."

A long time ago, a young Frank Robinson was arrested for carrying a concealed weapon. Cesar Cedeno was charged with manslaughter. Jose Canseco was caught with a semiautomatic handgun in his car. All three men (and scores of others in these pages) were given a second chance and allowed to continue playing in the major leagues.

But Pallone, who was not even *charged* with any crime, was considered too great a threat to stay a part of the game. He thought seriously about suing baseball to clear his name, but decided to accept a generous settlement instead and move on with his life.

For Pallone, one good thing resulted from the scandal—he came out of the closet and was able to live openly as a homosexual. "Now I don't have to hide anymore," he says. "Now I'm free."

Perhaps the most shocking revelation from Pallone—from a baseball standpoint—is the way he was treated by veteran umpires when he came up to the big leagues.

In 1979, when ballplayers were getting their first taste of free agency, fifty of the fifty-two major-league umpires went on strike for better wages. At the time, first-year umps made less than $18,000 a year.

Pallone was one of the eight minor-league umpires who accepted an offer to fill in during and after the strike. He had been in the minors for eight years and didn't know if he'd ever make the majors. After much mental anguish over crossing the picket line, he decided to take the opportunity.

From that moment on, Pallone and the other replacement umpires were labeled scabs and shunned by the union umps. Pallone says they refused to talk with him off the field and would humiliate him by walking out onto the field separately. If a scab ump was working behind the plate and the catcher appealed a checked swing call, the union umpire on the baselines would automatically reverse the decision to show him up.

It went further than that. One night Pallone received a call in his hotel room from someone who simply said, "You're a scab, Pallone. How's it feel to be a back stabber?" A few minutes later, he received a similar call. He disconnected the phone, but for the next half hour heavy objects crashed against the door. He tried to sleep, but a group of men had gathered outside the window to yell at him.

Another time he went to the ballpark and found that his shin-guard straps had been slashed, his hat shredded, and a padlock placed on the bars of his mask.

These are the men to whom we entrust the dignity of baseball. Pallone was enraged enough to take a swing at umpire John Kibler and throw a chair at Nick Colosi's head, smashing a hole in the door of the umpire's dressing room.

American League crew chief Don Denkinger told the press, "I will not ride with them [the scabs]. I will not eat with them. I will not have idle conversation with them." Eddie Montague said, "They'll never be accepted. And I mean never."

Once an umpire makes a decision, it is said, he's not about to change his mind.

EDDIE WAITKUS
You Can't Get a Man with a Gun

On June 14, 1949, Ruth Ann Steinhagen checked into the Edgewater Beach Hotel on Chicago's Lake Shore Drive. She was nineteen, a pretty six-foot brunette. Any ballplayer's dream girl. She signed the register "Ruth Ann Burns."

Once settled in her room, Steinhagen ordered three drinks from room service and slipped the bellboy $5 to deliver the following message to another guest—Eddie Waitkus, the twenty-nine-year-old first baseman for the Philadelphia Phillies, in town for a series against the Cubs:

> *It is extremely important that I see you as soon as possible. We're not acquainted, but I have something of importance to speak to you about. I think it would be to your advantage to let me explain this to you as I am leaving the hotel the day after tomorrow. I realize this is out of the ordinary, but as I say, it is extremely important.*

Then she went to sleep.

Waitkus, a bachelor, knew the score. Ballplayers constantly receive invitations from strange women on the road. When he returned from dinner at around eleven, he called Steinhagen's room. She asked him to come by in thirty minutes.

At eleven-thirty, Eddie knocked at the door of room 1297-A.

"Come in for a minute," Steinhagen said. Waitkus startled her by breezing past and sitting down in the only chair in the room.

"I have a surprise for you," she said, walking quickly to the closet. She pulled out a .22-caliber rifle and waved it at Eddie's chest.

"Baby, what's this all about?"

"Get up and move toward the window."

Waitkus did as he was told. It didn't look like this night was going to turn out the way he'd thought.

"For two years you've been bothering me," Steinhagen said, aiming the gun, "and now you're going to die."

(A note to the reader: This dialogue may sound like it was invented for dramatic effect. If it was, it wasn't by me. It appeared in the pages of the *New York Times* three days after the incident.)

Before the gun exploded Waitkus cried, "What in the world goes on here?" The bullet tore a hole in his chest and the impact knocked him against the wall. He went down, rolling onto his back. A pool of blood formed on the floor around him.

"Baby, what did you do that for?" he gasped. "You like this, don't you? But why, in the name of Heaven, did you do this to me?"

Steinhagen knelt beside him and took his right hand in hers. Things weren't working out as she had planned. She had intended to stab Waitkus with a paring knife hidden in her skirt pocket and then shoot *herself* with the gun. When Waitkus walked right past her into the room, she panicked. After shooting him, she didn't have the courage to kill herself. Instead, she called the front desk and informed them that she had just shot a man.

Steinhagen was rushed to the police station and booked for assault with intent to murder, while Waitkus was rushed to Illinois Masonic Hospital. The bullet had entered under his heart and lodged in the muscles near his spine. His right lung collapsed, and doctors frantically administered two blood transfusions and oxygen in a desperate attempt to save his life.

The Waitkus shooting startled the nation in 1948, and provided the inspiration for Bernard Malamud's 1952 baseball novel *The Natural*, which was made into a movie starring Robert Redford. Actually, the incident more closely mirrors John Lennon's assassination in 1980, when an obsessed fan gunned down the ex-Beatle.

"I just became nuttier and nuttier about the guy," Steinhagen said after she was arrested. "I knew I would never get to know him in a normal way . . . and if I can't have him, nobody else can. And I then decided I would kill him."

Previously, she had been obsessed with actor Alan Ladd and long-dead composer Franz Liszt. Steinhagen's mother told the police that Ruth had become "baseball crazy" when she saw Waitkus play for Chicago two years earlier. Just sixteen, she fell madly in love with the first baseman, dreaming of him at night, praying for him and even building a shrine to him in her bedroom. His number was 36, so she bought records made in 1936. She started eating baked beans because he'd been born in Boston. When she found out that Waitkus was Lithuanian, she went so far as to learn how to speak the language.

Mrs. Steinhagen had urged her daughter to see a psychiatrist, and Ruth did. But she only got worse, suffering a nervous breakdown in December. A week before the shooting, she had complained about a "funny feeling" across the back of her head.

"I'm sorry Eddie has to suffer so," she said. "I'm sorry it had to be him. But I had to shoot somebody. Only in that way could I relieve the nervous tension I've been under the last two years. The shooting has relieved that tension. I've never been so happy in my life."

Steinhagen, as might be expected, was sent to a mental institution. Dr. William H. Haines diagnosed her as suffering from a split personality disorder.

Amazingly, Eddie Waitkus not only recovered but came back to play baseball again. The year after the shooting he played all 154 games for the Phillies, won the Comeback Player of the Year award and got four hits in the World Series (the Phils lost in four games).*

But for the rest of his life, Waitkus was uncomfortable about meeting new people. He was treated for alcoholism. When Steinhagen was released from the mental hospital three years after the shooting, he fought to keep her locked up.

Said Waitkus: "She had the coldest-looking face I ever saw."

JOE DIMAGGIO AND MARILYN MONROE
An American Obsession

No discussion of sex and baseball is complete without mention of Joe DiMaggio, who bedded and wedded the most famous sex symbol of our age. The romance of the slugger and the star was a Hollywood press bonanza, but a sad and tragic episode in both their lives.

---

* Four other players survived gunshot wounds. Shortstop Charlie Gelbert of the Cardinals shot himself while hunting in 1932. The same thing happened to White Sox pitcher Monty Stratton in 1938. Hank Bauer of the Yankees was hit at Iwo Jima in 1945, and a young woman shot Cub shortstop Billy Jurges in 1932.

As soon as he arrived in New York in 1936, Joe began to woo showgirls. A blond actress, Dorothy Arnoldine Olsen (Dorothy Arnold), became the first Mrs. DiMaggio when she was introduced to Joe on the set of *Manhattan Merry-Go-Round*. He had three lines in the 1938 film. Joe and Dorothy were married on November 19, 1939.

It couldn't have been for love. Dorothy complained that Joe preferred to spend his evenings hanging out with the boys at Toots Shor's. Joe couldn't help noticing that Dorothy was using his name to advance her career. (It didn't help. Her best-known film was *Secrets of a Nurse*.) The union lasted four years, and it was Dorothy who asked for a divorce on grounds of cruelty.

DiMaggio was puttering around in the spring of 1952, his first spring training after retiring from baseball. He happened to see a newspaper photo of White Sox outfielder Gus Zernial ("the new DiMaggio") posing with a gorgeous starlet named Marilyn Monroe. In the photo, Marilyn was wearing high heels, white shorts, and a tight top and holding a baseball bat. She was shooting *Monkey Business* at the time.

DiMaggio, one of the few men in the world to wield this kind of clout, made a few phone calls and lined up a blind date with Marilyn. They met for dinner at Villa Nova, a restaurant in Hollywood.

Some accounts of the first meeting of "Mr. and Mrs. America" howled that Joe had "struck out." According to Roger Kahn's book *Joe & Marilyn*, the pair made love in the back seat of a car just hours after they met.

The next day, DiMaggio said, "This is the first time I ever called up a girl the morning after I laid her to see how she was." This, to Joltin' Joe, was true love.

They were married January 14, 1954, at San Francisco City Hall. Marilyn signed the marriage certificate as Norma Jean Mortenson Dougherty. As a wedding gift, she gave Joe nude photos of herself. After the ceremony, the couple fled to a Paso Robles motel for their honeymoon.

Desperate for any information about the consummation, reporters discovered that DiMaggio had requested a room with a television, causing every male in America to wonder why anybody spending his wedding night with Marilyn Monroe would want to watch TV.

When they finally met the press and were asked how they were enjoying married life, Joe got off his best line: "It's got to be better than rooming with [Yankee pitcher] Joe Page."

By all indications, the marriage of Joe DiMaggio and Marilyn Monroe would have been long and happy had sex been the only component. Marilyn would giggle to friends that "Joe brings a great bat into the bedroom" or "Joe's biggest bat isn't the one he uses on the field." Marilyn used to say that Joe's body reminded her of Michelangelo's *David*.

Hers wasn't too shabby, either. Between the two of them, they gave every man and woman in America a fantasy to enjoy.

In all other respects, however, they were a mismatch. He was neat. She was a slob. He loved San Francisco. She preferred Los Angeles. She thrived on publicity. He was introverted, even cold.

He read the sports pages, if he read at all. She aspired to be an intellectual. His career was over. Hers was at its zenith. She wanted to be what she was—a movie star. He wanted the most beautiful housewife in the world.

"She's a plain kid," Joe said. "She'd give up the business if I asked her. She'd quit the movies in a minute."

Joe was insanely jealous and couldn't appreciate that making men tremble was Marilyn's line of work, just as making opposing pitchers tremble had been his. She gave him good reason to be jealous, having affairs with at least four men during their relationship. There was talk of physical abuse (Marilyn called DiMaggio "Joe the Slugger").

Toward the end of their marriage, Joe stopped by the set to see Marilyn shoot the famous scene in *The Seven Year Itch* in which her skirt flies up over the subway grating. Watching the first take, DiMaggio was furious about Marilyn's revealing underwear and insisted she change into something more . . . opaque.

As Roger Kahn tells it, later that night restaurateur and close friend Toots Shor tried to console DiMaggio by saying, "Aw, Joe. What can you expect when you marry a whore?" (It has been widely rumored that Marilyn worked as a prostitute before she was discovered.) At that, Joe stormed out of his favorite watering hole and didn't speak to Shor for a long time.

———

The marriage of Joe and Marilyn lasted 274 stormy days, and they were hounded by gossip columnists during every one of them. The day the pair separated, more than a hundred press people swarmed across their lawn begging for quotes.

While the marriage was collapsing, Joe hired private detectives to keep an eye on Marilyn and perhaps gather evidence to be used in the divorce case. This led to what became known as the notorious "Wrong Door Raid" of November 5, 1954.

Late that night, DiMaggio and close buddy Frank Sinatra were doing some serious drinking in a Sunset Strip restaurant called Villa Capri. Phil Irwin, a young detective hired to shadow Marilyn, spotted her car outside the Beverly Hills apartment of an actress friend. There had been suspicions that Marilyn was having a lesbian affair. Irwin called his boss, Barney Ruditsky, who called Sinatra at Villa Capri. DiMaggio became furious and demanded that they go see what Marilyn was up to.

What happened next is fuzzy. Some accounts of the incident have Ruditsky purposely breaking down the door of an apartment he knew Marilyn was not in. Others say Sinatra and DiMaggio themselves busted down what they thought was the door of Marilyn's actress friend. Even a Los Angeles grand jury probe couldn't decide who was telling the truth.

In any case, a fifty-year-old woman named Florence Ross Kotz was wakened abruptly when several boisterous men smashed down the door to her apartment. The men ran around shooting pictures until they realized they were at the wrong address and stumbled out in a panic. Kotz sued DiMaggio and Sinatra and received a quiet out-of-court settlement of $7,500.

Clearly, DiMaggio could not put Marilyn behind him when their romance was over. He remained obsessed with her right up until her death, and beyond. He was spotted hanging around her apartment late at night, like a fan waiting for an autograph. Until the end, he hoped they could get back together again.

Marilyn, too, had more than physical feelings for Joe. In 1961, she checked herself into Payne Whitney, a mental hospital in New York. Frustrated and frightened, she threw a chair through a window and was put in a straitjacket. When she was allowed one phone call, it was DiMaggio's number she dialed. Joe flew cross-country and pulled the strings necessary to free her.

When Marilyn died tragically in 1962, it was DiMaggio who paid for the crypt and made the funeral arrangements. He made it a point to bar his old friend Frank Sinatra, as well as Dean Martin, Peter Lawford, and Marilyn's other Hollywood cronies from attending. In Joe's view, she would still have been alive if they hadn't led her to drugs and secret affairs with the Kennedys.

Three times a week, from 1962 to 1982, a pair of red roses was faithfully delivered to Marilyn Monroe's crypt courtesy of Joe DiMaggio. To this day, he refuses to talk about her.

In his book *Goddess: The Secret Lives of Marilyn Monroe*, Anthony Summers reveals that the following letter was found after Marilyn's death:

> Dear Joe,
>   *If I can only succeed in making you happy—I will have succeeded in the bigest [sic] and most difficult thing there is— that is to make one person completely happy. Your happiness means my happiness.*

MORE SEX SCANDALS

Van Lingle Mungo, 1941

The Brooklyn Dodgers pitcher was one of the fastest in the game during the 1930s; he was clocked at 118 mph by a timing device (undoubtedly faulty) at West Point. He once struck out seven men in a row, and in 1936 he led the league with 238 strikeouts. (He also led the league in walks in 1932, 1934, and 1936.)

Mungo was most famous as a serious drinker and carouser who was constantly getting into trouble. He paid about $15,000 in fines over his fourteen-year career, which is the most he ever made in salary for one season.

His most famous fracas occurred in the third week of spring training in 1941. The Dodgers were training in Cuba and staying at Havana's Nacional Hotel. Mungo talked two women—the hotel singer Lady Vine and the female half of the Latin dance team Gonzales & Gonzales—into going to bed with him.

When his wife didn't come home all night, Gonzales—the *male* half of Gonzales & Gonzales—went looking for her. He found her, along with Lady Vine and Van Lingle Mungo, in bed. A fight naturally ensued. Mungo managed to push the male Gonzales, a former bullfighter, out of the room and bolted the door shut.

Gonzales left and came back waving a butcher knife, but by then the Dodgers had snuck Mungo out of the room and hidden him in a vegetable bin in the cellar. The police and Cuban soldiers were swarming over the hotel with a warrant for the pitcher's arrest, and Gonzales was hunting for him with the knife.

Leo Durocher, then managing the Dodgers, described the incident in his autobiography: "All you could hear, wherever you turned, was 'Mungo . . . Mungo . . . Mungo.' "

The Dodgers arranged for a seaplane to smuggle Mungo out of Cuba. Then they fined him and sent him to the minors. Mungo was also sued by the Gonzales dancers, prompting him to complain, "Don't anybody ever get into trouble but me?"

The next year he was traded to the New York Giants. He served in the military in 1944, and then came back to finish his career with a sparkling 14–7 record in 1945.

Mungo died in 1985, but was memorialized forever in the 1970 song "Dodger Blues." The song's lyrics consist entirely of names of old ballplayers, and each chorus ends with a haunting "Van Lin-gle Mun-go . . ." It's on a recent album titled *Baseball's Greatest Hits*.

Jim Rivera, 1952

"To the best of my knowledge," said Ford Frick, "this is the first time a commissioner ever had to make a decision on a morals charge."

Frick put White Sox rookie outfielder Jim "Jungle Jim" Rivera on probation for one year after he had been accused of raping a woman in Chicago. The charge was dismissed by a grand jury, but the commissioner said Rivera would be punished because baseball had "an obligation to the public to maintain the highest standards of morality among all men who are connected with the game."

Rivera went on to play ten years in the majors, with a lifetime batting average of .256. He led the American League with sixteen triples in 1953 and twenty-five stolen bases in 1955.

Edward Bouchee, 1958

The Philadelphia Phillies first baseman was arrested in his hometown of Spokane, Washington, for indecent exposure before a six-year-old girl. Bouchee, twenty-five, admitted exposing himself four other times, with girls aged ten, eleven, fourteen, and eighteen.

He was placed on three years' probation and spent two months receiving psychiatric treatment at the Institute of Living in Hartford, Connecticut.

"Bouchee has responded completely to treatment and is now ready to take his place in society," said Commissioner Frick when the ballplayer was reinstated on July 1.

A lifetime .265 hitter, Bouchee hit .285 with fifteen home runs the next season. He was traded to the Cubs in 1960 and finished his career as one of the original "amazin' " New York Mets in 1962.

Pete Rose, 1963

"You know why I get all the women?" Pete Rose used to joke. "Because I always go in head first."

Before his rookie season, the Cincinnati Reds played a series of exhibition games in Mexico City. One night at a strip club, Rose got up onstage and had sex with one of the performers.

Rose married Karolyn Englehardt that winter, but he remained a notorious womanizer throughout his career. He kept girlfriends in every National League city, and in a few potential expansion cities as well.

One of his mistresses, a Tampa woman named Terryl Rubio, hit him with a paternity suit in 1979. Her baby girl was curiously named Morgan, the last name of one of Rose's longtime teammates. Rose didn't contest the suit and settled out of court. At the time, somebody hung a huge banner at Candlestick Park that read "PETE ROSE LEADS THE LEAGUE IN PATERNITY SUITS."

Karolyn Rose was incredibly tolerant for sixteen years, though on one occasion at Riverfront Stadium she punched a woman who was wearing a diamond pendant necklace identical to one Pete had given her. The woman, Carol Woliung, was a *Playboy* bunny and Philadelphia Eagles cheerleader. She became the second Mrs. Pete Rose after Pete and Karolyn divorced in 1984. Karolyn received a $1.25-million settlement.

"Hey, just give her a million bucks and tell her to hit the road," Pete told *Sports Illustrated*, on his method of ending a marriage.

Seattle Pilots, 1969

One of the startling revelations in Jim Bouton's *Ball Four* (1970) was that the Seattle players had a running prank in which they kissed one another. One player would put a hand over another player's mouth and kiss the hand. From a distance, it looked like a real kiss.

"Then we got a little drunk on a bus one night and the guys started kissing without bothering to put their hands up," Bouton wrote. "And then *that* became a joke. We'd kid about how many guys had kissed other guys."

Baseball Commissioner Bowie Kuhn got so bent out of shape that Bouton used his reaction as one of the blurbs on the back cover of his book: "You've done the game a grave disservice. Saying players kissed on the Seattle team bus—incredible!"

Cleon Jones, 1975

Police in St. Petersburg, Florida, were surprised to find the New York Mets star outfielder sleeping nude in a 1961 Ford station wagon at five-thirty on a Sunday morning. With him was twenty-one-year-old Sharon Ann Sabol, an unemployed waitress, who was also nude.

Jones and Sabol were charged with indecent exposure. Sabol was also charged with possession of a marijuana cigarette and marijuana pipes.

When asked why he and Miss Sabol were sleeping in a car on the busiest street in St. Petersburg, Jones replied, presumably with a straight face, "We ran out of gas."

Jones had led the "Miracle Mets" of 1969 to the World Championship with a .340 average. He was in St. Petersburg recovering from a knee operation. The next season, the Mets traded him to the White Sox, where he played just twelve games and retired.

New York Yankees, 1979

There's no need to go to card shows and pay money to get autographs of baseball players. Just pull down your pants and hang a moon. A twenty-year-old blond woman boarded the Yankees' bus in Chicago after a game against the White Sox and had most of the team sign their names on her naked behind.

The incident made the papers when *Chicago Sun-Times* columnist Mike Royko interviewed the mother of a nine-year-old Yankees fan who was trying to get autographs at the same time.

"I couldn't believe it," the mother said. "They wouldn't give autographs to any of the kids, but they were signing their names to that girl's bare butt."

Afterward, the girl was followed off the bus by manager Billy Martin, who asked her if he could take her picture. The girl pulled down her pants right on the street and posed.

The incident was confirmed by Yankee publicity man Mickey Morabito, who said, "You travel with this team and you see everything."

Julio Valdez, 1983

This is perhaps the only time in baseball history that a player was arrested in the middle of a game. Valdez, a utility shortstop with the Red Sox, was sitting in the dugout during the seventh inning of a game against the Seattle Mariners and was notified that detectives with the Boston Vice Squad were waiting in the clubhouse with a warrant for his arrest.

The twenty-six-year-old Valdez was handcuffed and charged with statutory rape. A month earlier, he had had sex with a fourteen-year-old runaway in his hotel room near Fenway Park.

Valdez was cleared when the girl admitted she had lied to him about her age. "I told Julio I was seventeen," she told the *Boston Globe*. "He didn't know how old I was. If I told him I was fourteen, I would never be with him."

"I feel like a new man," Valdez said.

He still had two other problems. One, he was married. Two, he was hitting .120. The Red Sox sent him down to the minors and his big-league career was over after sixty-five games.

New York Yankees, 1984

In his autobiography, *Winfield: A Player's Life*, Dave Winfield described a party in which the team invited a hundred women to a penthouse overlooking the Detroit River. At midnight, two Yankees and a character called "Vapor Man" entered. All three were naked except for shaving cream and enormous dildoes.

"A few women demanded to be let out, and they bolted right then," wrote Winfield. "Others shrieked—in distress or pleasure—as the guys went after them, getting shaving cream all over their dresses and hair." He never revealed what happened next.

Marla Collins, 1986

The Chicago Cubs ball girl from 1982 to 1986, Collins was fired when she posed for a nude pictorial in the September issue of *Playboy*. Before being dismissed, the twenty-eight-year-old had been so popular that she landed an endorsement contract for athletic shoes. Collins said she had planned to make 1986 her last season anyway. She was besieged with offers for personal appearances.

Ball girls, by the way, made their entrance into baseball in 1971 when the flamboyant Oakland A's owner Charley Finley hired fourteen-year-old Sheryl Lawrence and thirteen-year-old Debbi Sivyer. Sivyer won the hearts of the fans, serving the umpires lemonade and chocolate-chip cookies she baked herself. Later, she married and became a multimillionaire by founding Mrs. Fields Cookies.

Oakland A's, 1987

Several businessmen in St. Paul, Minnesota, supplied thirteen- to seventeen-year-old prostitutes to friends and associates, including members of the Oakland Athletics, according to a year-long investigation by the *St. Paul Pioneer Press Dispatch*.

One girl, who was sixteen, told police she was taken to the bar of the Hyatt Regency Hotel in Minneapolis, where she talked with men who were introduced as A's players and staff. She then went with an A's official to his room and was paid $125 for sex. Another girl went with another member of the team. The incident took place in early summer of 1986, when the A's were in town to play the Twins and were staying at the Hyatt Regency.

The investigation stopped there, and the names of the ballplayers were not disclosed. Darrell Craig Lewis, the pimp for several of the girls, pleaded guilty to soliciting for prostitution and was sentenced to nine months in jail.

Dave Winfield, 1988

Ruth Roper, the mother of actress Robin Givens and mother-in-law of boxing champ Mike Tyson, claimed Yankees outfielder Winfield gave her a sexually transmitted disease in 1985. Winfield denied all allegations but agreed to an out-of-court settlement when Roper filed a lawsuit against him.

A year later, Winfield's problems with women made the papers again when his longtime girlfriend sued him for palimony. Sandra Renfro, who lived with Winfield from 1982 to 1983 and had a daughter with him, claimed their relationship was a marriage in common law. A Texas jury agreed, and Winfield was ordered to pay Renfro $1.6 million.

"I expect a lot of children were fathered by Ty Cobb's generation," complained Winfield's lawyer. "But nobody wanted half of six thousand dollars a year."

Bryn Smith, 1989

The Montreal pitcher was in West Palm Beach, Florida, to play golf in the pro-am PGA Seniors Championship when he went out one night looking for some action. Unfortunately, West Palm Beach police picked that night for a sting operation.

Six female officers posed as hookers on a busy street and received offers from Smith and 115 other men. He was charged with solicitation and paid a $250 fine.

"Don't come into our city looking for prostitutes," warned Police Chief Billy Riggs.

The incident didn't hurt Smith's golf game. He shot rounds of 76 and 73 and won the tournament.

Luis Polonia, 1989

After a game in Milwaukee, New York Yankees outfielder Polonia met a girl at the team bus and invited her to his hotel room. The girl, it was later revealed, was fifteen years old.

Her mother contacted the police, who knocked on Polonia's door at the Pfister Hotel between one and two in the morning. He opened it, and the girl charged him with sexual assault.

Polonia was arrested and spent sixty days in jail. There he watched the Oakland Athletics, with whom he had played for the first half of the season, playing in the World Series. "I was really down watching them having fun and I was in jail," he said after he returned to baseball. "Really, the only thing that kept me going was I knew I was going to get half a share [of the World Series money]."

He was traded eight months later to the California Angels.

Jose Uribe, 1989

The San Francisco Giants shortstop was detained in his native Dominican Republic so that he could stand trial on a rape charge. A woman complained that he had threatened her with a gun and forced her to have sex with him. Uribe spent three days in jail and was freed.

It had been a difficult year for Uribe. Seven months earlier, his wife, Sara, had died a day after giving birth to their third child. Uribe went on the disabled list because of emotional distress.

Boston Red Sox Fans, 1991

"Listen up, sports fans," wrote *Boston Globe* columnist Bella English. "There's a new game at Fenway Park this season. Call it Fondle the Doll. Call it Perverts on Parade."

Fans in the Fenway bleachers had begun bringing life-size inflatable female dolls to the ball park and simulating sex acts with them during Red Sox games. English said that men would pass the dolls around and fans would scream, "Yeah, yeah, do her!"

"The message of the doll-fondling is that the violation of women is okay, a sport even," English wrote.

A year earlier, vendors at Foxboro Stadium had sold "Lisa Dolls" after *Boston Herald* sportswriter Lisa Olson was sexually harassed by New England Patriots players in the locker room.

Rickey Henderson, 1991

Shortly after becoming the all-time major-league stolen-base leader, the married Oakland outfielder was accused of slugging a twenty-three-year-old blonde, a married ex-model, in his New York hotel room.

Sandra Salarimatin had attended the Yankees-Oakland game this particular evening and had been drinking heavily when she came home and got into a fight with her husband, Jahangir. She walked out and went to the Grand Hyatt hotel, where Henderson was staying. She met him in the hotel bar and after last call at two in the morning went up to his room. When she wanted to leave, he slapped her with the back of his hand, bruising her eye and back.

So she said, anyway. Henderson said it was all lies and Salarimatin refused to press charges. Her husband, a karate expert, threatened to track Henderson down and avenge his wife, but he apparently changed his mind.

Toppsy Curvey, 1991

Baseball hadn't seen anything like her since Morganna "The Kissing Bandit" Roberts terrorized the game in the 1970s.

The California Angels had men on first and second in the top of the second when this ridiculously endowed woman leaped out of the stands at Yankee Stadium. She made a mad dash for the pitcher's mound and planted a wet one on the cheek of Yankees right-hander Scott Kamienicki.

Kamienicki claimed the woman hadn't thrown off his game, but after they had hauled her away, Luis Sojo smacked his next pitch for a two-run double. Kamienicki was yanked after five innings.

Twenty-four-year-old Toppsy Curvey, whose real name is Laurie Stathopulos, was publicizing her exotic dance show at a nightclub called Fantasy Island in Nyack, New York. She received a summons for trespassing, and after the game she autographed pictures of herself outside Yankee Stadium.

Toppsy made Morganna look *small*. "I swear to God," an anonymous Yankee told the *New York Post*, "it looked like two pigs in a sleeping bag wrestling."

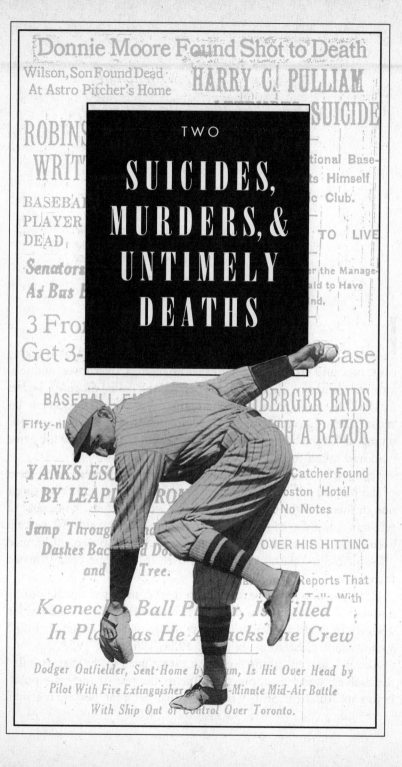

Donnie Moore Found Shot to Death

Wilson, Son Found Dead
At Astro Pitcher's Home

HARRY C. PULLIAM SUICIDE

ROBINS
WRIT

BASEBA
PLAYER
DEAD

Senator
As Bus

3 Fro
Get 3-

tional Base-
ts Himself
c Club.

TO LIVE

the Manage-
ald to Have
nd.

ase

TWO

SUICIDES, MURDERS, & UNTIMELY DEATHS

BASEBALL E
Fifty-n

BERGER ENDS
TH A RAZOR

YANKS ESC
BY LEAPI RO

Jump Throug
Dashes Bac Do
and Tree.

Catcher Found
oston Hotel
No Notes

OVER HIS HITTING

Reports That
ll With

Koenech Ball Pit r, Is illed
In Pl as He A cks he Crew

Dodger Outfielder, Sent Home by m, Is Hit Over Head by
Pilot With Fire Extingaisher Minute Mid-Air Battle
With Ship Out of Control Over Toronto.

> *"I won over two hundred games, but what happened to me in August of 1920 is the only thing anybody remembers."*
>
> —New York Yankees pitcher Carl Mays, the only man in major-league history to throw a ball that killed another man

Loren Coleman is the Bill James of suicide. Instead of tracking runs, hits, and errors, Coleman tracks hangings, overdoses, and self-inflicted gunshots. After he published a book called *Suicide Clusters* in 1987, the researcher with the Human Services Development Institute of the University of South Maine conducted a two-year study on major-league baseball players throughout the history of the game who had taken their own lives.

These are some of the statistics Coleman uncovered: 45 percent of the players who killed themselves were pitchers, and every single one of them a right-hander; 13 percent were catchers, who, next to pitchers, play the most stressful position on the field; 50 percent used guns; 22 percent used poisons or overdosed; 5 percent jumped off something; 3 percent hanged themselves; and 2 percent drowned themselves.

Only one player (Willard Hershberger) committed suicide during a season in which he was playing. Players who experienced sudden declines in performance were particularly at risk. Coleman found some suicide clustering—in 1927, 1934, 1945, and 1962.

About 1 percent of the men who ever played in the majors killed themselves, which is about the same as the rest of the male population in America. Still, Coleman considers that percentage high because he believes the minor leagues act as a screening process that ordinarily weeds out players who can't take the stress of being a celebrity athlete.

Coleman found that more than half the baseball suicide victims did the deed within ten years after leaving the game. Seven did it within *one* year. This has led him to conclude that baseball needs a counseling program to help players adjust to the real world.

"When they leave baseball, they too often don't have a coping mechanism," he says. "They're just left to drift by themselves."

In 1988, Coleman wrote to Commissioner Peter Ueberroth, warning that a suicide was statistically likely to happen within the coming year. He suggested a program—funded by Major League Baseball —that would identify and help players at risk. Ueberroth replied that Major League Baseball did not wish to be involved.

Within nine months, three major-league ballplayers killed themselves—Carlos Bernier, Virgil Stallcup, and Donnie Moore.

It's impossible to predict precisely who will commit suicide. It might have been expected that one of the Black Sox players, disgraced for a lifetime, would have killed himself. None of them did. Fred Snodgrass, Fred Merkle, and Ralph Branca—baseball "goats" for life— didn't kill themselves. After dropping the third strike that blew the 1941 World Series for the Dodgers, catcher Mickey Owen didn't kill himself. (But go figure—ten years later the man who threw the pitch, Hugh Casey, stuck a gun in his mouth and blew his brains out.)

It's a tragedy when *anyone* takes his own life. The saddest story, I think, is that of Bruce Gardner. He was a college pitching star with USC in the late 1950s. When he was just eighteen, the White Sox offered him a bonus of $66,000 to sign with them. Pressured by his mother and his coach, Gardner elected to finish his college education first.

After graduation, Gardner signed with the Dodgers for $12,000 and won twenty games in the minors in 1961. Then he got a sore arm and was washed up in baseball at twenty-five. He never forgave his college coach for taking away his shot to pitch in the big leagues.

On the night of June 7, 1971, Gardner hopped the fence of his old college baseball field in Los Angeles—where he had been a star. He lay down near the pitcher's mound. Holding his USC diploma and his All-America plaque, he shot himself in the head.

On the ground next to him was this typewritten note:

> *I saw life going downhill every day and it shaped my attitude toward everything and everybody. Everything and every feeling that I visualized with my earned and rightful start in baseball was the focal point of continuous failure. No pride of accomplishment, no money, no home, no sense of fulfillment, no attraction. A bitter past, blocking any accomplishment of a future except age. I brought it to a halt tonight at 32.*

DONNIE MOORE
The Pitch He Couldn't Forget

Even if Tonya Moore *hadn't* given her husband a .44 semiautomatic for Christmas, he probably would have found a way to kill himself. But with the gun, he could kill *both* of them.

Baseball is only a game, but it should never be said that ballplayers don't take it seriously. Donnie Ray Moore's berserk shooting spree on July 18, 1989, was a direct result of a home run he'd given up three years earlier—when he was one strike away from pitching the California Angels into their first World Series appearance.

Moore was born in 1954 and raised in Lubbock, Texas, a prodigy who could hit .400 and throw a curveball for strikes in high school. He met and married Tonya when he was nineteen. By 1985 Donnie Moore was one of the best relief pitchers in baseball, saving thirty-one games and pitching two perfect innings in the All-Star game.

The Angels rewarded him with a three-year, $3-million contract. Some of the money went to buy a Mercedes and a million-dollar home in suburban Anaheim, where Donnie lived with Tonya and their three children, Demetria, seventeen, Donnie Jr., ten, and Ronnie, seven.

Donnie wasn't quite as overpowering on the mound in 1986, but he did save twenty-one games for the Angels, plus the division clincher and Game 3 of the memorable American League playoffs against the Boston Red Sox. It was Game 5 that proved his undoing.

The Angels held a 5–2 lead going into the ninth inning in front of the home crowd at Anaheim Stadium. They had already won three games to Boston's one and every fan knew they were just three outs away from the World Series.

Mike Witt, the starter, was still on the mound for the Angels. He gave up a single to Bill Buckner (a name to remember), then struck out Jim Rice for the first out. Don Baylor slammed a home run over the left-field wall, making the score 5–4. Dwight Evans popped up for the second out.

At this point, manager Gene Mauch pulled Witt and brought in left-hander Gary Lucas to dispose of Rich Gedman and nail the season down. Lucas promptly hit Gedman with the first pitch. The tying run was now on base and the winning run at the plate—Dave Henderson.

Henderson hadn't started the game. He came in after center fielder Tony Armas sprained his ankle in the second inning. In the sixth inning, Henderson looked to be the goat of the game when he dove for a long drive off the bat of Bobby Grich and accidentally tapped the ball over the fence for a two-run homer. He had also struck out.

Mauch called on his closer—Donnie Moore. A strikeout would be a nice way to win the American League Championship.

Moore's first pitch was out of the strike zone, and Henderson took the next one for a strike. Moore blew the next one by him, and Henderson swung like he didn't have a clue.

The crowd was ready to get crazy and cops with motorcycle helmets stood poised in the dugouts, waiting to charge the field and keep the celebration orderly. Champagne bottles were ready in the Angel clubhouse.

One more strike and it would all be over. Donnie Moore could stand on the mound as the game's hero while his teammates mobbed him.

It takes a certain personality to be a relief pitcher, especially the team's closer. You come into every game with the pressure on, and you walk off the mound either a hero or a goat. Donnie Moore loved to get the ball when the game was on the line.

"If you can go out and take all the glory, then the days you're a goat you've got to handle that, too," he was quoted as saying, in a posthumous profile in *Gentlemen's Quarterly.*

A fastball in the dirt evened the count at 2–2. Moore threw his split-finger fastball, and Henderson fouled it off. Then he fouled off another fastball. It looked like Henderson was getting his confidence. The crowd was screaming with each pitch.

Catcher Bob Boone gave four fingers, the sign for the split-finger fastball. Moore rocked back and threw it, catching a little bit too much of the plate. Henderson got the thick part of the bat on it and all heads turned to watch the flight of the ball. It landed eight rows over the left-field wall. The crowd of 64,223 people fell quiet.

"You're looking at one for the ages here," said broadcaster Al Michaels as Henderson circled the bases and the Red Sox players went crazy. Seconds before they'd been one strike away from elimination. Now they were ahead.

Moore finished up the inning and the Angels even struggled back to tie it in the bottom of the ninth. But in the eleventh, Moore loaded the bases and gave up a sacrifice fly to the pesky Henderson for the game winner. Boston won the next two games and advanced to the World Series.

"I blew it today," Moore told reporters after the game. "I'm a human being and I didn't do the job." He also said of his pitch to Henderson, "I'll think about that until the day I die."

That was the beginning of the end for Donnie Moore. A closer is supposed to *close*. Moore continued blowing games in 1987 and 1988. Arm troubles nagged him, and he had an operation to remove a bone spur on his spine. Fans booed him every time he took the mound, letting it be known that they resented his collecting a million dollars a year when he wasn't getting the job done. Mike Port, the Angels' general manager, sniped at him in the press. The team released Moore at the end of the 1988 season. He pitched for the Omaha Royals in 1989, a Triple A team, but not effectively.

He had other problems, too. After sixteen years of marriage, Tonya moved out and got an apartment. Donnie had been beating her since they were nineteen, a fact not mentioned in a 1987 *Cos-*

mopolitan profile of Tonya titled "Secrets of a Successful Marriage." His agent had recently filed a grievance, claiming Moore owed him $75,000 in commissions. To make matters worse, Donnie Moore had turned thirty-five, the age at which most pitchers stop earning money throwing baseballs and start making money by writing their names on them. On June 12, he was released by Omaha.

A month later, Tonya came over to the house to show it to a prospective buyer. The buyer never showed, and Donnie and Tonya spent the morning arguing in front of the children. Things calmed down and Tonya was getting ready to leave when Donnie came into the kitchen holding a gun. He pointed it at his own head.

"What? In front of your kids?" Tonya asked.

Donnie then turned the gun toward her and pulled the trigger. The bullet went through Tonya's neck. Frantic, she ran into the laundry room, and Donnie fired several more shots, two of which hit her in the chest. She managed to crawl into the garage and into the back seat of the Mercedes.

Their seventeen-year-old daughter, Demetria, jumped into the car and drove to Permanente Hospital in Anaheim. Doctors were able to save Tonya's life. Amazingly, her worst injury was a collapsed lung.

Meanwhile, Donnie pointed the gun at his own head and, with his ten-year-old son, Donnie Jr., staring at him, blew his brains out.

There was no note. Donnie hadn't been drinking.

Tonya spent two months in a mental hospital.

With all his personal problems, it is generally believed that the biggest factor in Donnie Moore's death was the home run he gave up to Dave Henderson. Friends said he was obsessed with his failure to get that third strike.

"He could not live with himself after Henderson hit the home run. He kept blaming himself," said Moore's agent, Dave Pinter. "He felt he was the next Ralph Branca." (Branca pitched for twelve years in the majors but will always be remembered for giving up Bobby Thomson's "Shot Heard 'Round the World," which won the 1951 pennant for the Giants.) Pinter claimed that three hours before the suicide, he had urged Moore to get psychological counseling.

A strange twist to end the saga: A week after Moore was one strike away from the World Series and blew it, Boston was one strike away from *winning* its first World Series in seventy years and blew it when first baseman Bill Buckner let a squibbed grounder roll through his legs.

The New York Mets went on to win the Series the next day. For millions of fans, Donnie Moore's one-pitch mistake faded from memory, and Bill Buckner will probably be remembered as the biggest goat in baseball history.

WILLARD HERSHBERGER
He Should Have Wasted a Pitch,
Instead of Himself

The summer of 1940 was one of the hottest in this century, with temperatures consistently hitting the nineties and frequently reaching three figures. More than five hundred people died in the heat that year, and you could say that Cincinnati Reds catcher Willard Hershberger was one of them.

At 167 pounds, "Herky" was slight for a catcher. He was in his third season with the Reds, mostly backing up future Hall of Famer Ernie Lombardi. In July Lombardi sprained an ankle, so Hershberger was pressed into service as a full-time catcher for the first time.

On August 3, the Reds were in Boston for a doubleheader against the Boston Bees. At 11:30 A.M., Hershberger's roommate, Bill Baker, suggested they go to the ballpark together. Hershberger, scheduled to play the second game, said he'd be along later.

The first game started and Hershberger hadn't shown up, so Gabe Paul, the team's traveling secretary, called his room at the Copley Plaza Hotel. It was 1:10 P.M.

"I'm sick and can't play," Hershberger said, "but I'll come out right away anyway."

When the game was over and Hershberger *still* hadn't arrived, another call was placed to the room. This time there was no answer. A close friend of Hershberger's, Cincinnati businessman Dan Cohen, was instructed to go to the hotel to get him. Hershberger's lateness could be grounds for disciplinary action.

The door was locked, so Cohen got a maid to let him inside. There he found Hershberger, slumped over the bathtub, shirtless and quite dead. His jugular had been slashed. A "safety" razor belonging to Bill Baker was on the floor. There were several uncashed paychecks in Hershberger's pocket, but no suicide note.

Curiously, towels were all over the bathroom floor. Hershberger had obviously leaned over the tub when he slashed his throat so that the blood would go down the drain. He appeared to have been very careful not to make a mess.

Of the eighty major-league players who have killed themselves (see the list beginning on page 54), Willard Hershberger was the only one to do it while he was still an active player, in the middle of baseball season.

Why did he do it? He was batting a solid .309, and the previous season was his best ever (.345). The Reds were doing well, leading the National League by six games (they would go on to win the World Series).

As with Donnie Moore, one unfortunate pitch may have pushed Willard Hershberger over the edge.

Three days before he killed himself, Hershberger was catching a game at the Polo Grounds in New York. Cincinnati was leading the Giants 4–1 with two outs in the ninth. Bucky Walters got two strikes on Bob Seeds and was one strike away from pitching a brilliant two-hitter.

Then the roof fell in. Seeds walked, and Burgess Whitehead slammed a home run, also on a two-strike pitch. That made it 4–3. Mel Ott walked, again with two strikes. The tying run, represented by Harry Danning, came to the plate. Like the previous three hitters, Walters got two strikes on him. The count was 0–2, and once more it looked like the game was wrapped up.

Instead of wasting a pitch or two, Hershberger called for a fastball. Walters shook him off. Hershberger flashed the same sign. He *insisted* on a fastball. Walters gave it to him, and Danning ripped it into the upper deck to win the game for the Giants.

Hershberger watched the drive go out, believing it was his fault Cincinnati had lost the game. Chances are if he had called for another pitch or a better location, the Reds would have won.

After his next game, Hershberger sat down and talked with Cin-

cinnati manager Bill McKechnie in his hotel room. He told Mc-
Kechnie that he felt responsible for the team's loss. He was letting
the Reds down, he said, and he believed his teammates thought so
too. He couldn't take the pressure of being the team's starting
catcher.

He also told the manager that he had attempted suicide, but hadn't
had the courage to go through with it. McKechnie talked with the
depressed catcher for two hours, and wouldn't let him leave until
he thought Hershberger had cheered up somewhat.

If the same situation were to occur today, most managers would
realize the seriousness of the situation and see that the player got
immediate psychological counseling. Hershberger had sent out many
of what are now considered obvious warning signs of suicide: He
had recently taken out an insurance policy and bought a house for
his mother. He was losing weight and under a lot of stress. He
suffered from insomnia and headaches. He had even talked with
teammates about suicide the day before he did it.

But the most obvious danger signal had occurred eleven years
earlier, when Willard's *father* committed suicide. Three weeks after
the stock-market crash in 1929, Claude Hershberger sat on the edge
of the bathtub in his home, pointed a shotgun at his chest, and used
a cane to push the trigger. The explosion woke the family in the
middle of the night, including Willard, still in high school.

When Willard decided to do himself in, he made it a point not to
leave the mess his father had left in the family bathroom.

When Hershberger didn't show up between games of that doubleheader on August 3, McKechnie held a brief team meeting. He asked
the players to take it easy on Hershberger—to lay off the pranks
and not pester him about how he was feeling. Four innings later,
word got back to the stadium that Hershberger had taken himself
out of the game permanently.

Side Note: Years after finding Willard Hershberger's body in the
Copley Plaza Hotel, Dan Cohen killed himself.

HARRY C. PULLIAM
National League President Couldn't
Take the Pressure

The job of National League president requires a person who can deal with ruthless, often corrupt team owners and a pushy press. The president has to be able to handle any crisis and take the heat from all sides on controversial issues.

Harry Clay Pulliam didn't have these qualities. He was a quiet and nervous man. Early baseball writer Francis Richter described him as "a dreamer, a lover of solitude and nature, of books, of poetry, of music and flowers." Pulliam never married, and he lived in a room by himself at the New York Athletic Club.

He was born in Kentucky four years after the Civil War ended. After getting a law degree from the University of Virginia, he worked in the newspaper business back home in Louisville, where he met Pittsburgh Pirates owner Barney Dreyfuss. That led to a job with the Pirates, and in 1903 Harry Pulliam was named National League president. He also took on the jobs of secretary and treasurer.

Things went smoothly until 1907, when the strain of performing all three duties affected his health. John Heydler took over as secretary and treasurer, leaving Pulliam free to concentrate on his job as president.

The lighter load didn't help. Pulliam started falling apart. He became convinced that the team owners were conspiring against him. (He may have been right.) He got a lot of flak for siding with the umpires in "The Merkle Affair," when Fred Merkle failed to touch second base and cost the New York Giants the 1908 pennant. He made some enemies among powerful team owners—Charles Ebbets, Garry Herrmann, John T. Brush, and his old friend Barney Dreyfuss. He took criticism to heart, believing that the league's success or failure was entirely his responsibility.

In February 1909, Pulliam suffered a nervous breakdown at a banquet for National League owners. "My days as a baseball man are numbered," he sobbed. "The National League doesn't want me as president anymore." He was granted an indefinite leave of absence.

"Pulliam's health has been impaired for some time," the *New*

York Times wrote, "he being frail, nervous and unable to withstand the heavy drain upon his constitution."

Friends advised him to try a mineral springs treatment in the Midwest. Pulliam took a few months off, traveling the Western states instead. He returned to work on June 28.

The hornets' nest of baseball was still there. One month to the day after returning to work, Harry C. Pulliam calmly got up from the dinner table at the New York Athletic Club, walked up to his room on the third floor, stripped to his underwear, lay down on a sofa, and shot himself in the head.

No one heard the gunshot, but a "telephone boy" noticed that the phone in Pulliam's room was off the hook around 9:30 P.M. A bellboy was sent upstairs to check things out. The door was unlocked. The smell of gunpowder permeated the room. Pulliam was on the floor in a corner, moaning and barely alive.

A doctor, J. J. Higgins, was summoned. He leaned over Pulliam and asked, "How were you shot?"

"I . . . am . . . not . . . shot," Pulliam replied with great effort. Then his head fell back and he lost consciousness.

The bullet had entered his right temple, gone through his head, and struck the wall. "In holding the revolver to his head he had brought it so close that the powder had burned him severely," reported the *New York Times* in grisly detail, "and it was said that his right eye had been blown out by the discharge."

Pulliam, who was forty, was too severely wounded to be moved to a hospital. He died the same night.

THE COMPLETE LIST OF ALL 97 PLAYERS, MANAGERS, AND OTHER BASEBALL FIGURES WHO HAVE COMMITTED SUICIDE

This chronological list was compiled from material provided by Bill Deane at the National Baseball Hall of Fame and Museum, Loren Coleman of the Human Services Development Institute of the University of South Maine, and other sources. Brief notes have been added where information was available. An asterisk indicates that the player had been active in the majors during the twelve months before his suicide.

Fraley Rogers (1881) Gun.

Jim McElroy (1889) Morphine or opium.

Frank Ringo (1889) Morphine.

Ernie Hickman (1891) Gun.

Edgar McNabb (1894)* Gun.
First he shot his lover, the actress Louise Kellogg, who was married to another man. She survived; he didn't.

Terry Larkin (1894) Razor.
His wife complained about his drinking one day in 1883, so he shot her in the mouth. Then he picked up a razor from the mantel and slashed his throat. A policeman broke down the door at that point, and Larkin shot him too. Recovering in a New York hospital, Larkin intentionally banged his head against a steam register at the foot of his bed. He was strapped down, and when the doctors left the room he begged a policeman, "For God's sake hit me in the head and put an end to my suffering."

Three years later, Larkin tried to shoot his boss, a Brooklyn saloon owner. *The Baseball Encyclopedia* says that Larkin died—mercifully—on September 18, 1894.

Cannonball Crane (1896) Drank poison.

Marty Bergen (1900)* Razor.
His hip had been broken in a close play at the plate, a collision that ended his career. His father came to visit one morning and found that Bergen had murdered his two children and his wife with an ax and then had slit his own throat.

Dude Esterbrook (1901) Jumped from a train.
He was en route to a mental hospital.

Jim Galligan (1901) Razor.

Win Mercer (1903)* Inhaled illuminating gas.
The twenty-eight-year-old Tigers pitcher Mercer had been appointed player/manager a few days earlier. He checked

into the Occidental Hotel in San Francisco as "George Murray" and left this note to his fiancée:

> *Dearest Martha,*
> *With tears streaming from my eyes, I pen these few lines to you, the dearest and sweetest little girl in the whole world. The act I am about to commit is simply terrible, but I cannot help it, dearie. I am to blame—nobody else—so I am going to face it as rigid as I have many other wrong acts. Please forgive me, dear Martha. I love you till the last. Oh, if I could only kiss you once more, I would be satisfied to go.*

Dan Mahoney (1904) Drank carbolic acid (phenol).

Bob Langsford (1907) Drank carbolic acid.

Chick Stahl (1907)* Drank carbolic acid.

The only big-league manager to kill himself, Stahl, thirty-four, had resigned from the Red Sox two weeks earlier, but was talked back into his job. He killed himself during spring training in Indiana. He had been a teammate of Marty Bergen (see above).

Stahl's final words were "Boys, I couldn't help it. It drove me to it." Nobody knows exactly what "it" was. There has been speculation that Stahl was a homosexual, that he was having an affair, and that his wife of one year, Julia, was addicted to drugs. A year later, Julia was found in a doorway in a poor neighborhood of Boston, dead from an alcohol and drug overdose. It was her second try at suicide.

Five years before he killed himself, a twenty-year-old stenographer named Lulu Ortman had tried to shoot Stahl in Fort Wayne, Indiana, after he told her he no longer wanted to see her. A 1986 article in *Boston* magazine suggested Stahl had another lady friend who had become pregnant and threatened to talk unless he married her.

Ike Van Zandt (1908) Gun.

Reddy Foster (1908) Gun.

Edward Strickland (1909) Gun.

The twenty-six-year-old pitcher shot his girlfriend first.

Nicholas Mathewson (1909) Unknown.
He was Christy Mathewson's twenty-two-year-old younger brother.

Harry Pulliam (1909) Gun.
He was National League president from 1903 until his death.

Dann McGann (1910) Gun.
Two years after his thirteen-year baseball career was over, he'd had enough. He was thirty-three. His brother had killed himself the previous summer.

Charles Nelson Brown (1910) Hanging.

James Payne (1910) Unknown.
He did it while his wife and mother watched.

Randolph Blanch (1911) Gun.
He was a Pennsylvania sportswriter.

Thomas Senior (1911) Gun.
He was a thirty-two-year-old minor-league umpire.

Dick Scott (1911) Razor.

Walt Goldsby (1914) Gun.
After his major-league career was over, he was a minor-league manager and umpire.

Charlie Weber (1914) Gun.

Eddie Hohnhurst (1916) Unknown.

Carl Britton (1916) Unknown.
He was a forty-year-old minor-league pitcher.

E. F. Egan (1918) Unknown.
He was a minor-league manager. His suicide happened shortly after his wife had died.

Patsy Tebeau (1918) Gun.
He played thirteen years and managed eleven in the big leagues. In 1894, in the middle of his career as a manager, while drunk, he was beaten up, robbed, and forced to pay $250 blackmail to avoid a lawsuit in Cleveland. He was running a saloon in St. Louis when he shot himself.

Lew Meyers (1920) Strychnine.

Art Irwin (1921) Jumped.

In poor health, the former player and manager leaped from a steamer into the Atlantic Ocean while on a trip from New York to Boston. The body was never found. Later it was discovered that Irvin had had a wife and family in Boston and another one in Hartford.

Irwin has been credited with inventing the padded fielder's glove and the football scoreboard.

Noel Bruce (1921) Gun.

A minor leaguer, he was fifty-six.

Clay Dailey (1921) Unknown.

Minor leaguer. He killed himself after being cut from the Louisville team in spring training.

John Wakefield (1924) Unknown.

Minor leaguer. Did it after an argument with his girlfriend.

Jake Wells (1927) Unknown.

Bill Gannon (1927) Drowning.

Danny Shay (1927) Unknown.

Tony Brottem (1929) Gun.

He was depressed after his release from the minor leagues.

Zeke Rosebrough (1930) Gun.

Con Lucid (1931) Unknown.

Carl Sitton (1931) Gun.

Bill Grey (1932) Gun.

Pea Ridge Day (1934) Gun.

He was depressed after an operation failed to restore his pitching arm. Day's mother also committed suicide.

Charlie Dexter (1934) Gun.

Guy Morrison (1934) Gun.

Walt Kuhn (1935) Gun.

Emmett McCann (1937) Gun.

Benny Frey (1937)* Carbon monoxide.
> He had recently been sent down to the minors after an eight-year career and decided to retire instead. Police found him in his car, with a rubber hose going from the exhaust pipe to the window.

Willard Hershberger (1940)* Razor.

Charlie Hollocher (1940) Gun.
> As a rookie sensation with the Cubs in 1918, he led the league in at-bats, hits, and total bases. He hit .340 in 1922 and .342 in 1923. But throughout his seven-year career, he complained of severe stomach pains that kept him out of the lineup a good part of the time. At age forty-four, he shot himself in the throat in St. Louis.

Ralph Works (1941) Gun.
> He shot his wife first.

Harvey Hendrick (1941) Gun.

Lyle Bigbee (1942) Gun.

Chet Chadbourne (1943) Gun.

Harry McNeal (1945) Gun.

Hank Eibel (1945) Gun.

Morrie Rath (1945) Gun.

Ferdie Moore (1947) Gun.
> First he shot a gambling associate.

Luke Stuart (1947) Gun.

Jake Powell (1948) Gun.
> Shot himself in a police station.

Bert Hall (1948) Hanging.

Tim Bowden (1949) Gun.

Wattie Holm (1950) Gun.

Frank Pearce (1950) Gun.

Hugh Casey (1951) Gun.
> He was good friends with Ernest Hemingway, who would also shoot himself.

Wally Roettger (1951) Razor.

Skeeter Shelton (1954) Gun.

Jim Oglesby (1955) Gun.

Limb McKenry (1956) Gun.

Fred Anderson (1957) Gun.

Gib Brack (1960) Gun.

George Davis (1961) Hanging.

John Mohardt (1961) Cut femoral artery (thigh).

Fred Bratchi (1962) Drank battery acid.

Otto Miller (1962) Jumped.

Cy Morgan (1962) Razor.

Johnny Niggeling (1963) Hanging.

Paul Zahniser (1964) Gun.

Stan Pitula (1965) Carbon monoxide.

Stover McIlwane (1966) Gun.

Lew Moren (1966) Cut throat.

Art Garibaldi (1967) Gun.

Emil Kush (1969) Carbon monoxide.

Murray Wall (1971) Gun.

Del Bissonnette (1972) Gun.

Don Wilson (1975)* Carbon monoxide.
 He pitched two no-hitters for Houston and once struck
 out eighteen men in one game. They found him in his
 1972 Thunderbird, parked in his garage in Houston. The
 gas tank was empty. His five-year-old son was found in
 an upstairs bedroom—another victim of the fumes. Wilson's death was ruled accidental.

Danny Thomas (1980) Hanging.
 He was a deeply religious man who would not play on
 Sundays. He only lasted one year in the majors, as an
 outfielder with the Brewers.

Francisco Barrios (1982)* Heroin overdose.
 He had been released the previous year after eight seasons
 with the White Sox. The previous June he had been ar-

rested for possession of cocaine, and had entered a Chicago drug and alcohol treatment center.

Carlos Bernier (1989) Hanging.
He played outfield for Pittsburgh in 1953. Killed himself in Puerto Rico on April 6—eight days before the opening of baseball season.

Virgil Stallcup (1989) Gun.
He was an infielder for the Cincinnati Reds in the 1940s and 1950s.

Donnie Moore (1989)* Gun.
He shot his wife first. She survived.

Charlie Shoemaker (1990) Gun.

Jim Magnuson (1991) Alcohol poisoning.

Suicide Squeeze

Poor Johnny Mostil tried his best to make this list: In 1927, he slashed his neck, wrists, legs, and chest but failed to kill himself. An outfielder with the White Sox, Mostil had led the American League in walks, stolen bases, and runs in 1925. The next year—the season before he tried to kill himself—he hit .328. He came back after the suicide attempt to play two more years. He died of natural causes in 1970.

LEN KOENECKE
Death at 10,000 Feet

Baseball's most spectacular killing occurred in the early morning hours of September 17, 1935, when Brooklyn Dodgers outfielder Leonard Koenecke was bludgeoned to death on a small plane flying between Detroit and Buffalo.

In 1934, his first full year in the majors, Koenecke hit .320 and set a National League record for fielding. But the next season he was repeatedly disciplined for "breaking training," a common euphemism for drinking. After the Dodgers were shut out by the Cardinals on September 16, the twenty-nine-year-old outfielder was released, despite a respectable .283 batting average.

Ballclubs didn't travel by plane in 1935, just thirty-two years after the Wright Brothers had left the ground. But after getting his release, Koenecke boarded an American Airlines plane in St. Louis, heading for Buffalo, where he had played in the minors.

When Koenecke boarded the plane, stewardess Eleanor Woodward noticed that he was carrying a bottle and appeared to be intoxicated. Several minutes into the flight, Koenecke began arguing with a passenger. When Woodward approached him, he knocked her down with one punch. Then he offered to fight another passenger. When the plane touched down in Detroit, Koenecke was ordered off. Part of his fare was refunded.

From there, he chartered a little three-seater to Buffalo with pilot William Joseph Mulqueeney. Mulqueeney's friend Irwin Davis was also on board.

Koenecke sat up front with Mulqueeney and remained quiet for the first few minutes of his trip, but soon he began to nudge Mulqueeney with his shoulder and grab at the controls of the plane.

"I told him to cut it out, that I had no time to play," Mulqueeney told the press afterward. Koenecke continued to bother him, so Mulqueeney ordered him to the rear with Davis. Within minutes, the two men were rolling on the floor of the plane and punching one another. The plane was rocking back and forth. When Koenecke sank his teeth into Davis's shoulder, Davis yelled for help.

"I had to come to a decision," Mulqueeney said. "It was either a case of the three of us crashing or doing something to Koenecke."

Mulqueeney looked around for something he could use to hit Koenecke. Spotting a fire extinguisher, he grabbed it with one hand while he struggled to hold the controls with the other. By this time, the plane was off course and veering wildly. Mulqueeney had lost all sense of direction.

"I watched my chance, grabbed the fire extinguisher and walloped him over the head," he said.

With Mulqueeney's first swing, Koenecke managed to knock the fire extinguisher out of his hand. Mulqueeney retrieved it but on the second swing hit Davis by accident. On the third swing, he smashed Koenecke with a good thunk.

The feisty outfielder still had some fight in him, so Mulqueeney gave him three or four direct hits for good measure. The struggle lasted about fifteen minutes, until Koenecke was finally subdued.

It was pitch dark, the plane was damaged, and there was a dead ballplayer lying on the floor of the "blood-spattered cabin," but Mulqueeney managed to land the plane successfully on a racetrack near Toronto.

"I guess I was in a trance," Mulqueeney said later, "but when I hopped out of the cockpit I thought I was about to be attacked by wolves."

It was just police dogs. Officers climbed on board and found Koenecke, dead of a brain hemorrhage with his face severely battered. Mulqueeney and Davis were arrested for manslaughter and put in jail pending trial. After they told their stories and alcohol was found in Koenecke's body, the jury deliberated five minutes and decided that the two men had acted in self-defense.

"Koenecke was deliberately attempting to commit suicide and trying to do it in one grand, glorious finish," claimed Edward Murphy, the lawyer representing Mulqueeney and Davis. "He wanted to die a spectacular death."

LYMAN BOSTOCK
On the Last Day of His Life, He Went 2 for 4

When California Angels outfielder Lyman Bostock reached third base on September 23, 1978, he was greeted by White Sox third baseman Eric Soderholm, a former teammate. Bostock had started the season in a hitting slump, and Soderholm asked how he had pulled himself out of it.

"Eric, I got my life straightened out off the field," Bostock told Soderholm, "and that turned it around for me on the field."

Eight hours later, Lyman Bostock lay dead, his head filled with shotgun pellets.

Bostock's potential as a hitter wasn't spotted right away. He was the 596th player chosen in the 1972 draft. But he tore up the minor leagues and was hustled up to the Minnesota Twins in 1975. He would be the first major-leaguer in the family. His father, also named Lyman, had been a first baseman in the Negro Leagues.

Bostock hit .282 over ninety-eight games as a rookie. The next season, he hit .323. In 1977 he did even better—.336. Gene Mauch, who managed the Twins at the time, said the kid had as much talent as Pete Rose.

Minnesota certainly got its money's worth. The year he hit .336, Bostock's salary was $20,000. He decided to see what he was worth as a free agent, and the day before his twenty-seventh birthday he signed a contract with the California Angels that would pay him $450,000 a year for the next five years. Suddenly, he was one of the highest-paid players in the game.

To the real fan, money and salaries aren't baseball. Bostock's paycheck is only noted here because it made history, of sorts. In an era when hitters demand salary increases after batting .225, Lyman Bostock was perhaps the only player to give money *back* when he felt he wasn't doing the job.

After signing that fat contract, Bostock started the 1978 season in a terrible slump: two singles in thirty-nine at-bats. He felt that he had let down his team and his fans, so he requested that the Angels not pay him his salary for the month of April. Gene Autry, who owned the team, refused his offer. Bostock donated the money to charity.

Seven months later his average was all the way up to .294, thanks in part to a 2-for-4 day against the White Sox. After the game that Saturday, Bostock went to visit his uncle Thomas Turner in Gary, Indiana. He often stayed with Turner when the team was playing in Chicago.

That evening, Bostock was riding in a car with Turner and Turner's godchildren, Joan Hawkins and Barbara Smith. The women were sisters. Lyman and Barbara were sitting in the back seat.

A car pulled alongside Turner's. Barbara could see her husband, Leonard Smith, was driving. The two had quarreled earlier in the day and were planning to be divorced. Barbara asked Turner not to stop the car. He drove through two red lights before he was forced to stop at a large intersection—5th Avenue and Jackson Street.

Leonard Smith hopped out of his car and walked briskly to Turn-

er's car. He was carrying a .410-gauge shotgun. There was no conversation. Smith pointed the barrel at the back window and blasted
away. Bostock crumpled, blood pouring from his right temple. Barbara had been hit also, but not badly. Smith fled.

Three hours later, one of baseball's most promising young players
was dead.

It didn't appear that Barbara Smith was cheating on her husband
with Lyman Bostock. They had met twenty minutes earlier. Bostock
had simply been in the way of an angry bullet meant for Barbara.
Leonard Smith was arrested for murder the next day in his home,
six blocks from the shooting. He was found not guilty by reason of
insanity and spent six months in a mental institution.

"I'm shocked. I'm sorry. I'm angry. I'm sick," said Bostock's old
manager, Gene Mauch. "People don't realize the strong feelings of
admiration and respect that develop on a ballclub. I thought the
world of that man."

MAJOR-LEAGUE MURDERS

This chronological list was provided by Bill Deane at the National
Baseball Hall of Fame and Museum. An asterisk indicates that the
player was active in the majors during the twelve months before his
death.

Andy Swan (1885)* Shot.

Ted Firth (1885)* Unknown.

Mox McQuery (1890) Shot.
    By a thug.

Frank Bell (1891) Shot.

Frank Bowes (1895) Shot.

Fleury Sullivan (1897) Shot.
    During a political argument.

Mother Watson (1898) Shot.

Samuel White (1899) Hit with a baseball bat.
    He was umpiring a minor-league game in Alabama when
    he got into an argument with a player who had been

heckling him. The player smashed the bat against his head, ending the dispute.

Ora Jennings (1901) Hit with a baseball bat.
See Samuel White above. This time it happened in Indiana.

John Ryan (1902) Kicked to death.
While making an arrest.

Pat Hynes (1907) Shot.
On his birthday, Hynes went out for a few beers. He was shot by the bartender in a dispute over how much credit he had.

George Craig (1911) Shot.
By a burglar.

Bugs Raymond (1912)* Hit with a baseball bat.

Jerry Harrington (1913) Stabbed.
While trying to break up a barroom brawl.

Charlie Weber (1914) Shot.

Ed Irvin (1916) Thrown out of a saloon window.

Larry McLean (1921) Shot.
At six foot five, McLean was the tallest catcher ever. He had a spectacular 1913 World Series for the New York Giants, hitting .500, but became such an aggressive drunk afterward that he was out of baseball by 1915. Six years later he and Jack McCarthy (who played in the National League from 1893 to 1907) started a fight in a Boston bar and the bartender shot McLean dead. McCarthy was injured.

Chief Johnson (1922) Shot.

Frank McManus (1923) Unknown.

Dolly Stark (1924) Shot.

Drummond Brown (1927) Shot.

Ed Morris (1932) Stabbed.
Friends were throwing a farewell party at a fish fry for Morris, a veteran Red Sox pitcher. He got into an argument with a gas station owner, who plunged a knife twice into Morris's chest.

Len Koenecke (1935)* Battered with a fire extinguisher in a plane.

Ray Treadway (1935) Shot.

Gordon McNaughton (1942) Shot.
By a jealous husband in a Chicago hotel.

Frank Grube (1945) Shot.
By a prowler outside his home.

Hi Bithorn (1952) Shot.
A policeman in Mexico tried to arrest him. Bithorn made a run for it and the cop shot him.

Howie Fox (1955) Stabbed.
In a bar fight.

Eddie Gaedel (1961) Beaten.
He was the famous three-foot, seven-inch midget sent up to hit for the St. Louis Browns in 1951. Ten years after making baseball history, he was mugged on a Chicago street corner, staggered home and died of a heart attack. The mugger got away with $11. Only one baseball person showed up at the funeral—Bob Cain, the pitcher who had faced Gaedel in his famous at-bat.

Tim McKeithan (1969) Shot.

Mickey Fuentes (1970)* Shot.
In a bar fight in Puerto Rico. It was right after his rookie season.

Bob Baird (1974) Shot.
During a quarrel with a woman.

Lyman Bostock (1978)* Shot.

Luke Easter (1979) Shot.
One of the first black men in the majors, Easter hit twenty-eight, twenty-seven, and thirty-one home runs in 1950–1952. He was a chief steward for TRW Inc. in Euclid, Ohio, when he was accosted by two robbers outside a bank. He had just cashed payroll checks for his company totaling $5,000. Blasts from a sawed-off shotgun and a pistol killed him instantly.

Bob Schultz (1979) Shot.
   In a bar.

David Short (1983) Beaten.
   His body was found in the trunk of a car.

Luis Marquez (1988) Shot.
   During a family quarrel.

. . . AND MURDERERS

Baseball has had its share of player/murderers, the most famous being Hank Thompson and Cesar Cedeno (see Chapter 7: Crime). Charlie Sweeny, who pitched six years, was charged with murder in 1894 after he shot a man named Con McManus in a bar. In 1917, ex-shortstop Danny Shay got into an argument with a waiter in an Indianapolis hotel over the amount of sugar in the bowl at Shay's table. Shay pulled out a gun and shot the waiter. He was charged with murder, but pleaded self-defense and was acquitted. The fact that Shay was a white man and the waiter black probably had something to do with the verdict.

Baseball's first and only execution (as far as I have been able to determine) took place on November 28, 1895, when Charles "Pacer" Smith was hanged in Decatur, Illinois. Smith, who pitched for the Cincinnati Red Stockings in 1876–1877, had shot and killed his five-year-old daughter and his seventeen-year-old sister-in-law. He fired two shots at his wife as well, but missed, and she escaped.

"The tragedy was the culmination of several years of domestic infelicity," reported *Sporting Life* magazine, "coupled with a career of drunkenness and immorality on the part of Smith."

The jail was packed with spectators as Smith climbed the scaffold. "I am sorry," he said, with tears trickling down his face. "Goodbye." Deputy Sam Stabler adjusted the noose and M. Holmes put a black cap over Smith's head. Sheriff Jerry P. Nicholson pulled the trap at 11:54 A.M.

Smith's longtime catcher, Frank Harris, was supposed to be hanged the same day on a separate murder charge, but he received a reprieve from the governor of Illinois.

DEATH THREATS

*"I sincerely feel that somebody is going to end up
getting shot on the field."*
—Billy Martin, 1975

From a letter Henry Aaron received in 1973:

> *Dear Hank,*
> *You are a very good ballplayer, but if you come close to Babe*
> *Ruth's 714 homers I have a contract out on you. Over 700*
> *and you can consider yourself punctured with a .22 shell. If by*
> *the all star game you have come within 20 homers of Babe you*
> *will be shot on sight by one of my assassins on July 24, 1973."*

Death threats, like rain delays, are an unfortunate nuisance in the
life of a professional baseball player—especially a player who is
controversial or involved in momentous events.

Henry Aaron finished the 1973 season one home run short of
Babe Ruth's career total of 714, forcing him to endure six months
of waiting to break the record. That year he received nine hundred
thirty thousand letters, more than any nonpolitician in the country.
Dinah Shore was second with sixty thousand, but it was doubtful
that any of them threatened to kill her.

When he got close to Ruth's record, Aaron needed police protection to and from the ballpark. He would register at hotels under
different names.

The FBI was informed of a plot to kidnap his daughter Gaile at
college, and FBI agents swarmed all over Fisk University disguised
as maintenance men. Aaron's parents in Mobile, Alabama, received
calls from people saying they'd never see their son again. Aaron
would tell his teammates not to get too close to him in the dugout.
He never knew when someone might take a shot.

"I lived like a guy in a fishbowl," he said later.

Roger Maris, another private person, had received threats on his
life in 1961 when he approached Ruth's other "unbreakable" mark
of sixty home runs in one season. Had Maris been black, it would
have been a lot worse.

When he broke the color barrier in 1947, Jackie Robinson received dozens of death threats. At one point he turned down all personal appearances and speaking engagements because he feared for his life. A teammate went so far as to suggest that the Dodgers could foil an attempt on Jackie's life by having every player on the team walk out on the field wearing number 42—Robinson's number.

Curt Flood, another black pioneer, got mail and telephone threats during his lawsuit challenging baseball's reserve clause. During a series against the Yankees, he found a black funeral wreath in his locker. That's when he quit baseball for good.

Ty Cobb routinely received threats on his life, especially in 1909 after he spiked the popular "Home Run" Baker in Philadelphia. Cobb, the story is told, was warned that he would be shot as he stood in the outfield. No guns went off, but every time a car backfired outside the stadium, he jumped.

In 1973, the Oakland A's received a letter warning that if Reggie Jackson played in the playoffs or World Series, it would be the last thing he ever did. The letter was signed "The Weathermen." Jackson not only played, but also became the Most Valuable Player during the Series, even though he was accompanied by two FBI agents wherever he went.

Later he said gallantly, "If I had got knocked off, I'd rather it be on the field."

Baseball has had to cope with bomb threats on several occasions. When President Lyndon Johnson came to celebrate the opening of Houston's Astrodome on April 9, 1965, somebody called a local radio station and said he was going to blow the place up. Nothing ever happened.

At 8:57 P.M. on July 3, 1960, a man called United Airlines in New York and said that planes carrying the New York Yankees and Detroit Tigers would crash. Both planes were searched and no bomb was found.

In 1975, a United Airlines 727 carrying the Kansas City Royals was forced to make an unscheduled landing at Salt Lake International Airport when an unidentified male called Oakland Airport and said there was a bomb on the plane.

It stands to reason that umpires have been threatened. People bet a lot of money on baseball games, and a controversial call can influence the outcome.

During Game 3 of the 1975 World Series, Larry Barnett made a disputed interference call in the tenth inning that led to a Cincinnati victory. The next day he received a letter demanding that he pay $10,000 or get "a .38 caliber bullet in your head" if Boston lost again. The letter writer also threatened Barnett's wife and daughter.

After the famous 1988 bumping incident that resulted in Pete Rose's suspension for thirty days, umpire Dave Pallone received a call in his hotel room: "Pallone, you screwed up, you asshole. If you go on the field tomorrow, you're dead. I'll kill you."

To date, no death threat has ever been carried out. Any time a player or umpire has been assaulted or murdered, it has been totally without warning.

But it would be unwise for baseball to develop a false sense of security. Before the sixth game of the 1972 World Series, a woman waiting in line at Riverfront Stadium overhead a man say, "If Gene Tenace hits a home run today, he won't walk out of this ballpark." Tenace, a career .241 hitter, was the star of the Series, slugging four home runs, driving in nine runs and hitting .348.

The woman informed stadium officials and led police to a thirty-two-year-old man from Louisville, Ohio. In his possession was a bottle of whiskey and a loaded pistol.

RAY CHAPMAN
Hit by Pitcher

In an average baseball game, approximately 200 pitches are thrown. Over a 162-game season, that works out to a quarter of a million or so pitches. So in major-league baseball's long and glorious history, close to 30 million pitches have been thrown. And only one of them ever killed a man.

It happened on August 16, 1920. This is the story of Ray Chapman and Carl Mays.

As the shortstop with the Cleveland Indians, "Chappie" was one of the most popular players of his day. Having played more than a thousand games in his nine-year career, he was still one of the fastest men in the game in 1920, and one of the best bunters.

Before the season began, Chapman had taken a wife—Kathleen Daly, the daughter of a wealthy Cleveland businessman. His best man at the wedding was Tris Speaker, Cleveland's player/manager and one of the greatest ever to play the game. The newlyweds planned for Ray to retire after the 1920 season and devote himself to business and raising a family. But first, he wanted to lead the Indians to the World Series—Cleveland had never even won a pennant.

Carl Mays came up to the big leagues to pitch for Boston in 1914 —the same year as Babe Ruth. The two men were also traded to the Yankees over 1919–1920.

Mays was a submariner—an underhand pitcher whose knuckles would sometimes scrape the ground as he cut loose. His delivery looked like "a cross between an octopus and a bowler," wrote *Baseball Magazine*. Coming in at such an odd angle, the ball was hard for hitters to pick up, and Mays became one of the best right-handers in the American League. He had a reputation for pinpoint control, averaging less than three walks a game. In twenty-six innings of World Series play, he didn't issue a single base on balls.

He also had a reputation for being a headhunter. Mays wasn't afraid to throw inside and "dust off" a hitter now and then. He led the league in that category in 1917 and came in second the next two years. By the middle of 1920, he had downed fifty-four batters in his career.

"If the batter is hugging the plate, and many of them do this, he is likely to get hit," Mays used to say.

Mays was widely disliked around the league, even by his own teammates. He would berate fielders who made errors behind him, and more than once accused teammates of "laying down" when he was on the mound. During one game, Mays was disturbed by fans banging on the dugout roof. He whipped a baseball into the stands, hitting a man. The fan complained to the police after the game, and Mays would have been arrested had he not already left town.

One incident in spring training of 1920 shook Mays up. His only real friend on the Yankees, Chick Fewster, was hit above the ear with a fastball thrown by Jeff Pfeffer of the Dodgers. Fewster lay in the dirt for ten minutes, and when he regained consciousness he didn't remember what had happened. He couldn't speak for a month and spent that time in a wheelchair. After that, Mays couldn't bring himself to hit the inside corner, and he wasn't effective for the first half of the season.

But by August 16 he regained his aggressiveness and wanted to win badly. He would be going for his 100th career victory that day at the Polo Grounds, and it was a big series. The Yankees were half a game behind Cleveland and it was getting late in the season.

The Indians took an early lead in the second inning on a home run by Steve O'Neill. They got two more runs in the fourth. Stan Coveleski held the Yankees scoreless.

Chapman led off the fifth. He had always struggled hitting Mays. In the first inning, he dropped down a sacrifice bunt, and in the third he popped up to Wally Pipp at first. Mays got a ball and a strike on Chapman, and then let go of the pitch he wished he could take back for the rest of his life.

"The ball sailed directly toward Chapman's head, but he made no effort to move," wrote Mike Sowell in his excellent book on the 1920 season, *The Pitch That Killed*. "He remained poised in his crouch, apparently transfixed as the ball flew in and crashed against his left temple with a resounding crack."

The *New York Times* reported, "The crack of the ball could be heard all over the stands and spectators gasped as they turned their heads away." Sportswriter Fred Lieb wrote, perhaps exaggerating, "I could see the left eye hanging from its socket."

The ball rolled back to the mound and Mays, thinking it had struck Chapman's bat, tossed it to first. Chapman took two staggering steps up the baseline, then crumpled to the ground. Seeing the blood pouring out of Chapman's ear, umpire Tommy Connolly ran to the stands shouting for a doctor.

Tris Speaker, who was on deck, rushed to Chapman's side, as did the entire Indians team and several Yankees. Mays stayed on the mound.

Chapman was conscious and tried to speak, but no words came out. He struggled to his feet and began walking toward the clubhouse in center field. Before reaching second base, he collapsed and was carried off the field.

In the clubhouse, Ray was able to put together a few words. "I'm all right," he said. "Tell Mays not to worry."

Mays didn't. He calmly mowed down the Indians in order in the sixth, seventh, and eighth innings. Yankee manager Miller Huggins pinch-hit for Mays in the bottom of the eighth.

The Indians held on and won the game 4–3. Mays did *not* get his 100th victory that day.

In the clubhouse, Chapman was not doing well and an ambulance was summoned to take him to St. Lawrence Hospital. "Ring . . . Katy's ring," he kept repeating. Finally, trainer Percy Smallwood retrieved Ray's wedding ring, which had been put aside for safe-keeping. He put it in Ray's hand, which seemed to bring some comfort to the struggling shortstop before he lapsed into unconsciousness.

At the hospital Chapman's vital signs continued to deteriorate. At ten o'clock, the decision was made to operate. The procedure to remove a one-and-a-half-inch piece of Chapman's skull lasted from 12:29 to 1:44 A.M. Dr. T. M. Merrigan saw that Chapman's brain was damaged both on the left side, where the ball had hit, and on the right side, where the brain had smashed against the skull.

When she received word that Ray had been hit, Kathleen rushed to New York by train. She was escorted to the Ansonia Hotel, where Tris Speaker was staying. She only needed one look at Speaker's face to know Ray was dead. Chapman had died at 4:40 A.M. on August 17.

Mays was informed in the morning. He was summoned to the office of the Manhattan district attorney to describe the incident and was absolved of any guilt.

Tris Speaker took Chapman's death the hardest. At Kathleen's parents' house before the funeral, he collapsed and suffered a nervous breakdown. Ordered to bed by a physician, he lost fifteen pounds. Jack Graney, Chapman's roommate, became hysterical and had to be physically restrained. At the funeral, he fainted. Neither of the two was able to serve as pallbearer.

Several Yankees attended the funeral, but not Carl Mays. "I knew that the sight of his silent form would haunt me as long as I live," he said.

Chapman's body was returned to Cleveland and buried under a simple tombstone in Lake View Cemetery.

With Mays's reputation, many people in and out of baseball decided he had thrown at Chapman's head intentionally. There were rumors of bad blood between the two.

The *Cleveland Press* called for Mays to be banished from baseball. Players on the White Sox, St. Louis Browns, Boston Red Sox, and Detroit Tigers talked seriously about refusing to play if Mays was on the mound. Mays stayed secluded at home with his wife, Freddie, and their newborn baby.

Carl Mays blamed the umpire, Connolly, for the tragedy. He claimed there was a rough spot on the ball and that it should have been thrown out of the game. Outraged umpires immediately countered that Mays routinely dragged baseballs across the pitching rubber to roughen up the surface. (This was the first year the spitball, scuffball, and other "freak" pitches became illegal.) Nobody will ever know for sure if the ball that killed Chapman had been tampered with—it had been removed from play and was never recovered.

After the beaning, sportswriters speculated that the death of Chapman would affect Mays so deeply that he would lose his effectiveness as a pitcher. Years earlier, another Yankee pitcher named Russ Ford had beaned Roy Corhan of the White Sox so seriously that Corhan was not expected to live. Ford became so upset that he had to leave the team for a while. He was never the same pitcher again.

That didn't prove to be the case with Mays. One week after the tragedy, he pitched a shutout (although twice he shouted "Look out!" after releasing pitches he thought had gotten away from him). Mays finished the season at 26–11. The next year was the best in his career: 27–9.

In fact, there's a good chance Carl Mays would be in the Hall of Fame if he hadn't thrown that 1–1 fastball to Ray Chapman. He pitched for fifteen years, winning 208 games while losing only 126. His lifetime ERA was 2.92. Those are better numbers than many Hall of Fame pitchers put up, including Mays's teammates Waite Hoyt and Herb Pennock.

The Cleveland Indians went into a losing streak after Chapman's death but recovered and went on to win the pennant in one of the most exciting races in baseball history. They also defeated the Dodgers in the World Series, fulfilling Chapman's dream without him. Cleveland would not win another pennant for a quarter-century—around the same time protective batting helmets came into regular use.

Kathleen Chapman was another tragedy of Mays's underhand fastball. She didn't attend another baseball game for the rest of her life, which ended just eight years later—she committed suicide by drinking cleaning fluid. Her daughter, Rae, born six months after Ray died, caught the measles and died the following year.

Carl Mays's wife also died tragically, of complications after an eye infection. She was only thirty-six.

The one to live the longest was Carl Mays. For fifty years after the incident, he had to live with the notoriety of being the only major-league pitcher to have killed a man with a baseball. To the end, he insisted that it wasn't on his conscience—that Chapman had crowded the plate and ducked into the path of the ball.

"I won over two hundred games," he said. "But what happened to me in August of 1920 is the only thing anybody remembers."

EARLY ON-FIELD FATALITIES
"Fell Dead After Making a Home Run"

The tragedy of Ray Chapman was baseball's most famous fatality, but certainly not the only one. Below the major-league level, *hundreds* of players have been killed during games.

Inexperienced pitchers have poor control. Young hitters don't have the skill to judge the break of a curve or duck away from high, inside fastballs. Accidents happen. During a 1947 semipro game in Pennsylvania, the left fielder and center fielder of the Pennsburg team were struck by lightning bolts and died.

In 1915 alone, fifty-nine people were killed playing baseball, according to an article in the *New York Times* that year. Thirty-eight of the fatalities involved batters being hit on the head by a ball, six were the result of fights, six stemmed from "overexertion," and three were caused by collisions. Just about every year before and after, a few players have been killed in baseball accidents.

The first professional baseball player to die as a result of the game was the first professional baseball player—Jim Creighton of the Brooklyn Excelsiors. He took a big cut at a pitch in 1862, missed, and "sustained an internal injury occasioned by strain."

It's difficult to pinpoint the first amateur to be killed in a ballgame, but this short, sad article appeared in the *New York Times* on June 12, 1877:

DEATH ON THE BASE-BALL FIELD

RICHMOND, June 11.—A young man named John Emmett Crowder, while playing in a base-ball match this afternoon, fell dead after making a home run. Death was caused by apoplexy.

Dozens of similar stories ran in the *Times* during baseball's early years, under headlines like "DEATH CAUSED BY A BASEBALL" and "DIES OF BALL GAME INJURY." Over time, the *Times* realized there was drama in these tragedies and began to report them as in-depth news stories.

These are a few of the most touching tragedies:

• July 11, 1887. Headline: "THE SAD DEATH OF LITTLE EDDIE M'DADE."

McDade, according to the *Times*, was catcher for the Mount Vernon Baseball Club, a group of men who worked in the Manayunk mills around Philadelphia. When they got out of work at 1:00 P.M., they would don uniforms and play ball. McDade was just fifteen years old.

Eddie McDade was there, and he looked pretty in his light blue cap, white shirt, with "Mount Vernon" braided across his bosom, the red belt, white knickerbockers, blue hose, and canvas shoes. Eddie had caught out one batsman: Tommy Muldoon had hit for a base, and Mike Curley held the willow, when Eddie put on his mask and came up to the plate to keep the runner from stealing second base. Pitcher Jimmy Watson was shooting the dollar and a quarter League ball in great style, and the clever little catcher gave him good support.

Mike Curley split the air twice when he made a swing at the curving ball. It was a foul tip, and instantly young McDade threw back his head and put up his gloved hands, but he missed the ball and he dropped to the ground. The ball had struck him in the neck. He was gasping for breath as he arose to his feet and pushed off the mask.

The crowd of three hundred gathered around McDade as he staggered around the field. A close friend named Billy Carlin took him in his arms and carried him to a wagon.

"Billy, get a doctor, I'm gone," McDade said. "It's my last game." Then he fell over, unconscious.

The crowd went to the McDade home, to which a doctor had been summoned. An incision was made in Eddie's neck below the break, and a gutta-percha tube inserted to allow the young man to breathe.

The tube was short, and it slipped and worked unsatisfactorily. The boy died at 7:50 o'clock.

• August 16, 1885. Headline: "KILLED ON THE BALLFIELD."

Louis Henke, first baseman for an Atlanta team, was at the plate in a game against Nashville. He got good wood on the ball and started for first base.

Marr, Nashville's first baseman, assumed a position to meet him, and standing with bent knee, Henke ran against him with tremendous force. He rose, staggered, and fell. The audience not realizing the gravity of what had happened cried out 'Run, run; make for home!' But it was no use, for Henke was terribly hurt.

Henke was taken into a tent by the field, where he "writhed in frightful contortions" as the game continued. Doctors rushed him to a nearby hotel, where it was determined that he had a ruptured liver. A telegraph was sent to Henke's wife, who was in Cincinnati.

All night long the members of the club surrounded the dying man. Between Henke and Bittman, the second baseman, a strong friendship existed. One would never sign to play with a club unless the other was taken also. Henke, observing his friend by his side this evening, whispered to him: "Bitt, do not play to-day; I feel that I am dying."

"What shall I tell your wife for you?" Bittman inquired.

"Just tell her I got hurt in yesterday's game and died from it," he replied as he again closed his eyes, and in three minutes he was dead.

• October 2, 1904. Headline: "CAUGHT THE BALL AND DIED."

John Garcia was probably the first black man to die playing baseball. The *Times* described the twenty-eight-year-old as "so dark that he easily passed for a Cuban, whether he was or not."

On this day he was catching in a game in Jamaica, New York, with a crowd of two thousand people in the stands. In the second inning, a batter lofted an extremely high foul pop directly over the plate. Garcia pushed him aside and circled under the ball.

"Let him have it! Let him have it!" yelled the Captain of the Giants, whose shouts were re-echoed by several other players.

There was a moment of silence, a loud report when the ball struck Garcia's hand. Then Garcia fell over on his face like a log.

"Not o-u-t," the umpire drawled, inaudibly, as he saw the ball rolling away from Garcia's hand.

"He's hurt! He's hurt!" came from a hundred throats as players and spectators began to crowd around Garcia.

Several teammates hoisted Garcia up and ran across the field to St. Mary's Hospital, which was right across the street. The doctor tore open the catcher's shirt to feel for a heartbeat.

"No use," he said. "He's dead. His heart has given out." According to the *Times,* "the excitement of the game, perhaps the tension he was under while he was waiting for the ball to land, had killed him."

ED DELAHANTY
Niagara Falls, and So Did Big Ed

Some people have said Big Ed Delahanty killed himself. Others said he was murdered under mysterious circumstances. Most likely, he was just a damn fool who screwed up and got himself killed.

Delahanty was the home run king when there weren't any home runs. He slugged nineteen in 1893—an amazing number for the dead ball era. He banged out four homers in one game in 1896.

He also hit for average. Over sixteen seasons, mostly with Philadelphia, he averaged .346—fifth highest in major-league history. He led the National League in 1899 by hitting .410, and when he jumped to the new American League in 1902 he hit .376 and won his second batting title.

But Big Ed was having some personal problems. Forty-two games into the next season, he was suspended after a game in Detroit, most likely for drinking. He was having marital problems too, and disputes over money (his salary was $4,000 a year). At thirty-five, his baseball career was coming to an end. On July 2, 1903, Delahanty decided to go to New York to visit his estranged wife.

He boarded a New York Central train on its way from Chicago to New York, which passed above Lake Erie on the Canadian side. He was probably drunk when he got on the train, and he became progressively more disorderly as the trip went on. When the train reached Fort Erie on the Canadian side of the Niagara River, and was about to cross the International Bridge into the United States, the conductor ordered the famous baseball player off. Canadian law specified that ejected passengers be turned over to a constable, but nobody bothered in Delahanty's case.

Several guards and bridge workers with lanterns tried to stop him, but Delahanty shoved them aside and began running across the bridge after the train. It was nighttime by then, and the big man most likely tripped and lost his balance. He fell through the rails and was swept over Niagara Falls. A week later, his mangled body was fished out of the river.

Reports of the star's death plunge shrouded it in mystery, most likely because it would not have been acceptable to say the American

League batting champion got so loaded that he fell off a bridge. All sorts of motivations were provided for his suicide or murder. It was said that Delahanty was carrying $1,500 in diamonds, and they were not on the body when it was discovered.

"Many believed he had fallen off the bridge and drowned in the waters of the Niagara," speculated a 1962 children's book called *The Greatest in Baseball.* "Others wondered if he had been the victim of foul play."

"Foul play, my butt," wrote baseball statistics guru Bill James in *The Bill James Historical Baseball Abstract.* "There isn't a mugger in the world stupid enough to try to make a living by lurking around train bridges in the middle of the night."

Whatever happened, Delahanty lived on, in a way. His younger brothers Frank,* Jim, Joe, and Tom all played in the major leagues—a total of forty-one years for the entire family. But only Big Ed achieved superstar status. He was inducted into the Baseball Hall of Fame in 1945.

MORE UNTIMELY DEATHS

This list was provided by Bill Deane of the National Baseball Hall of Fame and Museum. An asterisk indicates the player was active in the majors during the twelve months before his death.

Al Thake (1872)* Drowned.
  Fell out of a boat while fishing.

William E. Smith (1886) Broke his back in a diving accident.

John Ake (1887) Drowned.
  He was trying to row the Mississippi River.

John Glenn (1888) Shot.
  A policeman hit him accidentally while protecting him from a lynch mob.

Jim Gallagher (1894) Accidental fall.

---

* Frank Delahanty also died after a fall, in 1966.

Bill Colgan (1895) Train accident.
  He was coupling railroad cars.

Emory Nusz (1898) Train accident.
  He fell from the train, under the cars.

Walter Plock (1900) Bridge accident.

John Traffley (1900) Brain injury.

Fred Zahner (1900) Drowned.

Ed Knouff (1900) Broke his back fighting a fire.
  He died of complications three years later.

Charlie Snyder (1901) Fractured his skull.
  While he was being evicted from a hotel.

Doc McJames (1901)* Thrown from a carriage.

Jim Duncan (1901) Drowned.

Dave Eggler (1902) Hit by a train.

Hardie Henderson (1903) Hit by a trolley car.

Ed Delahanty (1903)* Drowned.
  He fell over Niagara Falls.

Al Mays (1905) Drowned.

Pete Dowling (1905) Hit by a train.

Nat Hicks (1907) Asphyxiated by gas in a hotel room.

Mike Dorgan (1909) Blood poisoning.
  It was a result of an old ballplaying injury to his leg.

Jack Horner (1910) Fractured his skull.
  After he slipped in his bath.

Jerry O'Brien (1911) Drowned.

Will White (1911) Drowned.

Ed Cermak (1911) Hit in the throat with a baseball.
  He played just one major-league game, for Cleveland in
  1901. He went 0 for 4. The accident happened while he
  was umpiring in the Cotton States League.

Ed Glenn (1911) Fell into a pit in a locomotive shop.

Rube Taylor (1912) Streetcar accident.
  His skull was crushed under the wheels.

Charlie Waitt (1912) Fell while washing a window.

Fred Corey (1912) Asphyxiated by gas in a hotel room.

Charlie Sprague (1912) Head injury.

Joe Stewart (1913) Fell out of a window.

Willie Mills (1914) Railroad accident.

Heinie Reitz (1914) Hit by an auto.
He was the first of many players who would die in automobile accidents.

Otis Johnson (1915) Shot while hunting.

John Dodge (1916) Hit by a pitched ball.
He played in the majors for Philadelphia and Cincinnati in 1912–1913, but was in the minors when this accident occurred in Mobile, Alabama. At least four other minor-leaguers have been killed by pitched balls: Joe Yeager (1906), Charles Pickney (1909), Jesse Batterson (1933), and Otis Johnson (1951).

Bob Unglaub (1916) Crushed in a railroad shop.

Reddy Mack (1916) Fell and fractured his skull.

Willie Sudhoff (1917) Brain injury.

Jack Glasscock (1917) Auto accident?
The Baseball Enclyclopedia lists Glasscock, a seventeen-year National League shortstop, as having died in 1947 at the age of eighty-eight. *The Bill James Historical Baseball Abstract* says Glasscock and his wife were killed when their car was hit by a train on December 21, 1917. James also says that another major-leaguer, Bill Gleason, was run over by a fire truck in St. Louis and died the same day Glasscock did. *The Baseball Encyclopedia* says Gleason died in 1932. Believe whomever you prefer.

Bill Gleason (1917) Run over by a fire truck?
See above.

Carl Druhot (1918) Shipyard accident.

Ralph Sharman (1918) Drowned.

Larry Pape (1918) Complications from an old baseball injury.

Eddie Grant (1918) Killed in World War I.
> The first major-league baseball player to be killed in battle. The ten-year veteran played third base for Cleveland, Philadelphia, Cincinnati, and New York. He died in the Argonne, France.

Robert "Bun" Troy (1918) Killed in battle at Meuse, France.

Alex Burr (1918) Killed in battle in France.

John McCloskey (1919) Mine explosion.

Bob Clark (1919) Burned.

Harry Blake (1919) Burned.

Ray Chapman (1920)* Hit by a pitched ball.

Dick Bayless (1920) Copper mine explosion.

Socks Seybold (1921) Auto accident.

John Coleman (1922) Hit by an auto.

Jim Scoggins (1923) Brain tumor.
> He pitched one game in the majors, in 1913. He was the losing pitcher, even though he didn't give up a single hit. The tumor developed after he was hit in the head by a ball.

Wild Bill Donovan (1923) Train wreck.
> He was on his way to the winter baseball meetings.

Tony Boeckel (1924)* Auto accident.

Jim Hughes (1924) Fractured his skull falling from a trestle.

Emil Huhn (1925) Team bus accident.

Charlie Irwing (1925) Hit by a bus.

Marv Goodwin (1925)* Military airplane crash.
> A pitcher, he went 0 for 2 for Cincinnati that season and became the first major-league player to die in an airplane. He had been a flying instructor in World War I.

Otis Clymer (1926) Auto accident.

Germany Smith (1927) Hit by an auto.

Jack Ridgway (1928) Auto accident.

Danny Claire (1929) Burned.

Denny Williams (1929)* Auto accident.

Tom Crooke (1929) Bus accident.

Dan Long (1929) Railroad accident.

Rupert Mills (1929) Drowned.

Walt Lerian (1929)* Truck accident.
    He was crushed when a truck jumped the curb and pinned
    him to a wall.

Gus Sanberg (1930) Burned.

Guy Tutwhiler (1930) Train accident.

Sandy Piez (1930) Drowned after his car skidded off a bridge.

Charlie Ferguson (1931) Drowned.

Mark Stewart (1932) Hit by a drunken driver.

Lon Knight (1932) Asphyxiated by gas.

Doug Neff (1932) Drowned after falling off a boat.

Howard Freigau (1932) Drowned.

Tommy Dowd (1933) Drowned.

Fred Wood (1933) Hit by an auto.

John Kane (1934) Auto accident.

Rowdy Elliott (1934) Fell from a window.

Dan Dugdale (1934) Hit by a truck.

Adrian Lynch (1934) Auto accident.
    Drove his car into a ditch.

Joe Ward (1934) Auto accident.

Charlie Sullivan (1935) Auto/train accident.

Rex DeVogt (1935) Auto accident.

Irv Hach (1936) Fell from a truck.

Braggo Roth (1936) Auto/truck accident.

Fred Olmstead (1936) Auto accident.

Eddie Foster (1937) Hit by a hit-and-run driver.

Harry Wolverton (1937) Hit by a hit-and-run driver.

Hi Jasper (1937) Fell off a truck.

Gene Connell (1937) Auto accident.

Andy Bednar (1937) Auto accident.

Rube Benton (1937) Auto accident.

Earl Clark (1938) Auto/streetcar accident.

Still Bill Hill (1938) Auto accident.

Mike Donovan (1938) Shot by a fellow employee at work.

Tiny Chaplin (1939) Auto accident.

Pete Henning (1939) Auto accident.

Axel Lindstrom (1940) Concussion after a fall on the street.

Harry Krause (1940) Auto accident.

Patsy McGaffigan (1940) Drowned.

Rube Kisinger (1941) Train accident.
He was on duty as the bridge engineer.

Joe Boehling (1941) Fell from a porch.

George Gilpatrick (1941) Fell and fractured his skull.

Al Montgomery (1942)* Auto accident.
After a rookie season in which he hit .192 for the Braves, he was killed driving to Boston after spring training.

Cad Coles (1942) Drowned.

Harry Spies (1942) Hit by an auto.

Bob Bescher (1942) Auto/train accident.

Slim Love (1942) Hit by an auto.

Frank Connaughton (1942) Hit by an auto.

Chad Kimsey (1942) Drove a truck into a bridge.

Elmer Gedeon (1944) Plane shot down.
In World War II combat, over France. A former track star, he passed up a chance to run in the 1936 Olympics to play baseball. When war broke out, he enlisted.

Ed Brandt (1944) Hit by an auto.

Bill Hobbs (1945) Shot in a hunting accident.

Harry O'Neill (1945) Killed in the battle of Iwo Jima.
He caught one game for the Philadelphia Athletics in 1939.

Hick Cady (1946) Burned.

Bill Fincher (1946) Shot.

Johnny Grabowski (1946) Burned.

Chris Hartje (1946) Burned.
  Was involved in a Spokane team bus accident.

Emil Bildilli (1946) Drove a car into a tree.

John Woods (1946) Drove a car into a parked truck.

Jimmy Sheckard (1947) Hit by an auto.

Tom Sullivan (1947) Hit by an auto.

Bill Keen (1947) Auto/train accident.

Woody Crowson (1947) Bus/truck accident.

Phil Stremmel (1947) Carbon monoxide poisoning.

Frank Browning (1948) Burned.

Pete Knisely (1948) Fell from a trestle.

Chick Bowen (1948) Fell out a window.

Roy Ellam (1948) Hit by a falling weight.

John Carden (1949) Electrocuted.

Marty O'Toole (1949) Fell down stairs.

Bill Steele (1949) Hit by a streetcar.

Nub Kleinke (1950) Drowned while fishing.

Duke Kenworthy (1950) Drowned while fishing.

Jing Johnson (1950) Auto accident.

Vance Page (1951) Fell and fractured his skull.
  He tumbled from the roof of a tobacco barn he was
  repairing.

John Cameron (1951) Burned.

Rube Vinson (1951) Fell from a window while washing it.

Ray Jacobs (1952) Auto accident.

Burt Keeley (1952) Fractured hip.

Bob Neighbors (1952) Missing in action.
  While in captivity, in Korea. He had played shortstop for
  seven games with the St. Louis Browns.

Arky Vaughan (1952) Drowned.
  His fishing boat overturned.

Les Channell (1954) Fell at home.

Earl Whitehill (1954) Auto accident.

Rube DeGroff (1955) Auto accident.

Tommy Sewell (1956) Drowned.

Tommy Gastall (1956)* Drowned.
> It happened after his plane crashed into Chesapeake Bay. A twenty-four-year-old catcher, he had yet to hit .200 in two seasons with Baltimore. His body was found five days later.

Charlie Peete (1956)* Plane crash.
> Two months after Tommy Gastall drowned, Peete's plane went down in Venezuela. It happened after his first season with the Cardinals, when he got ten hits in fifty-two at-bats. He was on his way to play winter ball. His wife and three kids also died in the crash.

Dixie Leverett (1957) Fell from a tree.

Charlie Babington (1957) Died of injuries from a fall.

Ivy Griffin (1957) Auto accident.

Walt Lonergan (1958) Fell and fractured his skull.

John Phillips (1958) Electrocuted.

Bill McAfee (1958) Plane crash.
> Long retired, he was returning from the All-Star game.

George Quellich (1958) Auto accident.

Snuffy Stirnweiss (1958) Train wreck.
> The Jersey Central train ran through an open drawbridge and plunged into Newark Bay. Stirnweiss had won the American League batting title in 1945 and led the league in stolen bases in 1944.

Joe Berry (1958) Auto accident.

Walt Meinert (1958) Fell loading a shaft at work.

Mel Ott (1958) Auto accident.

Howie Fitzgerald (1959) Auto accident.

Boileryard Clarke (1959) Hip fracture.

Terry Lyons (1959) Asphyxiated.
> By gas administered by his dentist.

Ed McFarland (1959) Fell.

Fritz Clausen (1960) Fell.

Uke Clanton (1960) Auto accident.

Bob Thorpe (1960) Electrocuted.

Bill Thompson (1962) Complications from a broken hip.

Johnny Scalzi (1962) Auto accident.

Bill Bell (1962) Auto accident.

Possum Whitted (1962) Hip injury.

Dave Shean (1963) Drove his car into a fence.

Karl Drews (1963) Hit by an auto while changing a flat tire.

Ed Hock (1963) Drowned.

Dinny McNamara (1963) Hit by an auto.

Ted Pawelek (1964) Auto/truck accident.

Ken Hubbs (1964)* Plane crash.
> He had had his pilot's license for two weeks when he took off in a snowstorm and smashed his Cessna into a frozen lake near Provo, Utah. Hubbs was the National League Rookie of the Year in 1962, when he went seventy-eight consecutive games without an error. He died at twenty-two.

Fred Vaughn (1964) Auto accident.

Lefty Scott (1964) Fractured skull.

Ed Pipgras (1964) Auto accident.

Al Wingo (1964) Truck/auto accident.

Jim Joe Edwards (1965) Auto accident.

Jay Dahl (1965) Auto accident.

Dick Newsome (1965) Auto accident.

Jack Niemes (1966) Auto accident.

John Grady (1966) Auto accident.

Bing Miller (1966) Heart attack.
> After an auto accident while returning from a baseball game.

Frank Delahanty (1966) Fell.

Tom Gulley (1966) Drowned.

Jimmie Foxx (1967) Choked on meat.

Al Benton (1968) Burned.

Ned Porter (1968) Explosion on a cabin cruiser.

Don Rudolph (1968) Crushed by a dump truck.

Nestor Chavez (1969) Plane crash.
> He pitched just two big-league games, for the San Francisco Giants in 1967. He was on his way to spring training when he became a victim of one of the worst crashes in aviation history—155 people were killed.

Milt Gray (1969) Auto/train accident.

Joe Grace (1969) Auto accident.

Danny O'Connell (1969) Car skidded and struck a pole.

Curt Roberts (1969) Hit by an auto while changing a flat tire.

Paul Edmondson (1970)* Auto accident.
> He was on his way to spring training after his rookie season.

Sherry Robertson (1970) Auto accident.

Joe Wyatt (1970) Shot in a hunting accident.

Herman Hill (1970)* Drowned.

Rube Melton (1971) Auto accident.

Chico Ruiz (1972)* Auto accident.

Roberto Clemente (1972)* Plane crash.
> His DC7 had just taken off from Puerto Rico with five people on board. The plane was loaded with medicine and food to bring to survivors of a massive earthquake that had hit Managua, Nicaragua, on December 23. Nicaraguan dictator Anastasio Somoza had pocketed the $30 million in aid sent by the United States, which was why Clemente was flying supplies in personally. He criticized the Somoza government, and it has been speculated that the plane had been tampered with.
>
> Clemente's body was never found. His empty black briefcase and a brown sock washed up on the beach.

Pat Hardgrove (1973) Auto accident.

Frankie Frisch (1973) Cardiac arrest.
The seventy-four-year-old Hall of Fame manager of the St. Louis Gas House Gang had been injured a month earlier when his car slammed into an embankment in Maryland after a rear tire blew out. He had married for the second time less than a year earlier.

Eddie Solomon (1973) Auto accident.

Johnny Weekly (1974) Auto accident.

Irv Medlinger (1975) Plane crash.

John Bottarini (1976) Drowned.
His boat overturned.

Bob Moose (1976)* Auto accident.
He was on his way to his own birthday party in Martin's Ferry, Ohio. He was twenty-nine, and had gone 3 and 9 for Pittsburgh that season. Moose pitched a no-hitter against the Mets in 1969.

Danny Frisella (1977)* Dune buggy accident.
It flipped over in the desert near Phoenix on New Year's Day.

Mike Miley (1977)* Auto accident.

John Chambers (1977) Drowned.
His fishing boat overturned.

Dick Farrell (1977) Auto accident.

Bob Klinger (1977) Auto accident.

Mike Gazella (1978) Auto accident.

Thurman Munson (1979)* Plane crash.
He was practicing landings in his new jet when the plane hit the ground 1,000 feet short of the runway near Canton, Ohio. Two passengers in the plane survived and tried to pull Munson out of the flaming wreck, but failed.

Wenty Ford (1980) Auto accident.

Dick Hoover (1981) Auto accident.

Al Bool (1981) Tractor overturned.

Randy Bobb (1982) Auto accident.

Bob Hall (1983) Hit by an auto.

Ray Sanders (1983) Auto accident.

Lynn McGlothen (1984) Asphyxiated.
> He was overcome by smoke in a mobile-home fire. A woman with him was also killed.

Gonzalo Marquez (1984) Auto accident.

Joe Wood (1985) Carbon monoxide/soot inhalation.

Norm Cash (1986) Drowned.
> He was drunk and fell off a boat.

Joe DeSa (1986) Auto accident.
> Head-on crash in Puerto Rico. He was twenty-seven.

John Burrows (1987) Burned.

Fred Newman (1987) Auto accident.

Jim Brewer (1987) Auto accident.

Dick Stello (1987) Hit by an auto.
> The nineteen-year National League umpire was crushed to death when one of the two cars he was standing between was hit by another car. The accident took place in Lakeland, Florida.

Carl Hubbell (1988) Auto accident.

Specs Toporcer (1989) Fell.

Billy Martin (1989) Auto accident.

Don Bessert (1989) Alcohol poisoning.

Bo Diaz (1990) Crushed.
> He was adjusting the satellite dish on the roof of his house when it fell on him.

Aurelio Monteagudo (1990) Auto accident.

Jim Hardin (1991) Plane crash.

BALLPLAYERS AND TRAIN WRECKS

Before the days of airplane travel, it was commonly believed that baseball teams were blessed with some kind of dumb luck that prevented trains they were traveling on from crashing. People would go so far as to seek out trains with baseball teams on them, and make it a point *not* to take out insurance if they happened to be sharing a train with baseball players.

The following appeared in the 1893 edition of *Reach's Official Base Ball Guide*:

> *Baseball Players and Railroad Accidents*
>
> Some one has figured it out that base ball players are very lucky railroad travelers. So far as known there has never been any prominent base ball player killed in a railroad accident or even injured seriously, though every season scores of them travel thousands of miles.
>
> Last season the Cincinnatis were in a wreck on the Baltimore and Ohio Railroad near Grafton, but none of them were injured. The Chicago and St. Louis teams had a narrow escape also last season. While going west from New York on the P., Ft. W. and C. Railroad in Indiana part of their train was ditched. The Cincinnatis a few years ago got caught in a wreck in southern Indiana, yet all escaped. The same team, with the exception of one player, was on a hotel elevator at Dayton in 1885, when the elevator fell three stories. Again they escaped with only a few severe bruises. The old Metropolitan met with several railroad accidents in their time—once on the Louisville and Nashville Railroad near Louisville, and again on the Hudson River road. In the latter wreck a number of people were killed.
>
> A careful investigation of the percentage of injuries and deaths to the total number of people who are traveling constantly will show that this freedom to base ball players from injuries on railroads is not more extraordinary than that which follows other classes of people. Probably the fact that base ball teams do most of their traveling at night, and ride almost always in heavy sleeping or parlor cars, accounts for much of the immunity from serious accidents which they enjoy; for sleeping and parlor cars on account of their weight are not so easily derailed or telescoped as are the day coaches.

A year after that was written, thirty-nine-year-old Charlie Bennett, a fifteen-year veteran catcher for Boston, saw his career come to an end when he was run over by a Santa Fe passenger train in Kansas. He got off the train to speak with a friend and slipped under the wheels trying to get back on. Both his legs had to be amputated, one at the ankle and the other at the knee.

Bennett maintained a positive attitude about his disability, and lived to be seventy-three.

WHAT IF AN ENTIRE TEAM IS KILLED?
"The Show" Must Go On

What if an entire major-league baseball team was wiped out in a single tragic accident or natural disaster?

It could happen. There have been many plane crashes in which groups of athletes have lost their lives—three accidents in 1970 alone.* In 1948, the entire Sanitago baseball team was killed when its DC-3 airliner crashed into a hill north of Ciudad Trujillo in the Dominican Republic.

Even before teams traveled by plane, there were accidents in which entire clubs were wiped out or *almost* wiped out. On March 21, 1925, the Washington Senators were heading for an exhibition game when the wheels of the team bus broke through a wooden bridge near Sarasota. The team bus, which included future Hall of Famers Walter Johnson, Goose Goslin, and Stan Coveleski, dangled precariously over the Manatee River. Projecting girders prevented the bus from falling.

Two weeks later, after a game in Charlotte, North Carolina, the New York Yankees' bus came to the top of a steep hill, the brakes failed, and the bus started rolling backward.

"It gained momentum as it rolled and the occupants saw it was a case of jump or broken necks," reported the *New York Times*. "They dove through the windows to safety." Babe Ruth was not on that bus, having collapsed in Asheville, North Carolina, two days earlier (see chapter 1).

In 1946, another bus accident killed nine members of the Spokane team in the International League. An approaching car on the wrong

---

* Plane crashes killed thirty-eight players on the Marshall University football team, fourteen players on the Wichita State football team, and four parachutists in Montana.

side of the road forced the bus to swerve, and it plunged five hundred feet over the Cascade Mountains near Seattle.

The 1989 earthquake that rocked Candlestick Park just before Game 3 of the World Series brought the possibility of a team disaster to national consciousness. But baseball had been prepared decades earlier. As soon as teams began to travel by air routinely in the 1950s, plans were put in place to deal with disasters.

In 1954, the American League adopted a plan that would take effect if six or more players were killed or disabled in an accident. First, it would be determined how many players would be required by the disabled club to put a team on the field. The other teams in the league would submit a list of ten players from their active list, forming a pool of available players. With financing from an insurance plan, the disabled team would be able to purchase up to twenty-one players for $75,000 each, with no more than three coming from any one team.

In this way, the team that suffered the loss would not have to rebuild with minor-league-caliber players, and the other teams would not be seriously weakened.

It wasn't until 1965 that the National League adopted a similar system, called the Emergency Team Replacement Plan. The differences were slight: It would not take effect unless *seven* players were lost, the other teams would provide a list of *twelve* players, only *two* could be chosen from any one team, and the purchase price would be *$100,000*.

"When a team has to put down twelve players, or almost half its active roster, you get some good men on the lists," Cincinnati Reds president Bill DeWitt said. "A club that's been wiped out would have a real chance to get started again."

It was suggested to DeWitt that if the pool of available players contained the stars of the game, some demented team owner might be tempted to shoot down a plane carrying his own team so that he could restock it with better players. DeWitt had no comment.

LIVE LONGER—PLAY SHORTSTOP

Do ballplayers live longer than the rest of us?

The answer is no, according to "The Mortality Experience of Major League Baseball Players," a 1987 study published in the *New England Journal of Medicine*. The study was conducted by Dr. John Waterbor of the University of Alabama, who wanted to see whether there was any proof for the accepted idea that physically fit people have a longer life expectancy than the general population. He used major-league baseball players because careful records have been kept on everyone who ever played the game. Also, he's a Phillies fan.

Records were gathered on 985 men who played their first games between 1911 and 1915. The average age at death was 70.7 years. While Waterbor didn't find that baseball players live longer, he did find that life expectancy was correlated with length of career, statistical performance, and field position.

"If you played longer, you lived longer," says Waterbor, "and if you played *better* you lived longer." Infielders lived the longest, followed by outfielders and pitchers. Catchers died younger than any other players, a fact Waterbor attributes to body type.

There was "an excess of deaths" from heart disease, cancer of the rectum and pancreas, and gastric and duodenal ulcers. Fewer deaths than expected came from chronic nephritis and motor vehicle accidents. Catchers had an excess of deaths from cancer of the pancreas, pitchers from Hodgkin's disease; outfielders seemed prone to ulcers and neurologic deficits from vascular lesions of the central nervous system.

DEATH ON THE DIAMOND

Catch this 1934 MGM movie on late-night TV sometime. Mickey Rooney and Robert Young star in the story of three St. Louis Cardinals players who are mysteriously murdered—one of them by poisoned mustard on a hot dog. In the happy ending, the hero pitcher makes a spectacular throw to conk the villain on the head with a baseball.

Credit and blame for the flick go to Edward Sedgewick, who directed it, and Cortland Fitzsimmons, who wrote the novel it was based upon.

There was also "Death on the Diamond," a television show broadcast by CBS on July 17, 1953. Ralph Bellamy starred as a sensational rookie who was murdered.

WHERE ARE THEY BURIED?
Gravesites of the Hall of Famers

The following list was provided by Bill Deane of the National Baseball Hall of Fame and Museum.

Alexander, Grover C. (Elwood Cemetery, St. Paul, Nebraska)

Anson, Adrian "Pop" (Oakwoods, Chicago, Illinois)

Averill, Earl (G.A.R., Snohomish, Washington)

Baker, Frank (Spring Hill, Easton, Maryland)

Bancroft, Dave (Greenwood, Superior, Wisconsin)

Barrow, Edward (Kensico, Valhalla, New York)

Beckley, Jake (Riverside, Hannibal, Missouri)

Bender, Chief (Ardsley Park, Ardsley, Pennsylvania)

Bottomley, Jim (I.O.O.F., Sullivan, Missouri)

Bresnahan, Roger (Calvary, Toledo, Ohio)

Brouthers, Dan (Wappingers Falls, New York)

Brown, Mordecai (Roselawn, Terre Haute, Indiana)

Bulkeley, Morgan (Cedar Hill, Hartford, Connecticut)

Burkett, Jesse (St. John's, Worcester, Massachusetts)

Cartwright, Alexander (Nuuanu, Honolulu, Hawaii)

Chadwick, Henry (Greenwood, Brooklyn, New York)

Chance, Frank (Rosedale, Los Angeles, California)

Charleston, Oscar (Floral Park, Indianapolis, Indiana)

Chesbro, Jack (Howland, Conway, Massachusetts)

Clarke, Fred (St. Mary's, Winfield, Kansas)

Clarkson, John (City, Cambridge, Massachusetts)

Clemente, Roberto (body never recovered)

Cobb, Ty (Village, Royston, Georgia)

Cochrane, Mickey (cremated, ashes scattered over Lake Michigan)

Collins, Eddie (Linwood, Weston, Massachusetts)

Collins, Jimmy (Holy Cross, Buffalo, New York)

Combs, Earle (City, Richmond, Kentucky)

Comiskey, Charles (Calvary, Evanston, Illinois)

Conlan, Jocko (Green Acres Memorial Gardens, Scottsdale, Arizona)

Connolly, Tommy (St. Patrick's, Natick, Massachusetts)

Connor, Roger (Old St. Joseph's, Waterbury, Connecticut)

Coveleski, Stanley (St. Joseph, South Bend, Indiana)

Crawford, Sam (Inglewood Park, Inglewood, California)

Cronin, Joseph (St. Francis Xavier, Centerville, Massachusetts)

Cummings, Candy (Aspen Grove, Ware, Massachusetts)

Cuyler, Kiki (St. Ann's, Harrisville, Michigan)

Dean, Dizzy (Bond, Bond, Mississippi)

Delahanty, Ed (Calvary, Cleveland, Ohio)

Dihigo, Martin (Cienfuegos, Cuba)

Duffy, Hugh (Old Calvary, Mattapan, Massachusetts)

Evans, William (Noilwood Mausoleum, Cleveland, Ohio)

Evers, John J. (St. Mary's, Troy, New York)

Ewing, Buck (Mt. Washington, Cincinnati, Ohio)

Faber, Red (Acacia Park, Chicago, Illinois)

Flick, Elmer (Crown Hill, Twinsburg, Ohio)

Foster, Rube (Lincoln, Chicago, Illinois)

Foxx, James E. (Flagler Memorial, Miami, Florida)

Frick, Ford (Christchurch Columbarium, Bronxville, New York)

Frisch, Frank (Woodlawn, Bronx, New York)

Galvin, James (Calvary, Allegheny, Pennsylvania)

Gehrig, Lou (Cremated, Kensico, Valhalla, New York)

Gibson, Josh (Allegheny, Pittsburgh, Pennsylvania)

Giles, Warren (Riverside, Moline, Illinois)

Gomez, Lefty (Novato, California)

Goslin, Goose (Baptist, Salem, New Jersey)

Greenburg, Hank (Hillside Memorial, Los Angeles, California)

Griffith, Clark (Fort Lincoln, Suitland, Maryland)

Grimes, Burleigh (Clear Lake, Clear Lake, Wisconsin)

Grove, Robert (Memorial, Frostburg, Maryland)

Hafey, Chick (St. Helena, St. Helena, California)

Haines, Jesse (Bethel, Phillipsburg, Ohio)

Hamilton, Billy (Eastwood, South Lancaster, Massachusetts)

Harridge, Will (Memorial Park, Skokie, Illinois)

Harris, Bucky (Pittston, Pennsylvania)

Hartnett, Gabby (All Saints, Des Plaines, Illinois)

Heilmann, Harry (Holy Sepulchre, Southfield, Michigan)

Hooper, Harry (Mt. Calvary, Santa Cruz, California)

Hornsby, Rogers (Hornsby Bend, Texas)

Hoyt, Waite (Spring Grove, Cincinnati, Ohio)

Hubbard, Cal (Milan, Missouri)

Hubbell, Carl (New Hope, Meeker, Oklahoma)

Huggins, Miller (Spring Grove, Cincinnati, Ohio)

Jackson, Travis (Waldo, Waldo, Arizona)

Jennings, Hugh (St. Catherine's, Scranton, Pennsylvania)

Johnson, Ban (Spencer, Indiana)

Johnson, Judy (Silverbrook, Wilmington, Delaware)

Johnson, Walter (Union, Rockville, Maryland)

Joss, Adrian (Woodlawn, Toledo, Ohio)

Keefe, Timothy (City, Cambridge, Massachusetts)

Keeler, Willie (Calvary, Queens, New York)

Kelley, Joe (New Cathedral, Baltimore, Maryland)

Kelly, George (Holy Cross, Colma, California)

Kelly, Mike "King" (Mt. Hope, Boston, Massachusetts)

Klein, Chuck (Holy Cross, Indianapolis, Indiana)

Klem, Bill (Graceland Memorial Park, Miami, Florida)

Lajoie, Nap (Cedar Hill, Daytona Beach, Florida)

Landis, Kenesaw Mountain (cremated, Oakwoods, Chicago, Illinois)

Lindstrom, Fred (All Saints, Chicago, Illinois)

Lloyd, John (City, Atlantic City, New Jersey)

Lombardi, Ernie (Mountain View, Oakland, California)

Lyons, Ted (Big Woods, Edgerly, Louisiana)

Mack, Connie (Holy Sepulchre, Philadelphia, Pennsylvania)

MacPhail, Larry (Elkland Township, Cass City, Michigan)

Manush, Heinie (Memorial, Sarasota, Florida)

Maranville, Rabbit (St. Michael's, Springfield, Massachusetts)

Marquard, Rube (Hebrew, Baltimore, Maryland)

Mathewson, Christy (City, Lewisburg, Pennsylvania)

McCarthy, Joe (Mt. Olivet, Tonawanda, New York)

McCarthy, Tommie (Old Calvary, Mattapan, Massachusetts)

McGinnity, Joe (Oak Hill, McAllister, Oklahoma)

McGraw, John (New Cathedral, Baltimore, Maryland)

McKechnie, Bill (Manasota, Sarasota, Florida)

Medwick, Joe (Saint Lucas, St. Louis, Missouri)

Nichols, Kid (Mt. Moriah, Kansas City, Missouri)

O'Rourke, Jim (St. Michael's, Bridgeport, Connecticut)

Ott, Mel (Metairie, New Orleans, Louisiana)

Paige, Satchel (Forest Hills, Kansas City, Missouri)

Pennock, Herb (Union Hill, New York, New York)

Plank, Ed (Evergreen, Gettysburg, Pennsylvania)

Radbourn, Hoss (Evergreen, Bloomington, Illinois)

Rice, Sam (cremated)

Rickey, Branch (Rush Township, Stockdale, Ohio)

Rixey, Eppa (Greenlawn, Milford, Ohio)

Robinson, Jackie (Cypress Hills, Brooklyn, New York)

Robinson, Wilbert (New Cathedral, Baltimore, Maryland)

Roush, Edd (Montgomery, Oakland City, Indiana)

Ruffing, Red (Hillcrest, Bedford Heights, Ohio)

Rusie, Amos (Washelli, Seattle, Washington)

Ruth, Babe (Gate of Heaven, Hawthorne, New York)

Schalk, Ray (Evergreen, Chicago, Illinois)

Simmons, Al (St. Adalbert, Milwaukee, Wisconsin)

Sisler, George (cremated, Oak Grove, St. Louis, Missouri)

Spaulding, Albert (cremated, Byron, Illinois)

Speaker, Tris (Fairview, Hubbard, Texas)

Stengel, Casey (Forest Lawn, Glendale, California)

Terry, Bill (Evergreen, Jacksonville, Florida)

Thompson, Sam (Elmwood, Detroit, Michigan)

Tinker, Joe (Greenwood, Orlando, Florida)

Traynor, Pie (Homewood, Pittsburgh, Pennsylvania)

Vance, Dazzy (Stage Stand, Homosassa Springs, Florida)

Vaughan, Arky (Community, Eagleville, California)

Waddell, Rube (Mission Burial Park, San Antonio, Texas)

Wagner, Honus (Jefferson Memorial, Pittsburgh, Pennsylvania)

Wallace, Bobby (Inglewood Park, Inglewood, California)

Walsh, Ed (Forest Lawn, Pompano Beach, Florida)

Waner, Lloyd (Rose Hill, Oklahoma City, Oklahoma)

Waner, Paul (Manasota, Sarasota, Florida)

Ward, John (Rural, Babylon, New York)

Weiss, George (Evergreen, New Haven, Connecticut)

Welch, Mickey (Calvary, Queens, New York)

Wheat, Zack (Forest Hill, Kansas City, Missouri)

Wilson, Hack (Rosehill, Martinsburg, West Virginia)

Wright, George (Holyroad, Brookline, Massachusetts)

Wright, Harry (West Laurel Hill, Bala Cynwyd, Pennsylvania)

Yawkey, Thomas (cremated, Cambridge, Massachusetts)

Young, Cy (Methodist Church, Peoli, Ohio)

Youngs, Ross (Mission Burial Park, San Antonio, Texas)

WHATEVER HAPPENED TO TINKERS?
TO EVERS?
TO CHANCE?

Frank Chance: Severe headaches, perhaps caused by years of beanballs, induced him to undergo brain surgery. He died at age forty-seven on September 14, 1924, in Los Angeles. He had managed the Boston Red Sox the previous year.

Johnny Evers: Spent the last years of his life in a wheelchair. Died from a stroke at age sixty-six on March 28, 1947, in Albany, New York.

Joe Tinkers: Suffered from diabetes and a respiratory problem and had one leg amputated. He died on his sixty-eighth birthday, penniless and in an oxygen tent, July 27, 1948, in Orlando, Florida.

SAY IT AIN'T SNOW, DOC!
BASEBALL HERO DWIGHT GOODEN IS
KNOCKED OUT OF THE BOX BY COCAINE

Jenkins   odger,
Accord   e Habit

First Base   13 (AP) — Lo
Faces Ma   s World Serie
                           or $500 to hel
                           it, and recall

THREE
DRUGS

Cocaine Sale Is Put
In Pirate Clubhou

Baseball Orde *Gave Out Amphetamines*

11 Drug Users   Wiggins Died Of AIDS,
                   L.A. Newspaper Claims

Parker *Aiken's Recounts*
Admit   *Drug Addiction*
to
Co   *Tranquilizer Pills Help*
Us   *Bertoia to .397 Average*

DETROIT, May 16 (Æ)—The
disclosure that the major
leagues' top batter and several other professional athletes in Detroit were taking
tranquilizing drugs to ease
nervous tension drew both
praise and a warning today
from the new team physician
of the Detroit Tigers.
    Dr. Luther R. Leader says
nquilizing drugs that
p. Reno Bertoia
ffect on other

ertoia, a
ing both
a .397

SPOR

Ba

Some
during
By PETE A

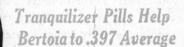

> *"A cloud called drugs is
> permeating our game."*
>
> —Baseball Commissioner
> Peter Ueberroth, 1985

There are no funny cocaine stories. There are no great anecdotes about mischievous ballplayers snorting an ounce of coke and then going out to slam the game-winning homer.

Drug stories are of a different kind: former Dodgers star Lou Johnson hocking his World Series ring for $500 to support his habit. San Diego infielder Bip Roberts getting an emergency call from his father, who is addicted to crack. Alan Wiggins going through rehab repeatedly, and then contracting AIDS and dying. Drugs rarely produce the kind of baseball folklore we'll sit around chuckling over decades from now.

When asked about drug use in baseball in 1969, National League president Warren Giles told *Sports Illustrated*, "It has never come up, and I don't think it ever will." American League executive Bob Holbrook said, "Baseball players don't use those types of things."

Like hell they don't. Ballplayers have gotten hooked on drugs since the days of Billy Earle, a catcher who played in the 1890s for Pittsburgh, St. Louis, and Brooklyn. Earle got himself addicted to morphine and became a derelict living in the streets of Washington.

When Reno Bertoia of the Detroit Tigers admitted in May 1957 that he was using tranquilizers to ease his nervous tension, it was front-page news.* Today, with ballplayers regularly doing pot, coke, crack, speed, painkillers, and steroids, tranquilizers sound like popcorn.

"Baseball players will take anything," Jim Bouton wrote in *Ball Four*. "If you had a pill that would guarantee a pitcher twenty wins but might take five years off his life, he'd take it."

---

* The twenty-two-year-old third baseman was leading both leagues with a .397 average at the time. He finished the season at .275, his best year ever.

There were a few isolated drug cases in the early 1980s (Darrell Porter, Ferguson Jenkins), but the problem wasn't taken seriously until a good chunk of the Kansas City Royals were arrested, convicted, and jailed on drug charges in 1983.

"There were times I didn't care whether we won or lost," said first baseman Willie Aikens, who hit .302 in 1982 and would never top .205 thereafter. "I began to plan my day around when I was going to get high."

Besides Aikens, pitcher Vida Blue and outfielders Willie Wilson and Jerry Martin admitted they had attempted to purchase cocaine. In exchange for guilty pleas, the government agreed not to press charges for intent to *distribute* coke.

All four were sentenced to a year in jail, with nine months of the sentence suspended. It was a harsh penalty for first offenders convicted of a misdemeanor. However, the players were conveniently permitted to go to jail right after baseball season was over, and finish their terms in time for spring training.

While alcohol has destroyed many ballplayers, it's a legal substance and there's only so much that can be done to prevent a player from abusing it without infringing on his personal freedom. Baseball—and society—perceives illegal drugs as a much more serious menace.

It looks bad for the game when guys are checking in and out of rehab clinics. Fans don't want to pay to see million-dollar-a-year players stumbling around the field. And of course, there's the possibility that a ballplayer could owe so much money from supporting his habit that he could be induced to throw games.

The drug problem, probably more than anything else, has destroyed the myth of the athlete-hero in America. The number of players caught with drugs in the mid-1980s proved definitively that just because a guy can throw a ball ninety miles an hour or hit it four hundred feet doesn't mean he has a lick of common sense.

He's not invulnerable to the problems the rest of us have to deal with. He can get addicted, he can get caught, and he can get put away. Physically addictive substances reach out and grab the fit and fat, rich and poor, black and white, benchwarmers and Hall of Famers.

Sadly, ballplayers don't even necessarily *want* to be our heroes anymore. "All I signed a contract to do is play baseball, and that's my job," said Willie Wilson, who won the American League batting title in 1982 and went to jail in 1983. "I didn't sign a contract to take care of anybody else's kids or to be a role model for anybody else."

THE 1985 PITTSBURGH DRUG TRIAL
Cocaine in the Clubhouse

"Baseball is not on trial here," Assistant U.S. Attorney James Ross told the jammed courtroom in Pittsburgh.

Of course it was. After four players on the Kansas City Royals were sent to jail in 1983 for cocaine use, baseball could no longer ignore the widespread drug problem that was threatening the integrity of the game. Montreal Expos president John McHale told the *New York Times* that eight players on his team were heavy cocaine users in 1982, and that it cost the Expos the National League Eastern Division title.

The star player on that team, Tim Raines, admitted in graphic detail how serious his problem was. Raines said he didn't want to leave cocaine in his locker or a jacket, so he kept a gram in the hip pocket of his uniform. Between innings, he'd have a quick snort and sometimes take a nap in the dugout. Raines touched a nerve with fans when he said he always slid head first, not to get to the base safely, but so that he wouldn't damage the stash in his pocket.

In the spring of 1985, a federal grand jury indicted Philadelphia Phillies caterer Curtis Strong and six other alleged drug dealers. But when stars like Keith Hernandez, Jeff Leonard, John Milner, Dave Parker, Lonnie Smith, Dale Berra, and Enos Cabell were called to testify against Strong—under grants of immunity—everyone forgot about the sleazy dealers.

At Strong's trial in September, America learned that major-league ballplayers bought cocaine in hotel rooms, elevators, and the bathroom at Three Rivers Stadium in Pittsburgh. Drug dealers peddled their wares in team clubhouses and airplanes. Players admitted not only using cocaine, but also smuggling it and distributing it. They bought it while playing winter ball in Venezuela and snuck it through airport security in their gloves.

To get evidence, the FBI had placed a hidden radio transmitter on Pittsburgh's mascot Kevin Koch, better known as "The Pirate Parrot."

The media ate it up. "Not since the Black Sox scandal," said *Time* magazine, has the national pastime suffered such a loss of public esteem."

Four months earlier, New York Mets first baseman Keith Hernandez, one of the most accomplished and respected players in the game, had denied "any involvement in cocaine, ever." He threatened to sue Players Association mediator Kenneth Moffett after Moffett hinted that drug use had been a factor in the trade that sent Hernandez from the Cardinals to the Mets in 1983.

On the witness stand, Hernandez sang a different song. He said he had started using coke after his marriage broke up in 1980 (he hit .321 that season). He quickly got to the point where he was doing "massive" amounts and developed "an insatiable desire for more." Before long he had lost ten pounds and was waking up in the morning with nosebleeds, his body shaking. It took him three years to kick the habit. Hernandez said 40 percent of all major-league players used cocaine.

In the most dramatic moment of the trial, Hernandez described the drug as "a demon in me . . . I consider cocaine the devil on this earth." When he returned to Shea Stadium after testifying, the fans gave him a standing ovation.

"I had more money than I had ever known. I had a lot of free time," Hernandez later wrote in his book *If At First*. "I also think my basic personality might have led me to try cocaine: I was never one to look before I leaped."

The defense effectively portrayed the ballplayers as rich "hero junkies" who were using drug dealers as scapegoats. At one point, Curtis Strong's lawyer shouted at Dave Parker, "How is it that once you get immunity, you're not going to jail and won't lose your twenty-thousand dollar diamond rings, that you now remember?"

Both Parker and Dale Berra (Yogi's son) testified that Willie Stargell had distributed amphetamines to players. John Milner said, "Willie had the red juice" (an amphetamine mixture).

"Willie who?" asked the defense attorney.

"Mays," said Milner.

"Willie Mays?"

"That's right, the great one, yes."

Stargell and Mays, Hall of Famers both, denied any drug use.

The defense lawyers did a good job of making the ballplayers look bad, but they were unable to make their clients look good. All seven drug dealers were convicted and received prison sentences of up to twelve years.

On March 1, 1986, Baseball Commissioner Ueberroth came to a decision. Seven players—Keith Hernandez, Dale Berra, Joaquín Andújar, Dave Parker, Jeff Leonard, Lonnie Smith, and Enos Cabell—were suspended from major-league baseball for one year because they had "in some fashion facilitated the distribution of drugs in baseball."

The suspension would be lifted if the player agreed to donate 10 percent of his salary for one year to drug abuse programs, perform 100 hours of public service for each of two years, and submit to random drug testing for the rest of his career.

Four players—Al Holland, Lee Lacy, Lary Sorensen, and Claudell Washington—would be suspended for sixty days unless they contributed 5 percent of their salaries to drug abuse programs.

All the players accepted Ueberroth's punishment, which was light, considering that a week earlier the National Basketball Association had banned New Jersey Net Michael Ray Richardson for *life* because of his drug use.

Ueberroth cleared only one player implicated in the trial—Dodgers third baseman Bill Madlock. Dale Berra had named Madlock as passing out amphetamines.

After the trial, drugs became a part of baseball much like exploding scoreboards and the seventh-inning stretch. Every hitter who went into a slump or pitcher who had a couple of bad outings was suspected of being on coke. Drug testing came to play a part in contract negotiations. In 1986, the Yankees offered pitcher Mike Armstrong $295,000 to play if he agreed to a drug-testing clause. If he refused, the figure would be $35,000 less. Ueberroth sent a letter to every major-league player requesting that he accept voluntary testing. The Players Association fought testing tooth and nail, claiming the tests were unreliable and an infringement of personal liberty.

For all the hoopla over the Pittsburgh case, Ueberroth's disciplinary action came off as a public relations gesture that gave the *illusion* that baseball was getting tough on drugs. Two years later, Atlanta outfielder Lonnie Smith said he had only been tested twice since Ueberroth's decision. He admitted that he had paid less than half of his $85,000 fine and nobody had even asked him about the rest. Nobody bothered to check to see whether he had performed 100 hours of community service. He called his punishment "a joke."

Baseball continues to struggle with the question of whether drug use is a disease or a crime. While pitcher Dwight Gooden was given understanding and treatment when he was caught using cocaine, his teammate Keith Hernandez—who was never even caught—was given the choice of being thrown out of the game for a year or paying a $135,000 fine. And players convicted of drunk driving—who are a real threat to people other than themselves—are rarely punished *or* sent for treatment.

THE COCAINE ALL-STARS

The list of major-league ballplayers who have been named, arrested, convicted, treated or have admitted using cocaine would stock a pretty good All-Star team, if not a Hall of Fame. Unless otherwise noted, the following were not charged or convicted of any crime.

> *Willie Aikens:* Convicted of trying to buy cocaine. Spent eight weeks at Shepherd and Pratt Clinic in Baltimore and eighty-one days in jail at the Federal Correctional Institution in Fort Worth.
>
> *Joaquín Andújar:* Suspended for one year and fined after the Pittsburgh drug trial in 1985.
>
> *Dusty Baker:* Named as a cocaine user at the 1985 Pittsburgh trial.
>
> *Len Barker:* Accused of buying cocaine by drug dealer Anthony Peters.
>
> *Steve Bedrosian:* Received counseling for cocaine dependency.
>
> *Dale Berra:* Suspended for one year and fined after the Pittsburgh drug trial in 1985.

Vida Blue: Convicted of possession of cocaine. Rehabilitated at CareUnit in Orange, California. Did three months in prison and paid a $5,000 fine. He tested positive for cocaine use while under parole, and again several times while trying to make a comeback in 1986.

Juan Bonilla: Treated at CareUnit.

Enos Cabell: Suspended for one year and fined after the Pittsburgh drug trial in 1985.

Mike Caldwell: Accused of buying cocaine by drug dealer Anthony Peters.

Bernie Carbo: Named by Keith Hernandez as a cocaine user at the Pittsburgh drug trial.

Joe Charboneau: Accused of buying cocaine by drug dealer Anthony Peters.

Donn Clendenon: Addicted to freebase cocaine in 1987, according to sportscaster Howard Cosell.

Al Cowens: Named as a cocaine user by convicted drug dealer Mark Liebl.

Dick Davis: Named as a cocaine user by drug dealer Anthony Peters.

Dennis Eckersley: Named as a cocaine user by convicted drug dealer Mark Liebl.

Barbaro Garbey: Arrested for possession of cocaine in 1985.

Dwight Gooden: Tested positive for cocaine in 1987, went through rehab at the Smithers Alcoholism and Treatment Center in New York.

Keith Hernandez: Suspended for one year and fined after the Pittsburgh drug trial in 1985.

Al Holland: Suspended for sixty days and fined after the Pittsburgh drug trial in 1985.

Don Hood: Named as a cocaine user by convicted drug dealer Mark Liebl.

Steve Howe: Addicted to cocaine, went through rehab six times.

LaMarr Hoyt: Was arrested at least four times for intent to distribute cocaine, drunk driving, leaving the scene of an accident, possession of marijuana, and importing a controlled substance (seventy-nine Valium pills, forty-six Quaaludes, three grams of pot) across the Mexican border into the United States. Went through rehab at Hazelden Center in Minnesota in 1986; sentenced to a year in jail in 1988.

Ferguson Jenkins: Convicted for possession of marijuana, cocaine, and hashish in 1980. Inducted into the Baseball Hall of Fame in 1991.

Lou Johnson: Received treatment for cocaine addiction.

Lee Lacy: Suspended for sixty days and fined after the Pittsburgh drug trial in 1985.

Ken Landreaux: Treated for chemical dependency at The Meadows, an Arizona rehab center.

Ron LeFlore: Named as a cocaine user by convicted drug dealer Mark Liebl.

Jeff Leonard: Suspended for one year and fined after Pittsburgh drug trial in 1985.

Jerry Martin: Convicted of attempting to buy cocaine, served eighty-one days in jail at the Federal Correctional Institution in Fort Worth.

Gary Matthews: Named as a cocaine user at the 1985 Pittsburgh trial.

Denny McLain: Convicted and jailed for cocaine trafficking, cocaine possession, loan sharking, extortion, and bookmaking.

Eddie Milner: Underwent cocaine rehabilitation in 1987. Suspended for one year without pay as a repeat offender.

John Milner: Admitted buying cocaine in the Pittsburgh Pirates' clubhouse.

Paul Molitor: Named as a cocaine user by drug dealer Anthony Peters.

Otis Nixon: Arrested for cocaine possession in 1987 as a minor-leaguer. He blossomed into a star with the Atlanta

Braves in 1991. With three weeks left in the season, he tested positive for cocaine and was suspended for sixty days. Nixon had been hitting .297 and leading the league in stolen bases. He was replaced by Lonnie Smith, another member of the Cocaine All-Stars. Smith made a baserunning flub that cost Atlanta the 1991 World Series.

Dickie Noles: Acknowledged cocaine user.

Mike Norris: Named as a cocaine user by convicted drug dealer Mark Liebl.

John "Blue Moon" Odom: Convicted of selling cocaine in 1986.

Rowland Office: Named as a cocaine user at the Pittsburgh drug trial in 1985.

Dave Parker: Suspended for one year and fined after the Pittsburgh drug trial in 1985. Convicted drug dealer Shelby Greer said Parker boasted of smuggling cocaine into the United States from Venezuela by hiding it in a catcher's mitt.

Joe Pepitone: Arrested for possession of cocaine, heroin, Quaaludes, drug paraphernalia, and a loaded handgun in 1985. Spent two months in jail.

Pascual Perez: Charged with trafficking cocaine in the Dominican Republic and convicted of possession, he spent three months in prison in 1984.

Darrell Porter: One of the first players to admit a drug problem, in 1980. Treated at The Meadows for abuse of alcohol, marijuana, Quaaludes, amphetamines, and cocaine.

Tim Raines: Treated for cocaine dependency at CareUnit.

Chuck Rainey: Named as a cocaine user by convicted drug dealer Mark Liebl.

Pedro Ramos: Arrested in 1979 for possession of cocaine, drug trafficking, and possession of a concealed weapon.

J. R. Richard: Purchased cocaine through Dave Parker, according to Parker at the 1985 Pittsburgh drug trial.

Manny Sarmiento: Named as a cocaine user at the 1985 Pittsburgh trial.

Daryl Sconiers: Acknowledged cocaine user.

Rod Scurry: After five years of addiction, treated for cocaine dependency at Gateway Rehabilitation Center in Aliquippa, Pennsylvania, in 1984. "The stuff I was doing was enough to kill you," he said after rehab. He was arrested again in 1988 for buying crack in Reno.

Lonnie Smith: Suspended for one year and fined after the Pittsburgh drug trial in 1985. Treated for cocaine dependency at Hyland Center for Drug and Alcohol Abuse in St. Louis.

Eddie Solomon: Named as a cocaine user at the Pittsburgh drug trial in 1985.

Lary Sorensen: Suspended for sixty days and fined after the Pittsburgh drug trial in 1985.

Derrel Thomas: Named as a cocaine user at the 1985 Pittsburgh trial.

Mike Torrez: Named as a cocaine user by convicted drug dealer Mark Liebl.

Steve Trout: Named as a cocaine user by convicted drug dealer Mark Liebl.

Tom Underwood: Named as a cocaine user by convicted drug dealer Mark Liebl.

Claudell Washington: Suspended for sixty days and fined after the Pittsburgh drug trial in 1985. Treated for cocaine addiction at Merritt Peralta Institute in Oakland.

U. L. Washington: Named as a cocaine user by convicted drug dealer Mark Liebl.

Alan Wiggins: Arrested for possession of cocaine and treated at CareUnit. After several relapses, he died of AIDS in 1991.

Maury Wills: Arrested for possession of cocaine in 1983. He was cleared because of insufficient evidence, but admitted being addicted and was treated at CareUnit.

Willie Wilson: Convicted of trying to buy cocaine, served eighty-one days in jail at the Federal Correctional Institution in Fort Worth.

DWIGHT GOODEN
"We robbed him of his youth"

He came out of Tampa in 1984 with a 95-mph fastball and a curve that left hitters mumbling to themselves. Before turning twenty, he had struck out 276 terrified batters and was named Rookie of the Year. The next season he was even better, putting up an astonishing 24–4 record, 1.53 ERA, and 288 strikeouts. He became the youngest man to win the Cy Young Award. He was unhittable, and he had poise. They were already calling him the greatest pitcher who ever lived. He was also a serious, shy, hardworking kid—the perfect baseball idol.

A somewhat jealous old phenom named Bob Feller warned prophetically, "Give him a chance to mess up his life, and *then* see how good he is."

Dwight Gooden began messing up his life almost immediately after the 1985 season. Nobody expected Dr. K to top a career year like that, but he just wasn't the same. His fastball lost its hop. He was good, but no longer overpowering. The guys in the K Corner at Shea Stadium didn't have as much to do. A series of events unfolded that brought America's newest baseball hero crashing down to reality.

On December 27, 1985, police in Tampa received an anonymous tip that Gooden was carrying a large quantity of cocaine. It did not come as a surprise. Police surveillance reports had previously placed the pitcher at a known "drug bar" in Ybor City's Manila Bar & Restaurant.

His car was tailed for six hours, then pulled over and searched by drug-sniffing dogs. The police found $4,000 in cash, a holstered pistol, some empty beer cans, and a bag of baking soda. It seemed unlikely that Gooden would be making cookies, but baking soda is not cocaine and he was not arrested.

Nine days later, Gooden sprained an ankle shagging flies in Tampa. The Mets didn't find out about it until a week later, when an anonymous call was received from someone saying he had seen Gooden walking around on crutches.

In April 1986, Gooden, his sister, Betty Jones, and his fiancée, Carlene Pearson, got into an argument with a clerk at the Hertz counter in New York's LaGuardia Airport. Jones threw a soda in the clerk's face. Gooden said they were being harassed.

On October 28, New York City threw a ticker-tape parade to honor the Mets, who had won the World Series in an incredible come-from-behind fashion (with little help from Gooden—he lost one game in the playoffs and two in the Series). Dwight didn't show up. The Mets said he had overslept.

Two weeks later, Gooden announced that his engagement to Carlene Pearson was off. At the same time, he confirmed published reports that he was the father of a boy, Dwight Jr., who had been born to a high-school friend named Debra Hamilton eight months earlier.

Rumors of Gooden's drug use had become public by then. In an interview with the *Tampa Tribune*, he said he would request a drug-testing clause in his upcoming contract. "Drugs? No, I have never used them and I never will," he insisted.

At 10:50 P.M. on December 13, Tampa police spotted three cars weaving in and out of traffic on a four-lane thoroughfare, their drivers shouting at one another. One of the cars was a 1984 silver Mercedes with plates that read "DOC."

The police pulled over Gooden, his eighteen-year-old nephew, Gary Sheffield (the top draft choice of the Milwaukee Brewers that year), Gooden's seventeen-year-old cousin Dick Pedro, a high school teammate named Vance Lovelace, and a friend named Philip Walker.

According to police, Gooden was immediately abusive and refused to hand over his driver's license. An exchange of angry words turned into a fistfight. One cop was kicked in the head, another kneed in the groin. Gooden was struck with fists, knees, and flashlights and beaten to the ground with nightsticks before being handcuffed and shackled. At one point, Gooden reached backward and grabbed a cop's holster. Another cop pulled out his revolver and put the barrel under Gooden's chin.

The cops, all white, taunted the young black men. Officer David Bryant flashed a light in Gooden's eyes and pretended to be a broadcaster interviewing him. Officers Mark Townsend and Jim Thompson shouted, "Break his arm!" Gooden came away with bruises on his face, cuts on his arms and wrist, and a bloodshot eye. His blood alcohol level was .111—just over the amount necessary to be considered driving under the influence of alcohol.

Gooden was charged with resisting arrest with violence, battery, and disorderly conduct.* He pleaded no contest to the felony charges and was sentenced to three years on probation.

On January 30, 1987, ex-fiancée Carlene Pearson flew into La-Guardia Airport to meet Gooden, who was flying in from Florida. She was detained as she passed through the metal detector at the Delta terminal. Officers found a loaded, two-shot .38-caliber Derringer in her handbag. Pearson said she had obtained the gun the previous year from her "boyfriend," Gooden.

"I don't know where she got the gun," said Gooden. "I don't think it's possible she intended to harm me."

A police trace of the pistol found that it had been reported stolen in Tampa five years earlier. Pearson pleaded guilty to criminal possession of a weapon and was sentenced to five years on probation.

Finally, on April 1, a week before baseball season began, Gooden drove to his parents' home in Tampa. "You better sit down," he told them. "I have some bad news."

Despite everything that had been going on in Gooden's personal life, there was general shock when people learned that he had tested positive for cocaine. At first he denied it, then broke down in tears and told Mets general manager Frank Cashen that he had only used the drug once at a party two days before his urine test. Later, Gooden admitted he had begun using cocaine in high school, and he had been doing it about once a week during the off-season.

---

* Four of the Mets' five starting pitchers were arrested for fighting with police officers in 1987. Ron Darling, Bob Ojeda, and Rick Aguilera were involved in a brawl with uniformed cops in Cooters, a Houston nightspot. Darling was fined $200 and put on probation for one year. Charges against Ojeda and Aguilera were dropped.

Psychologists lined up to give explanations of why Gooden insisted on a drug-testing clause in his contract if he was doing drugs. He was in denial, some said—he thought he was invincible. He was sending out a cry for help, claimed others—he had a subconscious desire to be caught. Gooden had taped a "Just Say No" public service commercial a few months earlier.

Baseball Commissioner Peter Ueberroth told the Mets that unless Gooden accepted help, he would be suspended. "If the player is willing to help himself, he gets one chance," he said. "If he is unwilling to cooperate or if a problem occurs a second time, then we will take the penalty route."

Instead of being on the mound on Opening Day staring down the Pittsburgh Pirates, Gooden was in the Smithers Alcoholism and Treatment Center on Manhattan's Upper East Side. It's a Renaissance Revival mansion that was once the home of Broadway impresario Billy Rose. Writers John Cheever and Truman Capote had dried out there, among others.

The $200-a-day program is patterned after the twelve-step Alcoholics Anonymous program. Gooden got up at seven every morning, had twenty minutes for "meditation" followed by breakfast and "therapeutic duties" (such as listing the most painful consequences of addiction or writing a letter of farewell to drugs). Then there was a lecture and group therapy. After lunch, he would exercise, then attend more lectures and an educational film. Visitors were allowed on Sunday evenings.

After twenty-eight days, Gooden was released. It was determined that he was an occasional user and not addicted to cocaine.

Advocates of drug testing for athletes can use Gooden's case as ammunition. If he hadn't been tripped up by the test, there's no telling what might have happened to him. His is the classic "too much, too soon" story. After breaking into the majors, his yearly salary soared from $60,000 to $270,000 to $1.32 million. He made $350,000 from commercials for Polaroid, Toys Я Us, and Nike. Would *anyone* have been mature enough to handle such wealth at the age of twenty-one?

"The sudden fame and fortune he achieved is nice," Mets general manager Frank Cashen said. "But we sort of robbed him of his youth."

It may be too early to tell, but Dwight Gooden's rehabilitation looks to be successful. The first person he called when he left Smithers was Monica Colleen Harris, a childhood friend. They were married in Tampa in November of 1987. When he returned to the Mets, he went 5–1 and finished the season 15–7. In 1988, he posted a sparkling 18–9 mark. Shoulder problems ruined most of 1989, but he came back to 19–7 in 1990. There were no more "harassment" incidents with cops, clerks, or anybody else.

Although he doesn't throw quite as hard as he did as a teenage phenom, he's learned how to *pitch*. Through his first seven seasons, Gooden had a record of 119–46, the highest winning percentage of any pitcher in baseball history. In April 1991, he signed a three-year contract that will pay him $5.15 million a year. If he keeps his nose clean and recovers from arthroscopic surgery performed in 1991, Doc Gooden is headed for Cooperstown.

STEVE HOWE
The Thing That Wouldn't Die

Steve Howe reminds me of Rasputin, the Siberian monk whom assassins found so difficult to kill.

One night in 1916, Russian aristocrat Felix Yusupov gave Rasputin a glass of poisoned wine and a piece of cake filled with enough potassium cyanide to kill an ox. When Rasputin failed to topple over, Yusupov pulled out a pistol and shot him. The monk staggered into a courtyard, where he was stabbed several times and shot by other assassins. He *still* wasn't dead. The conspirators wrapped him in rope and threw him into the Neva River. Eventually Rasputin *did* die—from drowning.

Nobody has tried to kill Steve Howe except himself. His story is a brain-numbing series of cocaine binges, rehab clinics, and relapses. For all Steve Howe has been through over the last ten years, it's a miracle he's still alive, much less pitching in the major leagues. *Rolling Stone* described him as "John Belushi in a jockstrap."

Howe tried cocaine for the first time during his sophomore year at the University of Michigan. To say that he liked it would be an understatement. He also tried marijuana, mescaline, and LSD, the last of which caused him to believe he'd seen his stereo speakers *breathing*.

Drugs didn't seem to hurt his pitching—after just thirteen games in the minors he was called up by the Los Angeles Dodgers in 1980. At age twenty-two, he won the National League Rookie of the Year Award.

A hero in L.A., he didn't put up a fight when cocaine came to him. He was getting high two or three times a week, half a dozen lines at a time. And he wasn't the only one. "The list of nonpartyers on the 1980 Dodgers would be much shorter than the list of partyers," Howe revealed in his autobiography, *Between the Lines*.

The next season he was up to two or three grams a week and cocaine became his total preoccupation. He hid it from his wife, Cindy, and began staying out all night. On one binge he went through fifteen grams in three days.

He started getting paranoid. During a road trip to Chicago, he taped the curtains to the window frame of his hotel room so that nobody could see inside. When Cindy hugged him, he turned his head away because he was sure she was looking up his nose.

When he needed a toot, Howe would tell Cindy he was going out to buy milk and not return for days. In November, he was missing for nearly a week. Cindy called the Dodgers and a private investigator.

Despite it all, Howe had another great season in 1981. He helped the Dodgers win the World Championship, winning Game 4 and saving Game 6 of the World Series.

The next year he was even better. Incredibly, he managed to pitch sixty-six games in 1982 and turned in a 2.08 ERA. But Cindy and the Dodgers were on to him, so he checked into The Meadows in Wickenburg, Arizona (the same clinic where Dodger Bob Welch had been treated for alcoholism three years earlier). Wearing pajamas, he was put in a room for three days of detox. They took away his shaving lotion so he couldn't drink it, his razor blades so he couldn't kill himself.

Rehab didn't work, because Howe didn't think he had a problem. The day after he left, he raided a stash he'd hidden in his house and went right back to using cocaine.

Despite posting a 1.44 ERA in 1983, things started spinning out of control in Howe's life. He was earning $325,000 a year, but most of it went up his nose. He declared bankruptcy, separated from his wife, and started packing a gun. After a couple of bad outings, he broke down and wept in manager Tommy Lasorda's office.

On May 29, he checked into CareUnit, a rehab center in Orange County, California, that has been the temporary home of many ballplayers. When he got out a month later, Baseball Commissioner Bowie Kuhn and the Dodgers fined him $53,867—his pay for the time he'd been unavailable to his team. It was the largest player fine in baseball history at that point.

Howe started snorting again in mid-September and was quickly back to a couple of grams a day. After he left the team without permission, the Dodgers suspended him indefinitely.

He went back to CareUnit for another month. It didn't help. He didn't have the willpower to stop. On December 15 the baseball commissioner suspended him for the entire 1984 season.

Without baseball in 1984, Howe again took to drugs and was admitted to Palmdale Hospital, a Christian chemical dependency center. (A deeply religious man, Howe had accepted Jesus Christ into his life at about the same time he began using cocaine.)

When 1985 rolled around, the Dodgers decided they'd had their fill of Steve Howe, and Howe realized he had to get out of Los Angeles. He signed with the Minnesota Twins for $450,000. By now, drugs had started hurting his performance on the mound. He was no longer invincible, finishing the season with a 3–4 record and 5.49 ERA. After his third relapse in two and a half years, the Twins released him that September and he checked into yet another rehab clinic, St. Mary's Hospital in Minneapolis.

He had come to understand, he said, that "coke magnified feelings of inadequacy that I'd battled since adolescence."

Peter Ueberroth had become baseball commissioner in 1985, and drugs were number one on his hit list. When Howe approached major-league teams *this* time, many expressed interest in him but were oddly reluctant to offer a contract. At least three general managers told him, "I can't tell you why."

Howe believed that he was being blackballed—Ueberroth wanted him away from the game so he couldn't relapse, embarrass baseball, and spoil the commissioner's well-known political ambitions.

"Ueberroth couldn't fine me or order community service because

I didn't have a contract," Howe wrote in his autobiography. "But it was easy for him to secretly hit me with the ultimate penalty: banishment from major-league organizations."

Still hungry to pitch, Howe hooked up with a semipro team in 1986—the San Jose Bees of the California League. The Bees were a bunch of ex-big-league misfits with drug, booze, and other problems. Besides Howe, cocaine abusers Mike Norris, Daryl Sconiers, and Derrel Thomas were on the team, as well as amphetamine junkie Ken Reitz. A *Rolling Stone* article about the Bees said Reitz—the National League Gold Glove third baseman in 1975—had been so messed up on speed that he blew his car to bits with a shotgun because he thought somebody was hiding in the back seat.

Howe was spectacular with the Bees, but failed a urine test (he believed somebody tampered with it) and got booted out. He was going to play for the Seibu Lions in the Japanese Pacific League, but they thought better of it. He played for a month with the Tabasco Gonaderos in the Mexican League.

There's something about a 90-mph fastball with movement that makes front offices overlook the fact that a pitcher can't stop inhaling illegal drugs. The Texas Rangers offered Howe $175,000 to pitch for the team at the end of 1987. Ueberroth fined the Rangers $250,000 for bringing Howe up without his approval. Howe got into twenty-four games and went 3–3.

Surprise! Howe got high again and failed a drug test. The Rangers terminated his contract on January 17, 1988. It was his sixth suspension. He'd been in six treatment centers in six years. It looked like the end of the road for Steve Howe.

Three years later, this modern-day Rasputin floated to the surface. With cap in hand, he went around begging for a tryout with any big-league team. He was thirty-three—old for a pitcher—and an organization would have to be desperate or crazy to take a risk on a six-time junkie loser like Steve Howe.

The New York Yankees, coming off their worst record since 1912, agreed to give Howe a tryout. Amazingly, the old guy could still *bring it*. The Yankees signed him to a $150,000 contract that allowed them to back out if Howe so much as blew his nose funny.

As I write this at the tail end of the 1991 season, Steve Howe is not only back in the majors, he's the Yankees' ace reliever. He has won three games and lost one, with a stingy 1.52 ERA. At one point in the season, he had given up one earned run in sixteen innings. He's allowed seven walks in forty-seven innings.

I'm reluctant to close this section with one of those corny endings about a guy who overcomes adversity to win in the end. Tomorrow's newspaper could very easily show a photo of Steve Howe being taken to his seventh rehab center, suspended once again and perhaps thrown out of baseball for good.

However, it does seem that over the years Howe has slowly matured, set his priorities, and come to accept and like himself enough so that he doesn't have to shove powder up his nose in order to deal with life. It will be nice if that proves to be the case.

Throughout his career Steve Howe struggled to understand why, if he was a devoted Christian, his faith failed to help him overcome drugs. A breakthrough came when he attended a lecture in Philadelphia given by Father Leo, a priest and recovering alcoholic. "Deep down I believed I wasn't worthy of God's love and forgiveness," Howe wrote in his autobiography. Father Leo made him believe that "God gives us freedom of choice and makes us responsible for our actions."

DOCK ELLIS
The First Hallucinogenic No-Hitter

Baseball didn't pay much attention to the Summer of Love in 1967. Bob Gibson and the St. Louis Cardinals marched through the World Series, beating shorthairs like Carl Yastrzemski and the totally uncool Boston Red Sox. It's doubtful that many hippies turned on and tuned in to ballgames at Woodstock in 1969, even though the local nine—the New York Mets—were performing a true miracle that summer.

Baseball just wasn't part of the counterculture.

That makes it particularly shocking to think that Dock Ellis, the twenty-five-year-old pitcher for the Pittsburgh Pirates, threw a no-hitter under the influence of LSD on June 12, 1970.

Ellis and the Pirates flew into San Diego the day before. Dock rented a car and drove to Los Angeles, where he partied with a woman friend. They stayed up all night listening to Jimi Hendrix* records and dropping acid.

About noon the next day, it occurred to Dock that he played baseball for a living and was scheduled to pitch a game in San Diego in six hours. He got to the ballpark at five-thirty, popped some Dexamyl and Benzedrine to come down off the high, and went out on the mound.

"I can only remember bits and pieces of the game," he said later. "I was psyched. I had a feeling of euphoria. I remember hitting a couple of batters and the bases were loaded two or three times."

Dock wasn't stumbling around the mound or anything, but as no-hitters go, this one was sloppy. He walked two batters in the first inning and eight throughout the game. He hit one guy, and three Padre players stole bases. Pittsburgh second baseman Bill Mazeroski had to make a great diving catch in the seventh inning.

Still, it goes in the books as a "no-no," as Ellis called it. Pirates 2, Padres 0. Not bad for a guy in an altered state of consciousness.

Ellis didn't mention to reporters after the game that he'd just pitched the first no-hitter in baseball history on acid. He didn't even mention it in *Dock Ellis in the Country of Baseball*, the 1976 book he wrote with Donald Hall. Just before publication of the book, Ellis and Hall changed the manuscript, substituting the word "vodka" for "acid" and "coffee" for "Dexamyl and Benzedrine." Ellis had just been traded to the Yankees and didn't want to give the New York press a drug scandal to sink their teeth into.

It wasn't until 1984, when he was interviewed by the *Pittsburgh Press*, that Ellis thought it was safe to tell the truth. The 1989 edition of *Dock Ellis in the Country of Baseball* was updated and explained the whole story. If other pitchers got the idea of using hallucinogens to see if it would help them, they're not talking.

Ellis was one of the most controversial and outspoken players of the 1970s. Before his first spring training, he was convicted of car theft and spent a day and a half in jail. In the minors, another player called him "nigger" and Dock sliced the shape of a heart in the guy's chest with a knife. He got his chance to play in the majors, he said,

---

* Three months later, Hendrix would die from a drug overdose.

because a stray bullet struck and killed teammate Waco Jackson, a pitcher slated to be called up to the Pirates.

In 1972, he was sprayed with Mace and charged with disorderly conduct after a guard in Cincinnati refused to let him into the stadium without identification. Maybe that was why, in 1974, Ellis decided to knock down the entire Cincinnati Reds lineup. He hit the first three batters to face him—Pete Rose, Joe Morgan, and Dan Driessen—before he was pulled out of the game. The performance tied a major-league record.

Ellis played nearly his entire twelve-year career on drugs, especially amphetamines and cocaine. He also drank heavily, using vodka to come down from the high. "I was using everything," he told the *New York Times*. "I mean everything. For about eight or nine years. I was an addict."

After his glory days with Pittsburgh, Ellis was traded to the Yankees in 1976. He lasted only a year because his drinking and drug use were too obvious to overlook. Short stays with Oakland, Texas, the Mets, and Pittsburgh again only confirmed that he was in no shape to pitch in the majors.

"Baseball, I was through with it," he said. "All I lived for was to get high."

In September 1980, Dock checked into an Arizona treatment facility to dry out. Five years of psychotherapy in Los Angeles helped too. After spending two years at the University of California at Irvine, Dock Ellis became a substance abuse counselor and devoted his life to helping others avoid what he'd been through. He worked at Pasadena Community Hospital and the California Institute for Behavioral Medicine, a private clinic in Beverly Hills. He hasn't touched alcohol or drugs in more than a decade.

A few years ago, Ellis was approached by the Miller people to shoot a Lite Beer commercial with ex-Yankee Sparky Lyle. He was all set to do it, until the woman at the advertising agency asked if he drank the beer.

"Not really," he replied. "I used to."

"Would you sign a contract," she asked, "stating that you *will* drink some beer on camera?"

"I can't do that."

"What the hell am I talking to you for?"

ALAN WIGGINS
Baseball's First AIDS Victim

Alan Wiggins would have wanted to be remembered for the best day of his career—May 17, 1984. That was the day he stole five bases, tying a modern National League record (since broken by Otis Nixon). Instead, he'll be remembered for his roller-coaster ride of cocaine, suspensions, rehab centers, relapses, and finally death at the age of thirty-two from AIDS.

Wiggins escaped his childhood in the Watts ghetto by playing ball for Muir High in Pasadena and Pasadena City College. He was signed in 1980 by his hometown team—the Los Angeles Dodgers—and caught a lot of notice by stealing 120 bases for Lodi in Class A ball. San Diego general manager Jack McKeon happened to see Wiggins single, steal second, steal third, and score on an infield out during one game. When the youngster did the same thing again a few innings later, McKeon decided this was just the kind of kid the Padres could use. He drafted Wiggins for the $25,000 waiver price, and the next season the speedster was in the big leagues.

Wiggins's troubles began almost immediately. In 1982 he was arrested for possession of cocaine and suspended by Commissioner Bowie Kuhn for thirty days. He spent the time at the CareUnit facility in Orange County, California. The Padres warned him that if it happened again, they would get rid of him.

It did happen again the very next year, but Wiggins was just slapped with a brief suspension. Stealing sixty-six bases and hitting .276 in his first full season kept the switch-hitting outfielder on the roster. Wiggins worked with the San Diego Police Department counseling young people on drug abuse and made some public service announcements.

In 1984, he swiped seventy bases and acted as the catalyst that propelled San Diego into the World Series. The Padres lost to Detroit, despite Wiggins's .364 average. He beat out four bunts in ten post-season games and had clearly become one of the best lead-off hitters in the game. He had also been converted to a second baseman, and he performed well. San Diego was impressed enough to offer the twenty-six-year-old a four-year, $2.5-million contract.

But a few weeks into the 1985 season, Wiggins disappeared before a game and showed up two days later at a drug treatment center in Minnesota. This time, San Diego was fed up. It was announced that Wiggins would not be permitted to rejoin the team even if he successfully completed another drug rehab program. The fact that he had been hitting .054 did not make it a difficult decision.

"At some point, a person has to be responsible for his own actions," said Padres owner Joan Kroc. "Whatever it takes, we're going to have a clean team." She traded him to Baltimore in June.

Once again, he was sensational, stealing thirty bases in just seventy-six games and hitting .285. He bought a house in Baltimore, and it looked like he was there to stay.

In 1987 he relapsed again. He failed a drug test and he was suspended for the fourth time in five years. This time it was an indefinite suspension, and without pay. At twenty-nine—the age at which he should have been at his peak—Wiggins was washed up.

Nothing much was heard from Alan Wiggins until Thanksgiving Day 1990, when he was admitted to Cedars-Sinai Hospital in Los Angeles. Six weeks later he was dead. He was survived by his wife, Angie, and three children.

Officially, the cause of death was "tuberculosis, pneumonia, and other medical complications." A week after he died, however, the *Los Angeles Times* reported that Wiggins's doctors and one family member had revealed that the actual cause of death was AIDS, and that he had been suffering from the disease for three years. From a playing weight of 160 pounds, Wiggins had dropped to less than 70 pounds when he died. The only teammate who attended the funeral was Steve Garvey.

One day in 1987, Alan Wiggins gave an antidrug talk before a group of junior high school students in New York City. He told them a story, which sportswriter Ira Berkow printed in the *New York Times*, about his son.

"I warned him that he should not touch the hot iron, but he did and burned his finger," Wiggins told the students. "He doesn't touch the iron anymore, but he had to find out for himself, like I did. It's not the way to go."

AMPHETAMINES
The 1980 Phillies Had More Speed in the Locker
Room Than on the Basepaths

Ballplayers who feel they need some extra zip on the fastball or pop in the bat frequently take dextroamphetamine sulphate pills, more commonly known in baseball circles as "greenies." They're basically pep pills—amphetamines that increase heart rate and improve performance (though some say the effect is psychological). They have also been known to cause side effects such as mood swings, hallucinations, and delusions.

In his autobiography, *Catch You Later*, Johnny Bench said that Cincinnati pitcher Gary Nolan "would get a couple of Daps (Daprisals) in him and he'd start chirping away, just sitting in the dugout and talking a blue streak. His eyes would get all googly and he wouldn't answer a question, just stay as high as could be and pitch his head off."

In the early 1960s, amphetamines were routinely given to depressed housewives and to college students who needed to pull all-nighters. In those days, many major-league teams kept a jar of pills in the clubhouse so that players could reach in and grab as many as they needed. Speed was the most widespread drug in baseball up until the 1980s, when snorting cocaine made greenie-popping look like munching milk and cookies.

"I was not very happy to learn that they were being distributed in some baseball clubhouses," said Commissioner Bowie Kuhn. His antidrug efforts served, at the least, to drive greenies underground. Players began to make friends with doctors who would prescribe pills (greenies are perfectly legal with a prescription). Guys would bring an entire season's supply home with them after playing winter ball in Venezuela or the Dominican Republic, where pep pills are sold over the counter.

As many as half the players in the majors use amphetamines, according to some estimates. In the 1985 drug trials in Pittsburgh (see page 106), superstars Willie Stargell and Willie Mays were accused by former teammates of being regular speed demons. Both

Willies—who are Hall of Famers—denied the charges. John Milner said Mays kept a liquid form of speed called "red juice" in his locker when they were on the Mets together. "A shot of that stuff," Denny McLain once claimed, "and it makes you believe that you can throw a baseball through a house."

Pete Rose was one superstar who admitted—reluctantly, in a 1979 *Playboy* interview—that his boundless energy on the field was sometimes chemically induced. Rose deflected a series of drug questions, but *Playboy* finally said point-blank: "You keep saying you *might* take a greenie. *Would* you? *Have* you?"

"Yeah, I'd do it," Rose said. "I've done it."

Still, Rose's long-term amphetamine use was kept quiet. The year he broke Ty Cobb's record for base hits, two Cincinnati doctors were arrested and convicted of supplying huge quantities of amphetamines across Ohio. Rose was suspected of being a steady customer, Michael Sokolove has claimed in *Hustle: The Myth, Life, & Lies of Pete Rose*, but investigators were discouraged from pursuing him because of his popularity.

A year after that *Playboy* interview and weeks after the Philadelphia Phillies won the 1980 World Series, baseball's first drug scandal broke. Once again, Rose was involved.

An indictment was issued against Dr. Patrick Mazza, team physician for the Class AA Reading Phillies. Mazza was charged with twenty-three counts of prescribing amphetamines beyond the scope of the patient-doctor relationship and without conducting physical examinations. Also charged were a machinist named Robert L. Masley and his son—"runners" who picked up the drugs Mazza prescribed from local pharmacies.

Some interesting names appeared on Mazza's prescriptions: Pete Rose; Steve Carlton; Tim McCarver; Larry Christenson; Randy Lerch; Larry Bowa; Larry Bowa's wife, Sheena; Greg Luzinski; and Luzinski's wife, Jean. A good part of the major league's World Championship team seemed to require an awful lot of drugs.

At Dr. Mazza's trial, the "Philadelphia Seven" were called to testify and presented a united, if somewhat ridiculous, front. Rose, Christenson, and McCarver claimed they had never requested or received pills. Rose went so far as to say that he didn't know what a greenie was, despite the fact that he had admitted in *Playboy* that he used them. Phillies executive vice-president Bill Giles said he had never heard of Mazza—Reading's team doctor for eleven years. Jean Luzinski said she found amphetamines in her medicine cabinet at home one day, but didn't know where they came from. Investigators couldn't even find Steve Carlton to serve him with a subpoena.

It looked very much like some hopped-up baseball players were more than willing to send Dr. Mazza up the river to keep their own names clean. Sadly, Mazza told the court that he had been personal friends with several of the players. Robert Masley said he got together with Greg and Jean Luzinski about fifty times a year socially. He vowed never to speak to them again.

"What you have here are a bunch of ballplayers who are world champions," Mazza's lawyer said, "but who also are champions of lying." A state drug agent recommended that the Phillies be given lie detector tests, but was overruled. It was Dr. Mazza who was on trial, not the Phillies.

Mazza freely admitted he had prescribed Dexamyl, Dexedrine, and Preludin for two years. "They were made at the request of the ballplayers," he testified, "and were done in good faith." The reason Bowa's and Luzinski's wives were involved, he explained, was that the players did not want their own names to appear on the prescriptions. Masley testified that Larry Bowa required three or four pills for every game.

Mazza would have had the book thrown at him, but one courageous player took the stand and contradicted his teammates' testimony. Pitcher Randy Lerch admitted under oath that he had received 75 Preludin tablets from Mazza and paid $15 for them. Lerch also told the court that Luzinski had a chronic weight problem, Bowa "was running out of gas," Carlton and McCarver needed something to pep them up, and Rose needed some help with his thirty-eight-year-old body.

"I couldn't see an innocent man going to prison," Lerch told baseball writer Peter Golenbock. "The guy was getting set up to go away for maybe five years." Because of Lerch's testimony, the court ignored what the other Phillies had said and all charges against Mazza were dropped.

A month later, the Phillies rewarded Randy Lerch for his honesty—they traded him to Milwaukee.

STEROIDS AND OTHER MUSCLE DRUGS
Bulking Up with a "Canseco Shake"

Steroids were first developed by the Nazis, who probably hoped to build an army of bulked-up, bloodthirsty maniacs who would march across Europe and demolish everything in sight. The drugs didn't help Germany very much during World War II, but they've done wonders for many postwar weightlifters, bodybuilders, sprinters, and football players.

It's doubtful that steroid use will ever be as popular among baseball players, because monster muscles and body bulk don't necessarily guarantee success in their game. Muscles might help a slugger power a ball over the fence, but they won't help him hit it in the first place. If there was a drug that could guarantee a batter would hit .400 or a pitcher would consistently hit the outside corner, baseball players would do *anything* to get their hands on it.

But there is undoubtedly some steroid use in baseball. In 1987, the *New York Times* quoted an anonymous doctor who said he had been contacted by an American League trainer about obtaining steroids for several of his players. Any time a relatively small player bulks up during the off-season (Lenny Dykstra, come on down!), it's whispered that steroids must have been a part of his training regimen.

Steroids are derivatives of testosterone, the male sex hormone. The human body has at least eighteen steroid substances circulating through it naturally. There are two kinds of synthetic steroids, anabolic and cortical. Cortical steroids suppress inflammations, and are used to treat arthritis. Anabolic steroids promote tissue growth by creating protein.

Steroids do have medical uses. They're prescribed for cancer patients who have lost a lot of weight, and older people who have osteoporosis, anemia, and other endocrine disturbances. But not for healthy athletes.

A study in the *British Medical Journal* in 1988 found that stanozolol, the anabolic steroid that Canadian sprinter Ben Johnson was

The Sultan of Swat was *also* legendary because of his insatiable appetite for women. "One woman couldn't satisfy him," said sportswriter Fred Lieb. "Frequently it took a half a dozen." Ruth's famous "Bellyache Heard 'Round the World" in 1925 was most likely a dose of the clap. (National Baseball Library, Cooperstown, N.Y.)

Los Angeles Angels pitcher Bo Belinsky out on the town with blond bombshell Mamie Van Doren. After their breakup, he said, "I needed her like Custer needed Indians." (AP/Wide World Photos)

Jo Collins, *Playboy* Playmate of the Year for 1965. She married Bo Belinsky after his celebrated affairs with Ann-Margret, Tina Louise, Connie Stevens, Mamie Van Doren, and Juliet Prowse. Bo even went out with the Shah of Iran's former wife Queen Sorraya. (Reproduced by special permission of *Playboy* magazine; copyright 1964 by *Playboy*)

Red Sox star Wade Boggs and his mistress Margo Adams (TOP). They spent four years of road trips together, until Boggs decided he'd had enough and Adams decided she needed $100,000 to prevent her from sending pictures like this one to Boggs's wife. (Penthouse Int'l, 1989)

Margo Adams got her $100,000–by selling her story and posing for *Penthouse*. (Penthouse Int'l, 1989)

Umpire Dave Pallone. He was the
first man in baseball history to admit
publicly that he was a homosexual,
and he was fired shortly thereafter.

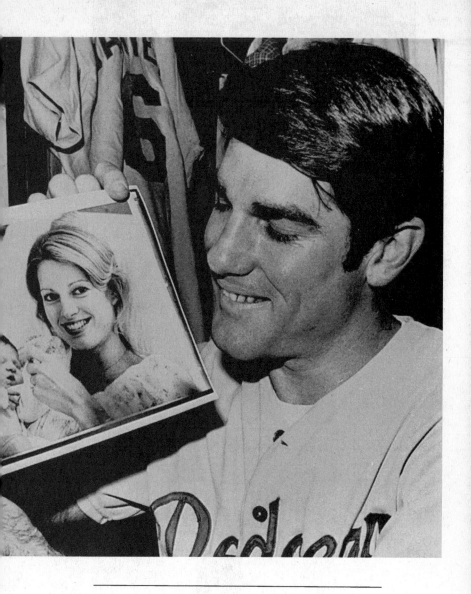

Squeaky clean boy-next-door Steve Garvey would father three children with three different women in the late 1980s. His first wife, Cindy (pictured here), would later say, "The guy is a sociopath." (AP/Wide World Photos)

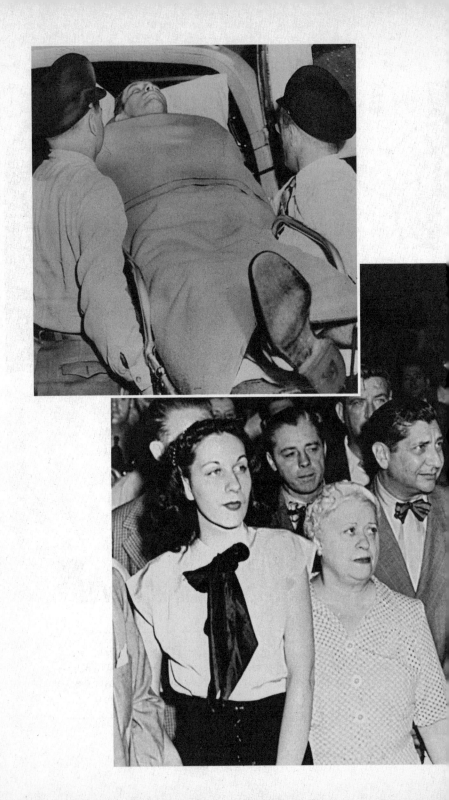

Philadelphia Phillies first baseman Eddie Waitkus (AT LEFT) being loaded into an ambulance after he was shot in the chest by an obsessed nineteen-year-old female admirer in 1949. The story inspired the book and movie *The Natural*. (UPI)

Ruth Ann Steinhagen (BELOW, FAR LEFT), the young woman who loved Eddie Waitkus (SEATED) so much that she tried to kill him. This photo was taken during the hearing at which Steinhagen would be judged insane. (AP/Wide World Photos)

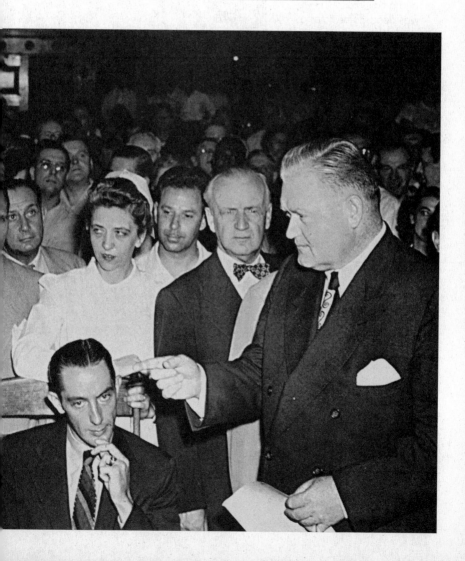

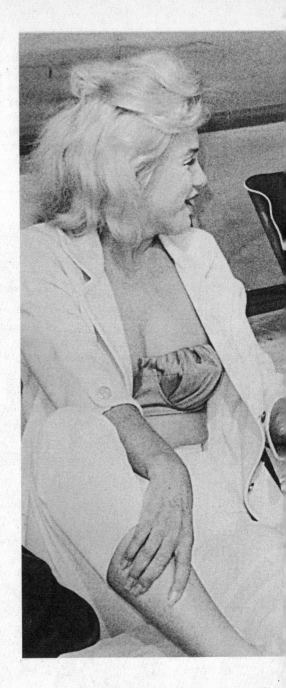

Marilyn Monroe and Joe DiMaggio, vacationing together near St. Petersburg in 1961—seven years after the breakup of their marriage. A year and a half later, Marilyn was dead. Three times a week for twenty years, a pair of red roses was delivered to her crypt courtesy of Joltin' Joe. (AP/Wide World Photos)

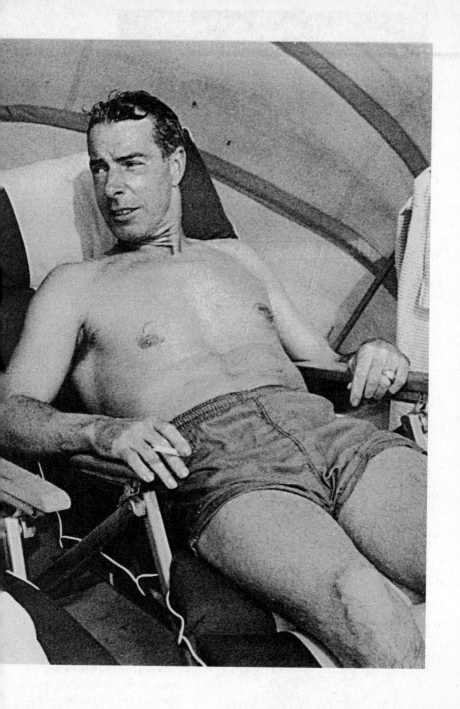

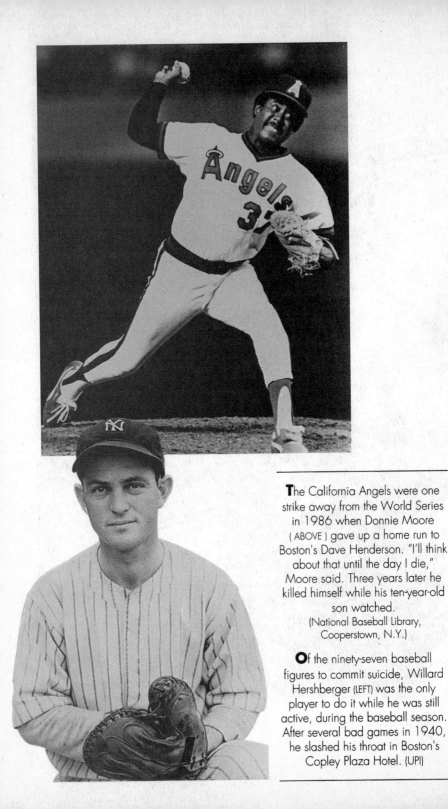

The California Angels were one strike away from the World Series in 1986 when Donnie Moore (ABOVE) gave up a home run to Boston's Dave Henderson. "I'll think about that until the day I die," Moore said. Three years later he killed himself while his ten-year-old son watched.
(National Baseball Library, Cooperstown, N.Y.)

Of the ninety-seven baseball figures to commit suicide, Willard Hershberger (LEFT) was the only player to do it while he was still active, during the baseball season. After several bad games in 1940, he slashed his throat in Boston's Copley Plaza Hotel. (UPI)

National League president Harry Pulliam (RIGHT). On June 28, 1909, he calmly got up from the dinner table at the New York Athletic Club, walked up to his room on the third floor, and blew his brains out. (National Baseball Library, Cooperstown, N.Y.)

Len Koenecke. After the twenty-nine-year-old outfielder was released in 1935, he went berserk on a small plane to Buffalo. To subdue him, the pilot slammed a fire extinguisher over Koenecke's head. He was dead on arrival. (UPI)

RAYMOND JOHNSON CHAPMAN

1891   1920

Ray Chapman was the only man ever killed while playing in a major league baseball game. He is entombed in Cleveland's Lake View Cemetery. (Collection of Mike Sowell)

New York Yankee Carl Mays (OPPOSITE) and his trademark submarine delivery. He would sometimes scrape his knuckles against the ground before releasing the ball. One pitch got away and killed Ray Chapman. (UPI)

Dock Ellis (having his "hair" combed by teammate Dave Giusti) was the first pitcher in baseball history to throw a no-hitter while under the influence of LSD. (UPI)

Ed Delahanty won the American League batting title in 1902, hitting .376. Less than a year later he fell (jumped? was pushed?) off a bridge and was swept over Niagara Falls to his death.
(National Baseball Library, Cooperstown, N.Y.)

Alan Wiggins, baseball's first AIDS victim, died in 1991. Seven years earlier he stole five bases in one game for the San Diego Padres.
(National Baseball Library, Cooperstown, N.Y.)

1951 and 1952 American League batting champ Ferris Fain (sliding) was arrested when police raided his barn in California and found a million dollars worth of marijuana. Fain said he never touched the stuff himself, though you have to wonder why a guy would slide into home and miss it by five feet. (AP/Wide World Photos)

caught using, increased the size of certain muscle fibers even if the user wasn't exercising the muscle. Athletes report that besides helping them bulk up, steroids also make them feel more aggressive, almost invincible.

Some experts, however, believe steroids do nothing at all. "It is my opinion that the positive results in increased strength and muscle mass that have occurred as a result of these drugs is far more closely related to the power of suggestion or mind over matter," says Dr. Donald L. Cooper of the National Collegiate Drug Education Committee.

The side effects of steroid use are considerable: In young people, steroids have been known to stunt growth. With men there is a risk of liver, prostate, and blood pressure problems. Women may experience a deepening of the voice, increased body hair, and reproductive problems.

But for many athletes, the possibility of winning a championship or earning millions of dollars makes these risks worth taking.

In any discussion of steroid use in baseball, the name of Oakland slugger Jose Canseco invariably comes up. In 1988, when he became the first player in major-league history to hit forty home runs and steal forty bases in one season, people started talking. No man could possibly be so strong *and* so fast (Canseco can run from home to first base in 3.8 seconds) without chemical help, many believed.

Canseco's alleged steroid use became news when respected baseball writer Thomas Boswell said on national television that the outfielder was "the most conspicuous example of a player who made himself great with steroids." Canseco vigorously denied using *any* drugs and threatened to sue Boswell. ("We can't do anything to him because he doesn't have any money," Canseco said after dropping the idea.)

After Canseco's Superman season, reporters began referring to steroids in print as a "Canseco shake." In the 1988 American League playoffs, 34,104 Red Sox fans chanted "STER-OIDS! STER-OIDS!" whenever Jose took the field. "I thought it was kind of fun," he said. "I flexed my muscles for them."

It's easy to see why Jose Canseco would be a prime suspect for steroid use. He's a big man—240 pounds—yet he has a 33-inch waist. (Sparky Anderson once said Canseco had "the physique of a

Greek goddess.") He swings a thirty-five ounce bat, probably the heaviest in baseball, and hits mammoth shots. Canseco once hit a *broken-bat* home run.

Sports Illustrated reported in 1990 that Canseco "was with a man who had been detained at various times for carrying steroids." Still, nobody has ever proven that Jose's muscles are the result of anything more than sweaty workouts.

Steroids seem to have become passé anyway. Recently, athletes started using a synthetic version of human growth hormone, sometimes called HGH and sold under the trade name Protropin. The drug has been shown to stimulate protein production and reverse muscle shrinkage. It was developed by Genentech, Inc., to treat dwarfism and costs about $15,000 a year. HGH has many of the same qualities of steroids, but scientists have yet to uncover harmful side effects.

And in 1991, a new drug hit the scene—recombinant erythropoietin, or EPO. It increases the body's ability to carry oxygen by increasing red blood cell count, which improves stamina. It's used to treat chronic anemia. EPO is an almost perfect duplicate of a hormone produced by the human kidney, so it's impossible to detect with any available test.

It does, however, have one side effect—death. Over the last four years eighteen Dutch and Belgian professional bicycle racers have died suddenly, and it is believed they were taking EPO.

MARIJUANA
Cha Cha, Spaceman, and
Burrhead the Farmer

A reporter once asked Tug McGraw to describe the difference between grass and artificial turf. "I don't know," the pitcher replied. "I never smoked artificial turf."

Marijuana, for the most part, has provided only an occasional amusement in the community of baseball. Players who use drugs have preferred to get themselves up with speed or coke, and down with beer and pretzels.

There have been a few isolated incidents, however.

Bill "Spaceman" Lee created a mini-controversy in the spring of 1979 when he casually mentioned during an interview that he used marijuana. It must have been a slow news day. The press jumped all over the confession, and Lee amended it by saying, "but only on my organic buckwheat pancakes at breakfast."

Baseball Commissioner Bowie Kuhn failed to see the humor and fined Lee $250 for that familiar crime, "conduct detrimental to baseball." Lee asked Kuhn for permission to donate the $250 to charity, and he sent it to an obscure Indian mission in Alaska.

"If I sent it to the charity of *his* choice," Lee said, "I'm sure it would have gone to Nixon."

Lee, perhaps baseball's most celebrated flake, fit the description of a stereotypical pot smoker. He advocated pyramid power, zero population growth, soyburgers, and Zen Buddhism. He said that pitching was a form of sexual expression. He once showed up late for a game because, he claimed, the early dew on the ground combined with the acorns in the outfield gave off an unpleasant odor. He also admitted he had pitched under the influence of hashish.

It figures that Lee pitched ten years with the most straitlaced team in sports, the Boston Red Sox. They probably wouldn't have kept him around if he hadn't won seventeen games three seasons in a row. After leaving baseball, Lee ran for president as the candidate of the Rhinoceros Party.

More seriously, Orlando "Cha Cha" Cepeda was convicted of smuggling 165 pounds of marijuana into his native Puerto Rico two years after retiring from baseball in 1974. Cha Cha received a five-year sentence and did ten months in jail. Afterward, he became a Buddhist (is there a pattern here?) and gave talks to kids about drug abuse. He admitted he had gotten high every night for ten years.

Cepeda was the National League Rookie of the Year in 1958, became MVP in 1967, and hit 379 home runs with a .297 average over seventeen seasons. It seems clear that the marijuana conviction has prevented the keepers of the Baseball Hall of Fame from voting him in.

But then, that didn't stop them from admitting Ferguson Jenkins, who was arrested in 1980 when customs inspectors found two ounces of marijuana, plus two grams of hashish and four grams of cocaine in his luggage at Toronto International Airport. Jenkins was suspended briefly by Bowie Kuhn, but issued a public apology and donated $10,000 to a drug prevention program. He was allowed to finish up his nineteen-year, 284-victory career, and joined baseball's immortals in the summer of 1991.

But the National Pastime's most notorious pothead was Ferris Roy "Burrhead" Fain.

You say you've never heard of him? While Joe DiMaggio and Ted Williams were getting all the attention, it was the Philadelphia Athletics' no-name first baseman who led the American League in 1951, hitting .344. The next season he did it again, with a .327 average.

Fain played for nine years, until bad legs forced him to quit baseball in 1955. He headed for El Dorado County in California, where the sun shines most of the time and you can grow just about anything.

Ostensibly, he made his living as a carpenter, and he built his own house next to a mountain lake. But in September 1985, the place was raided and the sixty-four-year-old Fain was arrested for cultivation and sale of marijuana. He plea bargained that down to cultivation alone and received a four-month house arrest sentence, plus five years on probation and a $7,500 fine.

People around El Dorado County didn't make much of Fain's arrest at the time. He had been suffering from diabetes and gout, and it was assumed that the old guy smoked a joint now and then to ease his pain.

Part of the plea bargain allowed police to search the Fain residence at any time without a warrant. On March 17, 1988, they did, this time finding a full-blown marijuana farm. The barn had been outfitted with a sophisticated lighting and irrigation system, as well as a network of wires that bypassed Pacific Gas & Electric meters.

There was pot, of course. More than a man could smoke in a lifetime. Police confiscated 400 live marijuana plants, processed pot, growing paraphernalia, and records that indicated sales. Altogether, there was about $1 million worth of marijuana. Ferris Fain truly had a green thumb.

Old Burrhead admitted that he grew the stuff only to sell it. The man had $1 million worth of dope in his barn and he never took a puff. That's proof positive that marijuana just doesn't make it as a baseball drug.

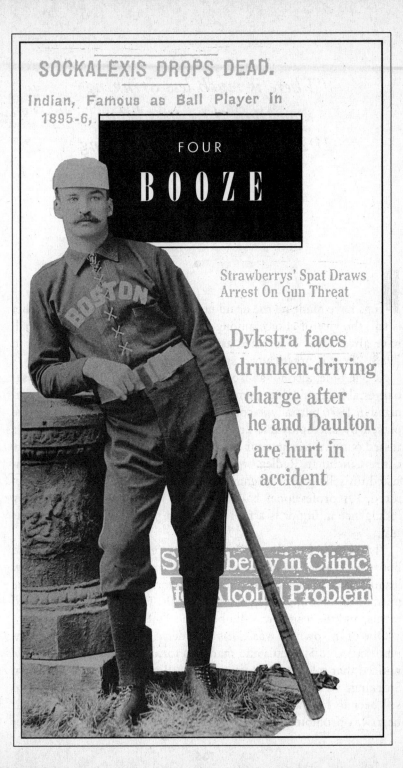

SOCKALEXIS DROPS DEAD.

Indian, Famous as Ball Player in
1895-6,

FOUR

BOOZE

Strawberrys' Spat Draws
Arrest On Gun Threat

Dykstra faces
drunken-driving
charge after
he and Daulton
are hurt in
accident

Strawberry in Clinic
for Alcohol Problem

> *"There is much less drinking
> now than there was before
> 1927, because I quit drinking
> on May 24, 1927."*
>
> —Hall of Famer
> Rabbit Maranville

Drugs have made all the headlines in recent years, but a liquid diet is still the vice of choice among ballplayers. "Alcohol and baseball have always had a charmed association," wrote *Time* magazine in 1988. "Beer is practically a synonym for the sport."

At one time, alcohol abuse was taken more seriously by the baseball establishment than gambling. The National League was organized in 1876 partially to counteract baseball's reputation as a game played by unemployable drunken louts. In 1882, ten players were tossed out of the league for life because of their drinking habits. The entire Cincinnati Redleg organization was disbanded because it insisted on selling beer at games. *Spaulding's Guide* that season lectured, "A professional ballplayer . . . who weakens his play by indulgence in liquor is a fool unfit for a position on any first class team."

That was before the alcohol industry realized that baseball and booze were a perfect match and virtually took over the game. A new league, the American Association, was formed to compete with the puritanical National League in the 1880s. Four beer barons owned teams, and the league was dubbed "the American Beerball League."

One of the owners was Chris Von der Ahe, a German immigrant who settled in St. Louis and made his fortune selling beer there. He noticed that saloons did particularly well when the St. Louis Brown Stockings were playing, so he thought it would be a good idea to sell beer to fans attending the games. When he was informed that beer was prohibited inside the ballpark, Von der Ahe got another idea—he bought the team. He eventually died from cirrhosis of the liver.

The St. Louis Cardinals were purchased in 1953 by August A. Busch Jr., president of Anheuser-Busch.* In time, beer ads were plastered all over the stadium—*Busch* Stadium. Beer jingles were played over the public address system. "Every Cardinals home game for years and years has been a nearly nonstop Budweiser commercial," wrote *Sports Illustrated* in 1988.

The New York Yankees also came of age on beer money when brewery tycoon Jacob Ruppert bought the team in 1915. Yankee Stadium could most accurately be called "The House That Beer Built."

Today, the beer industry just about owns baseball. The Labatt Brewing Company owns 45 percent of the Toronto Blue Jays and the TV rights to the Expos. The Mets and Yankees each make $4 million a year by selling beer to their fans. Baseball rakes in more than $33 million a year from beer advertising. Players spray booze all over each other to celebrate winning championships; then they retire to a life of leisure shooting beer commercials. Hell, Milwaukee named its team after the process of making beer.

An occasional five-second public service message advising fans to "know when to say when" hardly overcomes the message baseball pounds into every fan's head night and day.

While everyone has been raising a fuss about cocaine in baseball, there is little mention of alcohol abuse until tragedy strikes. In 1991, Hall of Fame pitcher Don Drysdale was arrested for drunken driving after an accident that injured a young woman. Philadelphia Phillies star Len Dykstra got loaded after a bachelor party and wrapped his Mercedes-Benz 500SL around two trees.

Dykstra was lucky. He walked away with a broken collarbone, broken cheekbone, three fractured ribs, a scratched cornea, and a punctured lung. Legendary jockey Bill Shoemaker drove drunk four weeks earlier and will be a quadriplegic for the rest of his life. Billy Martin is flat-out dead after a drunken car wreck in 1989.

Some of the greatest players in baseball—Hack Wilson, Grover Cleveland Alexander, Mike "King" Kelly, to name just a few—drank

---

* Busch bought the team when its previous owner—Fred M. Saigh—was sentenced to fifteen months in prison for income tax evasion.

themselves to death. Yet even as ballplayers check in and out of detox centers, we still chuckle over those wild and crazy jocks arguing about whether the beer tastes great or is less filling.

Baseball's quandary is that it wants to project a healthy image, yet it earns a fortune from a substance that slows reaction time, dulls the senses, and is totally incompatible with athletic excellence. Drinking and playing *any* sport don't mix. Even hard-core alcoholic players try to abstain when they have a game to play.

In the last few years, most stadiums have agreed to stop serving beer after the seventh inning, and some have set aside nondrinking sections in the stands. A few teams have banned booze in the clubhouse. It's doubtful, however, that baseball will ever do anything serious about the booze problem, like banning beer commercials entirely or beer sales at the ballpark. There's just too much money to be made.

MIKE "KING" KELLY
The Last Slide

Legend has it the Chicago White Stockings hired a Pinkerton detective in 1883 to keep an eye on their star catcher/outfielder Mike "King" Kelly, a renowned horseplayer, spendthrift, and carouser. The detective turned in a report saying that Kelly had been hanging out at a dive until three o'clock in the morning drinking lemonade.

Kelly angrily denied the charge. "It was straight whiskey! I never drank lemonade at that hour in my life!"

King Kelly was baseball's first superstar personality and the greatest sports hero of the 1880s. As one of the game's earliest and most notorious drunks, he began a tradition that continues right up to the present day.

But he could play the game. Kelly stayed sober enough to win the National League batting championship in 1884 (.354) and 1886 (.388). The following season—the first year stolen bases were recorded—he stole eighty-four. He once swiped six bases in a single game.

Kelly's trademark hook slide, a maneuver which few players had perfected before the turn of the century, was immortalized in the popular 1889 song "Slide, Kelly, Slide":

> *Your running's a disgrace*
> *Stay there, hold your base!*
> *If someone doesn't steal you,*
> *and your batting doesn't fail you,*
> *they'll take you to Australia!*
> *Slide, Kelly, Slide!*

The song became the basis for a movie in 1927. Kelly was also said to have inspired the poem "Casey at the Bat."

Playing in an era when the rules and structure of baseball were still taking shape, Kelly was known for being innovative and crafty. Some histories of the game credit him as the first outfielder to back up his infielders, the first to pick up a line-drive single and throw the batter out at first, and the first catcher to send signals to his pitcher. He also perfected, if not invented, the hit-and-run play.

One of his favorite plays as a catcher was to make a "wild" pickoff throw to first, throwing the ball into right field. The runner on first would take off, not realizing that Kelly had signaled the right fielder to come in and take the throw. Invariably, the runner was out by a mile.

He would wring every loophole out of the rulebook. If the umpire wasn't looking, Kelly would scoot from first to third by cutting across the pitcher's mound. The most oft-told Kelly story is the one about the time he was sitting out a game one day, probably with a hangover, when an opposing batter lofted a lazy foul ball toward the dugout. Seeing that his catcher had no chance to make the play, Kelly shouted, "KELLY, NOW CATCHING FOR BOSTON!" and stepped out of the dugout to snare the ball. A rule was quickly put into effect banning substitutions in mid-play.

A handsome man with a huge handlebar mustache, Kelly had a happy-go-lucky, uninhibited manner that shocked and thrilled the fans in the Victorian era. Today, we'd call him a hot dog. Whatever he did, he drew crowds. He would tell jealous teammates, "Why don't some of you dubs break a window and get yourselves talked about?"

Mostly, Kelly was known for consuming enormous quantities of booze. He considered it a point of honor to get smashed. He would drink before, after, and *during* ballgames. On one occasion a game had to be held up so that Kelly could finish hoisting a few with some fellows in the box seats.

When a reporter asked if he drank during games, Kelly replied, "It depends on the length of the game."

A fan in Indianapolis once heckled Kelly about the large salary ($5,000) he was drawing, so Kelly shouted back, "I'm eating strawberries and ice cream off the salary I earn performing for suckers like you."

"Yes," replied the fan, "and the bartenders get yours, all of it."

Cap Anson, his manager in Chicago, said Kelly had "one enemy, that one being himself." The Chicago management grew increasingly exasperated with his drinking problem, and in 1887 sold him to the Boston "Beaneaters" for the then astonishing sum of $10,000. It was "the baseball story of the century," according to David Quentin Voigt's history of the game, *American Baseball*.

As player/manager of the Beaneaters, Kelly preached what he practiced. When one of his players made several errors in a game, he gave the man money with instructions to go get drunk. "When sober," he said, "you're the rottenest ballplayer I ever saw."

He had a few good years with Boston, until the booze finally started to catch up with him. During his last season, he was in such bad shape that he had to be sent to a Turkish bath to sober up before each game. He was a pathetic figure at the end, staggering under fly balls and getting so tangled up in his own feet trying to run the bases that he would fall flat on his face. He played just twenty games in 1893.

He had never saved a dime when he was on top. Penniless, he tried a vaudeville act, and then opened a bar in New York. Neither was successful. He headed back to Boston in November 1894 and caught a cold that turned into pneumonia. Three days later he died at Boston Emergency Hospital. Five thousand people filed past his coffin in Elks Hall.

He had drunk himself to death at the age of thirty-six.

Legend has it that the day Kelly died, one of the men carrying his stretcher stumbled and the dying ballplayer tumbled onto the floor of the hospital. Lying there, Kelly issued his final words: "This is my last slide."

He was elected to the Baseball Hall of Fame in 1945.

BILLY SUNDAY
He Found God in the Gutter

One day in the summer of 1886, four players on the White Stockings were sitting on the curb of Van Buren Street in Chicago. Billy Sunday, Mike "King" Kelly, Ed Williamson, and Frank "Silver" Flint had been stopping in and out of State Street saloons all afternoon and were feeling no pain. As they sat in the gutter, a gospel wagon drove up and held a service.

Sunday listened intently. He recognized the hymns he'd heard in the little Methodist church near his boyhood home of Ames, Iowa. He remembered his mother singing to him. Sunday put his face in his hands for several minutes, then stood up and announced to his teammates, "Boys, it's all off; we have come to where the roads part."

With that, Billy Sunday renounced booze and baseball to devote his life to reforming drunks and other sinners. He would go on to become one of America's most famous and flamboyant evangelists.

Just a month after William Ashley Sunday was born in 1862, his father was killed fighting for the Union in the Civil War. Billy was a sickly child who had to be carried around on a pillow until he was two and a half years old. His mother couldn't handle her three young sons, so they were sent to Soldiers' Orphan Home in Iowa.

Growing up in various orphanages and foster homes, Sunday grew strong and took up the young sport of baseball. The White Stockings happened to play an exhibition game in Iowa in 1883, and manager Cap Anson noticed that Billy ran "like a scared deer." He asked the twenty-one-year-old to join the team. That was how it was done in those days.

Baseball Magazine in 1915 called him "one of the greatest ball players in the game." In truth, Billy Sunday was a pretty lousy ballplayer. With a lifetime batting average of .248 and a fielding average of .883, he was no great loss to the National Pastime. As a utility outfielder, Sunday only played about sixty games a year for eight seasons.

He didn't quit baseball right away. After all, he was making a whole $3,000 a year playing for the White Stockings. But he became more interested in spreading the gospel and less interested in runs, hits, and errors. His teammates were supportive. "Bill, religion ain't my long suit," King Kelly told him, "but if ever old Mike can help you, just let me know, for I won't knock you."

Shortly after Sunday found God in the gutter, Chicago was locked in an exciting game against Detroit. The White Stockings were ahead by a run in the ninth, and there was a full count on Detroit catcher Charlie Bennett. He lashed a screaming drive over Sunday's head.

"I saw it coming out to right field like a shell out of a mortar, and it was up to me," Sunday recalled. "There were thousands of people out in the field, for the grand-stand and bleachers had overflowed. I whirled and went with all my speed. . . . I was going so fast that day you couldn't see me for dust. I yelled to the crowd, 'Get out of the way!' and they opened up like the Red Sea for the rod of Moses. And as I ran I offered my first prayer, and it was something like this:

" 'God, I'm in an awful hole. Help me out, if you ever helped mortal man in your life; help me get that ball. And you haven't much time to make up your mind.' "

Needless to say, Sunday made the play, winning the game for Chicago. "I am sure the Lord helped me catch that ball," he claimed. "It was my first experience in prayer."

Sunday gave up baseball for good in 1891 (after stealing eighty-four bases) and began attending prayer sessions. Popular evangelist J. Wilbur Chapman asked him to be his assistant, and Sunday learned what it took to stir the emotions of impressionable audiences. When Chapman tired of the road, Sunday became a full-time preacher.

His style of ragtime religion turned preaching into performance art. He would run, leap, fall down on the stage, and break furniture as he condemned booze and other sins. Baseball would come into the act when Sunday went into a pitcher's windup and threw fastballs at the devil. To show sinners coming home for salvation, he would strip off his coat and perform his trademark—a head-first slide along the stage into "home plate" like a sinner trying to slide into heaven. The umpire—God—would dramatically call the bum out.

If only television has been around in those days.

One review of these performances read, "He storms and rages up and down the platform, whacking the pulpit and twisting and working his body until we are as much amazed at the physcial endurance of the man as at the resources of his tongue."

People all over the country flocked to Sunday's vaudeville sermons so that they could see him with their own eyes. He hit his peak during a series of New York revivals in April 1917, when he converted 98,264 souls. Donations from the newly faithful made Sunday a millionaire, and he became one of the most famous names of the early twentieth century.

Besides preaching the gospel, Sunday railed against foreigners, socialism, high fashion, draft dodgers, Kaiser Wilhelm, and playing baseball on Sundays. He never stopped shouting about the evil of demon rum.

With the end of World War I and the arrival of Prohibition, Sunday lost two of his primary targets, and his popularity waned during the Roaring Twenties. When the crowds stopped coming, he went back to tent preaching in small towns.

He died in Chicago in 1935, and the *New York Times* called him "the greatest high-pressure and mass-conversion Christian evangelist that America or the world has known." His fame as a preacher had far exceeded his accomplishments as a baseball player.

Today, Billy Sunday is mostly forgotten, but he was immortalized in the classic song "Chicago" ("Bet your bottom dollar you'll lose your blues in Chicago, the town that Billy Sunday could not shut down . . .")

Even if you don't know the song, Sunday's name lives on with another American classic that many believe was named in his honor—the ice cream sundae.

SHUFFLIN' PHIL DOUGLAS
The "Vacation" That Lasted a Lifetime

Phil Douglas wasn't a crook. He was a drunk. And because he was a drunk, he was kidnapped, drugged, institutionalized, and banished from baseball for the rest of his life.

That was the argument made in 1990, when friends and relatives of "Shufflin' Phil" petitioned Baseball Commissioner Fay Vincent to clear his name—sixty-eight years after his banishment and thirty-eight years after his death. The truth is, they were right.

Phil Douglas was a six-foot, four-inch Georgia boy who threw a nice assortment of pitches, including a spitter.* He was called "Shufflin' Phil" because of the lazy way he walked. At thirty-two, he had become one of the better pitchers in the National League. He was the hero of the 1921 World Series for the New York Giants, winning two games and fanning Babe Ruth four times.

Ever since he came up to the big leagues at twenty-one, Douglas had been a problem drinker. He would go on what he called "vacations"—binges during which he would get plastered and disappear for a week or so. Only a starting pitcher, who worked every four days, could get away with that behavior. Douglas bounced around to five teams in nine years as his managers became disgusted with his unreliability.

"There was no harm in that fellow," said Fred Mitchell, who managed Douglas when he was on the Cubs. "It was just that I never knew where the hell he was, or if he was fit to work."

Toward the end of the 1919 season, Shufflin' Phil was traded to John McGraw's Giants. McGraw got personal satisfaction out of signing hopeless drunks (such as Arthur "Bugs" Raymond) and using his own innovative form of alcohol rehabilitation, which involved threats, detectives, humiliation, fines, and drugs. He would become infuriated when these efforts failed to reform wayward players.

---

* Douglas was one of sixteen pitchers allowed to continue throwing the spitball until the end of their careers after the pitch was banned in 1920. Of those sixteen, Burleigh Grimes lasted the longest, retiring in 1934. So the last *legal* spitball was thrown fourteen years after the pitch was banned.

Douglas had a couple of decent seasons (15–10 and 14–10) for the Giants and finally seemed to be coming into his own in 1922, when he accumulated eleven wins and only three losses through July.

The incidents that led up to his banishment from baseball began on July 30, when Douglas lost a game to Pittsburgh at the Polo Grounds. After getting bawled out by McGraw, he went on one of his "vacations," and several days later even his wife had no idea where he was.

After much searching, five of McGraw's detectives found Douglas unconscious in an apartment near his home in Manhattan. Half-dressed, Douglas was dragged out of bed, threatened with blackjacks, and brought to the 135th Street police station, where he promptly passed out again.

"When I come to, I am in a sanitarium," Douglas told reporters after he was thrown out of baseball. "They give me knockout stuff, and won't let me telephone my wife."

The Giants had taken custody of Douglas at the police station and sent him to West End Sanitarium, a hospital on Central Park West. His clothes were taken away and he was given sedatives. His requests to be released were denied.

Five days later, he was finally let out of the sanitarium. He got drunk once again and went to the Polo Grounds, but the day's game was rained out. Going through his mail, he found a bill from the Giants for $224.30 to cover the sanitarium charges. Incredibly, after institutionalizing him and drugging him against his will, they wanted him to pay for it.

To make matters worse, McGraw called Douglas into his office, bawled him out again, and fined him $100, plus five days' pay.

It had been a rough week for Shufflin' Phil. He was certainly not in the best frame of mind when he walked out of McGraw's office, sat down, and wrote the following letter on New York Giants stationery to outfielder Leslie Mann of the St. Louis Cardinals:

Dear Leslie:
I want to leave here but I want some inducement. I don't want this guy to win the pennant and I feel if I stay here I will win it for him. You know I can pitch and win. So you see the fellows, and if you want to send a man over here with the

*goods, and I will leave for home on the next train, send him
to my house so nobody will know, and send him at night. I
am living at 145 Wadsworth Ave., Apartment 1R. Nobody will
ever know. I will go down to fishing camp and stay there. I
am asking you this way so there can't be any trouble to any
one. Call me up if you all are sending a man. Wadsworth 3210.
Do this right away. Let me know. Regards to all.*

Phil Douglas

While the wording of the letter is ambiguous, Douglas's point
seemed to be that he would take one of his "vacations" and hurt
the Giants' chances of winning the pennant if the Cardinals would
pay him. St. Louis was in the thick of the pennant race with the
Giants.

Almost as soon as it left his hand, Douglas had second thoughts
about the letter. He called Mann, he claimed later, and told him to
destroy the letter as soon as it arrived. Mann said this phone conversation never took place.

Meanwhile, the Giants were preparing to go on a road trip and
wanted Douglas to stay out of trouble. Each day for the next three
days, the team physician was sent to Douglas's home to administer
a sedative via hypodermic.

That Monday, Douglas worked out at the Polo Grounds and took
a train to join the team in Pittsburgh, where he was expected to
pitch the first game of the series. He was feeling good and told
sportswriter Frank Graham, "I been a sucker, but not anymore. You
wait and see."

By that time Leslie Mann had received the letter from Douglas.
He could have ripped it up or pretended it didn't exist. After thinking
it over for twenty-four hours, he decided it would be best to show
the letter to his manager, Branch Rickey.

"I told him it was a hot potato," Rickey said. "In fact, dynamite."

This was a year after the Black Sox had been banished from baseball
for life, and baseball was very fix-conscious. Rickey might also have
been thinking it would be nice if a Giant pitcher with a 11–4 record
was out of the rotation. In any case, Rickey convinced Mann to take
the letter to Baseball Commissioner Kenesaw Mountain Landis.

Landis took the next train to Pittsburgh and met McGraw and

Douglas in McGraw's room at the Schenley Hotel. Afterward, they sent Douglas out and McGraw dropped a bombshell on the press.

"We have the absolute goods on Douglas," he announced. "He will never play another game in organized baseball. . . . Personally, I am heartily glad to be rid of him. . . . Without exception, he is the dirtiest ballplayer I have ever seen."

"It's tragic and deplorable," added Landis.

Douglas's letter was shown to reporters, who printed it in their newspapers. The *New York Times*, a paper not known for exaggeration, wrote of the Douglas affair, "This is the biggest scandal in the history of baseball."

Shufflin' Phil didn't know what hit him. That night, while he was saying goodbye to his teammates in the hotel lobby, he spotted Landis and asked, "Is this all true, Judge, that I'm through for good?"

"Yes, Douglas, it is."

"Do you mean I can never play ball again?"

"Yes, Phil. I'm afraid that's just what it means."

Douglas took a train home and spent the next few days in bed. When he had composed himself, he called reporters and told his side of the story.

"I've never thrown a game in my life," he said. "I'm as innocent as a child." He explained that after being suspended, fined, and confined to the sanitarium, he thought he had been released by the Giants and hoped only to get some money to live on.

"McGraw had it in for me," Douglas complained. "I was desperate when I wrote the letter. . . . I've been put in an awful fix and don't know just what to do at present, but I'll prove my innocence in the end. I want the public to know that I am not guilty of any crooked baseball."

He hired a lawyer to petition Commissioner Landis for a hearing. Landis politely replied that he'd examine the matter if Douglas had any new evidence to offer. But Douglas was off on another bender and no evidence was submitted.

It wouldn't have mattered if Douglas had taken his vacation or not. The Giants won the pennant anyway, and then swept the Yankees in four straight games to win the World Series.

Douglas applied for reinstatement in 1936 and was turned down. He got odd jobs working as a laborer and did some maintenance

work with the Tennessee State Highway Department. There he had
the misfortune to get his foot caught in a lawnmower. Three strokes
followed, the second taking away his speech and the third killing
him on August 2, 1952.

When supporters petitioned Fay Vincent to reinstate Shufflin' Phil
in 1990, they pointed out that the cause of Douglas's letter was the
brutal rehabilitation program forced upon him, not any intention
to hurt his team.

The commissioner's office issued this response: "It is our opinion
that a resurrection of the Phil Douglas case today would not be
appropriate. The events surrounding the matter cannot be recreated
in sufficient detail to provide an adequate basis to reverse Commissioner Landis's decision. Commissioner Vincent cannot substitute his
judgement nearly 70 years after the fact for the judgement of a
commissioner with a reputation for the highest degree of integrity."

GROVER CLEVELAND ALEXANDER
Alcoholism Masked His Other "Sin"

It was perhaps the most dramatic pitcher/batter confrontation in
baseball history—Grover Cleveland Alexander versus Tony Lazzeri
in the seventh game of the 1926 World Series. Classic baseball—
the grizzled, alcoholic veteran for the Cardinals staggering out
of the bullpen at Yankee Stadium to face the rookie sensation, with
the championship of the world on the line.

"Old Pete," or "Alex the Great" as he was sometimes called,
claimed he learned to pitch by throwing rocks at chickens in his
native Nebraska. He broke in with the Phillies way back in 1911
and won twenty-eight games that first year. From 1915 through
1917, he won thirty or more each season. He became known, along
with Walter Johnson and Christy Mathewson, as one of the best
pitchers of his day. He also was probably the greatest alcoholic ever
to play the game.

When Alexander and Lazzeri had their famous confrontation, very
few people were aware that the two men shared something in
common—epilepsy. At the end of World War I, Alexander had been

drafted and sent to France, where exploding shells cost him the hearing in one ear and triggered his epilepsy.

There was a stigma attached to the disease in those days. For centuries, in fact, epileptics were believed to be victims of demonic possession. Even in the first half of this century, they were considered dangerous, incompetent, and unable to handle stress.

Alexander began drinking to mask the epilepsy, as alcoholism was a more socially acceptable condition. He was not, however, a man who could hold his liquor. When drunk, Alexander was so unsteady that it took him a few tries to shake hands. His wife had to hide her perfume for fear he'd drink it. During games when he wasn't pitching, he would sleep in the dugout, if he made it to the ballpark at all. Lazzeri never had a seizure on the field, but two or three times each season Alexander would collapse in a fit.

"He'd froth at the mouth and shiver all over and thrash around and sort of lose consciousness," recalled teammate Hans Lobert in Lawrence Ritter's *The Glory of Their Times*. "We'd hold him down and open his mouth and grab his tongue to keep him from choking himself. It was awful."

After the seizure, teammates would pour brandy down his throat (a brandy Alexander, so to speak), to help him get over it. A bottle was always in the dugout at the ready.*

Alexander had come to the Cardinals from Philadelphia in mid-season and won nine games, a big reason they reached the World Series. The Yankees had been heavily favored, but Alexander humbled them with complete-game victories in Game 2 and Game 6.

Accounts differ on how much celebrating Alexander did after winning Game 6, but most agree he was nursing a major-league hangover the next day and did not expect to be called on to pitch in the deciding game.

He was fast asleep in the bullpen when Babe Ruth hit a home run in the third inning. The Cards rallied and took a 3–1 lead, but the Yankees got a run back in the sixth against Jess Haines.

Time was running out on the 1926 season. The Yankees loaded

---

* Alexander's teammate, outfielder Sherry Magee, also suffered from epilepsy. He once had a seizure at the plate, thrashed his arms against the umpire, and was suspended for thirty days.

the bases with two outs in the seventh inning. Lazzeri stepped up to the plate. The rookie had driven in 114 runs that season, and he now had the opportunity to break the game open and be the hero in front of the home crowd.

Cardinals manager (and second baseman) Rogers Hornsby walked to the mound and motioned to the bullpen. Alexander may have gone nine the day before, and he may have been as loaded as the bases, but he was the best the Cards had. If they're gonna beat you, baseball wisdom dictates, let 'em beat your best.

Accounts of the day described it as gray and misty. A hush fell over the crowd when Alexander dramatically stepped out of the shadows of the left-field bullpen. He looked like a gunslinger—his cap perched to one side, his mouth slowly working a quid of tobacco. Alexander did everything slowly.

"Bases filled, eh?" he said to Hornsby casually. "I guess there's nothing much to do except give Tony a lot of hell."

Hornsby looked him in the eyes to see if they were clear and asked, "Can you do it?"

"I can try," the pitcher responded. Later, Hornsby said he knew that if Alexander could walk from the bullpen to the mound, he would be able to pitch.

Alexander had not warmed up in the bullpen, and he took just four throws off the mound—he didn't want to waste one of the few pitches left in his thirty-nine-year-old right arm.

The first pitch was low for a ball, and then Alexander split the plate for strike 1. Lazzeri jumped all over the next pitch, a high, inside fastball, sending a long drive down the left-field line. The ball had the distance to be a grand slam but curved foul by inches. With two strikes, Alexander served up a low, outside breaking ball. Lazzeri swung and missed for strike 3 and the battle was over.

Alexander held the Yankees scoreless for two more innings, and the Series ended when Babe Ruth was thrown out trying to steal second. The Cards mobbed Alexander coming off the mound, and St. Louis had ended its thirty-eight-year wait for a World Championship.

It's been said that Grover Cleveland Alexander would have been a better pitcher if he could have controlled his taste for alcohol. But how much better can one get? He was still winning ballgames when he was forty-two, and he finished his career with 373 victories—the third highest total in baseball history.

He would have won a few more, but went on a bender in the middle of the 1929 season. The Cardinals sent him to a sanitarium to dry out, but upon release he disappeared for two days and showed up at the ballpark reeking of gin. He was suspended for the rest of the season. The next year he went 0–3 and decided twenty years in the majors was enough for any man.

"I guess I just had two strikes on me when I came into the world," Alexander once said. "My father back in Nebraska was a hard drinker before me, and so was my grandfather before him. Sure, I tried to stop. I just couldn't."

Alexander and Lazzeri had more than epilepsy in common. They both made it to the Hall of Fame, and they both came to tragic ends. Just three years after he retired, Lazzeri died after falling down a flight of stairs in his home—possibly because of a seizure. He was forty-two.

Being a charter member of the Hall of Fame never helped Alexander put food on the table. He was down and out a year after his induction at Cooperstown, and the *New York Times* reported that he had been reduced to a sideshow attraction at a flea-circus museum on 42nd Street. Alexander shared the bill with "Sealo"—a young man who claimed to be half boy, half seal.

" 'Old Pete' found the going rough in the last few months," the paper reported, describing the act in which Alexander demonstrated fastballs, curves, fadeaways, and sinkers. "He shows all these deliveries, along with the sidearm 'slider' that struck out Lazzeri, and exhibits them about a dozen times each in an afternoon."

Eventually Alexander developed cancer and had to have an ear amputated. He died in 1950 in a rented room a few miles from his Nebraska birthplace.

A 1952 movie called *The Winning Team*, starring Doris Day and Ronald Reagan as Alexander, showed the pitcher getting hit in the head with a ball; the resulting dizzy spells were mistaken for drunkenness.

RYNE DUREN
The Not-So-Hopeless Drunk

It was another bad outing for Rinold George Duren Jr. in August 1965. Rhino had been sleeping off his daily hangover in the Washington bullpen when manager Gil Hodges called him in to pitch against his old teammates, the Yankees. Duren somehow found the mound and proceeded to hit two batters, walk one, bounce a wild pitch ten feet in front of the plate, and give up a bases-clearing double to Mickey Mantle. Mercifully, Hodges came back out and sent Duren to the showers.

Duren drank eight beers in the clubhouse, and then some vodka martinis at his hotel. Feeling sorry for himself, he walked outside, climbed to the top of a bridge, and decided to jump to his death.

He was up there, shouting incoherently, when a cop came along and radioed for help. In minutes Hodges arrived in a squad car. "Come on down," he said gently, "we'll get you help."

"I can't lick it," Duren sobbed. "I just can't beat it."

Today, ballplayers check in and out of rehab centers like they're Club Med resorts. Ryne Duren was one of the first to come out and admit he had a substance abuse problem. While he would never touch marijuana, amphetamines, or hard drugs, he had no problem becoming a self-destructive, abusive, pathetic falling-down drunk. Before getting cured, he would try to kill himself three times, burn down his house, ruin his family's lives, and spend time in a mental institution.

Duren grew up in Cazenovia, Wisconsin, where he got "snookered" for the first time when he was thirteen. He and a friend paid the town drunk to buy them liquor. The two boys went to a warehouse, got high, and threw up. The next day, Ryne only remembered the high. He drank almost continuously from that point on for the next twenty-five years.

Alcohol abuse ran in his family. Duren's aunt drank herself to death. His uncle then remarried, and the new wife drank *herself* to death as well. His uncle then drank *himself* to death.

As fate would have it, Ryne had a skill much in demand—he could throw a baseball in the neighborhood of 100 mph. He didn't get the chance to pitch in high school—he threw so hard his coach was afraid he would kill somebody. He did receive a baseball scholarship to the University of Wisconsin, where he achieved fame as the anchor of an undefeated fraternity chug-a-lug team.

Duren dropped out of college in 1949 when his high-school sweetheart, Beverly, became pregnant. They married, and Ryne was working in a factory when the St. Louis Browns offered him $250 a month to pitch. He threw a no-hitter in his first minor-league game.

Duren terrorized hitters, not just because of his speed but also because he wore "Coke-bottle" glasses and couldn't find the plate. He would rocket his last warm-up pitch over his catcher's head intentionally to keep hitters thinking about their life insurance. If they had known he was also drunk most of the time, they would probably have refused to step into the batter's box against him.

After doing time in the minors and playing a few games for Baltimore and Kansas City, Duren joined the powerhouse Yankees in 1958. He was one of the heroes of the World Series that year, when the Yanks became only the second team in history to come back to win after being down three games to one. Duren lost Game 1, but saved Game 5 and won Game 6. He struck out fourteen Braves in nine innings of relief.

In *Ball Four*, Jim Bouton told the world about Mickey Mantle's drinking habits, but it wasn't until the publication of Duren's *The Comeback* (in 1978) that the amount of alcohol abuse among the Yankees was revealed. Duren claimed that thirteen of his twenty-five teammates on the 1960 Yankees were either abusing themselves with booze or were downright alcoholics. This was the team that won the American League pennant by eight games and would have won the World Series if not for the dramatic Mazeroski home run in the bottom of the ninth inning of Game 7.

Duren estimated that 35 percent of the players in his day were alcoholics. "Some of the most wonderful players I performed with were downing a fifth of Scotch a day," he said. One "very famous" teammate drank a case of beer a day and consequently was a bed wetter.

As far as Mickey Mantle was concerned, Duren said that the best way to win favor with The Mick was to drink with him and not drunkenly embarrass yourself. During one celebration Duren got so loaded that Mantle and Whitey Ford came over and told him to stop drinking because he couldn't hold his liquor.* Stunned and hurt, he began drinking by himself.

"All I wanted out of life was for people to like me," Duren said. To that end, he would get smashed and do crazy things. He climbed up to the roof of a house and played trombone in the middle of the night. He threw furniture out of hotel windows. He once placed a call to Monaco and actually got through to Grace Kelly. He dumped a tub of ice water on a teammate, who responded by hanging Duren outside a sixteenth-story window by his heels.

In 1961, the Yankees traded him to the Los Angeles Angels. Over the next four years, he was shuttled to Philadelphia, Cincinnati, back to the Phillies, and on to Washington. The standard method of alcohol rehabilitation at that time was to trade the alcoholic to another team.

Eventually, word got around that Duren was a hopeless drunk, and nobody wanted him. A week after he tried to jump off the bridge, he was released from baseball for good and began a series of self-destructive acts. He fell asleep with a cigarette and burned his house down. He fell asleep while driving and hit another car stopped at a light. He blacked out and woke up face down in a swimming pool. He was arrested for drunken driving. His wife left him.

On New Year's Eve 1965, he tried to kill himself again by parking his car across a railroad track in San Antonio, Texas. He sat there drinking and waiting for a train to come along and run him over. The police showed up first and threw him in jail for disorderly conduct. He hung around skid row for a while and moved into a flophouse before checking himself into the San Antonio State Mental Hospital. After eighty-two days there drying out with tranquilizers, he went on the wagon for eleven months, but didn't have the strength to stay there.

After a stint at DePaul Rehabilitation Hospital, he tried to kill himself a third time by sitting in a Milwaukee motel room for ten

---

* When Mantle and Ford were voted into the Hall of Fame, New York restaurateur Toots Shor quipped, "It shows what you can accomplish if you stay up all night drinking whiskey."

days and attempting to drink himself to death. After lapsing in and out of consciousness for a week, he thought better of it.

"I realized that as a human being I was one big mess," he said, "but I felt helpless to do anything about it."

With a third try at rehab, Duren finally stopped drinking in May 1968. Since then, he has devoted his life to helping professional and college athletes deal with drug and drinking problems.* In 1972 he became director of the alcohol rehabilitation program at the Stoughton Community Hospital in Wisconsin. He married a nurse he met there.

Recently, Ryne Duren has become a crusader against alcoholism with Project SMART (Stop Marketing Alcohol on Radio and Television). He claims that the booze industry makes 75 percent of its revenue from people's pain and suffering, and that the government should identify alcohol as a drug, complete with warning labels on every bottle.

"Beer companies have the game of baseball in their hip pockets," he asserts. "Baseball people know where the revenue is coming from. You cut off the beer commercials and you cut off the single most important source of revenue in the game."

DARRYL STRAWBERRY
An Athlete for Our Times

It was the end of January 1990. On Sunday, blood tests proved he was the father of a child born to a woman in St. Louis. On Tuesday, he threatened his wife with a gun and was hauled off to jail. On Saturday, he was checked into a rehab center for alcohol abuse.

You might say it wasn't a great week for Darryl Strawberry.

It has become a racist cliché to portray black superstars as naturally gifted while white superstars receive credit for their hard work and knowledge of the game.

Strawberry, unfortunately, fits the stereotype. At six feet, six

---

* Sam McDowell and Don Newcombe are two other former alcoholic pitchers who became substance abuse counselors.

inches, with huge arms and a beautiful golf-like swing, he is perhaps the most natural talent ever to play baseball. Yet for all his ability, he has never hit .285 or forty home runs in a season. His monstrous homers are all too often solo shots, and they rarely come in crucial situations. He seems reluctant to dive for balls in the outfield. It's difficult to tell whether his running is a graceful lope or simply a lack of hustle.

Darryl Strawberry just never looks like he's trying. He's a good player, but not a great one, and there is a general impression that he has never reached his potential. If he manages to hit another 252 home runs over his second eight seasons, he may wind up as the only underachiever in Cooperstown.

Strawberry won little sympathy when he admitted he had a problem with alcohol in early February 1990. Because if there's one man who typifies the whining crybaby attitude that afflicts current ballplayers, it's Strawberry.

The Mets brought him up in 1983, perhaps a season before he was emotionally ready, and perhaps with a bit too much hype. The team had finished last in 1982, and here was a kid with enormous talent and a name that couldn't miss. He responded by hitting twenty-six home runs and winning the National League Rookie of the Year award. Sportswriters and fans practically anointed him a Hall of Famer at age twenty-one.

He began showing his other side at the end of 1986, the year the Mets won it all. Instead of celebrating the team's astonishing down-to-the-last-strike, come-from-behind victory in Game 6 of the World Series, Strawberry sulked because he had been taken out in the ninth inning (he batted .227 in the playoffs and .208 in the Series).

After the season he became estranged from his wife, who claimed that he had punched her.

A streak talker habitually plagued by foot-in-mouth disease, he threatened two of his teammates the following season. After he missed several spring training workouts and two regular season games because of illness, second baseman Wally Backman said, "Nobody in the world that I know of gets sick twenty-five times a year." Lee Mazzilli was quoted as saying, "He let his manager down, he let his coaches down and, most importantly, he let his teammates down."

"They rip me and they can't even hold my jock," Strawberry responded, tactfully. Of the five-foot, nine-inch Backman, he added, "I'll bust him in the face, that little redneck."

Later, New York tabloids discovered that while he had been out "sick," Strawberry had been in a Queens recording studio singing a rap record titled "Chocolate Strawberry" with the Brooklyn group UTFO.

Besides justifiable anger, jealousy was certainly a factor with Backman and Mazzilli, two players who squeezed out every ounce of their ability to stay in the majors. Echoing a feeling shared by just about every baseball fan, Mazzilli told *Sports Illustrated*, "I'd like to have Darryl's talent just for one year to see what I could do with it."

Strawberry had another altercation with a teammate during spring training in 1989. While the Mets' team picture was being shot, he took a swing at Keith Hernandez when the first baseman told him to "grow up."

Afterward, Straw walked out of camp and didn't return for two days, claiming the team was demeaning him by refusing to renegotiate his six-year contract ($1.8 million a year at the time). He went on to have his worst year ever, hitting .225, and then demanded $12 million to play the next four years for the Mets.

Next came that crazy week at the end of January. Nineteen months earlier, a baby boy had been born to a St. Louis woman named Lisa Clayton. She named him Eugene Michael Strawberry and claimed Darryl was the father. Strawberry's wife, also named Lisa, had a baby around the same time. Darryl didn't contest the blood test proving he was the father of the St. Louis boy and was ordered to pay $40,000 in back child-support payments, plus $2,000 per month.

Two days later, Darryl and Lisa Strawberry got into an argument in their home in Encino, California. He hit her with an open hand, and Lisa responded by slamming a metal rod against his wrist and rib cage. At that point, Darryl pulled out a .25-caliber semiautomatic pistol registered in his wife's name and threatened her with it.

Lisa Strawberry called the police, who arrived at 3:45 A.M. Darryl was arrested and charged with assault with a deadly weapon. He spent an hour in jail, then was freed on $12,000 bail. Lisa did not press charges.

Over the next three days, Strawberry holed up in a Los Angeles motel with Dr. Allan Lans, the Mets' team psychiatrist. The pair decided it would be best if Strawberry checked into the Smithers Alcoholism and Treatment Center, the same place where teammate Dwight Gooden had recovered from his celebrated cocaine abuse three years earlier (see chapter 3).

Alcohol seemed to explain a few things, anyway.

When the 1990 season was over (.277, thirty-seven home runs), Straw rejected the Mets' offer of $9.2 million for three years. He had been threatening for some time to leave New York and play in Los Angeles, his hometown. True to his word, he signed a five-year, $20.25-million contract with the Dodgers.

It wasn't about money, he told the press. He blamed the Mets management for all his problems in New York and described his eight years with the team as a "nightmare in Hell." It may or may not have been a coincidence that shortly after signing Strawberry, the Dodgers became the second major-league team to hire a full-time psychiatrist (the Mets had been the first).

"My life has changed," the twenty-nine-year-old Strawberry announced before spring training in 1991. "I accepted Jesus Christ."

Claiming that he had never been more at peace, he donated 10 percent of his salary to the church. After crashing into the outfield wall at Dodger Stadium and separating his left shoulder, he proclaimed that his minister had "laid hands" on the shoulder and healed it.

"I have a new life now," he said. "It no longer starts in the past. That life is dead."

Aftermath

At mid-season in '91, Strawberry was hitting .229 with eight home runs. He sat out the All-Star game to rest his sore shoulder. After the season he suggested teammate Kal Daniels be traded, and Daniels replied that Strawberry had "a mental problem."

ALL YOU CAN DRINK
"Beer Night" in Cleveland, 1974

It's unlikely that any major-league team will ever repeat "Beer Night"—baseball's most misguided promotion,* which took place Tuesday, June 4, 1974, in Cleveland. *Newsweek* called it "one of the ugliest incidents in the 105-year history of the game."

For some reason, it didn't occur to the front office of the Cleveland Indians that selling beer to the public for ten cents a cup might cause crowd-control problems. A total of 25,134 beer lovers showed up at Municipal Stadium for a game against the Texas Rangers that night, and by the time it was over they had knocked back 65,000 ten-ounce cups. That works out to nearly a quart of beer for every man, woman, and child in the ballpark.

The suds kicked in early in the game when forty fans jumped out of the stands and ran across the field, some of them performing somersaults. Next, a woman attempted to kiss umpire Nestor Chylak at home plate (she failed). A streaker was then chased over the right-field wall by policemen. He was wearing one strategically placed sock. If any foreign visitors were attending their first baseball game that night, they must have come away with a pretty warped view of the sport.

In the seventh inning, things started getting ugly. Drunken Cleveland fans began bombarding the Texas bullpen with beer, cups, tennis balls, firecrackers, and smoke bombs. Texas manager Billy Martin evacuated his players, which made the fans angrier. The fact that Cleveland was losing didn't help, either. Cherry bombs rained down on the field. A few creative fans tied firecrackers to strings, lit them, and dangled them into the Rangers' dugout.

The Indians came back with two outs in the ninth, when John Lowenstein hit a sacrifice fly, scoring Ed Crosby and tying the game at 5–5. Cleveland had the winning run on third when a half-dozen

---

* Second place: "Disco Demolition Night" on July 12, 1979, in Chicago's Comiskey Park. Fans who showed up with a disco record were admitted for ninety-eight cents, and the records were dynamited in a dumpster between games of the doubleheader. Unfortunately, fans rioted in the parking lot, heaved records from the upper deck, and set a bonfire in the outfield. The second game was called off, and thirty-seven fans were arrested.

fans suddenly leaped over the right-field fence and surrounded Texas outfielder Jeff Burroughs.

"They grabbed at my glove and took my hat," Burroughs said after the game. "I tried to call time but nobody heard me. I was getting scared because I felt the riot psychology."

When Burroughs brought both of his arms to his face like a boxer protecting himself, Billy Martin and the rest of the Rangers ran out to right field. Several of them waved bats over their heads.

"I saw knives and chairs and other things," said Martin, a man who had his own problems staying in control while under the influence of alcohol (see chapter 8). "We just couldn't let our teammate get beaten up."

Fans with chairs and broken bottles were pouring onto the field from all directions. Alarmed, a group of Cleveland players ran out to help the Rangers. (This was all the more remarkable because a week earlier the two teams had been involved in a bench-clearing brawl.)

Security guards rushed onto the field. In the riot, three Rangers were injured and Cleveland pitcher Tom Hilgendorf was hit on the head with a steel chair (aren't those things supposed to be bolted down?). So was umpire Chylak, who probably wished he'd stayed with the lady who only wanted to kiss him. He had blood all over him.

Later, Cleveland manager Ken Aspromonte said, "When Chylak got hit on the head, I knew we lost the game"—a rarely heard postgame interview comment.

Sure enough, Chylak invoked rule 3.18, which permits the senior umpire to declare a forfeit if the field is not cleared in a reasonable amount of time. The game went to Texas—only the ninth forfeit in major-league baseball since 1905.

"They were just uncontrollable beasts," Chylak observed. "I've never seen anything like it except in a zoo."

"That was the closest I ever saw to someone getting killed in baseball," claimed Billy Martin.

When the game was called, about five thousand people were on the field. Nine of them were arrested for disorderly conduct, and four were sentenced to three days in a workhouse. The streaker was a juvenile and was not charged.

With the wisdom that comes with being American League president, Lee MacPhail summed up Beer Night by saying, "There was no question that beer played a part in the affair."

MORE HEAVY HITTERS

Steve Dalkowski

The greatest pitching prospect of all time, Dalkowski never played a game in the majors—a combination which would drive any man to drink. He couldn't get the ball over the plate, but he could get it there *fast*. Legend has it that Dalko ripped a guy's ear off with a pitch. Ted Williams, who faced him in a spring training game, said he was the fastest pitcher of all time. Dalkowski was clocked at 98.6 mph once, and that was without a pitching mound.

After giving up baseball, he tried his hand at grape picking, forklift driving, and ditch digging, but found his true calling in elbow bending. Over the years he built up an impressive record of drunk and disorderly arrests and was last seen hanging around Bakersfield, California.

Tom Seats

"If any of my players don't take a drink now and then they'll be gone," Leo Durocher once said. "You don't play this game on gingersnaps."

Leo told the story of Seats, a pitcher with great stuff who couldn't seem to get anybody out for the Dodgers early in 1945. Durocher heard that Seats had a fondness for brandy, so as an experiment he slipped the pitcher a shot before a game and another one in the fifth inning.

"From there on in he was the best pitcher we had," Leo wrote in his book *Nice Guys Finish Last*. Seats would win ten games for the Dodgers that year.

At the end of the season, Dodger president Branch Rickey was congratulating Durocher on the improvement in Seats and asked the manager what he had done to bring it about. Durocher told him the truth.

"You . . . gave . . . a . . . man . . . in . . . uniform . . . whiskey?" Rickey asked in disbelief.

"Yes, sir."

"He will never pitch again for Brooklyn."

Seats never pitched again for *anybody*.

That was not the only time a manager used booze for medicinal purposes. When Tris Speaker signed up well-known drunk Ray "Slim" Caldwell to pitch for Cleveland in 1920, Speaker inserted a clause in Caldwell's contract that specified a strict training regimen: After each game he pitched, Caldwell was required to get drunk. The next day, he was not to report to the clubhouse. The following day he would run laps, and the day after that he would throw batting practice. He would pitch a game the next day and begin the cycle all over again.

Caldwell won twenty games in 1920, the only time he did it in his career.

Hack Wilson

Three years after Babe Ruth hit 60 home runs, five-foot, six-inch Wilson hit 56 for the Chicago Cubs. He batted .356 that season, drove in 190 runs, and won the MVP. He also gained his reputation as a "high-ball hitter."

Wilson would drink a quart of milk before each game, believing it would compensate for the quart of gin he had consumed the night before.

There are a few memorable Hack Wilson drinking stories that may or may not be true. On one occasion, his manager, Joe McCarthy, tried to demonstrate to Hack how drinking would hurt his performance. He dropped a worm into a glass of whiskey and asked Hack if he had learned anything from watching the experiment.

"Yes," Wilson replied, watching the creature drowning. "If you drink liquor, you won't have worms."

When he was with the Dodgers at the end of his career, Hack was seriously hung over one afternoon in Philadelphia and was just about asleep on his feet in right field. Manager Casey Stengel came out to make a pitching change. The frustrated starter, Walter "Boom Boom" Beck, disgustedly flung the ball toward the outfield.

Hack heard the ball hit the wall and woke with a start. He scooped it up and fired a strike to second base that would have surely beaten even the fastest runner—if only there had been a runner. (Note: This story has been told about virtually every hard-living outfielder who played the game.)

"I never played drunk," Hack used to say. "Hung over, yes, but never drunk."

Stories of drinking men aren't always funny. Hack went downhill quickly after his spectacular season. His wife left him in 1936 and accused him of "immoral cohabitation" with a woman named Hazel Miller. After the divorce was final, Hack married Miller and they became drinking partners.

By 1948, he was reduced to handing out towels at a public pool in Baltimore. That November, two months after Babe Ruth died, Wilson's landlady found him unconscious on the floor. He was taken to Baltimore City Hospital, where a nurse wrote him up as "white male huddled under a blanket, appearing acutely ill." Hack Wilson died the next morning of pulmonary edema and a sclerotic liver.

Wilson had earned about $250,000 playing baseball, but he died penniless. His body was unclaimed for three days, until National League president Ford Frick sent a check for $350 to pay for a coffin and simple service.

Wilson was elected to the Baseball Hall of Fame in 1979.

Lou Sockalexis

A Penobscot Indian from Maine, Sockalexis was tearing up the league for the Cleveland Spiders in 1897. His appearance on the field provoked fans into exuberant war whoops and rain dances. Two months into the season, when he was hitting .413, he was suspended and fined for drunkenness. Soon after, he beat a hasty retreat from a house of ill repute, leaping out of a second-story window and severely injuring his foot.

Being out of the lineup gave him plenty of opportunity to imbibe, and writers of the day began using him as an example of the evil of booze. He played just twenty-one games in 1898 and seven in 1899 and was out of the majors for good.

John McGraw once said Sockalexis was the greatest natural talent he had ever seen. Two years after Sockalexis died of heart disease at age forty-one, Cleveland renamed its team "the Indians" in his honor.

Mickey Mantle

It's common knowledge now that Mantle, the switch-hitting Hall of Fame slugger, drank well from either side of the plate. One of baseball's great debates centers around speculation about how many more home runs The Mick would have hit had he spent more time taking care of himself and less time loosening up with the boys after the game.

In *Ball Four*, Jim Bouton told the story of the time Mantle, injured and thinking he would not be playing the next day, got particularly wasted one night.

"He looked hung over out of his mind," Bouton wrote. "He could hardly see."

Unfortunately, a crucial moment in the game came up and Mantle was ordered to pinch hit. He grabbed a bat, dragged his aching body to the plate, and, amazingly, hit a monstrous home run into the left-field stands.

After staggering around the bases and acknowledging a tremendous standing ovation, he sat down with a thud and said, "Those people don't know how tough that really was."

Who knows—maybe Mickey would have hit more home runs if he had spent *more* time loosening up with the boys after the game.

THINKING ABOUT DRINKING

"I was the biggest, most hopeless and most violent drunk in baseball."
—Sam McDowell, 1985

"Either he was out very late, or he was out very early."
—Casey Stengel, commenting on legendary drinker/pitcher Don Larsen after he had wrecked his car at dawn during spring training in 1956. At the end of that season, Larsen pitched the only perfect game in World Series history.

"I'd give a hundred dollars for a cold beer."
"So would the Babe."
> —Ex-Yankees Joe Dugan and Waite Hoyt, as pallbearers at Babe Ruth's funeral, 1948

"The Babe drank like a man. And a gentleman."
> —Mrs. Babe Ruth, 1959

"We want beer! We want beer!"
> —Chant heard when Herbert Hoover was introduced during the 1931 World Series

"You can't drink at the hotel bar, because that's where I drink."
> —Casey Stengel, to his players

"They say some of my stars drink whiskey, but I have found that the ones who drink milkshakes don't win many ballgames."
> —Casey Stengel

"Anybody can play sober—I liked to get out there and play liquored up."
> —Bob Uecker, 1982

"In the old days, twenty-four of the twenty-five guys on every team were drunk. Today nobody hardly drinks anymore, and very, very few take drugs."
> —Sparky Anderson, 1984

"To say that Horace (Stoneham) can drink is like saying that Sinatra can sing."
> —Leo Durocher, 1975

"A drunk is a pitcher who's lost his fast ball. A confirmed drunk is a pitcher with a sore arm. An incurable drunk is a pitcher who hasn't won a game all season."
> —Leo Durocher, 1975

"It's not so bad. It's a great place to meet women."
> —Pitcher Bob Welch, about The Meadows, the Arizona clinic where he underwent alcohol rehabilitation, 1980

"As long as I could pitch a little, nobody cared that I was getting drunk."
> —Don Newcombe

"How dare you belittle my drinking?!"
> —Pitcher Red Evans to Leo Durocher, after the manager suggested Evans was drunk after six beers, 1939

"I have no data, but I would say that more problems occur and more human damage is done because of excessive drinking than because of drugs."
> —Bart Giamatti, 1988

"Pure elixir of malt and hops, beats all the drugs and all the drops."
> —"Smiling Mickey" Welch's formula for his pitching effectiveness, 1890s

"If they'd eat a blasted steak or drink a blasted beer once in a while, maybe their muscles wouldn't keep ripping off their rib cages."
> —St. Louis Cardinals manager Whitey Herzog, on why his pitchers kept getting injured, 1988

"Drink beer like a real man, not any more of that milk!"
> —Boston pitcher Roger Clemens, heckling recovering alcoholics Bob Welch and Dennis Eckersley, 1988

"Whenever a ball looks like this—ooo—take a chance on the middle one."
> —advice to players in a Cincinnati newspaper, 1903

DRINKING MEN

Baseball literature is littered with legends of celebrated drinkers. The following names often come up. Inclusion on this list does not necessarily suggest, however, that the player was an alcoholic.

Grover Cleveland Alexander	Sig Jakucki
Richie Allen	Hughie Jennings
Cap Anson	Mike "King" Kelly
Albert Belle	Ellis Kinder
Marty Bergen	Len Koenecke
Asa Brainard	Terry Larkin
Pete Browning	Don Larson
Ray "Slim" Caldwell	Larry MacPhail
Howie Camnitz	Mickey Mantle
Hugh Casey	Rabbit Maranville
Ty Cobb	Billy Martin
Harry Decker	Dennis Martinez
Ed Delahanty	Jack McCarthy
Jim Devlin	Joe McCarthy
Josh Devore	Jim McCormick
Mike Donlin	Sam McDowell
Phil Douglas	Willie McGill
Ryne Duren	Larry McLean
James Egan	Roger Moret
Red Evans	Van Lingle Mungo
Ferris Fain	Don Newcombe
Jack Farrell	Bobo Newsome
Jimmie Foxx	Cletus "Boots" Poffenberger
Gid Gardner	Darrell Porter
Josh Gibson	Charles Radbourne
Pumpsie Green	Arthur "Bugs" Raymond
Kirby Higbe	Dutch Reuther
Waite Hoyt	Flint Rhem

Dusty Rhodes	Patsy Tebeau
Jim Rooker	Lee Viau
Babe Ruth	Rube Waddell
Slim Salee	Paul Waner
Tom Seats	Bob Welch
Tex Shirley	Curt Welch
Lou Sockalexis	Mickey Welch
Billy Southworth	Earl Whitehill
Horace Stoneham	Nick Willhite
Charlie Sweeney	Hack Wilson
Jim Tabor	Harry Wright

PEEPERS AND KEEPERS

Over the years teams have hired what they called "keepers," usually a coach who would stay with a certain player at all times and see that he didn't get into mischief. Private detectives have also been used to shadow players when they were away from the diamond.

In the 1870s, Albert Spaulding had Pinkerton agents keep an eye on his fifteen-member Chicago White Stockings, only to find that seven men on the team were alcoholics. The St. Louis Browns once assigned a priest to go wherever outfielder Mike Kreevich went in a vain effort to keep him sober.

Rumors flew in 1948 that detectives hired by the Yankees had followed members of the team into a Bronx cocktail lounge and retrieved their fingerprints from martini glasses. Nothing ever came of it.

Granny Hamner, who played shortstop for the Philadelphia Phillies from 1944 to 1959, noticed one day that a man was following him wherever he went. Hamner alerted the police, who arrested the man for carrying a gun without a license. It turned out he was a detective hired by the Phillies management to watch Hamner.

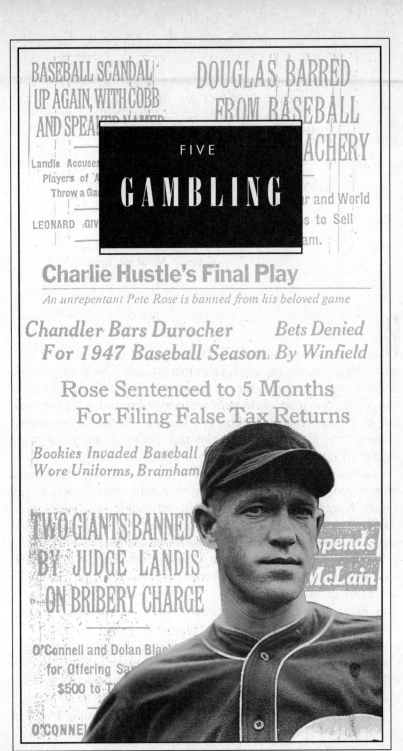

FIVE

GAMBLING

BASEBALL SCANDAL UP AGAIN, WITH COBB AND SPEAKER NAMED

DOUGLAS BARRED FROM BASEBALL ...ACHERY

Landis Accuses
Players of '...
Throw a Ga...

...ar and World
...s to Sell
...am.

LEONARD GIV...

Charlie Hustle's Final Play

An unrepentant Pete Rose is banned from his beloved game

Chandler Bars Durocher For 1947 Baseball Season

Bets Denied By Winfield

Rose Sentenced to 5 Months For Filing False Tax Returns

Bookies Invaded Baseball
Wore Uniforms, Bramham

TWO GIANTS BANNED BY JUDGE LANDIS ON BRIBERY CHARGE

...spends
...McLain

O'Connell and Dolan Blac...
for Offering Sa...
$500 to T...

O'CONNEL...

"They can't come back. The doors are closed to them for good. The most scandalous chapter in the game's history is closed."

—Baseball Commissioner
Kenesaw Mountain Landis,
about the Black Sox

Gambling pushes baseball's button. Many more lives have been ruined by drink, drugs, crime, and other vices, but baseball long ago decided that gambling is the most dangerous sin a person can commit. While Pete Rose sat in permanent banishment during the summer of 1991, Ferguson Jenkins and Gaylord Perry—one convicted of drug charges, the other an admitted cheater on the field—were welcomed into the Baseball Hall of Fame.

Gambling moved in on baseball early, as soon as the game changed from a gentleman's leisure activity to a professional sport in the 1860s. Wagering was a sign of gentility in those days. Fixing games, called "hippodroming," was commonplace. Sporting men would roam the crowd at games, giving odds and taking bets.

The *New York Times* wrote in 1872 that the purpose of baseball was to "employ professional players to perspire in public for the benefit of gamblers."

In *Eight Men Out*, Eliot Asinof wrote, "An outfielder, settling under a crucial fly ball, would find himself stoned by a nearby spectator, who might win a few hundred dollars if the ball was dropped. On one occasion, a gambler actually ran out on the field and tackled a ballplayer. On another a marksman prevented a fielder from chasing a long hit by peppering the ground around his feet with bullets."

To a gambling man, the only thing better than betting is betting on a sure thing. Invariably, attempts were made to influence the outcome of ballgames by offering money to key players. No amount of cash could motivate a player to give more than his best effort on the field, but a very small amount could induce him to play poorly.

Players who killed themselves with alcohol and drugs never hurt the integrity of baseball, but players who tossed games to gamblers did. It became clear to the men who ran the game that baseball would have to at least *appear* free of gambling to survive. The public certainly wouldn't pay to see contests in which the outcome had been predetermined (professional wrestling notwithstanding). The first action taken after the National League was formed was to boot out for life four players who had been caught throwing games.

Still, not enough was done to fight gambling. The Black Sox Scandal—baseball's darkest moment—was hardly an isolated incident. From 1900 to 1920 major-league baseball was awash in corruption by gamblers. When racetracks were shut down during World War I, baseball was allowed to continue and gamblers simply went where the action was. Games were tampered with. Players were bought. For every gambling scandal in these pages, there were probably two or three more that will never be revealed.

Even honest players, managers, and baseball officials looked the other way. It was easier to hush up the whole mess than it would have been to expose it and clean it up.

Baseball's first commissioner, Kenesaw Mountain Landis, thought otherwise, and banished the Black Sox players from the game for life. Landis painted gambling as a pure evil that became dynamite when mixed with baseball. He was so obsessed with baseball's attraction to gambling interests that he prohibited teams from announcing the next day's starting pitchers for a time because gamblers might get to them. During his twenty-four-year reign, society came to view gambling as evil too.

Today, baseball has to swim against society's tide. Gambling has become more acceptable than ever. Americans spend $278 billion a year doing it, not just at Las Vegas but at Atlantic City, church bingo games, and jai alai matches. You can get the odds for professional football, basketball, and baseball games in just about any newspaper. You can go to a racetrack or an off-track betting parlor. You don't even have to leave your home—now they have telephone off-track betting. Politicians are voting in favor of riverboat gambling on the Mississippi and casinos on Indian reservations.

It all sends a message that there's no longer anything morally wrong with risking money on games of chance. How wrong can gambling be when the governments of thirty-two states promote lotteries? It's no surprise, then, that many people wondered exactly what Pete Rose and George Steinbrenner did that was so bad.

Now that ballplayers earn millions of dollars a year, there's less fear that gamblers could offer them enough money to take the risk of throwing a game. The problem now is that players can use their *own* money to bet on games they participate in. Pete Rose fell into that trap, and he'll pay for it for the rest of his life.

THE BLACK SOX SCANDAL
A Day-by-Day Diary

Even people who are not baseball fans know that the "Black Sox Scandal"—when the 1919 Chicago White Sox threw the World Series to the Cincinnati Reds—was the biggest scandal to rock the game. Of all the incidents in these pages, this is the only one that seriously threatened to ruin baseball.

If you saw the movie *Eight Men Out*, you probably came away with an appreciation of the sets and period costumes, but little understanding of what actually happened. Eliot Asinof's book of the same title is much clearer than the film. With help from Asinof's research and other accounts of the scandal, what follows is a basic Black Sox diary. A few of the minor characters have been left out, in the interest of clarity.

September 18, 1919: It is three weeks before the World Series. Chicago first baseman Charles "Chick" Gandil calls a gambler named Joseph "Sport" Sullivan to his hotel room in Boston. The two have known each other for years, and Gandil occasionally supplies Sullivan with tips.

Gandil tells Sullivan the World Series can be bought. "I think we can put it in the bag," he says, adding that he will need $80,000 in cash (some accounts say $100,000).

September 19: It would be impossible for any one man to throw a World Series, so Gandil starts lining up accomplices. Shortstop "Swede" Risberg quickly agrees. Utility infielder Fred McMullin overhears the offer to Risberg and demands to be in on it too.

Gandil approaches pitcher Claude "Lefty" Williams. At first Williams refuses, but when Gandil says the fix is on anyway and Williams might as well get in on it, Williams joins the group. After much persuasion, pitcher Eddie Cicotte agrees, on the condition that he get $10,000 before the Series. (Between them, Williams and Cicotte won fifty-two games during the regular season.)

Why did these players sell out so easily? White Sox owner Charles Comiskey has received a lot of the blame for causing the Black Sox Scandal, and deservedly so.

Comiskey paid Risberg and Williams less than $3,000 a year—peanuts, even in those days. Cicotte, with his 29–7 record, earned less than $6,000. This was after thirteen years in the majors. Dutch Reuther, his opponent in Game 1, made twice that much after playing for only two years. Cicotte had an axe to grind, too. Before the season he was promised a $10,000 bonus if he won thirty games. As soon as he got close, he was benched. He felt no loyalty to Charles Comiskey.

Nor did the other players. In fact, in 1918, the White Sox came close to going on strike. With World War I still on, baseball expected lower attendance and salaries were cut. Attendance actually went up, but when the players asked for more money, Comiskey refused to discuss it.

There was no free agency in 1919. Baseball's reserve clause, which said that a player must accept whatever he is offered or find another line of work, was in effect. Comiskey took full and ruthless advantage of that, paying the best players in the world far below their market value. The White Sox were susceptible to the first smart gamblers to come along.

September 20: First baseman Gandil assembles Risberg, McMullin, Williams, and Cicotte, plus third baseman Buck Weaver (salary $6,000 a year) and outfielders Joe Jackson ($6,000) and

Happy Felsch ($4,000), in his room at the Ansonia Hotel in New York. It is not an enthusiastic "Let's throw the Series!" meeting, but the group agrees to see whether Sullivan can come up with the cash. They also agree that no money will change hands on a Friday—that would be bad luck.

September 21: Cicotte bumps into an old buddy—former ballplayer-turned-gambler William "Sleepy Bill" Burns. They discuss the fix and Burns begs Cicotte to let him handle the details. Burns wires an ex-fighter named Billy Maharg to come to New York and help out. Burns and Sullivan, note, are acting independently.

September 23: Burns and Maharg decide they need Arnold Rothstein, the most widely known gambler in America, to finance the fix. Rothstein had won $500,000 on the first Dempsey-Tunney championship fight, and once won $800,000 on a single horse race. The character of Nathan Detroit in *Guys and Dolls* is supposedly based on him.

Burns and Maharg visit Rothstein at Jamaica Race Track, where he is hanging around with his associate Abe Attell, a former featherweight champion of the world. Rothstein turns the two gamblers down, twice. Burns and Maharg give up on the idea of fixing the World Series.

September 24: Abe Attell contacts Burns and tells him that Rothstein has changed his mind (a lie) and will put up $100,000 as long as his name is kept out of it. Attell shows Gandil, Burns, and Maharg a telegram from Rothstein to this effect. The telegram, it is later revealed, is a fake.

September 26: Sport Sullivan also contacts Arnold Rothstein about financing the fix. Rothstein has more respect for Sullivan than for Burns and Maharg and now shows some interest. Rothstein sends his partner, Nat Evans, to meet with the players and see whether they can be bought.

September 28: Sullivan and Evans arrive in Chicago to meet with Gandil. Gandil wants to see some money, but Evans is reluctant to show it without any guarantee that the World Series will be thrown.

By this time, the players are becoming suspicious of the gamblers.

Williams has already told Gandil he doesn't want to be involved, and Jackson now wants $20,000 to participate.

September 29: Rothstein decides to finance the fix. He instructs Evans to give $40,000 to Sullivan to give to the players, and to put another $40,000 in the Hotel Congress safe in Chicago. The second $40,000 will be paid out if the Series goes according to plan.

Instead of giving $40,000 to the players, Sullivan takes $29,000 of it and bets it on Cincinnati. He gives $10,000 to Gandil.

Before going to sleep, Cicotte, due to pitch Game 1, finds $10,000 in large bills under his pillow. Presumably, it was put there by Gandil. He sews it into the lining of a jacket.

The White Sox—one of the best teams ever—are overwhelmingly favored to beat the Reds, which means a gambler can make a fortune betting on the Reds to win. Evans and Rothstein start getting as much money down on Cincinnati as they can. Evans gets George M. Cohan, the song-and-dance man, to put $30,000 on Chicago. Rothstein bets $90,000 with oil baron Harry F. Sinclair. They get $270,000 down all together.

Word of the fix starts getting around, at least in gambling circles. The odds in the Series begin to shift, from 8–5 to even money.

With the exception of Jackson, all the players meet in Cicotte's hotel room in Cincinnati with Burns and Attell. They are told that they will be paid in installments of $20,000 after each game they lose. The players are bitter, except for Cicotte, who has his $10,000.

Gandil receives a phone call from a newspaperman who says he's heard a rumor the Series has been fixed.

October 1: The World Series begins. Cincinnati is a pennant winner for the first time in fifty years, and this will be the first World Series after World War I. It will be played as an experimental best-of-nine series.

The lead editorial in today's *New York Times* hints at events to come:

> *Great things will be done today in Cincinnati. . . . The war against the Bolsheviki, the conflict in the Adriatic, the race riots, the steel strike . . . all fade into the background . . . the one great topic of transcendent interest is . . . the nerve-wracking*

World Series which has ruined the disposition of everybody who has any money on the outcome.

Before the game, Joe Jackson tells White Sox manager Kid Gleason that he doesn't feel well and asks to be taken out of the lineup.

Game 1: To show his compliance with the fix, Cicotte hits the lead-off batter with his second pitch. When Rothstein hears this in New York, he puts another $100,000 on the Reds. (Years later, he will say he never won a nickel on the 1919 Series.)

In the fourth inning, Cicotte takes an easy double-play grounder and throws high to second, losing the chance to get two. This starts a five-run rally, with most of the damage coming from Cincinnati's weakest hitters. Final score: 9–1, Cincinnati.

At night, Maharg and Burns go to Attell to get the $20,000 promised to the players. Attell refuses, saying the money is all out on bets.

Rumors are flying. At 11:00 P.M., Chicago owner Charles Comiskey calls Kid Gleason to his room to discuss the possibility that the Series is fixed. After midnight, Comiskey goes to National League president John Heydler's room and tells him his fears. Around 3 A.M., Comiskey tells American League president Ban Johnson. Johnson's response—"That is the yelp of a beaten cur!"—deserves to rival "Say it ain't so, Joe" as a Black Soxism.

October 2: In the morning, Gandil and the day's starting pitcher, Lefty Williams, meet with Burns, Maharg, and Attell. Gandil demands $20,000, and Attell again claims the cash is all out on bets. He says he'll have it after the game, and puts up an oil lease in Texas as collateral.

Game 2: Williams, a control pitcher, walks three men in the fourth inning and gives up three runs. Final score: 4–2, Cincinnati. After the game, Kid Gleason beats up Gandil in the clubhouse, and catcher Ray Shalk jumps Williams under the grandstand.

Burns and Maharg go to Attell's room to pick up the $40,000 they are now owed. Under pressure, Attell gives them $10,000. This money is turned over to Gandil, who is furious that the players are being stiffed.

October 3: Burns asks Gandil if the players are planning to win Game 3. "If we can't win for Cicotte and Williams," Gandil says, "we're not gonna win for no busher." The busher is rookie pitcher Dickie Kerr, who is not in on the fix. Burns and Maharg put every dime they have on the Sox to lose today's game.

Game 3: Dickie Kerr pitches the game of his life. Final score: 3–0, Chicago.

Burns and Maharg are broke. They go to Attell, who promises $20,000 to the players if they lose Game 4. He can't give them money in advance, he says, because they can't be trusted anymore.

Burns takes this information to the players, who tell him they've had it with the fix. Burns demands $1,000 from them—his fee for services rendered to this point. The players tell him to go to hell. Burns threatens to tell everything he knows.

October 4: Sport Sullivan is approached by a gambler who suddenly wants to put money on Chicago. Alarmed, Sullivan calls Gandil, who tells him the fix is off. Sullivan promises $20,000 before Game 4 and another $20,000 before Game 5 to put the fix back on.

The sum of $20,000 is delivered to Gandil, who gives $5,000 each to Risberg, Felsch, Williams, and Jackson. McMullin and Weaver receive nothing.

Game 4: In the fifth inning, Cicotte makes two errors, blows a ground ball to the mound, and deflects a cutoff throw to the plate. Final score: 2–0, Cincinnati.

October 6: Game 5: Williams takes the mound again. Anemic hitting and poor play by Happy Felsch combine for another Cincinnati victory. Final score: 5–0.

October 7: Sullivan never arrives with the promised $20,000. Game 6: Kerr pitches again. Final score: 5–4, Chicago.

October 8: Game 7: Thinking about his contract for next season, Cicotte ignores the fix and pitches to the best of his ability. Final score: 4–1, Chicago. Cincinnati's lead in the Series is cut to 4–3.

Arnold Rothstein, with $370,000 bet on Cincinnati, summons Sport Sullivan to his New York apartment. He instructs Sullivan to see that the World Series ends with a Cincinnati victory tomorrow. Sullivan contacts a man in Chicago identified only as Harry F.

At 7:30 P.M., Lefty Williams and his wife are returning from dinner when a man in a bowler hat approaches. He tells the pitcher that if he makes it past the first inning of tomorrow's game, "something is going to happen to you." The man threatens Williams's wife as well.

October 9: Game 8: In the first inning, Williams gives up four consecutive hits and three runs. He is removed from the game before getting two outs. Final score: 10–5, Cincinnati.

The World Series is over, with the Reds winning five games to Chicago's three. The winner's share is about $5,000 per man.

October 10: Joe Jackson asks to speak with Comiskey. He waits in Comiskey's office for hours before giving up and going home to Georgia.

Sullivan and Evans remove the $40,000 from the Congress Hotel safe. In Gandil's hotel room, $15,000 is handed to Risberg and $5,000 to McMullin, who only came to bat twice in the Series. Gandil is paid a total of $35,000 for masterminding the fix.

October 15: Comiskey releases a statement saying that anyone with "a single clue" about shady business involving the World Series will be paid $20,000. Jackson sends a letter to Comiskey saying he would like to discuss the Series being thrown, but the letter is ignored. Comiskey hires a detective to shadow the eight suspected players. The detective finds that Gandil, who has retired from baseball, has purchased a new house, a car, and some diamonds. None of this is made public, and during the winter the scandal seems to blow over.

Early September 1920: The day before a game between the Cubs and Phillies, Kansas City gambler Frog Thompson receives the following telegram from a Chicago pitcher: "BET $5,000 ON OPPOSITION." The telegram finds its way into the hands of sportswriter Otto Floto (these are real names), and an investigation into baseball's gambling problem begins. The 1919 World Series inevitably comes up.

September 21: Subpoenas are sent out to owners, managers, players, and writers to be heard by a grand jury. Even George M. Cohan gets one. New York Giants pitcher Rube Benton says he knew about the fix and names Gandil, Felsch, Williams, and Cicotte. The grand jury receives a letter saying that Lefty Williams's wife placed large bets against the White Sox during the Series.

September 27: Nearly a year after the World Series, the scandal finally breaks publicly. The *Philadelphia North American* runs an interview with Billy Maharg, who tells all and names names. The White Sox are quickly dubbed "The Black Sox." The plate umpire during the World Series, Billy Evans, says, "Well, I guess I'm just a big dope. That Series looked all right to me."

September 28: Cicotte confesses, in two hours and eleven minutes of spellbinding testimony. "I needed the money," he says. "I had sold out the other boys. Sold them for $10,000 to pay off a mortgage on a farm and for the wife and kids. . . . I had to have the cash in advance. I didn't want any checks. I didn't want any promises, as I wanted the money in bills. I wanted it before I pitched a ball. . . . That night I found the money under my pillow. . . . You could have read the trademark on it the way I lobbed it over the plate."

The eight players are indicted, and Comiskey sends each of them a telegram:

> *You and each of you are hereby notified of your indefinite suspension as a member of the Chicago American League base-ball club. . . . If you are innocent of all wrongdoing, you and each of you will be reinstated; if you are guilty, you will be retired from organized baseball for the rest of your lives if I can accomplish it.*

September 29: Jackson calls the Criminal Court building in Chicago and says he wants to confess. The story about the little boy outside the grand jury room actually happened, but his real words were "It ain't true, is it, Joe?" Williams and Felsch confess. Gandil denies everything.

Rothstein calls Attell and Sullivan to his apartment and suggests they all leave the country, at Rothstein's expense.

October 1: Instead of leaving the country, Rothstein goes to Chicago. He goes before the grand jury himself and blames the whole fix on Attell.

October 3: Attell reads in a newspaper what Rothstein has done. He goes to New York to confront him. While Attell watches, Rothstein hands his lawyer $50,000 and instructs him to make sure Attell is not called before the grand jury.

October 27: Arnold Rothstein is exonerated of any blame in the Black Sox Scandal.

November 11: Kenesaw Mountain Landis, son of a Union Army surgeon who lost his leg at the Battle of Kenesaw Mountain, is appointed baseball's first commissioner. His biggest priority is to restore faith in the game.

March 13, 1921: Landis places Jackson, Weaver, Williams, Felsch, Cicotte, Gandil, Risberg, and McMullin on the ineligible list.

July 5: The trial begins. The players who were paid pennies by Comiskey are now defended by the best lawyers money can buy. Later it is revealed that the defense is being paid for by Charles Comiskey.

July 23: The confessions signed by Cicotte, Jackson, and Williams are discovered to be missing from the Illinois State Attorney's office, along with their waivers of immunity. American League president Ban Johnson charges that Arnold Rothstein paid $10,000 to get this evidence. (In *Eight Men Out,* Asinof confirmed that this was the case.) The players repudiate their confessions. Jackson, who cannot read, says he was half drunk when he signed and believed that the paper contained only his address.

July 29: Final arguments. The State asks for five years in jail and a $2,000 fine for each defendant. The defense claims, among other things, that the players never signed any contract that obliged them to try to win ballgames.

August 2: They jury is instructed that to find the players guilty, it must be proven that they not only threw ballgames, but also intended to defraud the public. The jury deliberates for two hours. The verdict: not guilty. Bedlam breaks out, with the jurors hoisting the players on their shoulders and parading around the courtroom.

August 4: Commissioner Landis rules that the Black Sox, despite being acquitted, are banished for life. "They can't come back," he announces. "The doors are closed to them for good. The most scandalous chapter in the game's history is closed."

The *Saturday Evening Post* called the Black Sox Scandal "the biggest, sloppiest, crudest fix of a sporting event that ever was known to man."

The players, it is generally agreed, were pawns manipulated by their owner, double-crossing gamblers, and the criminal justice system. They didn't even think to hire lawyers before confessing. They signed waivers of immunity without even reading them. When they were told that the target of the investigation was the gamblers and not them, they believed it. By and large, the players were good young men who got sucked into a situation that spun out of control.

"They were the best," said second baseman Eddie Collins, who was never in on the fix. "There never was a ballclub like that one."

However, for all the *Field of Dreams* sentiment, it was the *players* who initiated the fix, not the gamblers. Shoeless Joe Jackson may have become a romantic figure, but he *did* take an envelope with $5,000 in it and complained that he didn't get $20,000. He had a spectacular Series, hitting the only home run and leading all hitters with a .375 average and twelve hits (a record that lasted until 1964), but he played so far out of position that he missed an easy fly ball in Game 4.

If anyone deserves to be reinstated to baseball, it's third baseman Buck Weaver. While he attended meetings with the other Black Sox, he never took a dime and was incapable of giving anything less than his best on the field. He hit .324 in the Series and got eleven hits. His only crime was not ratting on his teammates.

In the end, it wasn't Judge Landis who restored faith in baseball by banishing the Black Sox. It was Babe Ruth, who changed the nature of the game and led America into the Roaring Twenties.

The Aftermath

1928: Arnold Rothstein bets $600,000 that Herbert Hoover will beat Al Smith in the presidential election. Hoover wins, and Rothstein stands to collect a huge fortune.

Later that night, he is shot to death during a poker game at the Park Central Hotel in New York.

1951: Joe Jackson, liquor store owner, dies.

1956: Buck Weaver, drugstore owner, dies.

1959: Lefty Williams, gardener and nursery owner, dies.

1964: Happy Felsch, bartender, dies.

1969: Eddie Cicotte, game warden, dies.

1970: Chick Gandil, plumber, dies.

1975: Swede Risberg, dairy farmer, dies.

HAL CHASE
The Art of Throwing a Ballgame

When it came to throwing baseball games, the Black Sox were hopelessly obvious and amateurish. The master of the art was first baseman Hal Chase, who played for fifteen years in the majors and was banished from the game the same year the Black Sox threw the World Series.

Fixing games is a subtle art. If you want to lose a ballgame, you don't drop an easy fly ball. Everyone will immediately know what you're up to. The trick is to botch the play but make yourself look good at the same time.

Chase's technique was to be slightly out of position at a critical moment. He would arrive at the bag a split second late, turning a routine putout into an adventure. He would make a spectacular diving stop, and then toss the ball so quickly that the pitcher couldn't reach first base in time to catch it.

Chase was so good at fixing games that he was able to maintain a reputation as the best first baseman in baseball's first fifty years. He became a star as soon as he joined the New York Highlanders (who became the Yankees) in 1905. He was so swift, he would charge bunts and throw men out from the third-base side of home plate. He also won the National League batting championship in 1916, hitting .339.

"A more brilliant player does not wear a uniform," wrote the

Sporting Life. Babe Ruth named Chase to his All-Time Greatest Team. Nobody seemed to notice that Hal Chase averaged over thirty errors a year. (By comparison, Lou Gehrig made about twelve.)

The Black Sox had been corruptible. Hal Chase was simply corrupt. He didn't wait for gamblers to approach him; he arranged fixes himself and then put money down on the game. According to Eliot Asinof, author of *Eight Men Out*, Chase doubled his baseball salary with his gambling winnings.

As early as 1908, Chase was being accused in newspapers of throwing games. In 1910, George Stallings was the manager of the Highlanders. Chase thought *he* deserved the job, and was accused of "laying down" to lose games so that Stallings would be fired. Chase went to Frank Farrell, owner of the club, and complained. Farrell supported Chase, who happened to be one of the biggest drawing cards in the game. Stallings quit and Chase was made manager. He resigned the position the next season.

Frank Chance took over as manager, and he too accused Chase of throwing games. The Yankees traded Chase to the White Sox. A year later, he jumped to Buffalo in the Federal League, where he won the home run title. When that league collapsed, no American League team wanted him, and he became the property of the Cincinnati Reds.

He started getting a little too bold in 1918. Late in an August game, a rookie pitcher named Jimmy Ring was called in to bail the Reds out of a tough spot. Chase strolled over to the mound and said, "I've got some money bet on this game, kid. There's something in it for you if you lose." Ring ignored the offer, but he ended up losing the game anyway.

The next day, Chase slipped Ring $25. Christy Mathewson was managing the Reds that year, and Ring told him what Chase had done. Mathewson suspended Chase for the rest of the season. Chase denied all charges and filed a civil suit against the team for the salary he lost during the suspension.

On January 30, 1919, a hearing was held before National League president John Heydler. Chase showed up with three lawyers, a clerk, a stenographer, and an armful of his brilliant statistics. He claimed the $25 to Ring was a gift. Mathewson, who was serving overseas in the Army, couldn't attend the hearing to make his charges in person.* Heydler believed Chase was guilty but acquitted him for lack of evidence.

Chase was too slick to nail down. There was never any smoking gun, and there was no Judge Landis around yet to throw the book at players at the mere hint of foul play. Disgusted, Mathewson traded Chase to the New York Giants upon his return from the war.

Chase was thirty-eight years old and nearing the end of his playing career. He enlisted teammate Heine Zimmerman to join him in bribing Lee Magee, Fred Toney, Rube Benton, Jean Dubuc, and others on the Giants to throw games.

But National League president Heydler had not given up when he acquitted Chase in January. He kept looking for some hard evidence of gambling and at the end of the year he got it—a photographic copy of a $500 check Chase had received from a Boston gambler as pay for throwing a game the previous season. Chase was barred for life. So was Zimmerman.

Hanging around with all the other lowlifes in the Ansonia Hotel during the World Series, Chase acquired a reputation as the evil genius who masterminded the Black Sox Scandal. In fact, he merely got word that the fix was on and used the opportunity to make money (some say $40,000) betting on it.

But in some ways, Chase did bring about the Black Sox Scandal.

"The Chase case gave many players the idea that they could play dishonestly and not be discovered," sportswriter Hugh Fullerton wrote in the *New Republic* right after the Black Sox story broke. "They believed the club owners feared publicity so much that they would be safe. The club owners have always adhered to the policy of secrecy and have whitewashed every scandal and charge of crooked work on the grounds that it was 'for the good of the game.' Their policy encouraged the crooked ball players and tempted the weak ones who until then had remained honest. . . . Through it all, the officials in charge of baseball adhered to their policy of curing an evil by declaring it did not exist."

---

* While Mathewson was in France, he was exposed to poison gas in a bungled practice attack and had contracted tuberculosis by the time he returned. He died six years later at age forty-five.

Baseball has to take some of the blame for Hal Chase's crookedness. He played for more than a decade after charges against him first appeared. Three managers accused him of throwing games, but he was allowed to continue playing. Sportswriters were well aware of what Chase was up to, but they never made the story public for fear of libel suits.

His major-league career finished, Chase joined the Pacific Coast League in 1920, where he was banned after he offered a bribe to an umpire. He died in Colusa, California, in 1947.

THE TY COBB/TRIS SPEAKER AFFAIR
The Scandal That Nearly Ruined Them

Five days before the Black Sox threw the first game of the 1919 World Series, another game was fixed, bringing on a scandal that threatened to ruin two of the greatest players who ever played baseball—Ty Cobb and Tris Speaker.

The story didn't break until seven years later, when former pitcher Hubert "Dutch" Leonard described what took place that afternoon in 1919. Here's what happened, according to Leonard:

After their game on September 24, Cobb and Leonard of the Tigers and Speaker and Smokey Joe Wood of the Indians met under the stands in Detroit's Navin Field. The Tigers were battling to finish in third place and claim a slice of the World Series money.* Cleveland had already clinched second. If Detroit won the following day, they would finish third. All four men agreed that Detroit would win the next game.

Tris Speaker, according to Leonard, said, "Don't worry about tomorrow's game. We have got second place clinched and you will win tomorrow."

As long as they all knew the outcome of the game, the four decided to pool some money and place a bet on it. Cobb agreed to put up $2,000, Leonard $1,500, and Speaker and Wood $1,000 each. The bet was to be placed by ballpark attendant Fred West.

As expected, Detroit won the game 9–5. While the game was

---

* The difference between third and fourth place was about $500.

supposedly fixed, Cobb only had one hit in five at-bats, while Speaker had two triples and a single and scored two runs. Wood and Leonard did not play.

Cobb and Speaker were unable to get their money down in time, said Leonard, but he and Wood each won $130 on the bet.

The season over, the four players scattered to their hometowns, making it impossible to discuss the bet or divide up the winnings. After several days, Leonard received a letter from Cobb and one from Wood—letters which would later serve as evidence. These are the two letters in their entirety:

> *Augusta, Georgia, October 23rd, 1919*
> *Dear Dutch,*
>
> *Well, old boy, guess you are out in old California by this time and enjoying life.*
>
> *I arrived home and found Mrs. Cobb only fair, but the baby girl was fine and at this time Mrs. Cobb is very well, but I have been very busy getting acquainted with my family and have not tried to do any correspondence, hence my delay.*
>
> *Wood and myself were considerably disappointed in our business proposition, as we had $2,000 to put into it and the other side quoted us $1,400, and when we finally secured that much money it was about 2 o'clock and they refused to deal with me, as they had men in Chicago to take up the matter with and they had no time, so we completely fell down and of course we felt badly over it.*
>
> *Everything was open to Wood and he can tell you about it when we get together. It was quite a responsibility and I don't care for it again, I can assure you.*
>
> *Well, I hope you found everything in fine shape at home and all your troubles will be little ones. I made a this [sic] year's share of world series in cotton since I came home and expect to make more.*
>
> *I thought the White Sox should have won, but I am satisfied they were too overconfident. Well, old scout, drop me a line when you can. We have had some dandy fishing since I arrived home.*
>
> *With kindest regards to Mrs. Leonard, I remain,*
> *Sincerely,*
> *Ty*

Cleveland, Ohio, Friday
Dear Friend Dutch,
  Enclosed please find certified check for sixteen hundred and thirty dollars. [Note: This represents Leonard's $1,500, plus his share of the winnings, minus $30 for West.]
  The only bet West could get down was $600 against $420 (10 to 7). Cobb did not get up a cent. He told us that and I believed him. Could have put some at 5 to 2 on Detroit, but did not, as that would make us put up $1,000 to win $400.
  We won the $420. I gave West $30, leaving $390 or $130 for each of us. Would not have cashed your check at all, but West thought he could get it up at 10 to 7, and I was going to put it all up at those odds. We would have won $1,750 for the $2,500 if we could have placed it.
  If we ever have another chance like this we will know enough to try to get down early.
  Let me hear from you, Dutch. With all good wishes to Mrs. Leonard and yourself, I am.
  Joe Wood

From these two letters, it is obvious that a bet was made, almost certainly on a baseball game. There are two clear questions. First, why would Dutch Leonard want to bring down Ty Cobb and Tris Speaker? He seemed quite friendly with Cobb, judging by Cobb's letter. Second, why did he wait seven years to do it?

In the years after Cobb wrote the letter, Leonard grew to resent and despise the man. Cobb had become his manager at Detroit and overworked him to the point where he developed arm problems, then demoted him to the Pacific Coast League in 1925. Speaker, an old friend and teammate who had also become a manager, did not pick Leonard up for the $7,500 waiver price. Leonard believed— perhaps unfairly—that the two men had conspired to railroad him out of baseball. When his accusations were made public, he told writer Damon Runyon, "I have had my revenge."

Armed with these letters as solid evidence, Leonard tried to sell them to the press in 1926, but nobody was buying. He then brought them to American League president Ban Johnson, whose method of keeping baseball free of scandal was to make sure scandals never reached the public. Johnson and Detroit owner Frank Navin paid Leonard $20,000 for the letters.

Ban Johnson met with Cobb and Speaker (Wood had been out of baseball for six years) and told them he would keep the scandal quiet if they resigned as managers. Cobb turned in his resignation on November 3 and Speaker followed suit on November 29. Speaker told the Cleveland *Plain Dealer* that he was taking "a vacation from baseball I expect will last the rest of my life." Both superstars were also released by their teams as players. Since both were nearing the ends of their careers anyway, few suspected there was another reason they had quit.

The scandal would have died on the vine, but politics took over. Ban Johnson mentioned the mess before a meeting of American League club presidents, and the group voted to turn the evidence over to Baseball Commissioner Landis.

Landis and Ban Johnson were bitter rivals. Johnson resented this crotchety old judge coming in and ruling the game when *he* had been in baseball since 1887, founded the American League, and served as its president for twenty-eight years. Landis insisted upon supreme authority, and did not hesitate to humiliate those who challenged him.

On December 21, Landis issued a statement to the press detailing Leonard's charges against Cobb and Speaker. The newspapers geared up for the hottest story to hit baseball since the Black Sox Scandal.

Once the scandal was public, Ban Johnson backpedaled quickly, said he was shocked by it all, and announced that neither Cobb nor Speaker would ever return to the American League in any capacity. He denied any secret deal that allowed the two superstars to retire gracefully. Instead, he claimed they had been let go for incompetence. Speaker spent too much time betting on horse races, said Johnson, and Cobb was too violent in handling his men (eleven of Cobb's players, in fact, had asked to be traded in 1925).

Judge Landis decided to hold a hearing to get the facts. Leonard, who was living in California, refused to come to Chicago to make his accusations in person.

"Ballplayers who knew of Cobb's terrible temper told me that Leonard was afraid to come to the hearing for fear that Cobb would tear him apart physically," wrote sportswriter Fred Lieb.

Cobb and Speaker appeared before Landis with Wood and West on December 20. Cobb admitted that he wrote the letter, but claimed he had only been discussing a business proposition. Both he and Speaker denied that any meeting had taken place under the grandstand. Speaker said he knew nothing about the whole business until Leonard made his charges. Both insisted the game in question had been played squarely. Wood backed up the testimony of Cobb and Speaker.

Cobb also said he had bet on two baseball games in his life—the first two games of the 1919 World Series. He lost $150 betting on the Black Sox.

Fred West, the man who supposedly placed the bet, stated that the money had been bet on a horse, not a baseball game. The horse was named Panaman, and it had won. The fact that he was the only one to mention this cast some doubt on West's honesty, as well as everyone else's.

Cobb was a fierce competitor both on and off the field. He hired prominent lawyers and enlisted powerful friends like Senator Hoke Smith of Georgia to pressure Landis into exonerating him. He considered suing the commissioner's office for defamation. In his 1961 autobiography, Cobb said Landis knew he would "tear baseball apart" if the decision went against him. Presumably, he would reveal even more crookedness than had already been exposed.

"I have played the game as hard and square and clean as any man ever did," Cobb said. "All I thought of was to win. My conscience is clear. I will rest my case with the American fans and will match my record in baseball against that of anybody connected with the game."

"I have been in baseball twenty years," said Speaker. "All I ask of the public is their opinion based on these twenty years of hard, honest effort for the game I have loved."

Landis sat on the decision for two months. He had a lot to think about.

Whatever the truth was, three big factors were motivating him to let Cobb and Speaker off the hook. First, he was supposed to have cleaned up baseball seven years earlier. The last thing he needed was another gambling scandal to hang over baseball's head and his.

Second, to rule that the players were innocent after Ban Johnson had said they would never play again would further embarrass Johnson and perhaps even drive him out of baseball for good.

Third, Cobb and Speaker were two of the biggest drawing cards in the game. Public opinion was in their favor and baseball people had rallied around them. There would be no Hall of Fame for another decade, but baseball was becoming aware of its roots and legacy. And who knows, maybe Cobb *did* know something that would tear the game apart.

With all the ulterior motives and hidden agendas, it's doubtful that the evidence of the case had much bearing on the outcome. On January 27, 1927, Landis exonerated everyone involved.

"These players have not been, nor are they now, found guilty of fixing a ballgame," Landis told the press. "By no decent system of justice could such finding be made."

If this scandal had involved two less prominent players, they probably would have been drummed out of baseball for life. Cobb boasted in his autobiography that his lawyers had "dictated" the Landis announcement.

At age forty-one, Ty Cobb came back in 1927 to play one more great season, hitting .357 for Connie Mack's Philadephia A's. Speaker hooked up with the Washington Senators and hit .327. The next season, the two old-timers played side by side for Philadelphia and then retired. Both were inducted into the Hall of Fame, but neither was ever invited to remain in baseball as a manager or in any other position.

The real loser in the Cobb/Speaker affair was Ban Johnson. After covering up the scandal, then vowing neither man would play again, then being publicly humiliated by Landis, he suffered a breakdown. Three days before Cobb and Speaker were exonerated, Johnson collapsed twice, failed to recognize a close friend for nearly a minute, and walked around dazedly, mumbling to himself. All eight American League club owners voted to grant him an indefinite leave of absence. Johnson resigned permanently in October 1927.

Most fans long ago forgot that two of the greatest names in the game had come quite close to being disgraced for life. But Ty Cobb never forgot. Up until the end of his life, he kept a notebook with his personal "son of a bitch" list in it. Ban Johnson, Commissioner Landis, and Dutch Leonard were on the list, even though all three had been dead for years.

LEO DUROCHER
What Is "Conduct Detrimental to Baseball," Anyway?

Many fans are aware that Leo Durocher, the Brooklyn Dodgers' feisty manager, was banished from baseball for the 1947 season. Baseball books usually sum up the scandal by saying Durocher had engaged in "conduct detrimental to baseball" or that he had "consorted with gamblers."

It was never as simple as that. If the same situation occurred today, Durocher would not be suspended.

But Leo Durocher *did* consort with gamblers. When he played shortstop for the Yankees in the Babe Ruth era, he was often seen in the company of Meyer Boston, a big baseball bettor. Leo was pals with actor George Raft,* who happened to be tight with rum-runner Ownie Madden and mobster Bugsy Siegel.

Raft, a Californian, and Durocher, a New Yorker, would use each other's home as bases when visiting the opposite coast. In 1944, Leo was entertaining troops in Italy when Raft held a dice game in his apartment. A sucker was clipped for $18,000 and went to the police, touching Durocher with scandal.

Around the same time, Leo fell in love with Laraine Day, heroine of the then-popular *Dr. Kildare* movies. Her divorce was not yet final when they met, and some people considered Leo a homewrecker even after the two married.

Newspaper columnist Westbrook Pegler, a bitter opponent of Durocher, called him a "moral delinquent" in print. As a result, the Brooklyn chapter of the Catholic Youth Organization withdrew from the Dodger Knothole Club, an organization that sent one hundred fifty thousand kids to Ebbets Field each year. The CYO

---

* As a child, George Raft was a batboy for the New York Highlanders (later named the Yankees).

claimed Durocher was "a powerful force for undermining the moral and spiritual training of our young boys."

This was a time when gambling was again rearing its ugly head in the sports world. Five players and their manager were banned from baseball for life for throwing games in the Evangeline League. Two New York Giants football players had been caught throwing a play-off game at the Polo Grounds. Boxer Rocky Graziano had been approached with a bribe to throw a fight. A basketball point-shaving scandal had made all the papers.

Commissioner Landis, who had ruled baseball with an iron fist since the Black Sox Scandal, died in November 1944. His replacement, former Kentucky senator Albert B. "Happy" Chandler, was getting pressure to prove himself a staunch foe of gambling and counteract his image as a do-nothing stooge of the team owners.

In 1946, Chandler called Durocher for a meeting on a fairway at the Claremont Country Club in Berkeley, California. He pulled a slip of paper out of his pocket with a list of "undesirables" on it—Bugsy Siegel, handicapper Memphis Engleberg, casino owner Connie Immerman, George Raft, and other gamblers and mob figures. Chandler made it clear: If Leo was seen associating with any of these people, he would be out of baseball for life.

Durocher knew the commissioner was serious. Leo had come up to the big leagues four years after the Black Sox had been banished. Now forty years old and seeing the game as his life's work, he told Chandler he would stay away from the people on the list—even his old pal George Raft.

The Dodgers held their 1947 spring training in Havana, where gambling was legal. Durocher became a virtual hermit for fear of being connected in any way with mobsters. He had meals sent up to his room. He panicked when Memphis Engleberg and Connie Immerman stopped by his table during lunch to say hello. He was lounging around a pool when someone came over and said mobster Lucky Luciano wanted to meet him. Leo ran upstairs and hid in his room.

The Yankees were training in Havana that season alongside the Dodgers. During one game between the two teams, it became obvious to observers that Engleberg and Immerman—both known gambling figures—were sitting in the private box belonging to Larry MacPhail, co-owner and president of the Yankees.

Durocher and Branch Rickey were incensed. Leo couldn't even say hello to George Raft, while MacPhail was enjoying a ballgame with underworld figures. They mouthed off to reporters about this double standard.

Though he admitted that Engleberg was a longtime friend, MacPhail charged Rickey and Durocher was making "libelous and slanderous statements" and demanded an investigation and apology.

Commissioner Chandler held a hearing to discuss the matter on March 24 at the Sarasota Terrace Hotel.* A number of witnesses were called to testify about gambling in baseball. Durocher was questioned last, and he admitted that he had gambled on occasion with one of his pitchers, Kirby Higbe. He would beat Higbe playing cards and then every time Higbe won a ballgame, Leo would deduct $200 from the tab. There was no mention of Durocher's consorting with gamblers.

When the hearing was over, Chandler rose from his chair and walked over to Branch Rickey. "How much would it hurt you to have your fellow out of baseball?" he asked.

Rickey gasped, slamming a table with his fist. The commissioner reached into his jacket pocket and pulled out a handwritten letter from Supreme Court Justice Frank Murphy. The letter suggested Durocher be expelled from baseball.

On April 9, the day before baseball season was to begin, Durocher and Rickey were meeting in Rickey's Brooklyn office when a phone call came in. Rickey took it and listened for about a minute. Then he turned to Durocher and said, "Leo, the commissioner has suspended you from baseball for one year."

"For what?!" Durocher shouted.

"I . . . don't know."

This is the official statement from the commissioner's office:

> *This incident in Havana, which brought considerable unfavorable comment to baseball generally, was one of a series of*

---

* The same hotel where Jimmy Piersall suffered his nervous breakdown in 1952 (see chapter 6).

*publicity-producing affairs in which Manager Durocher has
been involved in the last few months.*

*Durocher has not measured up to the standards expected or
required of managers of our baseball teams. As a result of the
accumulation of unpleasant incidents in which he has been
involved, which the commissioner construes as detrimental to
baseball, Manager Durocher is hereby suspended from participating in professional baseball for the 1947 season.*

*Club owners, managers, players and all others connected
with baseball have been heretofore warned that association
with known and notorious gamblers will not be tolerated and
that swift disciplinary action will be taken against any person
violating the order. All parties to this controversy are silenced
from the time this order is issued.*

"Leo is like the fellow who passed a red traffic light and got the
electric chair," wrote Arthur Daley in the *New York Times.*

If anyone deserved to be disciplined, it was Larry MacPhail. Even
MacPhail was shocked at the severity of the punishment. When asked
for a reaction, he said, "Durocher's sentence marked the first time
that a baseball commissioner has fined or suspended a man without
stating, in writing, the specific charges against him."

It should be mentioned that Happy Chandler had won his position
as commissioner of baseball mainly through the support of Larry
MacPhail.

The commissioner refused to state specifically why he was sus-
pending Durocher, but hinted darkly, "If I ever opened my private
files on Durocher, the American people would say I acted too le-
niently." The files, if they really existed, were never opened.

Until Pete Rose was banished for life, Leo Durocher's year-long
suspension was the most drastic action taken against any major-
league manager. He was prevented from appearing on radio
programs, writing for publication, and making endorsements or public appearances. In those days, there were no baseball card shows
or Home Shopping Network where a disgraced baseball man could
go to hawk his memories.

The Dodgers considered suing Chandler and professional baseball
but decided against it because the commissioner's office had so much
power in those days. Even if they had won the suit, the case might
have been tossed back to Chandler, who could have banished Du-

rocher for life. The courts have always preferred to let baseball police itself.

The Durocher suspension would have aroused more outrage, but the very next day a more significant event for the Dodgers and baseball knocked it off the front page: A man named Jackie Robinson played his first major-league game.

Aftermath

- The Dodgers, with Burt Shotton as manager, won the pennant. The players voted Durocher a full share of their World Series money even though he was suspended for the entire season, but the commissioner refused to allow it.
- Durocher came back to manage the Dodgers in 1948. After seventy-two games and a 35–37 record, he was fired. He went on to manage for fifteen more years, for the New York Giants, Chicago Cubs, and Houston Astros, winning two pennants and one World Series. Many believe the 1947 suspension has kept him out of the Baseball Hall of Fame.
- When Chandler's contract came up for renewal in 1951, the commissioner was voted out of office, at least partly because of the way he had handled the Durocher affair. In 1971 he wrote an article for *Sports Illustrated* in which he said Durocher's squabbles with umpires and marital affairs contributed to the decision to suspend him. He maintained that Durocher "had been a discredit to baseball. He had performed the misdeeds of ten men."
- Leo Durocher published his autobiography, *Nice Guys Finish Last*, in 1975. "To this day," he wrote, "if you ask me why I was suspended, I could not tell you."
- Chandler and Durocher died within four months of each other, on June 15 and October 7, 1991, respectively. In his will, Durocher instructed his heirs to reject any posthumous induction into the Baseball Hall of Fame.

WILLIE MAYS AND MICKEY MANTLE
Guilt by Association

As if to show how phobic baseball had become about gambling, two of the sport's best-known and most beloved living heroes were forced to leave the game in the 1980s although they were not even accused of doing anything improper.

In 1979, Willie Mays was offered a job as "assistant to the president" of Bally's new Park Place casino in Atlantic City. Essentially the position consisted of glad-handing the high rollers casinos work so hard to cultivate. Joe Louis did it for years at Caesars Palace in Las Vegas. It's an ornamental, somewhat pathetic job, but certainly legal. Willie would also be doing work with various charities, but always as a shill for Bally.

The contract called for $100,000 a year for ten years, and Willie would only have to work ten days a month. As an employee of a Bally hotel, it would be illegal for him to gamble in the casino there.

For the five preceding years, he had held a public relations position with Ogden Corporation, a racetrack caterer. Mays was also working for the New York Mets as a goodwill ambassador and part-time coach, to the tune of $50,000 a year.

The slightest hint that baseball and gambling might be connected made the hair stand up on Commissioner Bowie Kuhn's neck. He had a strong sense of baseball history.

"There were people inside and outside the game who saw the 1919 Black Sox scandal as ancient history," Kuhn wrote in his book *Hardball*. "I did not. . . . If Mays were free to associate with and entertain the big gamblers in Atlantic City, how was I to keep our personnel away from gambling types?"

He issued an ultimatum to Mays: baseball or baccarat. If Willie took the job with the casino, he could no longer work for the Mets. It would be one or the other, but not both. Kuhn gave Mays a week to think it over.

Willie took the casino job and was out of baseball, just three months after he'd been elected to the Hall of Fame. Kuhn's telegram to him was careful to state that Willie was not guilty of any wrongdoing, but that "such associations by people in our game are in-consistent with its best interest."

The press and public were outraged at Kuhn for "banishing" one of the most popular men ever to play the game. Even Frank Sinatra chimed in with an opinion. "Mr. Kuhn told Willie Mays to get out of baseball," said the Chairman of the Board. "I would like to offer the same advice to Mr. Kuhn."

"I don't have anything to do with gambling," Mays said in defense of his decision. "I just play golf with the customers, and after that they take pictures and the customers put them on their office walls. . . . I've been a model for baseball during my twenty-two years in it. But now I have to think primarily of my family."

When it was pointed out that his access to ballplayers might make him a target for high rollers, Mays said, "A player has a lot of ways of throwing games. I'm not a player." He applied for reinstatement twice and was turned down both times.

Across the street from Bally's in Atlantic City is Del Webb's Claridge Casino Hotel. Del Webb co-owned the Yankees for years before selling the team to CBS in 1964. In the 1970s he inquired about buying the Chicago White Sox, but Commissioner Kuhn said he would have to divest himself of his casino operations. Webb decided to stick with gambling.

But if Bally had a big-name baseball star, Webb wanted one too. And who better than ex-Yankee Hall of Famer Mickey Mantle, who had been Willie Mays's rival all through their playing careers? Why not let the two ex-sluggers slug it out for suckers coming to lose their shirts at the Jersey shore?*

Mantle was offered the position of "Director of Sports Programs" at the Claridge, also for $100,000 a year.

A precedent had been set in the Willie Mays case. Mantle was warned that he too would be banned from baseball if he took the job.

"Some threat," sniffed Mantle. "What would I be banned from?"

The only baseball work Mickey had been doing was spending two weeks a year as a pseudo-hitting instructor with the Yankees. He

---

* Brooks Robinson appeared in a 1983 Bally's commercial, and former Yankee Sparky Lyle worked for the Claridge. Neither was disciplined by baseball.

made next to no money for it and was not particularly appreciated. His close friend, Yankee manager Billy Martin, told him, "If we want somebody to learn to strike out, we'll call you." (Mantle struck out 1,710 times in his career, eighth on the all-time list.)

As soon as the announcement was made that Mantle had accepted the casino job, he was handed a letter from Kuhn informing him that he was out of baseball. The commissioner told The Mick he regretted that Mantle had not taken another job, like the work Joe DiMaggio was doing for Mister Coffee.

"Nobody like Mister Coffee had offered to hire me," Mickey said.

Mantle pointed out that baseball operated under a double standard. DiMaggio was co-chairman of a golf tournament sponsored by the Riviera Hotel in Las Vegas. Several team owners owned racetracks and race horses. Why was he singled out for punishment?

By 1985, Mays and Mantle weren't the only ones out of baseball jobs. So was Bowie Kuhn. On March 17, the new commissioner, Peter Ueberroth, took the stage in the Astor Salon at the Waldorf-Astoria Hotel.

"I'm pleased to welcome back to baseball Willie Mays and Mickey Mantle, effective immediately," he announced. The two men came out together and shook hands with Ueberroth.

It was one of the only times in baseball history that a commissioner reversed the decision of a predecessor. Ueberroth tried not to embarrass Kuhn any more than was necessary.

"The world changes," Ueberroth explained. "I don't think we can start dictating who you can play golf with." Kuhn disagreed with the decision and said so publicly.

It's probably too soon to determine whether Bowie Kuhn was being overly fearful about the threat of gambling on baseball, or whether Peter Ueberroth took it too lightly. But within four years of Ueberroth's reversal, two major gambling scandals rocked the game—those involving George Steinbrenner and Pete Rose.

PETE ROSE

"I never bet baseball. I swear I never bet baseball."

We want so much to believe him. We want to believe that Pete Rose—a throwback to the days when men played baseball for love instead of money—was not corrupted by money. We want to believe him because it's so tragic for Pete Rose to be banned for life from the game that *was* his life.

Unfortunately, we can't believe him. He's lied to us too many times.

Rose said it wasn't his gambling that caused him to be called into the commissioner's office in February 1989. Then he admitted it was. He said he didn't know Ron Peters, a convicted bookie/steroid salesman/tax evader. Then it was discovered that Rose had left tickets for Peters at Riverfront Stadium. Rose said he didn't place bets with bookies on any sport, but twelve sources told *Sports Illustrated* that he had.

He said he wasn't involved in a Pik Six wager that paid $265,669 at Turfway Park in Florence, Kentucky. Then he admitted that, oh yeah, he was. He said he didn't dodge income taxes. Then he pleaded guilty to the charge and was sent to jail for it. He said he didn't have a gambling problem and wouldn't seek help for one. Then he admitted publicly that he was getting psychiatric help for his "sickness." He said he didn't sell off his baseball memorabilia. Then it came out that he'd sold the bat that made his record-breaking 4,192nd hit for $129,000. He put on nine separate uniforms during that game and peddled every one of them.

That all makes it very hard to believe Rose when he insists he never bet on baseball games.

Then there's the overwhelming evidence that Rose *did* bet on baseball—and that he bet on games he was managing. Nine people interviewed by the commissioner's office implicated Rose in baseball betting. There were betting sheets with Rose's fingerprints and handwriting on them. There was page after page of telephone records showing flurries of one-minute calls from Rose's office to known bookies. The calls came just minutes before ballgames, and during months when there was no sport to bet on except baseball.

The 225-page Dowd Report stated: "The testimony and the documentary evidence gathered in the course of the investigation demonstrates that Pete Rose bet on baseball, and in particular, on games of the Cincinnati Reds Baseball Club during the 1985, 1986 and 1987 seasons."

"He was attracted by criminality," wrote Michael Sokolove, author of *Hustle: The Myth, Life & Lies of Pete Rose*. "Just the whiff of it made his heart beat faster."

Pete Rose's father, Harry, loved to gamble, and he was already taking Pete to the racetack when the boy was eight years old. Pete's uncle Buddy was a pool hustler. When Rose was a brash rookie with a crew cut on the 1963 Cincinnati Reds, he was already a heavy racetrack bettor. He didn't have much money to gamble with in those days. He had a lot more by 1970, when he was a superstar. That's when baseball began a continuing investigation to keep track of what Rose was up to. But no serious action was taken until the canaries started to sing in the worst year of Rose's life—1989.

By January of that year, relations had turned sour between Rose and two of his closest associates, the previously mentioned Ron Peters and Paul Janszen, a convicted tax evader and cocaine trafficker. Janszen wrote to Rose's attorney requesting $34,000 he believed Pete owed him. Peters approached *Sports Illustrated*, looking to sell the story of Rose's gambling. The magazine turned him down, but word leaked out that Rose was in trouble.

The commissioner's office likes to think of itself as baseball's policeman, and on February 20, Rose was summoned to New York to meet with Commissioner Ueberroth and A. Bartlett Giamatti, who would be taking over the job on April 1. Rose was asked if he had ever bet on baseball games. He told the two commissioners he hadn't, and he thought the matter was closed.

On March 20, Ueberroth announced that his office "has for several months been conducting a full inquiry into serious allegations" about Rose. In the March 27 issue, *Sports Illustrated* ran the first of many articles on the trouble Rose was in.

The magazine said, among other things, that sources claimed Rose made hand signals from the Reds' dugout to Paul Janszen in the stands of Riverfront Stadium to indicate how Rose stood on his current bets. Ron Peters was described as Rose's "principle bookmaker" and was quoted as saying he had information that Rose had bet on baseball. Other cronies of Rose named in the article included convicted cocaine trafficker and tax evader Michael Fry and professional gambler Tommy Gioiosa, who would later be indicted for cocaine trafficking and tax evasion. Gioiosa's defense would be to claim that taking steroids had made him irrational.

In defending himself against the charges, Rose logically said that the men making such statements were an assortment of criminals and lowlifes who were talking to the authorities to reduce their own jail sentences and penalties for their criminal activity. There was some truth to that, though it didn't necessarily mean they were lying. It's tough to find upstanding citizens and credible witnesses in the field of illegal gambling.

Seventeen days after becoming commissioner, Bart Giamatti made a huge blunder in the Rose case, and it would not be unfair to say that the mistake was deadly. Giamatti wrote—or signed, anyway— a letter to federal judge Carl Rubin, who was scheduled to pass sentence on Ron Peters for drug charges. In Giamatti's words, Peters had provided baseball with "critical sworn testimony about Mr. Rose and his associates. In additon, Mr. Peters has provided probative documentary evidence to support his testimony and the testimony of others. Based upon other information in our possession, I am satisfied *Mr. Peters has been candid, forthright, and truthful* with my special counsel." (Italics added.)

In other words, Giamatti believed that Ron Peters was telling the truth when he said Pete Rose had gambled on baseball—before hearing Rose's side of the story. Giamatti, it could be argued, had prejudged Rose.

Rose's lawyers jumped all over that, and on June 19 they filed a lawsuit against the commissioner, Major League Baseball, and the Cincinnati Reds, claiming that Bart Giamatti was incapable of judging Pete Rose fairly. Rose's camp wanted a jury trial, where they believed he'd have a better chance of acquittal.

Plainly, it was a challenge to baseball's entire commissioner system, which gives the commissioner the power to act as judge, jury, and executioner in all cases.

Meanwhile, John Dowd, a Washington lawyer who acted as baseball's investigator, had submitted his findings, and they were devastating to Rose's case. The Dowd Report said that Pete Rose had placed bets on the Cincinnati Reds fifty-two times in 1987 alone. Rose bet $10,000 a day on baseball games and sometimes more. He lost so much money that he had to borrow $47,000 from a man operating a cocaine ring.

Paul Janszen had testified that Rose had told him he would consider throwing a game if he could make enough money on it. He also said Rose had volunteered to finance cocaine deals (the offer was turned down). There were stories of people coming right onto the field to collect gambling debts from Rose.

If there had been any doubt in the minds of the public that Pete Rose was guilty of betting on baseball, the Dowd Report erased them.

Rose and Giamatti played a public relations war throughout the summer. Both sides finally came to realize it would be in everybody's interest to hammer out some sort of agreement. For Giamatti's part, he didn't want to spend months in federal court trying to prove he had not prejudged Rose—he might lose and the whole commissioner system would go down in flames. As for Rose, he didn't have unlimited funds to fight a long drawn-out legal battle. Besides, his trial for tax evasion was approaching, and being a convicted felon would not help his case with baseball.

Rose claimed in his 1989 book *Pete Rose: My Story* that the commissioner offered him a deal that called for a seven-year suspension. He turned it down because the agreement required him to admit he had bet on baseball games—an admission that would certainly keep him out of the Baseball Hall of Fame forever. Rose was then offered a six-year suspension, and he turned that down too.

On August 22, Rose's wife, Carol, gave birth to their second child, a girl named Cara. That evening, Pete made $100,000 in four hours by hawking autographed balls ($39.94), bats ($229), and uniforms ($399.92) on the Cable Value Network (Rose could sign his short name six hundred times an hour). The next day he was paid *nothing* to put his signature on a piece of paper that would banish him from baseball for life.

According to the agreement, Rose was suspended permanently,

and could apply for reinstatement in one year.* Rose agreed not to challenge the decision of the commissioner in the evaluation of his reinstatement, to drop all litigation against Giamatti, and to admit the commissioner had acted fairly.

The one concession the commissioner made was this sentence: *"Nothing in this agreement shall be deemed either an admission or a denial by Peter Edward Rose of the allegation that he bet on any major-league baseball game."*

Rose was asked, and will be asked over and over again for the rest of his life, why he signed an agreement that banished him from baseball if he didn't bet on baseball. Rose's answer was that he felt he would be banned anyway—simply because he had associated with gamblers. In his mind, and in his lawyers' minds, he would be better off if he was suspended permanently with the words right on the page saying there had been no finding that he had bet on baseball.

He may have been right. The agreement didn't directly accuse Rose of betting on ballgames, and this is Pete Rose's key to future reinstatement.

"The matter of Mr. Rose is now closed," announced Giamatti. "It will be debated and discussed. Let no one think it did not hurt baseball. That hurt will pass, however, as the great glory of the game asserts itself and a resilient institution goes forward. Let it also be clear that no individual is superior to the game."

At the press conference afterward in the New York Hilton, Giamatti was asked if he personally believed Rose had bet on baseball. "In the absence of a hearing and therefore in the absence of any evidence to the contrary, I am confronted by the factual record of the Dowd Report," Giamatti responded, "and on the basis of that, yes, I have concluded that he bet on baseball."

Rose was stunned, and felt as if he'd been stabbed in the back. He had fought so hard for an agreement that stated there was no finding he had bet on baseball, and the commissioner had now blown it to bits.

Ever since the case had begun, Giamatti had been accused of

---

* This was not a special case. Anybody who is suspended permanently can apply for reinstatement a year later.

harboring a personal vendetta against Rose. It's extremely doubtful that he did. It is hard to believe that Giamatti, relatively new to baseball, would want to go through so much anguish to banish for life the most popular player in the game. What's more likely is that in his heart Giamatti—like the rest of us—believed Rose *did* bet on baseball, and was incapable of saying otherwise.

Rose had always been a fighter, but Giamatti showed he was a fighter too and wasn't going to let himself be pushed around no matter *how* many hits Pete Rose had.

Giamatti gave the fight his all. A week after kicking Rose out of baseball, he suffered a fatal heart attack. (Before it is said that Rose killed Giamatti, bear in mind that the commissioner was a chain-smoker who never exercised.)

In April 1990, Pete Rose got further into hot water when he pleaded guilty to two felony counts of filing false income tax returns, understating his income from baseball cards shows by $354,698 for 1985 and 1987. He spent five months in Federal prison in Marion, Illinois. He had a job in the prison's welding department.

Pete Rose and the Hall of Fame

The most heated debate in baseball concerns whether or not Pete Rose belongs in the Baseball Hall of Fame. Had all this unfortunate gambling business never come up, Rose would have been a shoo-in the first year he was eligible—1992.

According to the rules of the Hall of Fame, admission is based on "the player's record, playing ability, integrity, sportsmanship, character, contribution to the team or teams on which the player played and not on what he may have done otherwise in baseball."

I can only say what I think. Leaving Pete Rose out of the Baseball Hall of Fame would make it obviously incomplete, like a map of the United States with Texas missing. Putting Rose in after what he's done would certainly taint the Hall of Fame's grandeur—*if the rest of the members of the Hall were All-American boys like Christy Mathewson.*

Unfortunately, they are not. A glance at the first appendix in the back of this book shows that Cooperstown is already crammed to the rafters with gamblers, alcoholics, drug users, womanizers, cheaters, drunken drivers, Klansmen, and even ticket scalpers. It would be unfair to keep Pete Rose out after all the Hall of Fame has already let in.

If I were commissioner of baseball, I'd let Rose stew for a decade or so under suspension, to show him there are consequences for breaking the rules. Then, when he was sufficiently remorseful, I'd reinstate him and welcome him to Cooperstown. Even murderers are considered to have paid their debt to society after they do their time.

As long as I'm commissioner, I'd push through a change in the rulebook. Rule 21(d), which got Rose kicked out of baseball, goes like this:

> Any player, umpire or club or league official or employee, who shall bet any sum whatsoever, upon a baseball game in connection with which the bettor has no duty to perform, shall be declared ineligible for one year.
>
> Any player, umpire or club or league official or employee, who shall bet any sum whatsoever upon a baseball game in connection with which the bettor has a duty to perform, shall be declared permanently ineligible.

There should be some distinction between betting on your own team to win and betting on your own team to lose. While it is clearly unhealthy for baseball players to be betting on baseball in *any* form, betting on your team to lose strongly suggests criminal activity, while betting on your team to win is often good old-fashioned boosterism.

Penalties for the two offenses should be different. Throwing a guy out of the game *for life* because he put a few bucks on his own team to win is cruel and unusual punishment.

By 1991, Pete Rose had learned a thing or two about public relations. Instead of seeing him acting defiant on TV, we saw him doing his community service and playing with his wife and kids. Suddenly he sounded repentant. He wasn't a gambler; he had a "gambling disorder."

"I just hope that you will understand that I have a sickness," he said. "I first realized last October that I had a gambling problem and made that public in November. I have been able to stop gambling since then—but I will need help for the rest of my life."

Time will tell whether anybody is buying the new Pete Rose, who seems to be obviously aiming his pitch at reinstatement.

No one who has been banned for life from baseball has ever been reinstated. Black Soxers Joe Jackson and Buck Weaver fought for years to clear their names. Friends and relatives of Shufflin' Phil Douglas were still trying to get him reinstated forty years after his death.

Rose has a shot to be the first. Memories have become shorter and images more real. There's no film of Buck Weaver playing third base or Joe Jackson swinging his sweet swing (*Field of Dreams* and *Eight Men Out* don't count). Nobody remembers what a great pitcher Phil Douglas was.

Before long we'll forget the bets Pete Rose made, the sleazeballs he hung out with and crimes he committed. But we'll always remember—let's go to the videotape—Rose's dirt-eating head-first slides, his sprints to first base on walks, that brutal collision with Ray Fosse at the 1970 All-Star game. We want to remember Charlie Hustle, not Charlie the Hustler.

GEORGE STEINBRENNER
"The Boss" Walks the Plank

Roberto Kelly was up in the bottom of the fourth against Detroit when a murmur began circling through Yankee Stadium. The scoreboard read: July 30, 1990, 8:26 P.M. The murmur built steadily, and suddenly a guy in the upper deck behind home plate screamed, "It's over! It's over! Yes!" Fans began turning on portable radios. The murmur turned into a roar and the roar reached a crescendo as twenty-six thousand people became aware of the incredible news—George M. Steinbrenner III had been kicked out of baseball.

Yankees fans hadn't been so excited since the days of DiMaggio. People began chanting "NO MORE GEORGE! NO MORE GEORGE!" The standing ovation lasted ninety seconds. The whole scene had a very "Ding Dong, the Witch Is Dead" quality about it.

So ended the seventeen-year reign of terror that George Steinbrenner inflicted upon the game of baseball and on what was perhaps the greatest franchise in sports. "The Bronx Zoo," Sparky Lyle had called it. The era of Steinbrenner had been a baseball soap opera featuring musical managers (nineteen in eighteen seasons), general managers (thirteen), team presidents (ten), bad trades, meddling, dumb public statements, headline-hogging feuds, and rampant egomania.

Not since the resignation of President Nixon* had there been such unabashed glee at the fall of a public figure. All week long the New York tabloids had been drooling, "TOSS THE BOSS" and "T'ROW DA BUM OUT!" After Commissioner Fay Vincent's announcement that Steinbrenner was finished, *Time* magazine trumpeted, "July 30th may become a patriotic holiday in New York City and wherever the proud traditions of baseball are honored."

"The Boss," who had used the wealth of his American Ship Building Company to buy the Yankees in 1973 for $10 million, was undisputably the most despised man in baseball. Graig Nettles, when he played under Steinbrenner, said, "It might be good if we keep losing, because it's more likely Steinbrenner will fly in, and that increases the possibility that the plane will crash."

But George Steinbrenner wasn't kicked out of baseball because people didn't like him. His downfall began on December 2, 1986, when he took a call from Howard Spira, a small-time gambler with mob connections. Spira said he had incriminating information about George's arch-enemy and star right fielder, Dave Winfield.

"I'm anxious to hear what you want to tell me, what you have to say," Steinbrenner said, according to a taped telephone conversation that found its way to the *New York Times*.

From the moment Winfield signed his ten-year, $20-million-plus Yankees contract in 1980, Steinbrenner seemed out to get him. Winfield was a solid—often exceptional—ballplayer who averaged twenty-five home runs a year for the eight years he played on the Yankees. But he never filled Reggie "Mr. October" Jackson's

---

* Steinbrenner pleaded guilty in 1974 to fourteen felony counts of illegal contributions to Nixon's reelection campaign, as well as obstruction of justice. He was fined $15,000 and suspended from baseball for two years. Just before leaving office in 1989, President Ronald Reagan pardoned him.

shoes—at least when it came to pomp. Steinbrenner called Winfield "Mr. May," and he made certain that Winfield's photo did not appear on the cover of Yankees programs and yearbooks.

Part of Steinbrenner's problem with Winfield was the David M. Winfield Foundation, a nonprofit organization to help underprivileged kids that Winfield had started when he was playing with the San Diego Padres. Winfield's deal with the Yankees called for Steinbrenner to contribute $300,000 a year to the foundation. Steinbrenner fell behind in the payments, and Winfield sued him three times in seven years to get $450,000 that was owed. Steinbrenner sued Winfield right back, claiming Winfield had failed to make his own contributions, and that the organization had misused funds.

Howard Spira, a short, nervous, and obviously troubled young man, worked as a gofer for the Winfield Foundation from 1981 to 1983. When Winfield broke off their relationship, Spira contacted Steinbrenner. The Boss was all ears.

The two met in Tampa on December 30, 1986, and again in April 1987. What Spira had to say was that the Winfield Foundation *had* misused funds, that Winfield and his agent, Al Frohman, had concocted phony death threats to explain Winfield's poor play in the 1981 World Series, and that Winfield had loaned Spira $15,000 and held a gun to his head threatening to kill him if he didn't pay it back.

Steinbrenner paid Spira $40,000 for this information on January 8, 1990, a monumental blunder that would result in Steinbrenner's expulsion from baseball. When Spira demanded $110,000 more, Steinbrenner alerted the authorities. The FBI raided Spira's Bronx apartment and confiscated tapes he had made of telephone conversations. Two weeks later, on March 23, Spira was indicted by a federal grand jury for trying to extort money from Steinbrenner and threatening to harm Steinbrenner and Winfield.

After throwing the book at Pete Rose just six months earlier, the baseball commissioner's office geared up for another gambling scandal and investigation. This one wasn't nearly so wrenching. It was fairly cut and dried—Steinbrenner had paid a lowlife gambler $40,000, and there was even a check to prove it.

When asked why he had paid off Spira, Steinbrenner changed his story several times. First he said it had been "out of the goodness of his heart."

Then he claimed he had feared for his family. "You don't know what it's like when you've got a guy out there calling and threatening to kill people in your family," Steinbrenner told Commissioner Vincent.

Next, Steinbrenner said Spira had threatened to expose Yankees manager Lou Piniella's gambling habits. (Piniella said he went to the racetrack occasionally. Spira said Piniella was heavily into football betting.)

Finally, Steinbrenner said Spira's mother had cancer and he had felt sorry for the family.

None of that mattered. What mattered was that a team owner had paid off a gambler. Baseball poison.

"Did anybody say to you," Vincent asked Steinbrenner, " 'Suppose this guy takes the money and pays off gambling debts. You are now an owner in baseball financing a gambler'?"

"Well, I didn't, I never thought of that."

In closed-door meetings, Vincent—a Yankees fan—offered Steinbrenner a two-year suspension. Steinbrenner and his lawyers balked, and Vincent scribbled another arrangement on a yellow legal pad —there would be no suspension, but Steinbrenner would (1) acknowledge wrongdoing, (2) give up his majority ownership of the Yankees, (3) not challenge Vincent's ruling in court, and (4) agree to a lifetime ban on even *talking* about the Yankees with the new majority owner. Under this agreement, Steinbrenner would even have to get written permission from the commissioner just to *attend* a baseball game.

Incredibly, Steinbrenner accepted the second option. Like Pete Rose, he preferred to take a harsher punishment if he could control the wording of the agreement. Steinbrenner signed Vincent's agreement, on condition that the words "suspension" and "banned" not be used, and that he could name his thirty-three-year-old son, Hank, as the new general partner.

As it turned out, Hank didn't want the job. Robert Nederlander, a New York theatrical impresario, became the Yankees' new managing general partner. The word in New York is that Steinbrenner is still calling the shots behind the Yankees.

At the press conference after the big announcement, Vincent said Steinbrenner had acted in "a pattern of behavior that borders on the bizarre."

After Steinbrenner had been given the boot, Howard Spira went on trial for trying to extort $110,000 from Steinbrenner and threatening to harm him and Winfield. The evidence consisted only of Spira's weird letters and recorded phone calls. In one letter he referred to Steinbrenner as "George Von Steinhitler" and wrote, "If anything happens to my mother, George and Dave better both hire a lot of extra security because then I will really be out of control."

"If he thinks seven straight losses is a problem," Spira wrote to a Steinbrenner aide in 1989, "wait until I open my mouth. Dave is gone. George is next."

Steinbrenner was called to testify, and he came close to tears when he read the names of members of his family on Spira's telephone lists. When asked if his life had been destroyed by Spira, George responded, "As far as baseball is concerned, yes."

Yankees fans ate it up. A jury of ten men and two women convicted Spira on eight of ten charges.

Many believed that baseball botched the Steinbrenner scandal, just as it had botched the Rose scandal. *Sports Illustrated* did an investigation on its own and determined that baseball investigators had gone after Steinbrenner (a bad guy) with all their ammunition, but left Dave Winfield (a good guy) alone.

Winfield had a lot of problems and shady dealings that never made headlines because everyone was concentrating on stringing up Steinbrenner. For starters, Winfield's agent, Frohman, was a heavy gambler who would boast about his connections with the Colombo organized crime family. (Frohman died in 1987.) Albert Whitton, Frohman's chauffeur, served several months in prison for bookmaking in 1974.

Howard Spira was more than just a gofer for Winfield. When Spira went public in January 1989 about the $15,000 Winfield had lent him, Winfield told the New York *Daily News*, "Give me a break. I never gave him any money." Spira promptly produced a photocopy of the check. Winfield then admitted he made the loan, but said he couldn't remember what it was for.

But his agent's wife knew what if was for. She told *Sports Illustrated* that Winfield lent the money to Spira because he was "crying,
hysterical on bended-down knees" begging for cash. Mob bookies
were going to kill him if he didn't pay his debts.

And there were serious questions about Winfield's gambling. Two
sources, one of them *Village Voice* writer Allen Barra, said they had
overheard Winfield talking on the phone about his sports gambling
involvement and getting odds on sporting events. Another source
said he was present when bets were placed for Winfield with bookies.
A former secretary at the Winfield Foundation said that Albert Whitton had placed bets on sports events for Frohman and Winfield from
the foundation's office.

In addition to these troubling accusations, the Winfield Foundation *was* guilty of sloppy bookkeeping and worse. Steinbrenner's
lawsuit against Winfield was settled when the outfielder agreed to
pay $230,000 in "delinquent contributions" and reimburse the foun-
dation $30,000 in "inappropriately expended" funds.

To make matters worse for Winfield, he had personal problems.
He was ordered to pay his former common-law wife, Sandra Renfro,
$1.6 million, plus $3,500 a month for child support. And Ruth
Roper, the mother of actress Robin Givens, claimed Winfield had
given her a venereal disease (see chapter 1).

Clearly, Dave Winfield was no choirboy. But baseball's investigators took little interest in his activities, focusing all their attention
on Steinbrenner.

Finally, though Steinbrenner was certainly guilty of lousy judgment
and totally responsible for his actions, the baseball commissioner
could have nipped the scandal in the bud years earlier. Fay Vincent
said the commissioner's office had known about Steinbrenner's association with Howard Spira since 1987. Did it really serve the "best
interests of baseball" to ignore it?

BARBARO GARBEY
Fixed Games—and Got Away with It

For all its sensitivity to gambling and fixes, baseball welcomed a
known game-thrower into its ranks in 1984—Cuban refugee Barbaro Garbey, who played for the Detroit Tigers in 1984–85 and the
Texas Rangers in 1988.

Cuba was introduced to baseball as early as the 1860s, when
students attending schools in America returned with balls and bats.
The island has been a breeding ground for many American stars,
most notably Tony Perez, Minnie Minoso, and Tony Oliva.

Dictators Fulgencio Batista and Fidel Castro (who has been known
to pick up a glove and pitch now and then) were both fans. During
the 1960s, Castro made baseball Cuba's national sport and stopped
the flow of talent leaving the country for America.

Barbaro Garbey was a star for the Havana Industriales and Cuba's
national team in 1976–77. The next year, a scandal rocked the game
when he and seventeen other players and coaches were caught accepting money to throw games. They were suspended for life, and
the American press dubbed the group "The Black Bean Sox."

The following communiqué was issued by Cuba's National Sports
Institute:

> *Names of the players involved have been deleted from the
> record book, since they do not deserve the honor of appearing
> in the history of our nation's baseball. The players' zeal for
> profits, egotism, individualism, mercantile spirit and lack of
> respect for the people are attitudes that cannot be tolerated in
> a society of workers. Sports and athletics as merchandise are
> practices of a capitalist society that have been banished from
> our nation forever.*

Garbey would have been disgraced for life in Cuba, but he happened
to be in the right place at the right time: 1980 was the year of the
"freedom flotilla"—when one hundred twenty-five thousand people
were allowed to leave Cuba and come to the United States. Most
of them were refugees, but Castro took advantage of the evacuation

to get rid of several thousand criminals, mental patients, homosexuals, and others he regarded as undesirables. Dishonest baseball players were included in the group.

Baseball Commissioner Bowie Kuhn was aware that there might be some prospects among the refugees, and asked major-league teams to refrain from signing them. That didn't stop Detroit Tigers scout Orlando Pena from checking out the new talent at Fort Indiantown Gap, a refugee holding camp in Pennsylvania. He spotted Garbey, whom he described as "skinny, sort of starving."

"Get me out of here and feed me well," Garbey said, "and you'll see how good I can hit." The Tigers had had success with ex-cons Gates Brown and Ron LeFlore, and they signed Garbey for $2,500 on June 6, 1980.

The kid was right, he could hit. Garbey moved up the ranks of the minor leagues, batting .364 for Lakeland in the Class A Florida State League, and .286 and .298 for an AA team in Birmingham.

Garbey had left Cuba without his wife and two children, and suffered bouts of depression over it. He tried unsuccessfully to get them out through legal channels. Somebody offered to smuggle the family out for $37,000, but he didn't have the money. Depression and treatment by a psychiatrist didn't stop him from hitting, though. In 1983, he tore up AAA baseball, hitting .321 for Evansville.

The next season, Detroit overlooked the fact that Garbey had attacked a fan with a bat in Evansville, and brought him up to the big leagues. He started off the 1984 season hitting .392 in his first fifty-five at bats (Gates Brown was his hitting coach) and finished at .287. During the American League Championship Series he got three hits in nine chances.

Garbey never liked talking about his days in Cuba, but he did admit that he was paid to fix six games in 1978. He claimed he took money to keep games close, but not to lose them. He refused to say who paid him or how much but freely admitted his motivation—a monthly salary of ninety-five pesos. "How are you going to buy a television in Cuba that costs seven hundred pesos?" he asked.

Sources in Cuba gave *Sports Illustrated* a different version of Garbey's history. The magazine said Garbey didn't just shave runs, he also threw games, and he did it for two years.

Garbey's sister-in-law was tracked down and said, "I don't want to hear anything about him. We don't want to have anything to do with him."

After a mediocre 1985, Detroit traded Garbey to the Oakland A's, who sent him to their Triple A club in Tacoma. The same year, he was stopped by police for speeding. When the cop approached the car, Garbey tried to throw a folded dollar bill out the window. He was arrested for possession of cocaine.

Garbey came back to the majors to play thirty games for the Texas Rangers in 1988, but hit just .194 and was finished with baseball.

Cuba's Other Big-League Problem Child

Pedro Ramos got out of Cuba before Castro took over and pitched for fifteen years in the majors for five teams, compiling a 117–160 record with a 4.08 ERA.

In 1979, he was arrested and charged with possession of cocaine, drug trafficking, and possession of a concealed weapon. Two years later, while he was on probation, police pulled him over for driving while intoxicated. They found a pistol in the car's glove compartment.

Ramos was sentenced to three years in prison. He was paroled after serving half the term and got a job with a Florida detective agency.

SAY IT AIN'T SO, MASAYUKI
Scandals in Japanese Baseball

Japan was stunned on October 8, 1969, when it was revealed that Masayuki Nagayasu, a twenty-seven-year-old pitcher with the Nish-itetsu Lions, had been nabbed throwing games in exchange for money from gamblers.

Nagayasu, a mediocre right-hander with a 17–17 lifetime record, accepted $550 to $1,300 to throw easy pitches to opposing batters. When he tried to persuade teammates to do the same, they went to team officials, and Nagayasu was barred for life. After his banishment, Nagayasu disappeared and was rumored to have been kidnapped.

Like the Black Sox Scandal in America, the Nagayasu incident was just the tip of the iceberg. *Newsweek* reported in 1970 that gambling on baseball was one of the biggest sources of income for Japanese gangsters. Bets totaling $5,500,000 a day were being handled by two hundred gangs.

Except for the superstars, Japanese players are paid poorly and have been susceptible to the temptations offered by shady characters. In 1966, two members of the champion Yomiuri Giants were found guilty of consorting with a baseball betting gang called Uchikoshi-Kai. Around the same time, Shigeo Hasegawa, a slugger for the Nankai Hawks, became deeply indebted to gangsters and told friends he feared for his life. Shortly after, he was found murdered. A committee of the Japanese Parliament opened up a full-scale investigation into baseball corruption in March 1970, and three pitchers were suspended for life.

Scandal touched baseball in Japan as early as 1934, the year Babe Ruth and a group of American All-Stars came over for an exhibition tour against local Japanese teams. The tour was sponsored by Matsutaro Shoriki, publisher of a large Tokyo newspaper. Two days after Ruth went home, twenty-eight-year-old Katsuke Nagasaki walked up to Shoriki at the gate of the Yomiuri Building and stabbed him in the neck with a Japanese sword. He lived, but spent fifty days in the hospital.

Nagasaki was a member of the nationalist group Bushinkai, or "Warlike Gods Society," and had been arrested several times on assault charges. He said that he had attacked Shoriki for patriotic reasons—sponsoring the American tour, the assassin claimed, had caused money to leave Japan in a time of depression. And because the stadium where most of the games had been played had been built as a memorial to the emperor Meijii, Shoriki had "despoiled the sanctuary" for baseball.

"Yes, I knew Mr. Shoriki well and liked him," said Babe Ruth when he heard about the attack. "He was a fine host and full of energy and hustle. He wasn't in the game for money, but because he believed that baseball would be a good thing for Japan. . . . It must have been some crank."

While corrupt athletes and insane assassins can be found in both Japan and America, the differences between the two cultures do show up in baseball. It would be hard to imagine the general manager of an American major-league team committing suicide because his team wasn't winning. But that happened in Tokyo on July 19, 1988.

Shingo Furuya, GM of the Hanshin Tigers, chatted with his wife, Akiko, on the phone that evening. Instead of ending the conversation with his usual "oyasumi" ("have a good night's sleep"), he said simply "sayonara" ("goodbye").

Alarmed, Akiko called a taxi to drive her 300 miles to her husband's hotel in Tokyo. It was too late. The fifty-six-year-old Furuya had walked out onto the stairwell of the hotel and jumped eight floors to his death.

Three years earlier, his team had won the Japanese championship. But in 1988 they were in last place. Their best player, American Randy Bass, had returned home because his son was being treated for a brain tumor. The team's longtime hero, third baseman Masayuki Kakefu, wanted to retire.

In Japan, general managers have little power in team decisions but take most of the heat when a team is losing. Shingo Furuya didn't have the option of quitting his job and trying another career. Like most Japanese, he was employed for life. And like most Japanese, he was extremely loyal to his employer and took full responsibility for his company's fortunes. When the Tigers had a bad season, he decided suicide was his only option.

The Japanese trait of accepting responsibility is revealed more positively by the experience of an American player, Alan Bannister. Before he was drafted by the Philadelphia Phillies in 1973, Bannister led a college All-Star team on an exhibition tour of Japan. He was playing shortstop during one game when a perfect double-play grounder was hit to the right side of the infield. The second baseman flipped the ball to Bannister, who tapped the bag and threw to first. For one reason or another, the Japanese runner neglected to slide and Bannister's throw struck him on the side of the head. He died several days later.

Bannister felt terrible, of course, and considered leaving the tour to avoid offending his Japanese hosts. He was amazed when he returned to his hotel room after the tragedy and found it filled with flowers and gifts. During the rest of the tour, fans swarmed around him wishing him well, and he received a standing ovation at Tokyo Stadium.

Despite their own grief, the Japanese were concerned that the horror of killing a man with a baseball would cause serious damage to Bannister's psyche. At the boy's funeral, even his parents showed concern for Bannister's welfare. Bannister went on to play for several major-league teams from 1974 to 1985, averaging .270.

LESSER-KNOWN GAMBLING SCANDALS

New York Mutuals, 1865

After the Mutuals lost to the Brooklyn Eckfords 28–10, it was revealed that two players, Ed Duffy and William Wansley, had offered money to their shortstop, Thomas Devyr, to throw the game. The National Association banned Duffy and Wansley, but both were later reinstated.

The Mutuals had been founded by the notorious William "Boss" Tweed, who headed the corrupt Tammany Hall political machine in New York.

Louisville Grays, 1877

It was the year after the National League had been founded. The Grays were close to clinching the pennant when they began inexplicably blowing games. They finished in second place, two games behind Boston. Rumors of a fix were smoked out by Charles Chase, president of the team and owner of the *Louisville Courier-Journal*, who began an investigation.

Telegrams received by utility player Al Nichols were found to have the code word "sash" in them, which was interpreted as "sure as shit." Chase questioned his players and got confessions from

Nichols, outfielder George Hall, pitcher Jim Devlin, and shortstop Bill Craver. They admitted throwing games for a New York gambler named McCloud, who paid them as little as $10. The players claimed they had sold out because they had not been paid their salaries.

All were thrown out of baseball for life by William Hulbert, who was in charge in those pre-commissioner days. The Louisville Grays were disbanded before the next season. Afterward, Devlin was seen hanging around National League headquarters dressed in rags and begging to be reinstated.

1903 World Series

In 1924, American League president Ban Johnson made public a secret affidavit which revealed that baseball's first World Series between Boston and Pittsburgh might not have been played on the level.

Before the Series, a gambler named Anderson had approached Red Sox catcher Lou Criger in the lobby of the Monongahela Hotel in Pittsburgh and offered him $12,000 to throw games. Anderson claimed he had conned an oil millionaire to bet $50,000 on Boston, and that he wanted to put money on Pittsburgh.

Boston won the Series five games to three, though Criger made three errors. (Honus Wagner made six errors for Pittsburgh.)

Criger was seriously ill and believed he had weeks to live when he revealed the scandal to Ban Johnson in 1923. He recovered and lived until 1934.

Charles "Red" Dooin, 1908

It wasn't until the Black Sox Scandal became public in 1920 that Dooin, ex-catcher and manager with the Phillies, revealed that his team had been offered a huge bribe to throw the last seven games of the 1908 pennant race. Three pitchers on the Phillies had been approached in a Philadelphia café by gamblers, he said, who laid out $150,000 in cash on the table. To collect the money, the pitchers were asked to lose their games in the upcoming crucial series against the Giants. They refused.

After the first game of the series, Dooin was approached by a man in the clubhouse who showed him $8,000 in cash and said there was $40,000 more if he would sit out the remaining games. Dooin not only refused, but also had his burly first baseman Kitty Bransfield throw the man down a flight of stairs.

In the middle of the series, Dooin said, he was kidnapped, locked in a room, and hit over the head with a blackjack. He escaped and played the rest of the series.

The Phillies won several of the games in that series against the Giants, creating a tie for first place between the Giants and the Cubs. (The last game would be remembered for Giants first baseman Fred Merkle's "bonehead" failure to touch second base.) The Cubs won the one-game playoff for the pennant. The Phillies finished fifteen games back.

Four years later, at the time of the O'Connell/Dolan Scandal (discussed later in this section), Dooin revealed several other gambling scandals that had never been investigated.

"I saved organized baseball four times," he said. "They couldn't handle me and that is probably the reason I am not still in the game. There are too many stool pigeons. They want birds they can handle."

Umpire Bill Klem, 1908

Right before the playoff game noted above, umpire Bill Klem was approached by Giants team physician Joseph Creamer with an offer. "Bill," Creamer said, "you'll be set for life if the Giants win. Tammany Hall has assured me of that."

Klem told him that no amount of money in the world could tempt him, but Creamer persisted—even pressing bills into the umpire's hand as he was about to walk onto the field. In April 1909, Joseph Creamer was barred for life from entering any park in organized baseball. It was never determined who had backed him.

Connie Mack's Sell-Off, 1914

The 1914 Philadelphia Athletics were touted as one of the best teams ever. When they hit .172 and lost four straight to the Boston Braves in the World Series, there were rumors that games had been dumped for the benefit of gamblers.

The rumors only intensified when Philadelphia owner and manager Connie Mack sold off a large part of the team after the season. He got rid of Eddie Collins, Home Run Baker, Jack Barry, Eddie Murphy, and Jack Combs, as well as starting pitchers Chief Bender, Eddie Plank, and Bob Shawkey.

The Athletics came in last the next seven seasons. It would be fifteen years until Mack would have another pennant winner, and he would break up that team too.

Chicago Cubs President William Veeck, 1920

Minutes before the game against the Phillies on August 31, Veeck received this telegram: "DETROIT: COMMISSIONS OF THOUSANDS OF DOLLARS BEING BET ON PHILLIES TO WIN TODAY. RUMORS THAT YOUR GAME IS FIXED. INVESTIGATE."

Veeck and Chicago's manager, Fred Mitchell, decided at the last moment to pitch their ace, Grover Cleveland Alexander, in place of Claude Hendrix. As an added incentive, Alexander was offered a $500 bonus if he won the game. The Cubs lost anyway, 3–0. It was never determined who, if anybody, threw the game but the resulting grand jury investigation would expose the Black Sox Scandal of 1919 and tear the cover off gambling in baseball.

Carl Mays, 1921

A year after he threw the pitch that shattered Ray Chapman's skull and killed him, Mays very likely threw a game in the World Series.

Mays had pitched a five-hit shutout in Game 1. In Game 4, he was working on a shutout into the eighth inning when he gave up four hits and three runs. The Yankees lost the game 4–2.

That night, sportswriter Fred Lieb was contacted by a man who claimed that Mays had been offered "a rather substantial sum in cash" if he lost the game. The man explained that Mays's wife had flashed a signal to him at the start of the eighth inning. She wiped a white handkerchief across her face, indicating that the money had been handed over to her.

The story sounded fantastic, but Lieb took it to Commissioner

Landis, who hired a detective agency to investigate. Mays, who had also lost Game 7, was cleared of any wrongdoing.

However, years later Lieb revealed that both Yankees manager Miller Huggins and team owner Colonel Tillinghast Huston told him that they thought Carl Mays had thrown the 1921 World Series, and possibly the 1922 Series as well. (He lost Game 4, his only appearance.)

Record books show that Mays was rarely used by the Yankees in 1923, even though he was the highest-paid pitcher on the team. He didn't pitch an inning in the World Series that year, and the Yankees asked for waivers on him at the end of the season. Not a single American League team claimed him.

Mays went to the National League, where he had a 20–9 record for Cincinnati. He never got into another World Series, and it was never determined conclusively whether or not he had thrown games.

O'Connell/Dolan Scandal, 1924

Before the September 27 game that clinched the pennant for the New York Giants, Giant outfielder Jimmy O'Connell strolled over to Philadelphia Phillies shortstop Heinie Sand and said, "I'll give you five hundred dollars if you don't bear down too hard." Sand told his manager, Art Fletcher, who went to baseball authorities. O'Connell admitted offering the bribe, and claimed he got the idea from talks with his coach, Cozy Dolan, as well as second baseman Frank Frisch, first baseman George Kelly, and outfielder Ross Youngs. All were to chip in on the pot, said O'Connell.

On the eve of the World Series, twenty-three-year-old O'Connell and Dolan were banished from baseball for life. The others were exonerated. "They were all in on it and they deserted me when they found I was caught," claimed O'Connell.

The Giants won the game 5–1, and the pennant. They lost the World Series to Washington, four games to three.

American League president Ban Johnson refused to attend the World Series and called Landis a "wild-eyed nut" for not disqualifying the Giants entirely. Landis issued the famous reply: "Keep your shirt on." The two would have several more public conflicts until Commissioner Landis drove Johnson out of the game in 1927 (see "The Ty Cobb/Tris Speaker Affair" earlier in this chapter).

Return of the Black Sox, 1927

Seven years after he had been banished for life, Black Soxer Swede Risberg made fresh headlines by claiming that the 1917 White Sox had pooled their money and paid the Detroit Tigers $1,100 to throw four games. The fix was engineered by White Sox manager Clarence Rowland, according to Risberg, and even the incorruptible Ray Schalk and Eddie Collins were involved. Furthermore, Risberg claimed that when Detroit was fighting for third place, the White Sox did them a favor and "sloughed off" in two games against them.

When asked why he was dredging up the scandal a decade later, Risberg said, "I heard that the bosses of baseball said they wanted to clean the game up and I told my piece to help them."

Twenty-nine players were called to respond to Risberg's charge. A pool *had* been collected at the end of the 1917 season, it was freely admitted. But it wasn't a bribe, it was a *gift* to Detroit pitchers for beating Boston three out of four in a series. Collins and Shalk both admitted contributing to the pool, and several Detroit pitchers admitted they had received cash gifts. Eddie Collins said taking up such a collection was a common practice at the time.

The only player who backed up Risberg's version of the events was Chick Gandil, his fellow Black Soxer who had been banned from baseball for life.

On January 12, Commissioner Landis exonerated all parties. "It was an act of impropriety, reprehensible and censurable," he said, "but not an act of criminality."

At the press conference, he also instituted a new rule—banishment for one year for any player who offered a gift to players on another team for any reason.

Rogers Hornsby, 1927–1936

The Hall of Famer wouldn't drink, smoke, or even watch a movie for fear of losing his batting eye, but he was a notorious gambler.

He dodged a number of bullets that could have put him out of the game.

In 1927, Cincinnati bookie Frank L. Moore claimed Hornsby owed him $92,000 on horse race bets. Moore sued, and lost. Hornsby got off by claiming the bets had been made in a different state.

Hornsby was traded from the New York Giants to the Boston Braves that year, and had to issue denials that the trade was a result of his welshing on his gambling losses.

When chastised by Baseball Commissioner Landis, Hornsby said his gambling was no different from investing in the stock market. He knew what he was talking about, having lost $100,000 in the stock-market crash of 1929.

In 1932, a week after Hornsby had been fired as Chicago Cubs manager, Commissioner Landis investigated charges that the team had gambled heavily on horse races under his command. No disciplinary action was taken.

Hornsby was fired again in 1937 by the St. Louis Browns. The team's management objected to his betting on horse races.

Joe DiMaggio, 1940

Joltin' Joe, his salary a flimsy $32,000 after he hit .381, was having one of his celebrated salary wars with the Yankees. He consulted several close friends about his negotiations, one of whom was Joe Gould, a fight manager and gambler who liked to bet on baseball games.

Baseball Commissioner Landis, suspicious to the point of paranoia about gambling, announced that he intended to "inquire further" into the relationship between DiMaggio and Gould. DiMaggio assured the commissioner that Gould did not get a cut of his salary, and DiMaggio received no punishment for consorting with a gambler.

Landis's main concern seemed to be making sure that ballplayers would not begin using agents to help them in their salary negotiations.

"The big league bosses are afraid that the ball players will smarten up enough to hire fast-talking tough bargaining agents to speak for them," wrote sportswriter Bob Considine at the time. "And if that ever comes to pass the ball clubs would have to pay all the blokes what they're actually worth."

Phillies Owner Banished for Life, 1943

Less than a year earlier, thirty-four-year-old New York lumberman William D. Cox had taken over the Phillies. Now he was out of baseball for life, after it was discovered he had made fifteen or twenty bets ranging from $25 to $100 per game on Philadelphia to win.*

Cox first denied making any bets, then said he didn't know it was against the rules to bet on his own team. Finally he claimed he had only made small, sentimental wagers involving cigars, hats, and dinners.

Either way, he used poor judgment betting on the Phillies—they were one of the worst teams in baseball, finishing sixty-two and a half games out of first place in 1942 and forty-one games behind in 1943.

The Evangeline Scandal, 1946

The minor leagues have seen several gambling scandals, the most famous one occuring when four players and one manager in the Class D Evangeline League in Louisiana were banished from baseball for life. Those banned were manager Paul Fugit of Houma and his players Alvin Kaiser, Leonard Pecou, and Bill Thomas. Also banned was Don Vetorel of the Abbeville team.

They were accused not only of fixing games, but also of taking money that was handed into the dugout during games, setting back a bookie's clock by thirty minutes so that they could place sure-thing bets on horse races, and even allowing bookies to try on their uniforms. The *New York Times* described the team as "a combination baseball club and bookie hangout where the players did everything except stop in the middle of a double play to rush off and play the daily double."

---

* Cox was the second Phillies owner to be thrown out of baseball for life. In 1912, Horace Fogel was forced out after he alleged that collusion between National League umpires and John McGraw had fixed the pennant race in favor of the New York Giants.

The following year, Marion Allen McElreath of Muskogee was
banned for life for throwing games. The year after that, the same
fate befell Bernard DeForge, pitcher/manager for Reidsville of the
Carolina League, and Ed Weingarten, an official of the Florence club
of the Tri-State League.

After that, the minors remained free of scandal until 1982, when
catcher Angel Rodrigues with Alexandria in the Class A Carolina
League was suspended for a year. Rodrigues was accused of tipping
off rival Latin American batters, in Spanish, to the locations and
types of pitches.

Charley Finley, 1969

Back in 1941, Commissioner Landis ordered Boston Braves owner
Charles Adams to divest himself of either his baseball stock or his
racing stable. Adams sold the stable.

So Bowie Kuhn had a precedent to follow when Oakland Athletics
owner Charley Finley purchased 30,000 shares of Parvin-Dohrmann,
a company that owned the Stardust, Aladdin, and Fremont Hotels
in Las Vegas. Finley also held stock in the Del Webb Corporation,
which owned the Sahara and The Mint in Las Vegas.

Kuhn presented an ultimatum to Finley—baseball or gambling.
Finley sold his gambling stock.

Dizzy Dean, 1970

In 1948, the year after he threw his last pitch, Dizzy began taking
heat for his gambling. "I've bet on golf and horses and cards but
never on a ball game," he said when complaints reached Baseball
Commissioner Happy Chandler. "I have called bookmakers to ask
for odds on ball games. I have done that for friends in Texas. But
I never bet on a ball game."

In 1970, Dizzy was searched in his Las Vegas hotel room and
named as a "co-conspirator" in a federal indictment that sent ten
other men to jail for illegal gambling. Being a co-conspirator meant
the grand jury believed he was involved, but not sufficiently to be
indicted. Dean was "very cooperative with the Government," said

attorney James Brickley. As a result of the information he provided, three men were arrested in Biloxi, Mississippi.

Dean died four years later, in Reno.

Johnny Bench/Wayne Simpson, 1972

Bob Robertson, a first baseman for the Pittsburgh Pirates, couldn't buy a hit that season (his batting average was .193 for the year), so somebody tried to buy one for him. Cincinnati Reds pitcher Wayne Simpson received a call at his hotel room from someone named "Louie" who offered $2,000 if Simpson would "throw a fat pitch" to Robertson in the sixth inning of the July 22 game between the Astros and the Reds. Shortly after, Cincinnati catcher Johnny Bench got a call from the same man, who said, "Remind Simpson what I told him."

Simpson immediately informed his manager, Sparky Anderson. An investigation was made, but "Louie" was never found or heard from again.

"This whole thing shows there's nothing cleaner than baseball," said Sparky Anderson.

Interestingly, Robertson came up in the sixth inning of the game the next day and slammed a drive off the left-field wall. He was thrown out at second—by Pete Rose.

Len Dykstra, 1991

The Phillies center fielder was called in to testify at the trial of Herbert Kelso, a Mississippi man charged with running an illegal casino, conspiracy, money laundering, and perjury. Dykstra admitted playing high-stakes poker games at Kelso's house and writing checks of $21,000 and $29,000 to him. All together, Dykstra lost $78,000 and testified under oath that he had not paid back all his losses.

Kelso was acquitted.

"I learned my lesson," Dykstra said when he was put on probation for a year. Two months later, he nearly killed himself and teammate Darren Daulton when he got drunk and wrapped his Mercedes around a tree.

SIX

MENTAL PROBLEMS

HIS CAREER THREATENED BY DIZZYING ATTACKS OF VERTIGO, A BALLPLAYER STRUGGLES TO THE FIELD OF DREAMS

*"My heart was beating a
frantic tattoo on my ribs and
my head was splitting and my
eyes were smarting. My muscles
ached and my mouth was dry
and my throat burned and my
whole body was being pulled
every which way by a
thousand frenetic nerve ends
restlessly straining and
tugging and tumbling all over
each other."*

—Jimmy Piersall

While baseball deeply appreciates the fact that attitude, momentum, strategy, and psychological warfare help teams win, it has been painfully slow to recognize the effects psychological problems have on teams—and men. Only in recent years have psychologists and psychiatrists been employed to keep players in shape mentally.

Many players and managers remain suspicious of these characters with Ph.D.'s hanging around the locker room. Pitchers who will agree to any experimental surgery or drug to heal a sore arm will recoil with horror at the suggestion that they get counseling to heal a troubled mind. The stigma associated with going to a shrink is still strong in baseball.

———

In the old days, players didn't have psychological problems. They were just "wackos." There were no counseling programs, support groups, or telephone hotlines. Many turn-of-the-century ballplayers either killed themselves or went insane, most notably Pete Browning, who averaged .341 over thirteen years and died in a Louisville, Kentucky, insane asylum in 1905.

The first baseball official to go crazy was Charles H. Morton, president of the Ohio and Pennsylvania Baseball League. A headline in the March 17, 1909, *New York Times* read: "MORTON FOUND, DEMENTED."

Morton had disappeared just before the annual league meeting in Cleveland two months earlier. He was found wandering aimlessly about the streets of Chicago. Scraps of paper in his pockets indicated he had been in Texas and Mexico, but it was impossible to communicate with him.

"He mutters incoherently about Corpus Christi," the *Times* article reported.

Sports, and especially baseball, use hard facts and statistics to sum up a man's life. A pitch is a strike or a ball. A runner is safe or out. A guy wins twenty games or he doesn't. Psychology, which is forced to use interpretation and theory, has it much tougher.

Was Pete Reiser crazy? At twenty-two, the Dodgers outfielder was the youngest batting champ in National League history (.343 in 1941) and led the league in doubles, triples, and runs. But he was so reckless that he had to be carried off the field on a stretcher eleven times during his career. Several of those times he was in a coma, and once they gave him last rites.

Sometimes it's a thin line between giving it your all and having a subliminal death wish. Reiser might have been the best baseball player who ever lived if he hadn't smashed his body to pieces chasing fly balls. After 1942, he was plagued by dizzy spells and headaches for the rest of his career.

Was Joe "Super Joe" Charboneau crazy? It's hard to tell truth from legend, but the American League Rookie of the Year for 1980 was said to have fixed his broken nose with a vise grip, given himself a root canal with a razor and a pair of pliers, put three stitches in his arm with fishing line after being cut on barbed wire, and sliced a tattoo off his shoulder with a razor. He also ate a shot glass and was able to open a beer bottle with his eye socket.

At some point "colorful" becomes "eccentric," which becomes mentally unbalanced. Who knows where Charboneau fit on that continuum? It's easier to place him on the baseball continuum—after hitting .289 with twenty-three home runs and eighty-seven RBIs as a rookie sensation, he stopped hitting and was back in the minors the next season. Charboneau was last seen tending bar in Phoenix, where he could put his *real* talent to work—drinking beer through his nose with a straw. (He also had a bit part in the movie *The Natural*.)

Mental problems have even influenced the World Series. Pittsburgh Pirate left-hander Ed Doheny went 16–4 in 1902 and 16–8 the following year. Just before the first World Series he had a violent nervous breakdown and nearly killed the male nurse taking care of him.

"Doheny attacked and felled him with a poker and started to smash things right and left," wrote *Sporting Life* magazine. "His wife hurried to the neighbors for assistance, but Doheny defied them and threatened to kill the first man who attempted to take him. For more than an hour the madman held the crowd at bay."

The Pirates were forced to start Deacon Phillippe for five games of the Series and lost to Boston five games to three.

Doheny was taken to a mental hospital by force and never played another game.

JIMMY PIERSALL
"The best thing that ever happened to me was going nuts!"

Baseball's most publicized dive off the deep end took place in 1952, when Boston Red Sox outfielder Jimmy Piersall suffered a full-blown breakdown and was confined to a mental institution. His story became a book, *Fear Strikes Out*, which was made into a 1957 movie staring Anthony Perkins.

Psychologists argue about whether a child's heredity or environment is the cause of personality problems. Jimmy Piersall had both possibilities covered.

When he was in second grade, he came home from school one day to find his mother gone. She had been taken to Norwich State Hospital, a mental institution, after intentionally walking into traffic. She was in and out of Norwich for much of her son's youth. Whenever she came home, Jimmy would be afraid to go to school because he thought she might not be there when he got back.

His father, a house painter, was a terrifying man. "His sharp eyes would bore through me," Piersall recalled, "his face would redden and he would bellow at me in a voice that made the windows rattle." Obsessive in his desire to make Jimmy a ballplayer, the father once chastised the boy for saying how much fun it was to catch a ball.

"I don't want you thinking about fun," his father said during one of his baseball drill sessions. "When you grow up, I want you to become a slugger like Jimmie Foxx."

Piersall, understandably, developed into a nervous, constantly worried person. He suffered from headaches so severe that he couldn't get out of bed or sit through a movie.

But he could sit through a ballgame. His father's lessons paid off, and at seventeen Piersall received offers from the Yankees, Tigers, Dodgers, Braves, and Red Sox. He signed with Boston. They brought him up the last week of the 1950 season, and the twenty-year-old got a hit in his first major-league at-bat.

The Red Sox were grooming Piersall to become their center fielder after Dom DiMaggio retired, and they sent him back to the minors in 1951 to get more experience. He married, fathered the first of many children, and bought a house. But trouble was brewing. Jimmy worried incessantly, mostly about money. His father had recently suffered a heart attack, and Jimmy had taken on the responsibility of supporting the whole family.

Just before he was to report for spring training in 1952, he read in *The Sporting News* that the Red Sox were thinking of converting him into a shortstop. In his mind, he decided that meant the team really intended to get rid of him. Nothing could persuade him differently. He told his wife he wasn't going to report for camp in

Sarasota, Florida. She talked him into going, but he refused to bring his baseball glove along. He reasoned that without a glove, he would be unable to work out. He was losing touch with reality.

On January 15, 1952, he walked nervously into the lobby of the Sarasota-Terrace Hotel. For reasons that even he didn't know, he was terrified of being recognized by anyone. He paid the limousine driver, picked up his suitcase, and began walking across the lobby.

"My heart was beating a frantic tattoo on my ribs and my head was splitting and my eyes were smarting," he wrote in *Fear Strikes Out*. "My muscles ached and my mouth was dry and my throat burned and my whole body was being pulled every which way by a thousand frenetic nerve ends restlessly straining and tugging and tumbling all over each other."

The next thing he was aware of, he was strapped to a bed in the "violent room" at Westborough State Hospital in Massachusetts. For the first time since he was fifteen years old, he didn't have a headache. An attendant leaned over him and said, "Time to eat."

It was *August*. Incredibly, Piersall had completely blanked out eight months of his life. He had no recollection that he had played fifty-six games for the Red Sox, batted .267, stolen three bases, and hit eight doubles and one home run.

Unbeknownst to everyone, Piersall had suffered a breakdown at Sarasota that had been completely internal. To the outside world, he had acted quite normally. He hadn't passed out in the hotel lobby that day. He had checked in, gone through spring training and played well. When he woke up in Westborough, he could only remember walking into the hotel lobby in Sarasota. And he had no memory of his *external* breakdown, which occurred in July.

After coming out of this eight-month trance, Jimmy sat down and read the scrapbook of newspaper clippings his father had been collecting for him. He was amazed and embarrassed by some of the things he had done.

In May, he had been involved in two fistfights in one day—one with Billy Martin* of the Yankees, the other with his own teammate

---

* Fighting with Billy Martin was by no means an indication of insanity (see chapter 8).

Maurice McDermott. He had spanked the four-year-old son of Red Sox shortstop Vern Stephens. He had told the press his wife had walked out on him, though she hadn't. When informed that he would not be playing one night, Piersall had broken down and cried in the dugout.

He had started clowning for the fans. He did a hula dance in the outfield one day, provoking the entire crowd to make ukulele sounds. He had swung back and forth like a monkey while hanging by one hand from the dugout roof. On June 12, he made a base hit and while on first base had put on a vaudeville act imitating pitcher Satchel Paige by flapping his arms and making pig noises. (Paige was so rattled that he gave up six runs in the inning.)

The Red Sox sent Piersall to Birmingham in the Southern Association on June 28, hoping the change in scenery might calm him down somewhat. But he only got worse. He would come up to the plate without a bat and imitate the pitcher. On July 17, after being called out on a third strike, Piersall pulled a water pistol out of his pocket and shot it at home plate. He was suspended four times in twenty days and given pills to help him relax.

At the end of July, *Boston Herald* columnist Bill Cunningham happened to share a plane ride with Piersall and the two spoke at length. Afterward, Cunningham wrote, "I'm no authority on such matters, but my guess is he's heading straight for a nervous breakdown."

Sometimes it's a thin line between creative pranksmanship and mental disturbance. Eventually, the Red Sox management realized that Piersall wasn't a clown; he was sick. They talked him into "going off somewhere for a rest." He was sent to a private sanitarium, where he had another breakdown when attendants tried to give him shots against his will.* Piersall became violent and had to be transferred to another facility—Danvers State Hospital, where he received electroconvulsive shock treatment.

A New Orleans newspaper reported: "Jimmy Piersall, former Barons outfielder, who practically tore the ball park apart with his mad

---

* In the movie version, Piersall has his nervous breakdown after hitting a home run. He crosses home plate and screams, "I showed them!"

antics the last time he was here, will never play baseball again. Now a hopeless mental case, he will spend the rest of his life in an institution."

Finally he was sent to Westborough State Hospital, where he snapped out of it and returned to reality. Altogther he spent six weeks in mental institutions.

Piersall was released from Westborough on September 9, 1952, and was completely healthy by the time baseball season rolled around. Some fans called him "Nutsy" or "Wacko" or blew ambulance sirens when he appeared on the field. One fan in Cleveland took to shouting, "Hey screwball, look out for the man in the white suit!"

Piersall should probably be named Comeback Player of the Century. He went on to play for seventeen years in the big leagues, averaging .272 and hitting a hefty .322 in 1961. He became known for making "impossible" circus catches in the outfield. Casey Stengel chose him to represent the American League in the 1954 All-Star game.

In 1960, he started performing strange antics again. It looked like he was headed for another breakdown, but he consulted a psychiatrist and came out of it. After that, his only aberrant behavior was joyously running the bases backward to celebrate his 100th major-league home run.

After his playing days, Piersall held a number of jobs in baseball and served as play-by-play announcer for the Chicago White Sox until 1986. Despite heart problems, he was still participating in old-timers' games in 1990. Years after his mental problems were over, fans would still come up to him and ask him if he was crazy.

"Probably the best thing that ever happened to me was going nuts," he said. "Whoever heard of Jimmy Piersall until that happened?"

RUBE WADDELL
Wine, Women, and Fire Engines

George Edward "Rube" Waddell was a colorful eccentric whose antics provided countless stories that were a lot funnier before baseball historians pointed out that he was probably mentally retarded. He played from 1897 to 1910 and was elected to the Hall of Fame in 1946.

While Rube was on the mound, opposing managers would distract him by putting pets or children's toys—a rubber snake, a jack-in-the-box—outside the dugout and then call out for Rube to look at them.

"Rube would look over at the jack-in-the-box popping up and down and kind of grin, real slow-like," Detroit Tigers outfielder Sam Crawford told baseball historian Lawrence Ritter. "We'd do everything to get him in a good mood."

Pittsburgh manager Fred Clarke would throw Waddell off his game by telling Rube he would take him hunting after the season and perhaps give him a bird dog. Rube would start thinking about the dog and forget how to pitch.

In his *Historical Baseball Abstract*, Bill James wrote that Waddell would have been as great as Walter Johnson "if only he had had the sense God gave a rabbit." When he got serious, Rube was unhittable. He led the American League in strikeouts six years in a row, and he whiffed 349 batters in 1904. While Satchel Paige usually gets credit for sending his defense off the field and striking out the side, Waddell was actually the first to do it. On the field, he had a blazing fastball, the best curve of his era, and pinpoint control. Off the field, he had no control whatsoever.

"I roomed with that crazy character for a while," said Tommy Leach. "If they thought he was nutty later, they should have seen him then."

Waddell was most famous for having an inexplicable attraction to fire engines. When he heard fire bells in the middle of a game, he would suddenly dash off the field and chase them.

"He always wore a red undershirt," revealed Connie Mack, who managed Rube for six years with the Philadelphia Athletics, "so that when the fire bell rang he could pull off his coat, thus exposing his crimson credentials, and gallop off to the blaze, where he would try to direct operations by ringing commands, whether anybody obeyed them or not."

Rube was notorious for disappearing for days at a time, usually to go fishing. Posters would be pasted up all over town announcing that the great Waddell was to pitch on a certain date, and inevitably he wouldn't show up for the game. Several of his managers hired detectives to track him down.

They were likely to find him at a favorite fishing hole, working behind the bar in a saloon, or playing ball with a bunch of kids in a vacant lot. Connie Mack said Rube once disappeared for days, then finally showed up wearing a drum major's uniform and "a look of ineffable bliss on his face."

Frequently, a teammate was assigned to babysit Rube and make sure he got to the ballpark on days he was to pitch. His salary had to be doled out a few dollars at a time. If he had too much money in his pocket, he would be gone for weeks.

Rube had a flair for the dramatic. Sometimes he would make his entrance minutes before game time, jump out of the stands, march across the field, and put his uniform on as he made his way to the pitcher's mound.

Baseball folklore is filled with irresistible Waddell anecdotes. In his day, teams would save money by putting two ballplayers in a single hotel-room bed. One year, Waddell's roommate Ossie Schreck insisted on a clause in his contract that prohibited Rube from eating animal crackers in bed.

In New York City once, Rube was run over by a car. The driver must have thought he had committed manslaughter, because he stepped on the gas to leave the scene of the crime. But Waddell leaped up off the pavement, chased the car, and jumped on the running board.

"I'm the man you just ran over," he shouted to the astonished driver. "You hand me fifteen bucks, or I'll punch you in the eye. You ain't going to ruin my clothes and get away with it."

He had an interesting off-season job—he was a professional alligator wrestler.

His childlike innocence and pitching skill made him hugely popular, and he was asked to appear in a stage play called *The Stain of Guilt*. One reviewer wrote of his performance, "He is 'let out' for only two minutes in each scene—and the ensuing damage is awesome to behold."

Rube had to give up his acting career when his wife attempted to attach his wages for nonsupport. He was also arrested for throwing an iron at his father-in-law, and for committing bigamy. He did jail time for several of these offenses.

"He dived into the waters of matrimony with great abandon and led an exciting home life," was how Connie Mack put it in a 1936 *Saturday Evening Post* article.

It's doubtful that a man like Waddell could succeed in baseball today, when players who so much as wear their hair differently are branded "flakes."

In Waddell's day, there was much more tolerance for offbeat behavior. When he broke in with Louisville in 1899, there were no psychologists around to diagnose him. Nobody knew about IQ, neuroses, or learning disabilities. Freud was just starting out. Reporters in that era described Waddell as "a big kid," or sometimes a "bumpkin," "hayseed," or "buffoon."

Connie Mack probably understood the man better than anyone else. "The Rube was just naturally dizzy because he was born that way," said Mack. "It was his nature, and he couldn't help it."

In his first season with Mack, Waddell pitched the first game of an August doubleheader, going all the way to win a seventeen-inning marathon against Chicago. He also hit a game-winning triple. When he struck out the final batter, he turned cartwheels from the mound to the dugout.

Mack was so impressed by this exuberant performance that he told Rube he could go on a three-day fishing vacation if he pitched the second game of the doubleheader also. Waddell went out and threw a one-hit shutout. The story made headlines all over the country.

But even Connie Mack gave up on Rube after 1907. Heavy drinking made his already erratic behavior even worse. He eventually drank himself out of the game and died in 1914 in a San Antonio sanitarium. He was just thirty-seven. In some ways, it's almost a good thing that he never had to grow up and face adulthood without a game to play every few days.

"Waddell's inability to keep in condition discouraged most other managers and was indirectly responsible for his contracting tuberculosis, which caused his death," read his obituary in the *New York*

Times. "There was no better pitcher then he when he was in form, but he, as well as managers and club owners, was aware of his own inability to resist temptation."

Connie Mack summed up Rube's life better: "He had four passions and four only: He loved to fish. He loved the stuff that the vintners sell. He loved fires. And he loved to pitch ballgames. In about that order."

The Waddell Gambling Scandal

Rube had his best season in 1905, and just before the World Series, a group of New York gamblers offered him $17,000 not to play. He got out of the Series by claiming he had hurt his pitching arm stumbling over a suitcase on a train. He collected just $500 of the $17,000 and was double-crossed out of the rest.

Christy Mathewson (31–8 that year) pitched three shutouts to lead the New York Giants to victory over the Philadelphia Athletics in that year's World Series. It might have been a dream pitchers' duel if Waddell (26–11, 1.48 ERA) had taken the field. The scandal was never seriously investigated.

RUBE FOSTER
The Father of Black Baseball

During a 1902 exhibition game in New York, a twenty-three-year-old black man named Andrew Foster pitched against the great Rube Waddell and the Philadelphia Athletics. Waddell had gone 24–7 that year with a 2.04 ERA and was becoming a pitching legend. But Foster beat Waddell 5–2 that day, and Andrew's teammates gave him the nickname "Rube." He kept it for the rest of his life.

Rube Foster went from being a pitcher to manager to owner to founder of the first organized black baseball league. Then, after building a reputation as one of the greatest minds in black or white baseball, he lost his mind completely and ended up in a mental institution at the age of forty-seven.

————

The son of a minister, Foster came from Texas in 1902 to pitch for the Chicago Union Giants. He didn't have great natural talent, but he was six feet, four inches tall, weighed 200 pounds, and studied the game carefully. In short order, he made himself virtually unbeatable.

In 1905, he won fifty-one games in fifty-five starts. In 1910, he led the Leland Giants to an astonishing 126–6 season. Hall of Famer Honus Wagner called him "the smartest pitcher I have ever seen in all my years of baseball."

In those days, black teams would play doubleheaders and come home with $150 to be divided up among all the players. Foster persuaded Leland owner Frank Leland to let him handle the bookings and negotiations for the team. He was a savvy businessman, and immediately the take was bumped up to $500 a day. Soon Foster was managing the team as well.

After the 1910 season, Foster formed a partnership with white saloon owner John Schorling, who was the son-in-law of White Sox owner Charles Comiskey. Schorling believed money was to be made from black baseball, and leased the old White Sox ballpark when the Sox moved to Comiskey Park. He and Foster started the Chicago American Giants.

With Schorling's money, Foster's leadership, and most of the best black players around, the Giants became the leading black team of the decade. Often they would draw more fans on a Sunday afternoon than the Chicago Cubs or White Sox.

Foster retired as a player in 1915 to manage full-time. He was a master of baseball strategy, emphasizing the bunt, steal, and hit and run play. His ever-present pipe was used to relay signs, with a wave or puff of smoke. Foster's baseball acumen was so respected that New York Giants manager John McGraw briefly hired him as a pitching coach. It has been said he taught a trick or two to Christy Mathewson.

Black baseball in that era was chaos. The teams functioned mainly as loosely organized independent barnstormers. White booking agents got rich off of them, and players would jump from one team to another whenever a better offer came along. In 1920, Foster talked the black owners into cooperating, and founded the National Association of Professional Baseball Clubs—better known as the Negro National League.

Domineering, stern, and a shrewd businessman, Foster dominated his new league, to the extent that he would determine pitching rotations. He made it a point that star pitchers would always start on Sundays, when the largest crowd might come out for a game.

The NNL was sucessful, drawing 400,000 fans in 1923. More importantly, it made black baseball respectable and showed that blacks were ready to play on a major-league level even if whites weren't ready to admit them.

Foster laid down the foundation that would eventually enable Jackie Robinson and other black players to join the major leagues. He realized that breakthrough would be years down the road, however. His immediate goal was to have a *real* World Series, between the best black team in baseball and the best white team.

It was not to be. Baseball's first commissioner, Judge Kenesaw Landis, frowned on major-league teams even playing exhibition games against black teams. These had been common, and were frequently won by the black teams. When Foster went to the commissioner and asked why he was against such contests, Landis is said to have told him, "Mr. Foster, when you beat our teams, it gives us a black eye."

Foster worked tirelessly, usually fifteen hours a day, directing both the Giants and the league. In 1926, it got to him and he started behaving erratically. He was seen chasing imaginary fly balls outside his home in Chicago. He would walk down the street and suddenly break into a run for no reason. He locked himself in a bathroom and one of his players had to climb the roof and open a window to get him out. Several times he nearly died, once by falling asleep in a hotel room while a heating-gas jet was open. On another occasion, he hit a pedestrian while backing his car out of a garage. Sometimes he didn't recognize his own family. His wife said he had a delusion that he was invited to pitch in the World Series.

When she couldn't take it anymore, she had him committed to the state mental institution in Kankakee, Illinois. He spent the last four years of his life there, while the Negro National League collapsed.

Rube Foster died on December 9, 1930. He was the most famous black man in Chicago by that time, and three thousand mourners attended his funeral. A 200-pound baseball made of white chrysanthemums and red roses (for the seams) graced the proceedings.

He was named to the Baseball Hall of Fame in 1981.

MENTAL BLOCKS
The Search for a Cure for "Steve Sax Disease"

Wasn't it Yogi Berra who said, "Ninety percent of this game is half mental"?

In the ninth inning of the Dodgers' home opener in 1983, second baseman Steve Sax took a cutoff throw from right field and whipped it home. The ball bounded away and the runner scored.

Sax, the previous season's Rookie of the Year, started thinking about his throwing. He became fixated on it. Quickly he lost his timing altogether. For the rest of the season he inexplicably could not make the toss from second to first base—a throw any Little Leaguer can complete effortlessly. Sax could make spectacular plays, but not easy ones. He committed thirty errors that year and humiliated himself in front of millions with an errant toss in the All-Star game.

Mental blocks—or, as they have come to be called, "Steve Sax Disease"—have plagued a surprising number of players. During recent years, the problem has become an epidemic.

In almost all cases, the player forgets how to do what is perhaps the simplest task in the world—throwing a ball. The problem sounds almost laughable, but mental blocks have caused players of major-league caliber to give up careers in baseball.

Catchers and pitchers seem particularly susceptible. New York Mets backstop Mackey Sasser lost his starting job in 1991 because he had difficulty returning the ball to the pitcher. Sasser would pump the ball into his glove as many as six times, rock back on his heels and almost fall against the umpire, then launch a moon ball in the general direction of the mound.

Mets pitchers complained that he was upsetting their rhythm, and several runners timed the pumps in order to steal bases on Sasser.

On one occasion, the Expos bench taunted him by counting the pumps out loud and breaking into applause when he finally got the ball to the mound. That didn't help Sasser, who, as a recovering alcoholic, had enough problems.

He tried hypnosis, psychiatry, and throwing a *football* to the mound. In 1991, the Mets played him at third base and right field. They had good reason to keep Sasser in the lineup—he was the only catcher in the majors to hit over .300 in 1990.

Sasser described his experience as being in a cage in his own body. "I'd be ready to throw the ball back to the pitcher," he said, "and I'd see everything else, the outfield, the crowd, all swimming in front of my eyes."

An inability to toss the ball back to the pitcher may seem like an obscure problem, but it has also troubled catchers Johnny Edwards, Clint Courtney, Mike Ivie, Fran Healy, Dave Engle, Ray Fosse, Phil Lombardi, and Jim Hegan.

Healy used to hide the problem by going out to the mound for conferences after almost every pitch and putting the ball in the pitcher's hand. Lombardi got around it another way—he gave up baseball and now sells real estate in California.

Dale Murphy was a catcher at the beginning of his career and developed a mental block about throwing to second base. He made one throw that went all the way to the center-field wall on one hop. Twice he hit his pitcher in the back.

Murphy's solution was to become an outfielder. He went on to prove his defensive ability by winning five Gold Gloves and the National League MVP award in 1982.

In the late 1980s, Texas Rangers catcher Mike Stanley became obsessed with his percentage of throwing out base stealers—the main statistic catchers are judged by. It made him terrified of throwing the ball at all. Psychological counseling helped.

With pitchers, mental blocks are sometimes called "Steve Blass Disease." The Pittsburgh Pirate right-hander had a reputation for pinpoint control, and he threw a sparkling 19–8 season in 1972. The following year, Blass mysteriously couldn't get the ball over the plate. It never happened during practice, suggesting that he became fearful—perhaps subconsciously—of being hit by a line drive or of killing a batter with a fastball.

"You have no idea how frustrating it is," he said. "You're helpless. Totally afraid and helpless."

Blass tried Transcendental Meditation, psychotherapy, hypnosis, visualization, and even pitching from second base in practice. After his great season, he would win three more games and be out of baseball in two years.

Kevin Saucier was also driven out of baseball by his mental block. "Hot Sauce," as he was called, had a 1.65 ERA with the Tigers in 1981. The next season he developed such a fear of hitting batters that he dreaded going to the ballpark.

"I was afraid I was going to kill somebody," he said. He retired at age twenty-six to open a pizza parlor in Pensacola, Florida.

Alan Sothoron, who pitched for St. Louis from 1914 to 1926, had no trouble getting the ball over the plate—but he was incapable of throwing it to first to hold runners on base. He resorted to tossing it underhand. He was lucky he didn't have Rusty Staub or John Mayberry as first basemen. They both had a mental block about returning the ball to the pitcher after pick-off attempts.

After signing Ed Whitson to a $4.5-million contract in 1985, the Yankees discovered he had a mental block about pitching in Yankee Stadium. He just couldn't do it. They traded him back to San Diego, and he was effective again.

It was Wrigley Field that tormented Dodgers pitcher Jerry Reuss. Los Angeles hypnotist Arthur Ellen helped him get past the problem. Ellen also cured Maury Wills of the mysterious leg problems he developed after stealing a record 104 bases in 1962.

"People will say the pain was all in my mind," Wills said, "but that's the worst place to have it."

Darnell Coles made a few errors at third base for Detroit at the beginning of the 1987 season, became fixated on them, and had to switch to the outfield. "It got to the point where I wanted to cry," he said. "I really didn't want the ball hit to me. I wanted to die. Just crawl in a hole."

Various theories have been offered to explain mental blocks. Some psychiatrists propose that deep-seated emotional problems or childhood traumas can bring on a breakdown in motor function. But mental blocks rarely occur during practice, leading many experts to blame them on simple nervousness. Almost all athletes have experienced the fear that they'll wake up one morning and their skills will be gone.

Most psychologists agree that problems develop when an athlete thinks too much about what he's doing instead of just doing it naturally. It would be as if a musician started thinking about where his or her fingers were supposed to go.

"It's stage fright," Dr. Allan Lans, the New York Mets team psychiatrist, told the *New York Times*. "When you have stage fright, what are you afraid of? Embarrassing yourself. And when you get nervous, what do you do? You embarrass yourself. It's a cycle."

The most common advice players suffering from mental blocks receive is the toughest to follow—*just don't think about it.*

"It's like if somebody comes up to you and says, 'Don't think about an elephant for the next five seconds,' " laments Steve Sax.

Sax was so frustrated by Steve Sax Disease that he tried working out with a sock over his eyes and throwing to first base blindly. He finally cured himself in 1985 by visualizing himself making perfect throws. Unfortunately, that approach doesn't work for everybody.

MORE MENTAL CASES

Johnny Evers, 1911

A series of misfortunes and a natural tendency to be wound a bit too tight prompted Evers to suffer a nervous breakdown at the height of his career. Late in 1910, the middleman in Chicago's "Tinkers-to-Evers-to-Chance" infield was behind the wheel in an automobile accident that killed his best friend. A few weeks later Evers learned that a business partner had gambled away Evers's entire life savings, which he had invested in two shoe stores.

After suffering a nervous breakdown, Evers came back to have his best season in 1912, hitting .341. The next few years would see him survive pneumonia and the death of his daughter from a childhood disease. He lived just long enough to see his induction into the Baseball Hall of Fame in 1946.

Fred Perrine, 1913

"UMPIRE PERRINE IN INSANE WARD" headlined a *New York Times* article on September 13. With a dateline of Oakland, California, the full text read, "Bull Perrine, former American League umpire, was held at the receiving hospital here to-day on an affidavit of insanity sworn by his sister, Miss Margaret Perrine. His breakdown is attributed to a sunstroke suffered during a game in Cleveland in 1911."

A week later, the paper reported that Perrine had been committed to the Napa Asylum for the Insane.

Mickey Cochrane, 1936

One of the greatest catchers ever, Cochrane was also a good manager, bringing Detroit pennants in 1934 and 1935. The pressure of playing and managing must have been too much, for the next year he had a nervous breakdown.

The year after that, Yankees pitcher Irving "Bump" Hadley let loose a wild pitch that fractured Cochrane's skull in three places. Cochrane was unconscious and close to death for over a week. He recovered, but he never played again.

After one more season he gave up managing too. He was elected to the Hall of Fame in 1947.

Ernest "Babe" Phelps, 1940

Brooklyn manager Leo Durocher said his catcher was tired all the time because he stayed up all night checking his heartbeat. "It was Babe's theory that the body could continue to function if your heart missed a beat, or even two or three," Leo said, "but that if it missed four beats in a row you were dead."

Phelps was also the first man to be driven from the game because of fear of flying. In 1940, Brooklyn became the first team to travel by commercial airline. Phelps, who was nicknamed "Blimp" because of his shape, followed the team by train (this expanded his nickname to "The Grounded Blimp").

Phelps quit baseball in 1942, despite a .310 lifetime average. He hit .367 in 1936—the highest average ever for a catcher.

Years later Boston outfielder Jackie Jensen, who led the American League in RBIs in 1955, 1958, and 1959, left the game for the same reason.

Tony Horton, 1970

The previous season, the twenty-five-year-old first baseman had hit twenty-seven home runs and had driven in ninety-three runs for Cleveland. He asked for $100,000, which would have more than tripled his salary, and was turned down. The newspapers made him out to be a prima donna and the fans got on him.

Horton got off to a slow start in 1970 and started behaving strangely toward the end of the season. In the dugout during a game, he told his manager, Alvin Dark, "They're out to get me." When the third out was made in the ninth inning, Horton ran out to play first base even though the game was over.

It would be his last time on the field. He suffered a nervous breakdown and was institutionalized for a while, with orders not to watch ballgames on TV or listen to them on the radio. Dark called it "the most sorrowful, most tragic thing that happened to me in thirty years of professional baseball."

Alex Johnson, 1971

After bouncing around on four teams in six years, Johnson won the 1970 American League batting title, hitting .329 for the California Angels. The next season the sullen left fielder was benched four times, fined twenty-nine times, and finally suspended without pay "for failure to give his best efforts to the winning of games."

Johnson was accused of loafing in the field and failing to run out ground balls. On hot days during spring training, it had been reported that he would position himself not according to the hitter, but so that he could stand in the shadow of an outfield light post.

To make matters worse, there was some gunplay among the Angels. Johnson accused teammate Chico Ruiz* of pulling a gun on him twice in the clubhouse. The *Los Angeles Times* reported that three players on the team had been carrying guns and several others kept hidden knives. Tony Conigliaro had a shotgun in his locker. The team was owned by ex-singing cowboy star Gene Autry, who would sometimes give pistols to players as gifts.

After Johnson's suspension, his lawyer argued that Johnson was suffering from an emotional disturbance and should be placed on the disabled list—just like any player suffering from a physical ailment. "He's got a problem deep inside him that he won't talk about," Tony Conigliaro told *Sports Illustrated*. "He's so hurt inside, it's terrifying."

Johnson and his psychiatrist convinced an arbitration board that his problems were psychological, and he was restored to full play. It was a landmark decision—baseball recognized for the first time that players with nonphysical problems should be helped, not disciplined.

The Angels traded Johnson to Cleveland in 1972. He lasted one season and then spent a year each with the Rangers, Yankees, and Tigers before leaving baseball in 1976.

Jim Eisenreich, 1982

In the sixth inning of an April game, the Twins' rookie center fielder began to shake, twitch, and hyperventilate. Suddenly he ran off the field. The same thing happened again during the next four games. On May 7, Eisenreich ran into the clubhouse tearing at his clothes and screaming, "I can't breathe!" Boston fans threw bottles at him and hooted, "What inning are you leaving tonight?"

After he'd been touted as the hottest kid to come along for Minnesota since Tony Oliva, Eisenreich's rookie year was over after thirty-two games.

He returned for spring training in 1983 and hit .400, but he quit two games into the regular season when he felt his problem coming on. He tried again the next year—this time under heavy medication—but found himself falling asleep in the dugout. This time he lasted twelve games.

---

* Ruiz was killed in an auto accident a year later.

Eisenreich had been having these episodes since he was eight, but they'd never been this severe. He tried psychoanalysis, hypnosis, biofeedback, tranquilizers, and even humming to himself. It was finally determined that he had Tourette's syndrome, a rare neurological disorder. Medication and therapy helped him control it.

Eisenreich went to the minors for two years and came back when the Kansas City Royals took a gamble on his $1 waiver price. It may have been the best dollar the team ever spent. Eisenreich played full seasons in 1989 and 1990, hitting .293 and .280.

Dennis "Oil Can" Boyd, 1986

Four years after coming to the major leagues, baseball's skinniest player led the Red Sox in victories, ERA, starts, complete games, shutouts, and innings. He was a colorful character who would strut around the mound after strikeouts and take it hard when things weren't going well.

On July 10, Boyd threw a tantrum in the Red Sox clubhouse after learning that he had not been chosen for the American League All-Star team. He ripped his clothes out of his locker and threw them around, called his teammates names, and stormed out. He was suspended for three days.

Less than a week later, Boston cops stopped Boyd's silver Mercedes after receiving a tip that he had been involved in a drug transaction. He started throwing punches and threatened to shoot a police officer. He was booked on charges of disorderly conduct and assault and battery.

"I'm not a psychologist by any means," said teammate Tom Seaver, "but it seemed obvious that Dennis needed professional help."

Boyd checked into the University of Massachusetts Medical Center two days later for a comprehensive physical and psychological examination. No problems were detected, and if he was using drugs, he was never caught.

Maybe all Oil Can needed was to get away from Boston, a racially charged city that has shown itself to be less than hospitable to flamboyant black athletes (Reggie Smith, George Scott, Bill Russell, etc.). In 1990, the Can filed for free agency and signed with the Montreal

Expos. He went 10–6 with a 2.93 ERA and his personal life has been calm ever since.

Nick Esasky, 1990

After slugging 30 homers and driving in 108 runs for Boston in 1989, the first baseman signed a $5.7-million contract with Atlanta. During spring training, he experienced dizziness, fatigue, headaches, and nausea. He couldn't follow the ball. "It looked hazy, as if it had a glow," he said. He made five errors in his first nine games, striking out fifteen times in thirty-five at-bats. Terrified that he was going to get hurt, he didn't play another game all season.

Esasky consulted psychologists, neurologists, allergists, hypnotists, and ophthalmologists. For a time he thought he had Lyme disease. Like Jim Eisenreich, Esasky ultimately discovered he had a physical problem, not a mental one. The Dizziness and Balance Center in Wilmette, Illinois, discovered that his right inner ear was not functional, causing vertigo. As of the end of 1991, Esasky was undergoing various kinds of therapy and fighting to come back.

"The hardest part is the uncertainty," he told *Sports Illustrated*. "If it was a broken arm, there would be a time frame for it to heal, but you can't rehab inside your head."

So who'll be the next to blow? The odds would seem to favor two temperamental smoke throwers, Roger Clemens of Boston and Cincinnati's Rob Dibble. Typically, their fastballs explode and then they do.

During Game 4 of the 1990 American League playoffs, America got an eyeful of Clemens—like a cartoon character with smoke pouring out of his ears—giving umpire Terry Cooney a piece of his mind. He was ejected in the second inning and was half carried, half dragged from the Oakland Coliseum by his teammates. Two of the umpires said Clemens told Cooney, "I'm going to find out where you live. I'm going to get you." An anonymous Red Sox official said Clemens was stressed out and ready to snap. Articles started to appear suggesting that Clemens, the richest player in baseball, get help fast. There's such a thing as being *too* intense.

A year earlier, Clemens said in a Boston TV interview that "somebody's going to get hurt, and it's not going to be me" if reporters wrote about his wife or family.

Dibble is a piece of work who should delight Cincinnati headline writers for years to come. In 1991, he received a three-game suspension for throwing at Houston's Eric Yelding and a four-game suspension for throwing a ball four hundred feet into the Riverfront Stadium stands and injuring a schoolteacher.

Shortly after that incident, Dibble fielded a squeeze bunt off the bat of Doug Dascenzo that broke up a tight game. Baseball analysts will be arguing for years whether or not Dibble tried to drill Dascenzo on the legs with his throw to first.

In July, he admitted, "It has become apparent to me that I need professional counsel dealing with some of my emotions."

NERVOUS BREAKDOWNS

Ed Doheny (1903)

Chick Stahl (1907)

Harry Pulliam, National League president (1909)

Bob Carruthers (1911)

Johnny Evers (1911)

Tris Speaker (1920)

Hugh Jennings (1925)

Mrs. Babe Ruth (1925, 1928)

Mickey Cochrane (1936)

Tony Horton (1970)

Milt Wilcox (1986)

EX-WORLD SERIES STAR IN JAIL:
HOW I WRECKED MY LIFE—HOW I HOPE TO SAVE IT

After C...
The Un...

SEVEN
CRIME

...Is Shot
...Robbery

EAST ST. LOUI...
— A teen-age un...
baseball league w...
officiating after an...
edly fired severa...
during a game.

...s a highway overpass,
...wkins, a spokeswoman
...police.
...rno and the two others
...a citizen's arrest —
...eapon of their own
...rs who had fled in the
...l two...
...tom

A's Canseco Is Arrested

Pepitone Arrested
On Drug Charges

ARREST MARQUARD
FOR SPECULATING

Out t...
...on

— Mi...
...tana
...last
...d to

Odom Is Arrested

John (Blue Moon) Odom,
mer pitcher for the Oakland A...
arrested yesterday in Fountain...
ley, Cali... ...stigation of ass...
with a dea... ...olice sa...
Odom threatene...
held her at gunpoint wi...
Tuesday night in their apartme...
Fountain Valley about 35 miles...

...the
...tle
...as
...the
...into a
...n, Jack
...ntana
...a sur-

Ex-Ballplayer Gets 8⅓

Hold Cedeño

Girl Companion Is Killed
In Motel Fight for Gun

team members lobbed four canisters
of tear gas into the apartment. Odom

*"I don't know how you get to
where I am today from where I
was seventeen years ago."*

—Denny McLain in 1985,
after being sentenced to
twenty-three years in jail

Baseball's most famous crime story never happened.

This was the Flint Rhem kidnapping in September 1930. Rhem, a tall right-hander with the St. Louis Cardinals, was scheduled to start the first game of a crucial series against Brooklyn. There were two weeks left in the season and the Cards were a game behind the Dodgers.

Ebbets Field was jammed with fans anxious to see Flint Rhem face off against Dazzy Vance. Rhem had gone 20–7 in 1926 and had pitched well in 1930. The only problem was, he didn't show up. He didn't call, and nobody could find him. The police were brought in to begin a citywide search. Bill Hallahan took Rhem's place on the mound for the Cardinals. He pitched a ten-inning shutout, launching the team into a tie for first place.

Two days later, Flint Rhem finally appeared at the hotel where the Cardinals were staying in New York. "It was terrible, Sarge," he moaned repeatedly to manager Gabby Street. "It was just awful."

When he calmed down, Rhem explained that he had been standing outside the hotel waiting for a taxi when a car pulled up and two men called to him. He went to see what they wanted, and they pulled guns and pushed him into the car. Next they drove him to a roadhouse in New Jersey and forced him to drink whiskey all day and night at gunpoint.

"I kept begging them to let me go but it was one drink after another," Rhem said. "Rye, scotch, they didn't care how they made me mix it."

The men forced bootleg booze (this was during Prohibition) down Rhem's throat until he passed out, he said. Then they returned him to his hotel and warned him not to pitch against Brooklyn.

Rhem recovered from his ordeal and won two more games to help the Cardinals take the flag. The Philadelphia Athletics beat them in the World Series four games to two, with Rhem getting whipped badly in Game 2.

For the rest of his career—and the rest of his life, for that matter—people would ask Flint Rhem about the kidnapping. Why was there no official investigation? Where exactly in New Jersey had he been taken to? There were reasons to suspect he was lying. Flint knew his way around a whiskey bottle, and he could talk his way out of just about anything. After one night on the town with teammate Grover Cleveland Alexander, Rhem explained that he'd drunk more than his share only so that Alexander—a more valuable player—wouldn't get too intoxicated.

On the other hand, it was quite possible that gamblers might have wanted to keep Rhem out of action so that Brooklyn would have an edge in that big series.

It wasn't until thirty years later, when he was a farmer in South Carolina, that Flint Rhem admitted the truth—he had made the whole kidnapping story up. He'd gotten drunk the night before the big game and woke up "sicker than I have ever been in my life." He hid in his hotel room the whole time he was supposedly being held at gunpoint by kidnappers.

While the famous Flint Rhem kidnapping never happened, ballplayers have been convicted of auto theft, possession of weapons, loan-sharking, armed robbery, assault, and even murder. Sometimes their fame has helped them get off. Other times it has provoked judges to make examples of them.

DENNY MCLAIN
Troublemaker Extraordinaire

Williamston Kid was a long shot in the eighth race at Detroit Race Course on August 4, 1967. But a guy named Hubert Voshen thought enough of the four-year-old to put $8,000 on it. When the horse crossed the wire first, it set in motion a series of events that would eventually extinguish one of baseball's brightest stars.

In his brief heyday, Denny McLain threw high and hard. He was unbeatable in 1968, becoming the first pitcher to win thirty games in one season since Dizzy Dean did it in 1934. Nobody has done it since. The following year McLain won twenty-four and earned his second consecutive Cy Young Award.

His nickname was "Mighty Mouth," and he wasn't ashamed of his cocky reputation. When he wasn't pitching for the Detroit Tigers, McLain flew his own plane, promoted rock concerts, hustled golf, hosted a talk show, and performed as a concert organist. He described himself as an organist who also played baseball.

Despite his $200,000-a-year income, McLain could never seem to hold onto money. Around the clubhouse he was known as "Dolphin" or "Fish" because he would regularly lose card games and other bets. He put his savings in the hands of unscrupulous lawyers who made it disappear. Eventually he was evicted from his Michigan home, his office furniture was repossessed, and the IRS came after him for back taxes. At one point, his total assets were $413, and he owed $446,000.

"Giving me money," admitted McLain, "was like putting perfume on a pig."

Despite baseball's long-standing attitude toward gambling, in 1967 McLain invested $5,700 in a bookmaking operation. He and his partners handled bets on horse races and football and basketball games. He had the sense to stop short of baseball bets, but was brash enough to use the pay phone in the Tigers' clubhouse to conduct his bookie business. The full story came out as a result of an investigation conducted by *Sports Illustrated*, which published it in a February 1970 article titled "Downfall of a Hero."

It was through McLain's bookmaking operation that Hubert Voshen placed his $8,000 bet on Williamston Kid. When the horse came in, Voshen was due $46,000. McLain and his partners didn't have enough money to cover the bet.

Voshen, who owned a truck stop near Battle Creek, Michigan, naturally demanded to be paid. The bookies passed him around, telling him to go to others to collect the money. He received several phone calls asking him to be patient. One caller identified himself as Lou Boudreau, Denny McLain's father-in-law and a member of the Baseball Hall of Fame.

Frustrated, Voshen finally arranged an audience with Tony Giacalone, an alleged "enforcer" for the Detroit chapter of the Cosa Nostra. Giacalone invited McLain over to his boat on the Detroit River, where he exerted some pressure on the pitcher/bookie to pay his bills—by stomping two toes on his left foot, crushing them.

"Garbage," insisted McLain in his autobiography, *Nobody's Perfect*. "All of it." While he admitted being involved in the bookmaking operation, he claimed he had never met Tony Giacalone, he'd never been on any boat in the Detroit River, and no mobster had crushed his foot.

"The truth is that it was a common, household accident," McLain explained. His leg had fallen asleep while he was watching television, he said, and when he stood up he tripped and stubbed it. (Later he claimed he had hurt his toes chasing raccoons that had gotten into his garbage cans.)

Whatever caused the injury, his toes were hurt so badly that he missed several weeks at the end of the 1967 season. It was a tight race and Detroit missed winning the pennant by one game. McLain returned to the mound to pitch the final day of the season, when the Tigers were tied with the Red Sox for first place. He didn't last three innings, giving up four hits and three runs. Teammates blamed him for losing the pennant.

In the *Sports Illustrated* article, it was revealed that Tony Giacalone's brother Billy had bet heavily against the Tigers in that final game.

Eventually McLain and his partners raised the $46,000 to pay off Voshen, but the money was never delivered. In October 1968, Voshen played golf at the Marshall Country Club and went out for lunch. He got a phone call during the meal and rushed out to his car. An hour later, it was found wrapped around a tree on a highway outside Detroit. Voshen was dead.

"The pavement was dry, the visibility was good, the road straight," *Sports Illustrated* wrote suggestively.

McLain said that about 10 percent of the *Sports Illustrated* story was accurate. "The rest is a pack of lies and I should have sued *SI* at the time, but I was talked out of it."

Three days before the magazine hit the street, Commissioner Bowie Kuhn suspended McLain.*

"My biggest crime is stupidity," McLain said.

He returned to the mound on July 1, 1970, and pitched horribly for the rest of the season, finishing just one game in fourteen starts and giving up nineteen home runs. He went from 24–9 in 1969 to 3–5 in 1970.

During his suspension and after his return, McLain didn't act as though he was interested in returning to baseball's good graces. He threatened a parking lot attendant over a parking space. He dumped buckets of ice water and talcum powder over two sportswriters. He started accumulating guns (a .38-caliber revolver, a rifle, a .22 pistol, and others) and was accused of carrying one on a commercial airline and displaying one in a Chicago restaurant.

"Thousands of people in Detroit carry guns," McLain explained. "After all, Detroit is Murder City."

Kuhn suspended him again, this time for the rest of the season. He also suggested a psychiatric examination. McLain had one, at Detroit's Ford Clinic, and received a clean bill of mental health.

His right arm wasn't nearly as healthy. His fastball was gone, and the next year he led the majors by losing twenty-two games. In 1972, during a short stint in the minors, he was offered $25,000 to throw a game. He thought about it, but two days later was called up by the Atlanta Braves. He wasn't any good there either. Four years after his phenomenal thirty-one victory season, Denny McLain was out of baseball. He was not yet thirty years old.

"Life is just starting all over for me," he wrote in his autobiography. "I know it's not going to be utopian and I'll have some problems along the way . . ."

That was an understatement. Without the discipline of having to pitch every four days, McLain's life became even more chaotic. He

---

* McLain became the first player suspended for gambling since 1924, when Jimmy O'Connell and Cozy Dolan of the New York Giants were thrown out of baseball for life (see chapter 5).

declared bankruptcy in 1977. After letting his insurance payments lapse, his house burned to the ground and he lost everything, including his Cy Young Awards. His weight ballooned from 190 to 300 pounds and he suffered a mild heart attack.

In 1981, McLain took a job with mortgage broker First Fidelity Financial Services in Tampa, Florida. He helped a disco owner named Alton Dale Sparks obtain a $40,000 loan. When Sparks didn't keep up with his payments, he received threats from mobsters warning him they would cut off his ears.

To make matters worse, after a flight from Fort Lauderdale to Newark, investigators found McLain's golf bags stuffed with cocaine. ("I hate drugs," he had written in *Nobody's Perfect*. "I'm convinced the drug problem in this country is truly a major one and is largely responsible for our soaring crime rate.")

McLain was indicted in March 1984, and a jury found him guilty of racketeering, conspiracy to commit racketeering, loan-sharking, extortion, and possession of cocaine with intent to distribute. He was sentenced to twenty-three years in jail.

When asked if he had anything to say at his sentencing, McLain responded, "I don't know how you get to where I am today from where I was seventeen years ago."

The judge wouldn't even let him stay home on bail. He was immediately shipped off to Seminole County Correctional Facility in Sanford, Florida, and became inmate number 04000–018. He called the prison "the filthiest place on the face of the earth." Cockroaches and rats were so plentiful that inmates would throw them into the food as a protest. McLain was cracked over the head with a fire extinguisher by an inmate who had gotten tired of waiting for him to get off the phone. He considered suicide, but after six weeks he was transferred to the more civilized Federal Correctional Institution in Talladega, Alabama.

McLain had once said, "Money impresses me . . . I'm a mercenary . . . I want to be a billionaire." In jail, he earned eleven cents an hour mopping floors.

His conviction was overturned in August 1987 on a technicality —the trial had been unfairly rushed. After serving two years and five months, he was released. In a second trial he pleaded guilty to reduced charges and was sentenced to the time he had already served plus five years on probation. In an unusual punishment, the judge ordered him to revise his autobiography to reflect that he had pleaded guilty.

"It's about time you start getting things truthfully in order," she said.

The experience of being in jail was powerful enough to make McLain clean up his act. He worked as a publicity man for a hockey team in Indiana and a company that sold an alcohol-free wine cooler.

In 1989 he took a job playing the organ in a Michigan bar. The bartender was Leon Spinks, another shooting star who had trouble with the law. Onstage, McLain played the standards, performing among other songs a soulful rendition of "Yesterday."

JOE PEPITONE
He Wasn't Even Good at Breaking the Law

A week after Denny McLain was convicted in 1985, a Buick Riviera ran a red light and was pulled over at Rockaway Avenue and Newport Street in the Brownsville section of Brooklyn. Inside, plainclothes cops found $70,000 worth of cocaine, heroin, and Quaaludes, 140 glassine envelopes, drug paraphernalia, a loaded .22 Derringer handgun, and a vaguely familiar-looking guy wearing a black cowboy hat and black leather jacket.

"I'm Joe Pepitone," the man told the arresting officer, "formerly of the Yankees."

More famous for his hairpiece and blow-dryer than his play on the field, Pepi was baseball's rebel without a cause through the 1960s. In those days he was considered a harmless fun-lover who never lived up to expectations, but not a criminal.

Joe Pepitone grew up in a Brooklyn neighborhood where acting tough was a requirement for respect, if not survival. Willie Pepitone, his explosive father, beat him almost constantly for crimes as trivial as coming home five minutes late. If a kid at school beat Joe up, Willie's response was to beat Joe up again for getting beat up.

Major-league scouts noticed Joe when he was just fourteen, and by the time he was sixteen he could drive a baseball 410 feet. His father was a frustrated ballplayer himself, and became passionate about Joe's playing. If Joe struck out or made an error in a game, he would get a beating. Willie Pepitone would also beat up fans who heckled his son, as well as pitchers who threw at him.

It went on like that for years, until Willie almost blinded Joe by throwing an ashtray at his head. The ashtray hit a china cabinet and Joe had to go to the hospital to have glass taken out of his face. Joe endured a love-hate relationship with his father long after Willie was dead.

In 1958, two days after his father suffered a heart attack, Joe was at school when another boy walked up to him with a .38 pistol and said, "Stick 'em up." The gun went off and the slug ripped a hole in Joe's belly. He felt no pain, but collapsed on the floor. Nine hours of surgery saved his life, and at one point a priest was called in to administer last rites. In later years, Joe never tired of showing off the scars where the bullet had entered his front and exited his back.

Back home, Willie and Joe recovered from their misfortunes together, mostly yelling and arguing at each other. At one point, Joe told his mother that he wished his father would die. The next night, Willie Pepitone *did* die. He was just thirty-nine.

Joe believed he was responsible for his father's death—and at the same time felt relief that Willie was finally out of his life. These mixed emotions sent Joe into a depression. He suffered hot and cold flashes, and refused to leave his mother's apartment. He began having nightmares so regularly that he would get worried if he slept through a night without one. He was still having them twenty years later.

Some of the scouts who had been following Joe Pepitone lost interest after the shooting incident, but the Yankees signed him on August 13, 1958. He was touted as the next in the Ruth/Gehrig/DiMaggio/Mantle tradition. In 1962, the young slugger was brought up from the minors to assume the mantle of the fading Mantle.

It was almost too good to be true—a hometown Italian boy playing for the greatest baseball dynasty that ever existed.

A natural extrovert, Pepitone jumped into the celebrity party scene with both feet. He got up onstage at the Copacabana and danced with Tom Jones. He sang on *The Merv Griffin Show*. He met Frank Sinatra, partied at his house, and started drinking Jack Daniel's because Frank did. Pepitone also played some good baseball, hitting twenty-seven home runs in his first full season. But almost immediately, he began having problems with money, women, and crime.

Pepi wanted to live big, even if he hadn't yet put together the career to afford or merit it. He would blow $600 a night taking people out on the town and buy expensive cars on a whim. Once his paycheck totaled $15 because he had charged so much to the Yankees.

By 1965 he was $40,000 in debt and creditors hounded him everywhere he went. Men would walk up to him, ostensibly to ask for an autograph, and hand him a subpoena instead. Creditors would come to Yankee Stadium because they knew he would be there and repossess his car. Before one game, two burly guys approached him and suggested he pay off his tab at the Copa "or you're gonna have a problem."

The Yankees eventually got him a financial adviser, who put him on a strict allowance. When he had finally paid off all his debts two years later, he took charge of his finances again. Within months, he was $20,000 in the hole. The commissioner's office, uncharacteristically, ignored his money problems and his vulnerability to gamblers.

Pepitone was impressed by mobsters and had begun hanging out with them at the Copacabana shortly after joining the Yankees. The mobsters were proud to have a young ballplayer in their midst, especially a *paisan* from Brooklyn.

In his autobiography, *Joe, You Coulda Made Us Proud*, Pepitone could barely conceal his admiration for gangsters. "The wise guys, as we called them, were always nice, just people in a different business, doing their own thing and risking a lot of years in jail," he wrote. "As I look back, I really don't know if they were any worse than corporations that sell us inferior products at inflated prices." (The book was published ten years before Joe's arrest on the streets of Brooklyn.)

While it doesn't appear that he was ever pressured to throw a game, Pepitone wrote that his mobster friends came up with a way for him to get off the bench during his rookie year and take over the Yankees' first-base job:

"We're gonna help ya out with that little problem ya got wit [Moose] Skowron," one of them said.

"What? What do you mean?"

"We'll just get in touch wit him after a game, and the next day ya got the job. No problem. He won't play real good with cracks in his legs."

Pepitone told them he wanted to win the job on his own.

As a rising star with the World Champion New York Yankees, Pepitone had his choice of hundreds of willing women. The fact that he had gotten married when he was in the minor leagues didn't prevent him from taking full advantage. He would pick up a girl, have sex with her, then send her away and find another girl the same night.

After the 1964 season, he went partying in Miami for a month. His wife, Barbara, had detectives track him down and inform him that if he didn't come home, she would charge him with desertion. When he finally returned, all his clothes were in suitcases on the front porch.

His second wife, Diane, found slips of paper with 150 names of women Joe had been sleeping with, including some of her closest friends. After he left baseball in 1974, he got married for the third time, to a former *Playboy* bunny.

Pepitone loved the money and fame that came with being a major-league baseball player, but he never particularly liked baseball. "There's so much dead time in it," he complained. "It's the most boring sport in the world to watch."

He lost interest in the game by 1968 and bounced from the Yankees to Houston to Chicago. He lasted three games with the Braves in 1973 and fourteen with the Tokyo Yakult Atoms before hanging up his spikes for good. His disrespect for authority and total lack of discipline were even more glaring in Japan than in America.

Always looking for a way to make big money, Pepitone opened up hairstyling salons, restaurants, and bars. But everything he tried failed. The things he excelled at—hitting, throwing, and fielding—didn't interest him enough to give them his all. Finally he turned to drug peddling, and he wasn't particularly good at that either.

After being caught red-handed in the streets of Brooklyn in 1985, Pepitone could have gotten fifteen years to life in jail for criminal possession of a controlled substance and criminal possession of a weapon. He received a six-month sentence and only had to serve two months.

Sadly, the title of Pepitone's autobiography wasn't coined by fellow players, family, or the millions of fans he disappointed. "Joe, you coulda made us proud" was something a mobster said to him. He coulda made it to Cooperstown but instead ended up at Rikers Island.

HANK THOMPSON
Career Record—Assault, Car Theft,
Armed Robbery, Murder

Hank Thompson was having a beer with his sister one night in 1948 when he spotted Buddy Crow at the end of the bar. He remembered Crow from his sandlot days—a mean drunk who once stabbed a man and left him standing with his intestines in his hands.

"Hello, Mr. Moneyman," Buddy Crow said sarcastically. Thompson had become one of the first black players in the big leagues the year before. Crow's baseball career had gone nowhere.

"Have a beer, Buddy."

Crow went back to his table but quickly returned, waving a knife.

"I'm gonna get you," he said to Thompson.

Thompson pulled a .32 automatic out of his jacket pocket.

"Stop!" he yelled.

Crow kept coming, so Thompson pulled the trigger three times. Buddy Crow toppled over, dead.

The next day, Hank Thompson was at spring training. Such are the perks of playing professional baseball.

"I killed a man," Thompson recalled years later, "and the next day I was playing ball like nothing had happened." It would not be the last time Hank Thompson would be bailed out by baseball.

When Branch Rickey was looking for a man to break the color barrier, he wanted someone dignified, someone of impeccable background and morals to show white America that black men could be heroes too. Jackie Robinson was the right man for the job. Henry Curtis Thompson was not. As the third black man to make the majors, he faced the same pressures and problems that Robinson did. Thompson, however, didn't have the strength of character that Robinson had to overcome them.

Thompson's first arrest came at age eleven, when he was caught stealing jewelry from a car near his home in Dallas. He was sent one hundred miles away to Gatesville Reform School, where he started playing ball.

As a teenager, he hung around Dallas ballparks and asked if he could pitch batting practice for a Texas League team, the Dallas Steers. One of the Kansas City Monarchs—the premiere Negro League team—spotted him and suggested he go for a tryout. Within weeks, seventeen-year-old Hank Thompson was playing alongside future Hall of Famer Satchel Paige.

Thompson played with the Monarchs for two years, until he was drafted in 1944. He was sent overseas and served as a machine-gunner with the 1695th Combat Engineers at the Battle of the Bulge. His outfit kept the Germans boxed up in a village for three days, until three thousand of them finally surrendered.

"If there was a moment in my life I did something for society, that was it," Thompson told *Sport* magazine. "But you can't make three good days balance off the rest of a man's life."

When Sergeant Thompson got out of the service in 1946, baseball's color barrier was about to fall. After sixty years of keeping blacks out, major-league teams were actively looking for young black talent. On April 10, 1947, Jackie Robinson joined the Dodgers. On July 6, Larry Doby joined the Cleveland Indians. On July 16, Hank Thompson was eating breakfast before a Monarchs game in Madison, Wisconsin, when the team's traveling secretary tapped him on the shoulder.

"Get your stuff ready, Hank," he said. "You're going to the majors." He played his first big-league game two days later.

The last-place St. Louis Browns had signed Thompson (along with Monarch teammate Willard Brown) mainly to boost attendance. When Thompson didn't set the world on fire (.256 in twenty-seven games), the Browns released him and he rejoined the Monarchs for the '48 season. That's when he shot Buddy Crow.

The fact that Thompson had killed a man didn't bother the New York Giants, who signed him in 1949. With the help of the Giants, the murder charge against Thompson was dismissed, the killing ruled a justifiable homicide.

In New York, Hank Thompson became a star. He and Bobby Thompson were dubbed the "Tom-Tom Twins," and Hank hit eight home runs in the dramatic 1951 dash to the pennant that included Bobby's "shot heard 'round the world" in the final game of the season. In the 1954 World Series sweep of Cleveland, he hit .364.

Over his nine-year career, he played in 933 games, hitting .267 and 129 home runs. One day he hit three in one game. He went into the record book as the first black batter to face a black pitcher (Don Newcombe), as the first black man to play in both leagues, and as a member of the first all-black major-league outfield (with Hall of Famers Willie Mays and Monte Irvin).

As soon as he joined the Giants, Thompson started playing the big shot. He flashed $100 bills around in bars, bought a Lincoln Capri, and acquired racks of tailored suits. In the 1953 off-season, he was arrested for felonious assault in New York after a scuffle with a cab driver who hit him over the head with a sawed-off baseball bat. Thompson received fourteen stitches.

He had learned how to drink hard liquor in the Army and developed a serious alcohol problem. After most games, he would unwind with two or three Scotches before dinner and a whole fifth afterward. The booze began taking its toll, as Thompson slowed down and was nagged by injuries. The Giants sent him to the minors in 1957, and he was finished with baseball at age thirty-one.

He found nothing but trouble to get into. He had earned a quarter of a million dollars from baseball and blown just about every penny of it on booze, cars, and various women. When the big checks stopped coming, he missed the good life and had trouble coping with earning $85 dollars a week as a bartender.

In his first year out of baseball, he was arrested for stealing a car. The following year he was arrested again, for unlawful entry and third-degree assault. He had hit his girlfriend during an argument and taken $3 from her pocketbook.

Seven days in jail weren't enough to teach him a lesson. In 1961, drinking and in need of money to visit his mother in Fresno, California, he walked into a Harlem bar named Bill's Place and asked the bartender, "Do you know who I am?" When the bartender said he didn't, Thompson pulled out a .22-caliber pistol and said, "Good. This is a stickup. Put the money on the bar."

He was arrested a block away with $37 in his pocket. The charges were robbery, assault, carrying a concealed weapon, and armed robbery. Giants owner Horace Stoneham and baseball commissioner Ford Frick pulled some strings, and Thompson was released on probation.

It was a nice gesture, but the help he really needed was to get caught and put away for a good long time. In 1963, he took care of that. He grabbed two pistols from a friend's print shop and stuck up a Houston liquor store for $270. The cops caught him the same night flashing the money around a nearby nightclub.

It was his seventh arrest. This time baseball didn't come to the rescue. Hank Thompson was sentenced to ten years in the Texas penitentiary at Huntsville.

That's where he was in 1965 when he told his story ("How I Wrecked My Life—How I Hope to Save It") to *Sport* magazine. Prison seemed finally to have knocked some sense into Thompson. He became an active member of Alcoholics Anonymous and worked as an athletic coach for first offenders. He had plenty of regrets and remorse for his actions up until that point, and no excuses.

"The only person to blame is me," he wrote, "So if I blame drink, *I'm* the guy . . . who did the drinking. If I tell you I came from a broken home . . . so did millions of other kids. . . . If I tell you my father beat me with a strap . . . I'm in jail, not my father.

"Don't ask me to blame society, or the fact that I'm a Negro in a white world, or the fact I have a grade school education, or the fact I was washed up as a major leaguer when I was 31 years old. I'm the one who kicked society in the teeth."

It sounded as if Thompson was ready to start all over again at age forty, but by the time he'd pulled his life together it was too late. On September 30, 1969, shortly after he was paroled, he suffered a stroke in his mother's Fresno home. He never regained consciousness.

Hank Thompson's Tips for Kids

- Get advice about money, how to save it, how to invest it.
- Live a clean life.
- Stay away from those goodtime people who pretend to be your friends.
- Stay away from liquor.
- Stay healthy.
- Baseball is the cleanest sport we have, so treat it decent.

CESAR CEDENO
A Struggle . . . a Gunshot . . . a Corpse

It was probably for the better that Buck Weaver didn't live long enough to see the day of Cesar Cedeno. Weaver was banished from baseball for life simply because he didn't say what he knew about the Black Sox Scandal. Cedeno was convicted of involuntary manslaughter and never even missed a game.

A pure hitter who was touted as "the next Clemente" when he arrived from the Dominican Republic, Cedeno hit .320 for Houston in 1972 with twenty-two home runs, thirty-nine doubles, eighty-two RBIs, and fifty-six stolen bases. He also won the Gold Glove as a right fielder. Fans started calling the Astrodome "Cesar's Palace." Leo Durocher said the twenty-one-year-old was "better than Willie Mays at the same age."

It wasn't a fluke. Cedeno hit .320 again in 1973, with twenty-five home runs. Houston thought so much of his talent that they signed him to a ten-year contract worth $3.5 million.

But the most important statistic in Cedeno's career was registered right after the 1973 season: killed—1.

Cedeno had his share of problems with women. As a teenager, he had been married to a Puerto Rican woman and had a child by her. They divorced and he married an American named Cora. He also patronized prostitutes, who sometimes robbed him of money and jewelry. For protection, he started packing a .38-caliber Smith & Wesson.

He had a mistress too. At 2:00 A.M. on the night of December 11, 1973, Cedeno and nineteen-year-old Altagracia de la Cruz checked into a bungalow at the Keki Motel in a poor section of Santo Domingo. His wife was at their winter home, also in Santo Domingo.

Cedeno and Altagracia were seen arguing before they checked in. He had been drinking, and he ordered two bottles of beer from room service. Accounts of what happened next are fuzzy. Either Altagracia picked up Cedeno's gun to admire it, or she asked him if she could look at it and he refused. In any case, he tried to get the gun away from her and the two ended up wrestling over it.

Ten minutes after they had checked in, a gunshot was heard. Altagracia slumped to the floor, a bullet in her head.

Cedeno called the motel office and informed them, "A woman's been killed." Then he fled in his sports car. It wasn't until eight hours later that he returned with his father and turned himself in to the police. A photo of him with Altagracia was found near the girl's body.

"She asked for the revolver because she found it pretty," Cedeno testified at his pretrial hearing. "I answered 'no' because it was loaded and very dangerous. I tried to stand up to drink a glass of beer while she insisted that I let her hold it." He insisted that she had pulled the trigger and accidentally shot herself.

Cedeno was charged with voluntary manslaughter, which in the United States is equivalent to second-degree murder. His mother, father, and wife were at his side during the hearing.

It was not the happiest Christmas and New Year for Cesar Cedeno. He spent it in a jail cell with four other men accused of homicide.

After Cedeno had been in prison for twenty days, the postmortem parafin test showed gunpowder on Altagracia de la Cruz's right hand, indicating that Cedeno had been telling the truth—she had pulled the trigger. Charges were reduced from voluntary to involuntary manslaughter, and he was released on bail.

He was found guilty. The maximum sentence in the Dominican Republic for involuntary manslaughter is three years in jail. Cedeno's punishment was to pay a fine of 100 pesos.

"It's an injustice!" cried the victim's aunt, Felicia de la Cruz, when the sentence came down.

A woman had been shot dead, but all that seemed to concern anyone about the incident was how it would affect Cedeno's baseball career. Little was mentioned of Altagracia de la Cruz's three-year-old daughter (Cedeno was not the father). Two civil suits were filed on behalf of the girl and were settled out of court. Cedeno was back in the United States in time for spring training.

With the tragedy behind him, Cedeno refused to speak about it and insisted it would not affect his playing. It did, of course. It would be impossible for any young man to be involved in an episode like that and act as if nothing had happened.

Cedeno would play for thirteen more years, but he never had another great season and would only hit .300 once more. After 1974, he would never hit twenty home runs again. He was always a good player, but his potential for greatness died when Altagracia de la Cruz did.

For the rest of his career, Cedeno had to endure fans all over the country hollering things like "Who are you going to kill next?" Well known for his temper, he handled it well until 1981. During the first inning of a game in Atlanta, a spectator shouted "Killer!" at Cedeno and at his wife, who was sitting in the stands. Cesar climbed into the stands and attacked the man. He was fined $5,000.

If the de la Cruz killing had been Cedeno's only brush with the law, it could have been said that he had made one big mistake in life and was justified in losing his temper at an abusive fan. Unfortunately, trouble with the law became an almost yearly event, and Cedeno showed how hotheaded he could be.

In 1985, he was arguing with his girlfriend (another one) and lost control of his Mercedes, smashing into a tree in Houston. He refused to take a Breathalyzer test, and when the police tried to book him, he attempted to kick the window out of the patrol car. They had to handcuff him and tie his feet together. Cedeno was charged with driving while intoxicated, fined $400, and ordered to pay $7,000 for property damage.

In 1987, his first year out of baseball, a man bumped against

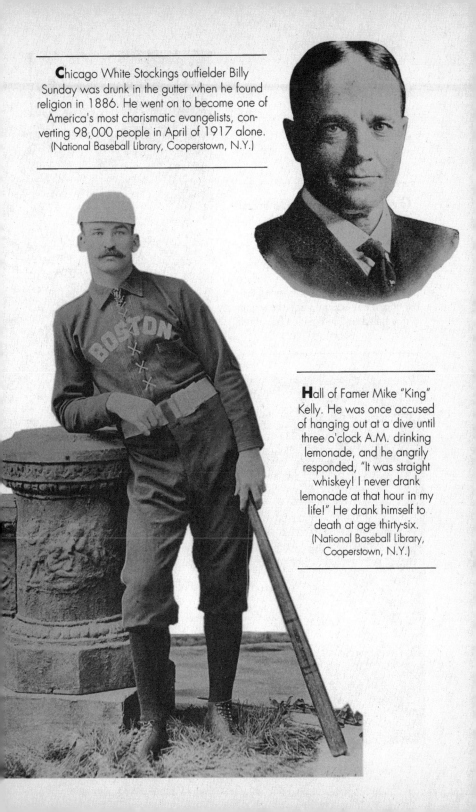

Chicago White Stockings outfielder Billy Sunday was drunk in the gutter when he found religion in 1886. He went on to become one of America's most charismatic evangelists, converting 98,000 people in April of 1917 alone. (National Baseball Library, Cooperstown, N.Y.)

Hall of Famer Mike "King" Kelly. He was once accused of hanging out at a dive until three o'clock A.M. drinking lemonade, and he angrily responded, "It was straight whiskey! I never drank lemonade at that hour in my life!" He drank himself to death at age thirty-six. (National Baseball Library, Cooperstown, N.Y.)

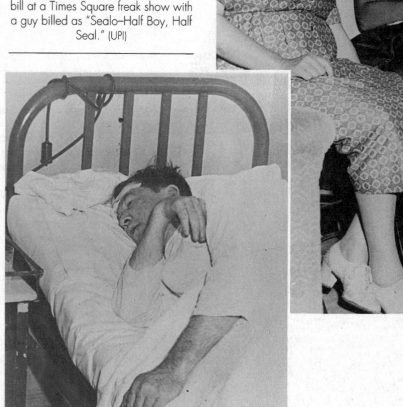

Grover Cleveland Alexander in an Evansville, Indiana, hospital after he was found unconscious in the street in 1936. "Old Pete" was a hopeless drunk in his playing days, and a year after he was inducted into the Hall of Fame he was reduced to sharing the bill at a Times Square freak show with a guy billed as "Sealo–Half Boy, Half Seal." (UPI)

Pitcher Ryne Duren (ABOVE, FAR RIGHT) obviously a man who needs a drink badly. Duren said that thirteen of his twenty-five teammates on the 1960 Yankees were abusing themselves with booze. He would try killing himself three times, burn down his house, and go to a mental hospital before beating the battle with the bottle. Today he counsels alcoholics. (UPI)

Leo Durocher (ABOVE, LEFT) with pal George Raft. Raft threw a dice game in Leo's apartment while the Dodger manager was out of the country. Baseball Commissioner Happy Chandler warned Durocher to stop hanging around with Raft and other gambling types. Leo heeded the warning, but Chandler threw him out of baseball anyway for the 1947 season. (UPI)

The 1919 Chicago White (Black) Sox (OPPOSITE, ABOVE) weren't smiling after the (1920) season was over. Banned for life were (*in the front row*) Cicotte (*3rd*) and Williams (*5th*); (*in the middle row*) Felsch (*5th*), Gandil (*6th*), and Weaver (*7th*); (*in the back row*) Risberg (*5th*), McMullin (*6th*), and Jackson (*9th*). (National Baseball Library, Cooperstown, N.Y.)

The Black Sox were amateurs compared with Hal Chase, master of the subtle art of throwing a ballgame (OPPOSITE, BELOW). One of the best first basemen ever, Chase was accused by three separate managers of selling out his team within a decade. He was finally caught and banned for life in 1919. (National Baseball Library, Cooperstown, N.Y.)

Jimmy Piersall (ABOVE) giving the boot to a fan who may have been even nuttier than he was. Several years earlier, Piersall suffered a nervous breakdown during his rookie season and woke up eight months later in the violent room at Westborough State Hospital in Massachusetts. (AP/Wide World Photos)

Mickey Mantle and Willie Mays (OPPOSITE) in their younger days. In their older days, they would both be forced to leave baseball by Commissioner Bowie Kuhn because they accepted jobs with casinos. When Peter Ueberroth became commissioner in 1985, he reinstated them. (National Baseball Library, Cooperstown, N.Y.)

Rube Foster, the father of the Negro Leagues (ABOVE). When he failed to recognize members of his own family in 1926 and started chasing imaginary fly balls outside his home in Chicago, he was put into a mental institution for the rest of his life. (National Baseball Library, Cooperstown, N.Y.)

Hall of Fame pitcher Rube Waddell (RIGHT). He would stop in the middle of games to go chase fire engines, and opponents would distract him with children's toys and stuffed animals. Known as a bumpkin in his day, Waddell was very possibly mentally retarded.
(National Baseball Library, Cooperstown, N.Y.)

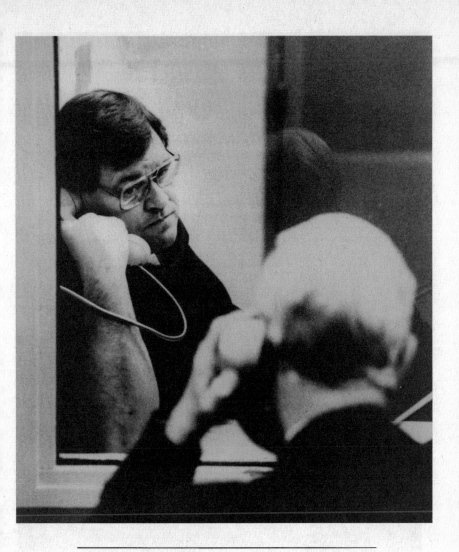

Former Tiger great Denny McLain doing time in Seminole
Correctional Institution for racketeering, loansharking,
extortion, and possession of cocaine with intent to distribute.
Back in 1968, he was the first pitcher to win 30 games in
one season since Dizzy Dean did it in 1934.
(AP/Wide World Photos)

Former Yankee Joe Pepitone being led into a Brooklyn police station after being arrested for possession of cocaine, heroin, Quaaludes, drug paraphernalia, and a loaded handgun in 1985. (AP/Wide World Photos)

Ron LeFlore (LEFT) was convicted of armed robbery and sentenced to five to fifteen years in the state prison of southern Michigan. And that was *before* he made it to the big leagues. (Southern Michigan State Prison)

Hank Thompson (BELOW) hit .364 in the 1954 World Series for the New York Giants. He was arrested seven times before, during, and after his baseball days—including once for homicide. Here he is leaving a police lineup after being arrested for robbing a bar of $37 in 1961. (AP/Wide World Photos)

Juan Marichal (ABOVE, AT LEFT) clubbing Dodger John Roseboro in
1965 while Sandy Koufax looks on. Roseboro came away with a
two-inch gash on his head. Marichal came away with a plaque in
Cooperstown. (UPI)

Is this the face (OPPOSITE, ABOVE) of a sane man? Two weeks before Ty
Cobb's first major league game, his mother accidentally shot and
killed her husband, thinking he was a burglar. Some say it drove
Cobb to both his achievements on the field and his lifelong anger at
the world. (National Baseball Library, Cooperstown, N.Y.)

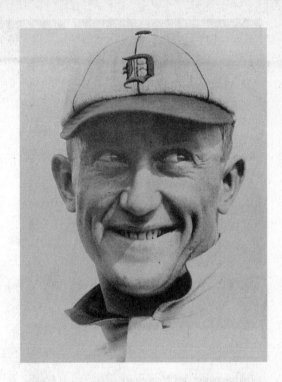

John McGraw (RIGHT):
compulsive fighter,
gambler, and baseball's
Jekyll/Hyde. (National
Baseball Hall of Fame)

The mysterious Moe Berg (ABOVE, SEATED), major league catcher for fifteen years and spy for the U.S. government during World War II. Berg couldn't hit, but he played a major role in the race with the Nazis to build the first atomic bomb. (National Baseball Library, Cooperstown, N.Y.)

George Brett getting a hug from Morganna "The Kissing Bandit" Roberts. Fans have not only run onto the field but have also been shot at the ballpark, died watching games on TV, thrown explosives into dugouts, and fallen off stadiums. See chapter 10. (AP/Wide World Photos)

Cap Anson, Chicago White Stockings manager and Hall of Famer, was largely responsible for erecting the barrier that kept black players out of organized baseball for half a century. (National Baseball Library, Cooperstown, N.Y.)

Sporting goods magnate and Hall of Famer Albert Spaulding foisted the myth that Abner Doubleday invented baseball on the American public. (National Baseball Library, Cooperstown, N.Y.)

Ford Frick, flanked by Babe Ruth and Lou Gehrig. Frick was a ghostwriter for Ruth and was summoned to his bedside the day before the Bambino died in 1948. Years later, when he was baseball commissioner, Frick would put a protective screen around Ruth's record of 60 home runs in a season to prevent Roger Maris from breaking it. (AP/Wide World Photos)

Cedeno in a Nassau Bay nightclub. Cedeno smashed a glass into the man's face and was charged with assault and resisting arrest.

In 1988, he attacked his current girlfriend (*another* one) in Webster, Texas. She ran outside with their four-month-old baby. Cedeno snatched the child and drove away. He returned shortly and beat up his girlfriend again, hitting her head against a wall. This time it took four policemen to get him into the patrol car. He was arrested for assault, causing bodily injury, and resisting arrest.

During the trial for the killing of Altagracia de la Cruz, Dominican ambassador to the United States Federico Antun described Cesar Cedeno as "a very nice boy; he never used bad words."

RON LEFLORE
The Convict Who Made the Big Time

In 1971, Ron LeFlore watched the All-Star game on television in the mess hall of the Southern Michigan State Prison.

In 1976, he *played* in the All-Star game, starting in left field for the American League.

LeFlore grew up in the crime-infested projects of East Detroit. He was smoking cigarettes when he was nine, drinking at eleven, smoking marijuana at thirteen, and using heroin and cocaine at fifteen.

"While other kids were home with their parents in the evening watching TV," he said, "I was hanging around dope houses or selling speed and stolen clothes to prostitutes and pimps."

Drugs cost money, and LeFlore got it by stealing. When he was just twelve, he stole $1,500 from an A&P store where he worked on weekends. A few years later, he was arrested for trying to crack the safe at a tobacco wholesale company. He spent a year and a half in reform school, where he was caught stealing copies of a biology test that he planned to sell to the other students.

Late one night around Christmas in 1966, LeFlore and two friends were hanging around O'Quinn's poolroom in Detroit when they decided to pull off a robbery. LeFlore was nineteen. He had been using hard drugs every day for nine months and needed some money to keep getting high.

The group got a .22 rifle and drove to a neighborhood bar called Dee's. It was a Thursday, the day the local Chrysler workers got paid and blew a good part of their paychecks at the bar. At closing time, LeFlore and his friends burst into the bar and forced the owner to lie on the floor while they emptied the cash registers. They also got a bag of money out of a safe. The job took ten minutes.

A silent burglar alarm had been tripped, and police from all over Detroit converged on the getaway car. LeFlore was hiding the money in a heat vent in his apartment when they broke down the door.

It wasn't until his trial that LeFlore learned the bag contained $35,000 in cash. He was convicted of armed robbery and sentenced to five to fifteen years at the Southern Michigan State Prison at Jackson.

Jackson State, as it was called, was not one of those country-club prisons. Goon squads of six or seven guards would come into LeFlore's cell in the middle of the night and beat him with fists and clubs. He saw a man being murdered in a dispute over another inmate's affections. He spent six and a half months in solitary confinement, part of it in total darkness.

To pass the time he would do sit-ups and push-ups, and got to the point where he could do 100 of each without stopping. His body responded to the exercise and so did his mind. He arrived at the realization that ghetto defiance wasn't getting him anywhere in life. He started taking classes in jail, got his high school diploma and quit using drugs.

Just as they do in the outside world, athletes get special privileges in prison—like early parole. LeFlore had never even hit a hardball with a bat, but he tried out for the baseball team and hit .569. The team had impressive numbers all around—the catcher was doing ten to twenty for armed robbery, the pitcher was doing ten to twenty for rape, and the second baseman was in for life on a murder rap.

LeFlore wrote to Detroit Tigers general manager Jim Campbell asking for a tryout and received a polite thanks-but-no-thanks response. But prison friends kept bombarding the Tigers with letters raving about him. On May 23, 1973, Tigers manager Billy Martin visited the prison. He was introduced to LeFlore, by then nearing parole, and invited him to a workout with the team when he got out of prison.

A month later, the day before his twenty-fifth birthday, Ron LeFlore walked into Tiger Stadium and jolted line drives all over the upper deck. He was timed at 6.1 in the sixty-yard dash and showed off an arm like a cannon. Having sat in prison for six and a half years, LeFlore signed a contract to become a professional ballplayer hours after being paroled.

He was sent to the Tigers' Class A team in Clinton, Iowa. When Tigers center fielder Mickey Stanley broke his hand, LeFlore was called up. One year and one week after his release from prison, he was a major-league baseball player.

Signing an ex-convict was not unprecedented in baseball. Detroit, in fact, had recruited Gates Brown out of the Ohio State Reformatory, where he was serving two years for breaking and entering (Why do you think they called him "Gates"?). Brown became a reliable pinch hitter and averaged an incredible .462 in 1968. He was still playing when LeFlore arrived, and he helped the rookie make the transition from prison yard to ballpark.

LeFlore was a little green in the beginning. He was caught trying to steal third with two out in the ninth and power hitter Willie Horton at bat. He misjudged a fly ball so badly that it bounced off his head for an inside-the-park home run. But he adjusted and became a good, if not great, player.

After years of outrunning the Detroit cops, stealing bases on American League catchers was a piece of cake. LeFlore averaged over fifty steals a season for nine years. He led the American League with sixty-eight in 1978. Playing for Montreal two years later, he stole ninety-seven and led the National League.

"Stealing was my specialty," he said. "As far back as I can remember, I was stealing things and getting away with it."

He could hit too. In 1976, he hit safely in thirty consecutive games, the longest American League streak in twenty-seven years.* He finished the season at .316 and signed a long-term contract that guaranteed $700,000 a year. He collaborated on a book about his life,

---

* In the middle of the streak, Ron's younger brother Gerald was shot and killed during an argument in Detroit. The autopsy revealed codeine, morphine, and methadone in his body.

Breakout: From Prison to the Big Leagues. It became a TV movie starring Lavar Burton.

With many players, success in the major leagues has corrupted the man. In the case of Ron LeFlore, it seemed as if baseball had rescued a man who appeared to be hopelessly corrupt. After a youth marked by almost constant criminal behavior, LeFlore made the big leagues and in his entire career was never even ejected from a game.

"With baseball," he said, "I finally had control of my life."

That would make a pleasant ending for the Ron LeFlore story, but there is more. Playing for the White Sox in 1982, LeFlore couldn't get along with manager Tony La Russa. He was accused of being out of shape, missing workouts, sleeping in the clubhouse during games, and lying to reporters.

Toward the end of the season, he was arrested in his Chicago apartment for unlawful possession of a controlled substance (seventeen amphetamine pills) and an unregistered firearm. He pleaded innocent and was acquitted when it could not be proven that the evidence belonged to him.

The following January, his forty-nine-day-old son, John Christopher, died at home, apparently of Sudden Infant Death Syndrome. "I felt what seemed like his last breath go into mine," LeFlore said. "I held his tiny body in my arms and I was looking death in the face."

LeFlore's other son, Ronald Alexander, had nearly drowned when he was twenty-three months old. The Florida Department of Health and Rehabilitative Services received a complaint from the county sheriff that the death of John Christopher may have been connected to child neglect or abuse. An investigation was conducted. No criminal charges were made.

Meanwhile, LeFlore was no longer producing on the field and the White Sox had just about had it. "I felt sorry for Ron about his son's death," said Tony La Russa, "but I didn't feel sorry for him when he was sleeping on training tables." LeFlore was released during spring training in 1983, his career in the majors finished.

Ron LeFlore may make it back to the big leagues once again. In 1988, he was working as a baggage handler for Eastern Airlines when he bumped into American League umpire Marty Springstead. LeFlore told Springstead he missed baseball, and Springstead suggested he become an umpire. LeFlore promptly paid $1,675 to enroll in the Joe Brinkman Baseball School.

That would be something—starting out a career criminal and ending up an umpire.

DAVE WINFIELD
The Fowl Ball That Got Him Arrested

When Dave Winfield was a college student, he spent a weekend in jail after he and a friend were caught stealing snowblowers from a warehouse in Minneapolis. But that was nothing compared to the trouble he got into in 1983 when he committed murder in front of 36,684 witnesses at Toronto's Exhibition Stadium.

Seagulls were always a problem in Toronto, flying around the field and annoying the players. In the middle of the fifth inning on August 4, one particularly pesky gull dive-bombed Yankee third baseman Graig Nettles, buzzed the pitcher's mound, and touched down in right center field.

Winfield, in center, was playing catch with left fielder Don Baylor. The Blue Jays were about to come to bat, so Winfield tossed his last warm-up throw in the direction of the gull to scare it away.

The bird apparently had never gotten the knack of playing on artificial turf. Winfield's throw short-hopped it right in the neck. It toppled over, dead.

"Right away I know he's a goner," Winfield said. "I feel awful."

The ball boy ran onto the field with a white towel and ceremoniously carried the corpse away.

Had the incident occurred in Yankee Stadium, the New York crowd would probably have gotten a good laugh over it. But the Blue Jays fans were also seagull fans. A murmur built in the stands. The crowd started booing and throwing things at Winfield. They were out for blood—Winfield's blood—for the rest of the game.

The Yankees went on to win 3–1 on a Winfield home run. He was in the dugout doing a radio interview when manager Billy Martin came over and said, "The police are waiting for you in the clubhouse."

A disbelieving Winfield was taken down to police headquarters in a squad car and booked on the charge of cruelty to animals. In official terms, he "unlawfully did willfully cause unnecessary injury to a bird, to wit; a Gull, by using a ball, contrary to the criminal code."

Bail was set at $500. The evidence in the case—the gull—was lying on a table in the police station with its feet sticking up in the air. Winfield peeked through the window and a dozen flashbulbs fired.

"I feel like John Dillinger holed up with the hostages," said Winfield. When he was escorted from the police station, he held his briefcase over his face, just like real criminals do on TV.

"What the hell good is a seagull?" asked Graig Nettles. "I think Winfield should have been given a medal for killing the damn thing."

Charges were dropped, but Dave Winfield's moment in history had arrived.* The next day he needed a police escort to get into the stadium. In Detroit, whenever he came to bat, everyone in the crowd stood up and flapped their arms. Winfield appeared on the cover of the spring training edition of *Yankee* magazine the next season with seagulls flying around his head.

Leave it to Billy Martin for the best observation on the incident: "That was the first time he hit the cutoff man all year."

Baseball for the Birds

The season after Winfield's "fowl ball," Rickey Henderson hit a nighthawk with a fly ball. Center fielder Rick Manning caught the ball, Henderson was out, and the bird's career was finished.

In 1987, Dion James of the Atlanta Braves hit a routine fly that struck a dove in Shea Stadium. Nobody caught the ball and James was awarded a ground-rule double. As a minor-leaguer, Eric Davis killed a bird with a fly ball in Oregon.

And back in 1947, St. Louis Browns pitcher Ellis Kinder was hit by a fish that had been dropped by a seagull.

---

* This would not be the last scandal involving Dave Winfield (see chapter 5: Gambling, "George Steinbrenner: 'The Boss' Walks the Plank").

MORE CRIMES AND CRIMINALS

Michael Donlin, 1902

The outfielder was charged in Baltimore with assaulting Minnie Fields, an actress, and her escort, Ernest Slayton. Both had black eyes, and Fields had been knocked unconscious. Donlin pleaded guilty, claiming he was drunk at the time and didn't know what he was doing. The sentence was six months in jail and a $250 fine.

Donlin came back to hit .351 the next season for Cincinnati. He played twelve years in the majors.

Rube Marquard, 1920

The Hall of Fame pitcher was arrested in the lobby of the Hotel Winton in Cleveland trying to scalp eight box seats for the World Series. Unfortunately, the person he was trying to scalp them to was an undercover policeman. The face value of the tickets was $52.80, and Marquard was asking $400. He was found guilty and fined $1 plus costs ($2.80).

The story became front-page news because this was the first World Series after the Black Sox Scandal and baseball was particularly sensitive about wrongdoing. Marquard pitched in Games 1 and 4 for the Dodgers, giving up one run over nine total innings and taking a loss in Game 1.

Afterward, Dodgers president Charles Ebbets announced that Marquard would never pitch for the team again. He didn't. They traded him to Cincinnati, where he went 17–14 the next season.

Benny Kauff, 1921

Kauff, who led the Federal League by hitting .370 in 1914 and .342 in 1915, was caught stealing a car with his brother and declared ineligible to play in organized baseball by Commissioner Landis. He never played again.

Comiskey Park Bombing, 1921

An explosive was hurled at the main entrance of the ballpark and
burst in the air, shattering windows and scattering debris all over
the sidewalk. There was speculation that the bombing had something
to do with the war against baseball gamblers, but no arrests were
made.

Paul Hines, 1922

Hines was long remembered for being the first man to pull off an
unassisted triple play, back in 1878. He led the National League
that year, hitting .358. After his sixteen-year baseball career was
over, he worked for the Department of Agriculture. He was arrested
on a pickpocketing charge in 1922, when he was sixty-nine.

The Nowak Kidnapping, 1938

Shortly after midnight on March 8, a car drove up to a Baton Rouge
boardinghouse where several young New York Giants recruits were
staying during spring training. After a short discussion, eighteen-
year-old second baseman Bill Nowak was whisked away and taken
to the nearby training camp of the Cleveland Indians.

"I cannot imagine how the Indians think they can get away with
anything like this," said outraged Giants manager Bill Terry. Both
teams claimed they had signed Nowak, but Cleveland had neglected
to place him on the club's reserve list.

In the long run it didn't matter who signed Nowak. He never
made it to the big leagues.

"Beanball Inc.," 1939

After Ducky Medwick and Pee Wee Reese had been hit by pitches
and knocked out of the lineup within two weeks, Dodgers chief
Larry MacPhail claimed there was a conspiracy among National
League pitchers to wipe out his team and kill its chances of winning
the pennant.

MacPhail brought in District Attorney Bill O'Dwyer, who had

just broken up the notorious Murder Inc. mob. The man in charge
of the Murder Inc. investigation, Burton Turkus, was assigned to
uncover the secrets of what came to be called "Beanball Inc." Turkus
interviewed the Dodgers for evidence.

No criminal charges were ever filed, but in 1941 the Dodgers
pioneered the use of protective batting helmets.

Frank Robinson, 1961

In the off-season, the twenty-five-year-old outfielder pulled out a gun
during an argument with a cook in a Cincinnati sandwich shop. He
was arrested for carrying a concealed weapon. He pleaded guilty
and paid a small fine.

During Robinson's first spring training game against the Braves,
Lew Burdette came out on the field wearing two guns in a holster
over his uniform.

Kirby Higbe, 1960s

Higby's best year was 1941, when he went 22–9 for the Dodgers.
In his 1967 autobiography, *The High Hard One*, he described his
life after baseball. This included getting caught passing bad checks
and spending sixty days in Richland County Jail in South Carolina.
After his release, Higbe became a prison guard and was caught
smuggling sleeping pills into the prison. He hid the pills inside
baseballs.

Pinky Higgins, 1968

Higgins played thirteen seasons for the Red Sox, A's, and Tigers in
the 1930s and 1940s, hitting .292. During a three-game stretch in
1938, he got twelve consecutive hits. He managed the Red Sox for
eight years, and was *The Sporting News* Manager of the Year in
1955. In 1968, drunk and out of control, he ran over and killed a
Louisiana state highway worker and injured three others.

Higgins was charged with negligent homicide and sentenced to
four years at hard labor in the Louisiana State Prison. He was paroled

after serving less than two months. The day after he was released, he died of a heart attack.

Roy Howell, 1972

After he was drafted by the Texas Rangers, Howell went home to Lompoc, California, to go deer hunting with a friend. They were standing by the highway waiting for their ride when some guys in a pickup truck drove by and opened fire. Howell was hit in the arm and required an operation, but he recovered and played eleven seasons at third base with Texas, Toronto, and Milwaukee.

San Francisco Giants, 1974

The team was hit by robbery twice in one series against the Mets in New York. First, while the Giants were winning a doubleheader on Tuesday, thieves broke into their hotel rooms. They stole a gold ring and three sets of cufflinks from manager Charlie Fox, and coach Ozzie Virgil lost a stereo and the watch he had received for winning the batting championship of the Dominican Republic in 1956. Two nights later, $700 worth of clothing, equipment, and baseballs was stolen from the Giants' clubhouse.

Maury Wills, 1984

Wills is generally credited with bringing the stolen base back to baseball. He led the league in that department every year from 1960 to 1965, and his 104 in 1962 broke Ty Cobb's supposedly unbreakable record of 96. He won the MVP that year and later became the third black manager in baseball history.

After baseball, he switched to stealing cars and snorting cocaine. When he was fired as manager of the Seattle Mariners in 1981, he went into a depression, living like a hermit for more than three years. He was arrested for cocaine possession in 1983, but the charge was dropped for lack of evidence.

The next year Los Angeles police spotted a 1981 Audi cruising along with a window wide open in the pouring rain. They checked out the license plate and found the car had been stolen. The window was smashed. They pulled the car over and found Wills inside. He was arrested for grand theft auto, and the police found a vial of cocaine and a water pipe in the car. He was cleared again—the car belonged to a former girlfriend.

Wills went through drug rehab at CareUnit in California and began a vitamin therapy program.

"I had no reason to go to bed at night and no reason to wake up," he told *Jet* magazine. "I was that close to death."

John "Blue Moon" Odom, 1985

Odom pitched for thirteen years and was one of the stars in Oakland's World Championship dynasty of 1972–1974. In 1985, he threatened to kill his wife and held her at gunpoint with a shotgun in their apartment in Fountain Valley, California. After several hours he released his wife, but refused to come out of the apartment. Hostage negotiation teams communicated with him by telephone, but it took a SWAT team lobbing four tear gas canisters through the window to get the ex-pitcher to surrender. No shots were fired and there were no injuries. Odom was arrested and charged with assault with a deadly weapon. The following year he was found guilty of selling cocaine.

James "Cool Papa" Bell, 1989

When Bell was inducted into the Baseball Hall of Fame in 1974, all the hats, balls, uniforms, and other memorabilia from his thirty-year career in the Negro Leagues became priceless overnight. In 1989, two men came to visit the eighty-six-year-old Bell, asking for autographs. While one of them kept Cool Papa and his wife busy, the other hauled out crates of stuff. Three weeks later, Bell suffered a stroke.

The two men, Ed Grybowski and Robert Retort, claimed they'd paid Bell $500 for the memorabilia. Bell said he felt "trapped" and afraid he would be hurt if he tried to stop them.

Grybowski and Retort were arrested for interstate transportation of stolen property. Charges against Grybowski were dismissed and Retort's trial ended in a hung jury. Though it appeared that they had pressured Bell into a deal, there was no proof a crime had been committed.

Jose Canseco, 1989

A passerby on the campus of the University of California at San Francisco peeked into the window of a red Jaguar and saw a 9mm semiautomatic handgun on the floor of the driver's side. Both car and gun belonged to Oakland slugger Canseco. He pleaded not guilty to illegal possession of a weapon and explained that he and his wife had received repeated telephone threats.

This was one of a series of incidents that made headlines for Canseco that year. He and his cousin David Valdez were at Detroit Metropolitan Airport when a metal detector showed Valdez was carrying a handgun. Canseco was clocked by police driving 125 mph in Miami, and he received four citations in one day in Phoenix—for running a red light, having false license plates, driving without registration, and failure to prove ownership or insurance.

Umpire Steve Palermo, 1991

After working third base in a Saturday-night game between the California Angels and Texas Rangers, the fourteen-year American League umpire went out for dinner at Campisi's Egyptian Restaurant in Dallas. Just before 1:00 A.M., four men robbed two waitresses at gunpoint in the restaurant's parking lot.

Palermo and several others gave chase, and one of the robbers shot the umpire in the stomach. He suffered nerve damage, and didn't take his first step for three months. Three men were charged with attempted murder and robbery. A fourth suspect was a juvenile.

Little League Shooting, 1991

It happened in East St. Louis, Illinois. When sixteen-year-old umpire Roderick Fisher called a runner out on a close play at the plate, the runner's coach charged onto the field and berated him.

"Why are you making all these bad calls?" screamed thirty-one-year-old Curtis Fair.

Fisher threw Fair out of the game, and the coach grabbed a bat and chased him, yelling, "I'll bust your head. I'll kill you."

Fair eventually left the field but came back ten minutes later with a .38-caliber revolver. Parents and their kids ran for their lives. Fair emptied the gun, but no one was hurt.

Prison Escape, 1991

Michael Michell, a convicted murderer, escaped from prison in Montana on January 19. He made his way to Seattle, where he decided to take in a Mariners game at the Kingdome. As he was standing at a souvenir stand, an old acquaintance spotted him—Jack McCormick, the warden of the prison Michell had escaped from. McCormick was on vacation, attending the ballgame with his son.

"Hi, Mike," said the warden. "How are you doing?"

Michell was arrested by officers at the Kingdome and currently faces two to ten years in jail for escape.

Dorian Gray Daughtry, 1991

The twenty-three-year-old former right fielder with the Seattle Mariners' farm team in Bellingham, Washington, was convicted of killing a nine-year-old girl with a stray bullet during a street gunfight in Brooklyn. The victim, Veronica Corales, was hit in the head while she was sleeping. Daughtry was sentenced to eight to twenty-five years in jail.

THEY DID JAIL TIME

Babe Ruth once spent an afternoon in jail on a driving violation. Ron LeFlore did eight years for armed robbery. The following is a list of major league ballplayers who spent at least some time in the slammer.

Willie Aikens

Cap Anson

Vida Blue

Cesar Cedeno

Orlando Cepeda

Ty Cobb

Michael Donlin

Ryne Duren

James Egan

Dock Ellis

Kirby Higbe

Pinky Higgins

Steve Howe

LaMarr Hoyt

Ron LeFlore

Billy Martin

Jerry Martin

Denny McLain

Dickie Noles

Mike Norris

Joe Pepitone

Pascual Perez

Luis Polonia

Pedro Ramos

Pete Rose

Babe Ruth

Sammy Stewart

Darryl Strawberry

Hank Thompson

Fred Toney

Rube Waddell

Willie Wilson

Dave Winfield

Twins Show Punch As Martin Knocks
CHEW UMPIRE'S EAR IN BASEBALL BRAWL

Lasorda, ... S LINKED
Fight at ... T IN CAFE

LOS ANGEL...
fight in a televis...
Los Angeles De...
Lasorda, and a...
and coach, Jim...
sorda with a blo...
Lasorda was...
from his nose, ...

...er Denies That
...Swing at Fan
...na 'Incident'

DETROIT TEAM
OUT ON STRIKE

4 Mets
Arrested
In Fight

Won't Play Until Cobb, Who
Beat Defenseless Cripple at
Game, Is Reinstated.

BALL GAME.

Ex-Yank ...r in ho... row
with ... ...

...ork Tl...
...who ...
...n had ...
...assist...

...a fan of
...er early
...ed as

...L... ...ME.

...ver

BA...

*"Sure I fought. I had to fight
all my life to survive.
They were all against me . . .
tried every dirty trick to cut
me down. But I beat the
bastards and left them in
the ditch."*

—Ty Cobb

Baseball fights are a time-honored ritual that would make a fascinating subject for anthropological study. Typically they begin when a batter has the audacity to hit a home run, which pitchers take as a personal affront to their dignity.

Beanballs often follow, usually aimed at the offending hitter but frequently at the head of the poor slob who happens to be next up—the baseball equivalent to closing the barn door after the horse has escaped.

If sufficiently angered, the hitter will get up off the ground, exchange several obscenities with the pitcher, drop the bat, and approach the mound. Almost as if his moves have been choreographed, the pitcher in turn drops his glove, puffs out his chest, and challenges the hitter to come and get him, all the while praying his $2-million arm will not be separated from his shoulder.

A few anemic punches may be thrown, but damage is rarely inflicted because tradition requires that every player on both teams charge out of the dugout and converge on the infield in a mock show of support for his teammate.

Next, there is much finger pointing, rough shoving, yelling, and holding back of incensed participants. Mostly, it's a lot of silly dancing around, which from the upper deck may appear to be actual combat. Ballplayers, who are forbidden to fraternize with their opponents on the field during batting practice, may take the opportunity to renew old friendships, shoot the breeze, or set up dates to socialize with their families over the weekend.

After five or ten minutes, cool heads prevail, and everybody returns to his original position as if nothing has happened. Nobody gets hurt. Everybody looks macho.

The game goes on. The reporters have something to spice up their stories. The fans feel as if they've gotten a little something extra for their money and come home with a story to tell their friends. The baseball fight ritual, as practiced here, is actually good for baseball.

There are variations on the charging-of-the-mound theme: The nightclub brawl. The locker-room argument. The old climb-into-the-stands-and-punch-out-a-heckling-fan routine. But prospective players should study the step-by-step sequence above if they hope to make it in the big leagues.

Of course, on rare occasion, ballplayers actually fight because they're mad at one another. Teammates Joe Tinker and Johnny Evers, forever linked by the famous poem "Tinker to Evers to Chance," got into a fistfight during a game in 1905 and barely spoke to one another again. Three players were *killed in* a 1935 free-for-all between two teams in Jalisco, Mexico.

There have been many memorable fights and fighters in baseball that have gone beyond the ritual described above. Here are some highlights.

THE MARICHAL/ROSEBORO WAR
Bat Day at Candlestick Park

The 1965 National League pennant race was one of the tightest ever. At one point, a game and a half separated four teams. Two of them were the Giants and the Dodgers—baseball's most bitter rivals for decades. When the Dodgers pulled into Candlestick Park for a four-game series at the end of August, tension was in the air.

The Dodgers won the first two games, both in extra innings. The third game went to the Giants. The next day 42,807 fans—Candlestick's largest crowd of the year—turned out to see baseball's most glamorous pitchers, Sandy Koufax (21–4) and Juan Marichal (19–9), face off for the first time all season.

On the first pitch of the game, Maury Wills dropped down a bunt and beat it out for a single. Ron Fairly doubled Wills home. The score was 1–0, Dodgers.

In his half of the first, Koufax struck out the side.

In the second inning, beanballs started to fly. Marichal decked both Wills and Fairly. Wes Parker doubled, and the Dodgers' soft-spoken catcher, John Roseboro, singled in the run. The score was 2–0, Dodgers.

If a guy is throwing at your teammates, baseball tradition dictates that you throw at *his* teammates. Koufax took the mound and threw his first pitch over the head of Willie Mays, all the way back to the screen. "I meant it to come a lot closer," he said later. Cap Peterson hit a home run off Koufax, cutting the Dodgers' lead to 2–1.

Juan Marichal led off the memorable third inning for the Giants. He took a strike and a ball, then suddenly wheeled around.

"Why do you do that?" he said to catcher Roseboro. "Why do you do that?"

You couldn't tell from the stands, but Marichal was complaining about Roseboro's habit of zipping the ball dangerously close to the batter's ear on his return throws to the pitcher. It was a subtle form of intimidation.

Roseboro didn't respond. Maybe he should have. Marichal took a step backward to give himself some swinging room, raised his bat as if he was splitting wood with an ax, and slammed it down on Roseboro's head. Koufax came running off the mound to grab the bat, but not before Marichal got off at least two more blows. Roseboro was sprawled on the ground, with a two-inch gash on his head bleeding profusely.

A sixty-man rumble followed. On-deck hitter Tito Fuentes, in his first week in the big leagues, tried to break up the fight, but Dodger Howie Reed went after Marichal. Orlando Cepeda grabbed a bat. Marichal taunted Roseboro, who now had blood all over his chest protector, asking him if he wanted more. Dodgers coach Danny Ozark attacked Marichal. Umpire Shag Crawford dragged Marichal away. Giants teammates cooled off Cepeda. Policemen took up guard positions at both teams' clubhouses. The Dodgers' trainer wiped the blood away from Roseboro's face, and the catcher charged after Marichal. He was caught from behind by Willie Mays, who held Roseboro's head in his hands, looking at his wounds with obvious concern.

"Johnny, Johnny!" Mays said. "I'm so sorry." Some said Mays had tears in his eyes.

When order was finally restored, Marichal and Roseboro were escorted from the park. An unnerved Koufax walked two batters, and Willie Mays hit the first pitch over the left center-field wall for his thirty-eighth home run of the season. It turned out to be the game winner.

With thirty-seven games left to play, the National League standings looked like this:

Los Angeles	.576
San Francisco	.575
Milwaukee	.574

Afterward, there was time to reflect on what had happened and offer up quotes for the reporters.

"I thought it had knocked Roseboro's eye out," said Dodgers manager Walter Alston. "There was nothing but blood where his left eye should have been."

"He's a goddam nut," Dodgers coach Danny Ozark said of Marichal. "A guy like that would hit a woman."

"The important four-game series with the Giants had been split," commented *Sports Illustrated*, "and so had catcher John Roseboro's head."

Willie Mays said the incident was caused by the Dodgers, who would move their bats back trying to tip the catcher's glove and get on base by interference. Earlier in the series, Maury Wills had pulled off this trick.

National League president Warren Giles was ridiculed for the slap on the wrist he gave Marichal—an eight-day suspension and $1,750 fine. Marichal missed two starts.

"Giles is gutless," snapped Maury Wills.

The press made some effort to characterize the fight as a racial riot. Marichal was Dominican, Roseboro black. But Koufax was Jewish, Fuentes Cuban, and Cepeda Puerto Rican. Race was not an issue. Baseball's melting pot had made it possible for men of all races and religions to join together and beat each others' heads in.

The fight had unnerved both clubs. The Dodgers went to New York and lost three straight to the pathetic Mets, who were thirty-two games out of first place. The Giants lost four straight to Pittsburgh. Both teams eventually recovered, and the Dodgers won the pennant by two games over the Giants.

Marichal made a public apology for his explosion, explaining, "I thought he was going to hit me with the mask." Roseboro, back behind the plate three nights after the brawl, was unmoved. He filed a $110,000 battery suit against Marichal. Four years later, he settled for $7,500 and retired from baseball.

Apparently, there are no long-term consequences of slamming a baseball bat against a man's skull. With a lifetime record of 243 wins and 142 losses, Juan Marichal was inducted into the Hall of Fame in 1983.

TY COBB
The Fight That Lasted a Lifetime

There's no way of knowing whether or not Amanda Cobb was having an affair in the summer of 1905. But Professor William Herschel Cobb, a respected Georgia educator, suspected that his wife was fooling around behind his back and decided to find out for sure.

On the night of August 8, he informed Amanda that he would be away on a business trip for the evening. He hitched his horse to his buggy and left the house. Amanda went upstairs, locked her window, and went to sleep.

Shortly after midnight she heard a noise on the roof outside her window. A shadowy figure was trying to open the window, and she quickly grabbed the shotgun that stood in the corner of the room. She fired both barrels, then rushed to the window to see who the intruder was. Lying in a pool of blood lay Professor Cobb. There was a gaping hole in his abdomen and his brains had been literally blown out of his skull. A revolver was found in his coat pocket.*

Less then three weeks later, eighteen-year-old Tyrus Raymond Cobb played his first major-league baseball game, for the Detroit Tigers.

Ty Cobb was naturally quick-tempered, but undoubtedly the tragedy of his mother killing his father influenced his behavior, propelling him to his achievements on the field as well as fostering his lifelong violent streak. He was arguably the greatest player ever to set foot on a diamond, and certainly the most combative.

Cobb has been described as psychotic by some historians, paranoid and suffering from a persecution complex by others. He was a bitter, lonely man with no sense of humor who over the course of his life became estranged from most of his family and his few friends.

"Trouble was he had such a rotten disposition that it was damn hard to be his friend," teammate Davy Jones told baseball historian Lawrence Ritter. "He antagonized so many people that hardly anyone would speak to him, even among his own teammates. A lot of times it seemed as though he was just asking for trouble."

"He came up with an antagonistic attitude, which in his mind turned any little razzing into a life-or-death struggle," said Sam Crawford, who played alongside Cobb in Detroit's outfield for years. "He always figured everybody was ganging up against him."

"Cobb wouldn't stand for nothin'," Ring Lardner wrote in 1915. "If somebody poured ketchup in his coffee, he was liable to pick up the cup and throw it at the guy nearest to him. If you'd called him some name on the field, he'd of walloped you with a bat, even if you was his best pal."

"He was the same off the field as he was on," according to Charley Gehringer; "he was always fighting with somebody."

You could count on a good Ty Cobb fight about once a year. He beat up a boy delivering groceries to his home. He beat up a close

---

* In his autobiography, *My Life in Baseball*, Cobb wrote that his father was shot by a member of his family but does not mention that it was his mother. John McCallum's 1956 biography, *The Tiger Wore Spikes*—written with Cobb's cooperation—mentions that Professor Cobb was shot but does not say by whom. Charles C. Alexander's *Ty Cobb* is the best portrait of the man and tells the true story in detail.

friend who left him with the check in a restaurant. He beat up a roommate who tried to use the bathtub first. Even the mild-mannered Lou Gehrig tried to fight him.

His teammates hated him, especially when he first arrived in the big leagues. Cobb started carrying a gun in 1906—his second season—and slept with it at his bedside. That year he suffered "some kind of emotional and physical collapse," according to biographer Charles C. Alexander. He left the lineup and spent a short time in a Detroit sanitarium. An operation was performed, most likely to remove an ulcer. He was just nineteen.

On the final day of the 1906 season, Tigers pitcher Ed Siever took a swing at Cobb, who decked him with a right to the jaw and then kicked him in the head. Cobb didn't fare as well against Tigers catcher Charley Schmidt, an ex-fighter who had once gone a few rounds with heavyweight contender Jack Johnson. An article appeared in an Atlanta newspaper quoting Cobb as saying he could beat up Schmidt or anybody else on the team. The two agreed to fight, observing formal Marquis of Queensberry boxing rules. Schmidt, who was known for being able to hammer a nail into a piece of wood with his fists, broke Cobb's nose and banged his eyes nearly shut. In his autobiography, Cobb said Schmidt snuck up from behind and attacked him.

Though he seemed to hate men of all races and religions, Cobb had a particular dislike for blacks, and sportswriter Fred Lieb suspected he was a member of the Klu Klux Klan. During spring training in 1907, a black groundskeeper nicknamed "Bungy" greeted Cobb by calling him "Carrie." Cobb slapped the man and chased him toward the Tigers' clubhouse. Bungy's wife ran out, yelling at Cobb. He grabbed her and choked her before teammates pulled him off.

The next year, he stepped on some new asphalt being laid down by city workers, and a black laborer named Fred Collins yelled at him. Cobb knocked Collins down and was summoned to court on an assault and battery charge. He paid Collins $75.

In 1909, a black elevator operator in a hotel got into an argument with Cobb and received a slap to the face. George Stansfield, the black night watchman, then hit Cobb with his nightstick. Cobb pulled a knife from his pocket and slashed Stansfield. Stansfield pulled out a pistol and knocked Cobb to his knees with a blow to the head. Hotel employees broke the fight up before it went any further.

In 1914, Cobb came home one evening and his wife told him about a dispute she'd had with a butcher who refused to take back twenty cents' worth of spoiled fish. Furious, Cobb grabbed his revolver and ran down to the butcher's store to demand that he call Mrs. Cobb and apologize. The butcher did, but his assistant, who was black, began arguing and waving a meat cleaver. Cobb hit the man over the head with the gun. That time he was thrown in jail overnight.

He was also arrested in 1925 after an argument with a waitress over a bill. The cashier, a woman, hit Cobb over the head with a large glass dish. The police were summoned and Cobb posted an $11 bond to be released.

Ty Cobb's most celebrated fight took place on May 15, 1912, when he vaulted into the stands in New York and pummeled a defenseless fan. The incident cannot be described more vividly than it was in the unbylined article that appeared in the *New York Times* the next day:

> *Everything was very pleasant at the Detroit-Yankee game on the Hilltop yesterday* [Hilltop Park, where the Yankees played] *until Ty Cobb johnnykilbaned a spectator right on the place where he talks, started the claret, and stopped the flow of profane and vulgar words. Cobb led with a left jab and countered with a right kick to Mr. Spectator's left Weisbach, which made his peeper look as if some one had drawn a curtain over it. Silk O'Loughlin* [the umpire], *without a license from the boxing commission, refereed the go. He gave the decision to Cobb and then put him out of the ring. The spectator went to a lawyer's office to make out his will.*
>
> *It all happened in the fourth inning. For three days a group of fans have been sitting behind the Detroit bench, enjoying an uninvited monologue for Cobb's discomfort. What they have been saying to the Georgia Peach has no place in a family newspaper or even one that circulates in barber shops only. The conversation yesterday got as rough as No. 2 sandpaper*

*and Cobb hurdled into the ring. He went right up into the stand
and started to drum a tune on the face of the vulgar person
who was leading the chorus of mining camp talk.*

*The scrap broke up the game for a while. Umpire O'Loughlin
and several Detroit players subtracted Cobb from his victim.
Cobb's execution was rapid and effective. Ty used a change of
pace and had nice control. Jabs bounded off the spectator's
face like a golf ball from a rock. Cobb was dragged back to
the bench and O'Loughlin sent him to the clubhouse. The
spectator got the gate.*

*Cobb delayed the game by vaulting into the stand, with the
intention of making his talkative adversary swallow his cruel
words. The man who got in front of Cobb's wallops refused
to present his card, so he will be called Otto Blotz for Short.
Mr. Blotz lost much dignity and a little blood, while Detroit
lost a good ball player just when they needed him.*

"Otto Blotz" had a real name—Claude Lueker. He was a law-
office flunky who had lost his left hand and three fingers of his right
in a printing-press accident a year earlier.

For the most part, the verbal abuse consisted of Lueker shouting
that Cobb was a "half-nigger," and Cobb responding that he had
enjoyed relations with Lueker's sister the evening previous. (The
Times reported this exchange as: "You're dopy!" "Yes, I'm dopy,
but I'll get you yet!")

Lueker claimed he was not the one who heckled Cobb and described the beating he suffered: "He struck me with his fists on the
forehead over the left eye, and knocked me down. Then he jumped
on me and spiked me in the left leg, and booted me behind the left
ear. I was down and Cobb was kicking me, when someone in the
crowd shouted, 'Don't kick him, he has no hands!' Cobb answered,
'I don't care if he has no feet!' "

Cobb was suspended, and history was made when his
teammates—despite their dislike of him—pulled off the first players'
strike in baseball history. To a man, Detroit refused to take the field
until Cobb was reinstated. Manager Hughie Jennings pulled together
a makeshift team of college and semipro players and paid them $10
each to play the day's game against the world champion Philadelphia
Athletics. With the real Tigers enjoying the show from the stands,
the paper Tigers were mauled, 24–2. The strike ended the next day

when Cobb thanked his teammates and told them he didn't want to jeopardize their careers. He was back in the lineup a week later.

At the end of the season, Cobb had another battle when three men stopped his car and inexplicably began punching him. Cobb leaped out and pistol-whipped one of the muggers senseless, receiving a stab wound in his back during the fight. The Detroit trainer cleaned him up and he got three hits the following day.

The chronology of Cobb's conflicts goes on and on, but I will restrict myself to detailing just one more memorable fight. During a game against Washington in 1921, Cobb, now a player/manager, was called out trying to steal second base by umpire Billy Evans. He flew into a rage and after the game went to the umpire's dressing room and challenged Evans to settle it man to man. Both men stripped to the waist and went at it under the stands while a group of Tigers and Senators watched. Five-year-old Ty Jr. was there to offer encouragement to his father, shouting, "Come on, Daddy!"

According to Sammy Barnes, a young Tigers infielder, it was the bloodiest fight he ever saw. Evans's right cheek and eyebrow were opened, and before it was broken up Cobb was banging the umpire's head against the cinders. Afterward, the two men shook hands. Once again, Cobb was suspended.

If Ty Cobb was playing today, he probably wouldn't be. It's difficult to imagine how such a tortured man would have adapted to celebrity today, when public figures are scrutinized so much more carefully than they were earlier in the century.

Cobb had his last big fight in 1959, when he was diagnosed with cancer. A bitter, paranoid man to the end, he kept a loaded Luger pistol with him in his hospital bed, as well as a brown paper bag with more than $1 million worth of negotiable securities in it. (Having invested in Coca-Cola and General Motors early, he was the first player/millionaire.) A daily quart of Jack Daniel's mixed with a quart of milk numbed his pain somewhat, but after two years he slipped away at the age of seventy-four.

One obituary read, "The only difference now is that he is a bad guy who is dead." Just three former ballplayers—Mickey Cochrane, Ray Schalk, and Nap Rucker—came to pay their respects.

———

"Sure I fought," Cobb said in a magazine interview months before he died. "I had to fight all my life to survive. They were all against me . . . tried every dirty trick to cut me down. But I beat the bastards and left them in the ditch . . . I fought so hard for my father, who was the greatest man I ever knew."

JOHN MCGRAW
The Little Napoleon

While most players known as fighters have been skilled at the craft, John McGraw was, by most accounts, a *lousy* fighter. His Hall of Fame career as a player and manager of the New York Giants was dotted with dozens of brawls, most of which left McGraw dazed and bleeding on the ground. He was an expert at destroying men with his mouth but not much of a threat when it came time to put up his dukes.

"It is highly doubtful that John McGraw ever won a fistfight," umpire Bill Klem once said. "And it is without question that he never ducked one."

In 1915, McGraw accused Texas League manager Patrick Newman of using "bush league language." Newman hauled off and clocked him, splitting McGraw's lip and knocking him unconscious. In 1920, a drunken argument with Broadway actor William Boyd resulted in McGraw being slammed over the head with a water carafe and kicked in the face. Arriving at the Polo Grounds the next day with two black eyes, he handed the team over to coach Johnny Evers and didn't come back for five days.

McGraw's heckling once got Philadelphia pitcher Ad Brennan so angry that Brennan walked off the mound and knocked him out with one punch. Even five-foot-four-inch teammate Wee Willie Keeler got the better of McGraw when the two men fought—naked—on the Baltimore Oriole clubhouse floor after a game in 1897 (McGraw had criticized the play of Keeler, who hit .424 and led the league that season).

McGraw was so inept a fighter that the men he battled sometimes weren't even sure it was a real fight. After one brawl with him, pitcher Bugs Raymond said, "Why, if I'd known the little bastard was serious, I'd have killed him."*

Actually, John McGraw *did* occasionally beat somebody up: in 1904 he socked a boy selling lemonade near the Giants' bench. The poor kid split his lip and loosened a few teeth when he hit the ground.

Because McGraw became a major-league manager when he was just twenty-five years old and managed for the next thirty-three years, it's sometimes forgotten that he was a top-notch third baseman and batsman. he hit .391 for the Baltimore Orioles in 1899 and stole seventy-three bases.

The "old Orioles" were perhaps the rowdiest bunch in baseball history, and they were known to trip opposing runners, throw equipment in their path, sharpen their spikes, and do just about anything to win a ballgame. As the leader of the Orioles, McGraw was commonly referred to as a "ruffian," "rowdy," or "hoodlum" in the press. He once offered to fight everybody in the Cincinnati ballpark. Anyone who dared refer to him by his hated nickname, "Muggsy," was almost certain to have a fight on his hands.

During one game in 1894, McGraw got into a fight with Boston third baseman Billy Nash. Both benches emptied, and the brawl spread to the stands. Within minutes, fires started breaking out and the entire ballpark burned to the ground.

It was because of the language and behavior of the Orioles that National League owners passed "The Brush Rule" in 1898. Subtitled "A Measure for the Suppression of Obscene, Indecent and Vulgar Language Upon the Ball Field," it was one of the first attempts to "clean up" baseball.

When he became a manager, McGraw's trademark was umpire baiting. "His ability to heap verbal abuse on the beleaguered arbiters was unmatched," wrote Charles C. Alexander in his book *John McGraw*. Umpire Arlie Latham said McGraw "eats gunpowder every morning and washes it down with warm blood."

His most celebrated battle with an umpire was a 1917 fistfight

---

* Attending a game as a spectator in September of 1912, Raymond got into an argument with a more adept fighter, who kicked him in the head and fractured his skull. Raymond died two days later.

under the stands at the Polo Grounds against Bill "The Singing
Umpire" Byron. Byron got some perverse pleasure from belting out
taunting rhymes while he dusted off home plate. One of his favor-
ites ran:

> To the clubhouse you must go,
> You must go, you must go,
> To the clubhouse you must go,
> My fair manager."

After the Giants lost a game to Cincinnati in the bottom of the
ninth, McGraw walked up to Bryon and said, "Take your hands
out of your pockets and I'll show you who's the better man." Words
were exchanged, and the pair went at it.

"The umpire went down, his mouth bleeding profusely," wrote
sportswriter Sam Crane. "He made no attempt to regain his feet."

It may have been McGraw's finest performance on the field of
battle. He was suspended sixteen days and fined $500.

McGraw invited hostility, sometimes merely to draw attention to
his team and increase attendance. "Sportsmanship and easygoing
methods are all right," he once said, "but it is the prospect of a hot
fight that brings out the crowds."

He would send telegrams with the Giants' itinerary to the next
city the team was to play. In those days the players would put on
their uniforms in their hotel and ride in open carriages to the ballpark. Newspapers would print the parade route, and McGraw and
his teammates were sure to be pelted with rocks and vegetables on
their way to the game.

It isn't necessary to dig too deep for explanations of McGraw's
combative nature. He experienced enough heartache in his life for
several men. At the age of twelve, he lost his mother, two brothers,
and two sisters to a diphtheria epidemic. Afterward his father beat
him so badly that he ran away and was taken in by a kind-hearted
widow. He got married in 1897, but two years later his beloved
Minnie died of acute appendicitis. She was just twenty-two.

McGraw was a sort of Jekyll-and-Hyde character. In a baseball
uniform, he was a terror to umpires, opposing players, and even his
own teammates. Yet he contributed financial help to down-and-out
ex-big leaguers like morphine addict Billy Earle, and he was one of

the first to attempt to bring black players into the game. He fought legendary verbal battles with umpire Bill Klem in the afternoon, but they were friends off the field and frequently dined together. After Minnie McGraw died, John became a devoted husband to his second wife, Blanche, until his death thirty-two years later. He died early in 1934, a little over a year after he managed his last game.

"He was a fighter, but he was also the kindest, best-hearted fellow you ever saw," said shortstop Al Bridwell, who played under McGraw between 1908 and 1911. "I got along with him fine," Bridwell told baseball historian Lawrence Ritter. "He only suspended me once for two weeks. It was on account of I socked him."

McGraw and Gambling

"McGraw loved to gamble, especially on horses," claimed his biographer Charles C. Alexander. He also bet on prizefights, pool games, and, yes, baseball. According to Alexander, McGraw won $400 betting on the 1905 World Series against the Philadelphia Athletics, a transgression that today would result in lifetime banishment from the game.

Baseball was not policed very strictly in McGraw's early days, and he seemed oblivious to the fact that a man in his position should steer clear of gambling interests. He kept close associations with many big-time sporting men, including racetrack and casino owners.

According to Alexander, gambling was "a fairly important part" of McGraw's life by 1900. He would attend early races at tracks around New York City, then rush to get to the Polo Grounds in time for the afternoon's game. On occasion he would send his players out to the track to get bets down for him.

In the winter of 1904, he was arrested for unlicensed public gambling when he hustled about $2,300 from passersby pitching silver dollars into a basket at a hotel in Hot Springs, Arkansas. The following year he became co-owner of a pool hall in Manhattan with a gambler named Jack Doyle. He opened another one in 1908. This time he had a silent partner in Arnold Rothstein, the man who put up the money to fund the Black Sox scandal.

McGraw was never seriously investigated or disciplined for his attraction to baseball's biggest sin.

BILLY MARTIN
Even the Urinals Weren't Safe

"Everybody looks up to Billy," it was said, "because he probably just knocked them down."

As a young man, Alfred Manuel Pesano considered a career as a middleweight boxer. Instead, he chose baseball and made fighting a lifelong hobby. Billy the Kid had a short fuse and focused his aggression on players, fans, writers, and, in his later years, inanimate objects. He was a good fighter and didn't hesitate to take on men much bigger than himself. (He weighed just 165 pounds.)

After playing for eleven years as a second baseman, mostly for the Yankees, Billy became perhaps the best manager in baseball. He would typically lead his team to a championship, then get into a highly publicized fight and get fired. His hirings and firings by the Yankees—five times altogether—became an annual ritual in New York, kind of like the swallows returning to Capistrano.

It was an open secret that Billy had a problem with alcohol, and nearly all his off-field scuffles took place in bars. "I didn't like to fight," he once said. "But I didn't have a choice."

This is a record of Billy's major bouts:

• May 1952 vs. Jimmy Piersall

During infield practice before a game in Boston, Martin and Piersall exchanged insults. When Piersall called him a "busher," Martin motioned toward a runway under the stands. The fight lasted a few minutes and was broken up by several Yankees and Red Sox.

Two days later, Piersall was sent to Birmingham and had his celebrated nervous breakdown (see chapter 6).

Outcome: Billy by TKO.

• July 1952 vs. Clint Courtney

After the Yankees traded him away, the St. Louis Browns catcher played particularly hard against New York. In the second inning of this game, he kicked a double-play ball out of Billy's glove. In the sixth inning, he slid hard into Yogi Berra. In the eighth, he tried to steal second. Billy got the ball in time and tagged Courtney hard in the face. Courtney charged, and Billy dropped him with one punch. The catcher bounced back up and Billy got off a few more blows before the fight was broken up.

Outcome: Billy by decision.

• May 1957: The Yankees vs. Edwin Jones

Billy was at the Copacabana in New York celebrating his twenty-ninth birthday with teammates Mickey Mantle, Whitey Ford, Yogi Berra, Hank Bauer, Gil McDougal, and Johnny Kucks. A 200-pound Bronx delicatessen owner named Edwin Jones was there too, celebrating the end of bowling season with his team, the Republicans, and their wives. Sammy Davis Jr. was appearing that night, and the ballplayers showed up in time for the 2:00 A.M. show.

The Yankees' version of the fight was that Jones leaned over to Bauer and called Sammy Davis "Little Black Sambo." When Bauer told him to shut up, Jones replied, "Who's going to make me?" Words were exchanged, the music stopped, and Sammy Davis shouted, "I wish you people would either keep quiet or leave. I'm trying to entertain."

One of the bowlers said, "Goddamn nigger trying to tell me what to do!" Bauer and Jones got out of their seats and headed for the rest room, with the Yankees and Republicans right behind. In the ensuing scuffle, Jones ended up unconscious with a broken nose, a fractured jaw, and a concussion. Bauer got credit for doing the damage. He was hitting .203 at the time and commented, "Hit him? I haven't hit anybody all year." The Yankees claimed it was the Copa bouncer who bounced Jones. "All of a sudden, we heard a crash," said Whitey Ford, "and by the time we got there, the guy was stretched out on the floor."

Each Yankee was fined $1,000 except for Kucks, who only had to pay $500. Martin got most of the blame, probably because of his growing reputation. He was traded to Kansas City a month later.

"Nobody never hit nobody nohow," quipped Yogi.
Outcome: Billy by default.

• August 1960 vs. Jim Brewer

The Cubs pitcher threw a fastball behind Billy's head, and on the next pitch Billy flung his bat at Brewer. "You little dago son of a bitch!" Brewer yelled. Martin charged the mound and punched Brewer. The fight didn't last long, but Billy's blow shattered Brewer's cheekbone and put him in the hospital for two weeks. He was out for the season and had to undergo two operations on his eye.

Brewer sued Martin for $1 million, prompting Billy to ask, "How does he want it? Cash or check?" Billy was fined $500 and suspended for five days. After a jury trial, Brewer was awarded $10,000, and Billy was paying it off for years.

Outcome: Billy by TKO, Billy traded to Milwaukee.

• July 1966 vs. Howard Fox, Minnesota Twins traveling secretary

There was an airline strike on, and the Twins were sharing a plane with the Yankees. After a long delay, the players had too much to drink and Fox asked Billy—now a coach—if he would calm his old team down. Billy refused, and they argued all the way to the hotel. There, Fox angrily tossed his room keys at Billy, who responded, "You do that again and I'm going to beat the living hell out of you!"

Fox, a bigger man, took off his glasses and said, "How about here, right now?" Billy got the better of it, popping Fox in the eye.

Outcome: Billy by decision.

• August 1969 vs. Dave Boswell

During his first year managing the Twins, Billy flattened Boswell, one of his own pitchers, outside a Detroit bar. The day before, pitching coach Art Fowler had told Billy that Boswell had only run two of his required twenty wind sprints. When Billy saw Boswell that night in a bar, he told

him he wanted to speak with him the next day. Boswell left,
saying he was going "to get that squealer, Fowler."

Twins outfielder Bob Allison tried to talk Boswell out of
it and said, "If you're going to hit somebody, why don't you
hit me?" Boswell obliged, knocking Allison cold with one
punch. Billy arrived, and Boswell went after him too, landing
a few punches. Billy, who was twenty pounds lighter, fought
back viciously.

"I started punching him in the stomach as hard and as
fast as I could," Billy wrote in his book *Number 1*. "I must
have hit him forty times." Boswell was out before he hit the
ground, with blood all over. He came away with chipped
teeth, a black eye, and twenty stitches in his face. Billy got
seven stitches in his right hand.

Outcome: Billy by KO.

• September 1974 vs. Burt Hawkins, Texas Rangers traveling secretary

Now managing Texas, Billy socked the sixty-year-old Hawkins during an argument over whether or not the team
should have a club for the players' wives.

Outcome: Billy by decision.

• June 1977 vs. Reggie Jackson

Billy pulled Reggie out of a game in Boston when Mr. October failed to hustle after a double hit by Jim Rice. In the
dugout, Billy threw one punch that missed. The whole scene
was acted out before NBC's grateful *Game of the Week*
cameramen.

During a game the next July, Billy flashed the bunt sign
to Reggie in order to draw the infield in, then took it off.
Reggie insisted on bunting and bumped the third strike foul
for a strikeout. This time Billy directed his anger toward
inanimate objects, smashing glasses and heaving a clock radio against his office wall after the game.

Outcome: Draw. The radio was permanently disabled.

• November 1978 vs. *Nevada State Journal* reporter Ray Hagar

When Hagar refused to show Billy his interview notes in a Reno bar, Billy flattened him. Hagar charged Billy with battery but dropped the charge after Billy offered a public apology and $8,000.

Outcome: Billy by TKO.

• October 1979 vs. Joseph N. Cooper

This was Billy's most famous bout, simply because everyone found it so amusing that Cooper made his living selling marshmallows. The fight took place in the lobby of the Hotel de France in Bloomington, Minnesota.

Cooper, who weighed more than 200 pounds, approached Billy in the hotel bar shortly after midnight. He identified himself as the "Marshmallow King" and told Billy he didn't deserve the Manager of the Year Award. "Well," Billy replied, "maybe you're not the best marshmallow salesman."

Cooper taunted Billy, until Billy put $300 on the bar and said he'd bet it against Cooper's penny that Cooper couldn't whip him. Cooper decided the odds were excellent. On the way outside, he threw a left. Billy fended it off and hit the salesman with a right. "He went down like a sack of coal," Billy said later. Cooper ended up with twenty stitches in his lip.

Outcome: Billy by KO, Billy fired.

• May 1981 vs. Terry Cooney, umpire

After Billy threw dirt at him and bumped him, Cooney charged Billy with assault.

Outcome: Cooney by fiat. Billy was fined $1,000 and suspended.

• August 1982 vs. an office wall

During a contract dispute with the A's, Billy locked his office door and went berserk, breaking a finger. "I must be getting smarter," he said afterward. "I finally punched something that couldn't sue me."

Outcome: Wall by TKO, Billy fired in October.

• May 1983 vs. Robin Wayne Olson

Olson, a California real estate investor, was pestering Billy at the bar of the Anaheim Hyatt. Olson offered to buy Martin a beer, and Billy called him a name. Olson threw a matchbook at Billy. When he tapped Billy on the shoulder to apologize, Billy grabbed him by the shirt and hit him in the jaw. Olson's lawyer said his client suffered abdominal bruises and lost hair from his scalp.

Outcome: Billy by TKO.

• June 1983 vs. Cleveland clubhouse urinal

Billy was in the middle of his worst feud with George Steinbrenner. The Yankees' boss had fired Billy's pitching coach and close friend Art Fowler, and he had accused Billy of talking to women sitting next to the Yankees' dugout and of taking a nap during batting practice. When Cleveland scored six runs in the first inning of the day's game, Billy went back into the clubhouse and destroyed the urinal with a chair.

"I was in such a pissed-off mood," he told third baseman Graig Nettles, "if I had gone out and had a couple drinks, there's no telling what might have happened."

Outcome: Billy by KO. He had to replace the urinal.

• September 1985 vs. honeymooner

Billy was talking with a newlywed couple in the lounge of the Cross Keys Inn in Baltimore. He even bought them a bottle of champagne. The honeymooners left, but minutes later the husband returned and said to Billy, "You told my wife she has a potbelly."

"I didn't say she had a potbelly," Martin replied. "I said this woman (indicating somebody else) had a fat ass."

The two men shoved each other around a bit until some Yankees came along to break it up. Martin and the honeymooner agreed to settle the dispute outside, but when Billy got there his prospective opponent was gone.

Outcome: No decision.

• September 1985 vs. Ed Whitson

A week later, Billy was sitting in the same lounge with Dale Berra and his wife. It was an hour after the Holmes-Spinks fight. The Yankees were suffering through an eight-game losing streak. Billy was informed that Whitson, one of his pitchers, was having words with a hotel guest. Billy went to intervene.

Whitson was already steamed because Billy had scratched him as the starting pitcher for a game and had told reporters that "Whatchamacallit" had a tender arm. Angry words were exchanged, and the next thing anybody knew Martin and Whitson were rolling on the floor trying to strangle each other. Whitson kicked Billy in the groin, prompting the manager to scream, "Okay, now you did it! Now I'm going to kill you!"

By 1985, Billy was past his prime as a fighter and should have been thinking about hanging up the gloves. Whitson whipped Billy soundly, giving the manager a broken right arm, a bruised right side, and some cuts. Whitson himself had a cracked rib and a split lip. The pair crashed to the pavement in the parking lot before it was broken up. "Martin was plainly on his way to Palookaville," commented *Time*.

In the middle of the fight, Billy got off a real howler: "What's the matter with him?" he asked of Whitson. "Can't he hold his liquor?"

Outcome: Whitson by TKO.

• May 1988 vs. a phantom enemy in a Texas topless bar

Billy's explanation for his battered and bloodied condition was that two strangers had assaulted him in the men's room. But the police investigation showed that Billy had received his injuries when he was thrown out of the bar and landed against a brick wall. Billy offered to take a lie-detector test to prove his story but later changed his mind. "I guess I can't go anywhere anymore," Billy said, as though he had been in church.

"Who would hit a sixty-year-old man?" asked Yankees first baseman Don Mattingly. "That's like beating up your grandfather." With that comment, Billy's fighting days were truly over.

Throughout his storied career, many people believed that Billy had a death wish. He finally self-destructed on Christmas Day of 1989 near his home in Binghamton, New York. His pickup truck skidded off icy Potter Hill Road, careened 300 feet down an embankment, and crashed into a concrete culvert. The truck stopped at the foot of Billy's driveway. He was not wearing a seat belt and died of a broken neck, compressed spinal column, and injuries to the brain and other internal organs. He was sixty-one.

Billy's longtime friend William Reedy was behind the wheel. The two had been drinking heavily for hours and apparently decided that Reedy was in better shape to drive. Reedy sustained a broken hip and was charged with driving while intoxicated. Billy's fourth wife, Jill, filed a lawsuit against him in 1990.

Spied on Japs and Jerries

Mighty Moe Mysterious, Mum

ST. LOUIS—Doodling   —Moe was   as the .243-
a white tablecloth   d down the   zone was i

Myste   sified

WASHINGTON—   s foremost spies dur-
cabled home that he   olar, Spy," published
scientist say German
"Fine, just fine,   traces the life of a
Roosevelt upon hear   entures included dis-
the catcher."   n a Swiss lecture hall
The passage is   g to assassinate Ger-
player-turned-spy.   Werner Heisenberg.
With help fr   t the professor was
Agency and the State Department, Louis Kaur—   near success in developing the atomic bomb. He
man, Barbara Fitzgerald and Tom

Former Ballplayer Became
Top CIA Spy

2-10-75

Moe Berg: Adequate
Catcher, Great Spy

*Catcher magna
cum laude*

ONE-MAN BRAIN TRUS

Moe Berg, a M   any Facets

Moe Berg had such manifold talents that h   I remember that I long ha
as unusual and remarkable a character a   one and address.
baseball ever produced. It's a sadde   said Moe. "I's
Moe died suddenly on Monday at   how to reach
who knew him best will grieve   me in care o
delightful companion and just t   Boston."
only a pleasure but often an edu   Cronin h
As a ballplayer Moe Berg   er him
but as baseball's Man of Distinc   alled
was an honor   reate
Sports   received a law
of   studied at the
The Times   world traveler
              speak either
              number is j
to valuable use as an
Donovan's Office of S
Moe was baseb
help him especiall
catcher, Buck C
afte

> *"Moe Berg was a most*
> *unusual sort of catcher."*
>
> —Franklin Delano Roosevelt

MOE BERG
The Spy Who Came in from the Bullpen

November 29, 1934. It was the sixth inning of an exhibition game in Tokyo.* While Babe Ruth, Lou Gehrig, Charlie Gehringer, and Jimmy Foxx were showing the youth of Japan how far a fastball could travel, backup catcher Moe Berg had another mission in mind.

Wearing a black kimono, he walked into a Tokyo florist shop and purchased a bouquet. He stepped outside and hailed a cab to take him to St. Luke's International Hospital. Holding the flowers in front of him, he told the receptionist—in fluent Japanese—that he had come to visit American Ambassador Joseph Clark Grew's daughter, who had just had a baby. He was directed to take an elevator to the seventh floor. Security guards allowed him to pass.

When the elevator doors opened, Berg headed for a stairwell exit. He climbed up to the roof of the building, one of the tallest in Tokyo. Setting down the flowers, he opened his kimono and took out a black movie camera that had been strapped to his hip. He put it to his eye and slowly scanned the Tokyo skyline, capturing images of industrial complexes, armament plants, oil refineries, railroad lines, and the Imperial Palace.

---

* Baseball was introduced in Japan in 1873 by Horace Wilson, a visiting university professor. The sport became a national sensation during the 1934 tour when Babe Ruth hit thirteen home runs in sixteen games.

After the Japanese attack on Pearl Harbor, a movement arose in Japan to abolish decadent American influences such as baseball. During fighting in the Pacific, American soldiers reported hearing the ultimate insult from the Japanese—"Fuck Babe Ruth!"

These efforts were only partially successful, as the Japanese were hopelessly addicted to the game. Japanese prisoners of war would ask for World Series scores and even fight over copies of *The Sporting News*.

The Americans went on to win the game, 23–5, and Moe Berg went on to help America win World War II: Seven years later, the film Berg had shot from the roof of St. Luke's was used as an aerial map in the massive B-25 firebombing of Tokyo that began on April 18, 1942. This was the start of Moe Berg's double life as the world's first and only ballplayer/spy.

"I call him the mystery catcher," Casey Stengel once said of Moe Berg. "Strangest fellah who ever put on a uniform."

In a day when many ballplayers couldn't read or write, Berg was regarded as something of a freak. Majoring in language, he graduated *magna cum laude* from Princeton in 1923 and led the school's baseball team to nineteen consecutive victories. Berg could curse out umpires in French, Spanish, Portuguese, Italian, Russian, Greek, Japanese, Chinese, Latin, and even Sanskrit. Upon his graduation, Princeton offered him a teaching position in the Romance languages department.

But Berg wanted to study at the Sorbonne in Paris under the renowned scholar Abbé Jean Pierre Rousselot. He didn't have the funds for such a trip, and when the Brooklyn Dodgers offered him $5,000 to play half a season, he jumped at it.

Good-bye Ivy League, hello National League. The baseball money paid for a trip to Paris in the off-season to study philology (linguistics).

April in Paris may be romantic, but so is April in Florida. Berg came home for spring training and decided to see how far he could go with baseball. His father, Bernard, a Russian Jew who had fled the czar, never forgave him for the decision. During Moe's fifteen years in the big leagues, his father didn't attend a single game.

Moe Berg was attracted to baseball because it challenged him more than any intellectual pursuit ever did. "He can speak ten languages," it was said, "but can't hit in any of them." In fact, the old baseball cliché "good field, no hit" was coined to describe Berg in a telegram from St. Louis Cardinals coach Miguel Gonzales. Berg socked all of six home runs in his career, the sixth one in his final game. His IQ was probably close to his career batting average—.243.

In 1926, while he was playing for the White Sox, Berg applied to Columbia University School of Law. Believing the administrators would think a major-league baseball player couldn't possibly be serious about a law career, he used his given name, Morris, on his application. He was accepted, completed his studies during the off-season, and passed the New York bar exam in 1929. The Wall Street law firm of Satterly and Canfield was happy to have a major-league ballplayer on staff. They made him a partner, and he used his knowledge of languages to become an expert in foreign contracts and international matters. Playing baseball accounted for about one-fifth of his income.

In February each year, Berg would inform his secretary that he would be out of the office for seven or eight months. Then he would turn into a plain mug called Moe and go play ball.

Originally a shortstop, Berg became a catcher in 1927 when all three backstops on the White Sox were injured over the course of four games. Berg jumped off the bench to volunteer and spent the next twelve years squatting behind the plate for the Indians, Senators, and Red Sox.

"I spent years attempting to master a number of foreign languages and what happens?" he would ask. "I turn out to be a catcher and am reduced to sign language."

While his hitting never set the world on fire, he was excellent defensively and handled pitchers well. He made one bonehead play that followed him for years. It was a tie game with one out and a runner on third. Moe caught a foul pop and, thinking there were three outs, nonchalantly flipped the ball toward the mound. The runner scampered home. From that moment on, Moe was constantly reminded that for all his education, he couldn't count past two.

Two days after Berg's last game in 1939, the Nazis invaded Poland, igniting World War II. Berg coached for the Red Sox in 1940 and '41 but felt his talents could be used for a more important purpose.

"Europe is in flames, withering in a fire set by Hitler," he told *New York Times* columnist Arthur Daley. "All over that continent men and women and children are dying. Soon we, too, will be involved. And what am I doing? I'm sitting in the bullpen, telling jokes to the relief pitchers."

Shortly after America entered the war, President Roosevelt gave approval for General William "Wild Bill" Donovan to form the Office of Strategic Services (OSS), a global spy network whose goal was to combat Nazi propaganda and engage in counterintelligence. Berg was recruited and joined the OSS in August 1943.*

"Do you know who they gave us?" an aide asked Donovan after Berg had joined the team. "A ballplayer named Moe Berg. You ever heard of him?"

"Yes," Donovan responded. "He's the slowest runner in the American League."

Moe Berg just about fit the stereotype of a perfect spy. His mastery of foreign languages enabled him to disguise himself and infiltrate nations all over the world. He was a bachelor and a loner. He always wore a black suit, white shirt, and black tie. He was good-looking, charming, and sophisticated, and a connoisseur of wine. His experience in baseball showed he could perform under pressure. He could keep a secret. And as a "dumb jock," he would be the last person suspected of espionage.

He had just one liability. While he was not a star player, many publications had written about this odd combination of athlete, linguist, and lawyer and had printed his picture as well. He was constantly in danger of being exposed. And traipsing around Europe was not the safest thing for a Jew to do in the early 1940s.

Like any good spy, he struck people as mysterious. He would take three baths every day—at 8:30, 4:30, and 11:30. He read dozens of newspapers, both American and foreign, and refused to let anyone touch a paper until he had finished reading it. He claimed that the unread papers were "alive" and others could look at them when they were "dead."

Moe had to learn how to fire a gun, and he had to carry one with him at all times. He also carried a vial of potassium cyanide—in case he should be captured and find it necessary to kill himself instantly.

He performed his early missions flawlessly. He was sent to Latin America to gauge the sympathies of nations to the south of the United States. He parachuted into Yugoslavia to determine which resistance group should receive American aid. He made a shortwave radio address in Japanese that was broadcast in Japan, urging the people to lay down their arms and overthrow their warlords.

---

* New York Yankees president Michael Burke was also in the OSS.

But Berg's passion was the atomic bomb. Throughout the war, government officials feared German scientists were ahead in the race to develop the bomb. Right up until the collapse of the Third Reich rumors persisted of some incredible *wunderwaffen*—a wonder weapon that would turn the war around and change the nature of modern warfare. Berg became obsessed with the German effort to develop nuclear weapons.

When the bombing of Berlin began in August 1943, the Nazis scattered their top atomic scientists around Germany and nearby occupied countries. Berg's mission was to pinpoint their locations and discover how close the Nazis were to a working A-bomb.

In Paris, Berg met with Frédéric Joliot-Curie, the well-known French physicist who produced the first chain reaction of uranium atoms. Joliot-Curie informed Berg that Germany was years away from perfecting an atomic weapon—important news for the Allies.

In Italy, Berg gained entry into Galileo Works, a German munitions plant. Dressed as a German army officer and equipped with fake identification papers, he was convincing enough to receive salutes from the soldiers. He even had the *chutzpah* to tell plant managers that Berlin was not satisfied with their production. Inspecting the plant, he was able to report back on new rocket weaponry that was being developed there.

Germany had a plant in Rjukan, Norway, that manufactured heavy water, a crucial ingredient for building a bomb. The plant had been partially destroyed by saboteurs, and in October 1943, Berg was assigned to drop into Norway and determine its status. His recommendations led to an air attack on the plant, wiping out most of the Nazis' heavy water production.

Berg's biggest coup was tracking down Nobel Prize winner Werner Heisenberg, Germany's foremost atomic scientist. Heisenberg had shocked the German scientific community when he announced in 1942 that it would be possible to build an atom bomb capable of destroying a city in a package no larger than a pineapple.

Berg learned that Heisenberg and most of Germany's other top atomic scientists were working south of Stuttgart in the towns of Hechingen, Bisingen, and Ringingen. The Allies wanted to bomb the region, but aerial photography didn't show enough detail. Berg got the assignment to go in personally, but his mission was canceled when intelligence showed how tightly the Nazis controlled the area.

If he couldn't go to Heisenberg, Berg reasoned, he would get Heisenberg to come to him. Berg went to Switzerland and had a sympathetic physicist invite Heisenberg to give a lecture at the Federal Institute of Technology. Surprisingly, Heisenberg took the bait. It would be the first time he had left Germany since America had entered the war.

The lecture took place on December 18, 1944. Berg passed himself off as a Swiss graduate student to get by the SS agents guarding the lecture hall. He took a seat in the front row. With a Beretta in his shoulder holster, Berg sat not ten feet away from the man touted as the architect of the Nazis' atom bomb. If Heisenberg said anything that indicated he was creating an atomic weapon, Berg's orders were to assassinate him on the spot. It was a suicide mission. Berg would certainly be killed seconds after he showed a gun.

Fortunately, Heisenberg's talk focused on basic physics. He said nothing about Germany's progress on the bomb, and Berg kept the gun in the holster. But after the lecture, when everyone broke into informal groups to chat, Berg circulated around the room and picked up crucial information about the German war effort: Most of Germany's research labs were in the southern part of the country. Hitler had *not* suffered a nervous breakdown after the recent assassination attempt, as was rumored. Most significantly, Berg overheard Heisenberg saying he believed Germany had already lost the war—an indication that the Nazi scientists were having trouble building their bomb.

Berg immediately cabled this information to OSS general Leslie Groves, who told the president. "Fine, just fine," said Roosevelt. "Let us pray Heisenberg is right. And, General, my regards to the catcher."

When Heisenberg returned to Germany, he began feeling heat from his superiors. Hitler believed his top scientist was not completely loyal and "made it very uncomfortable" for him, according to a U.S. government report.

Heisenberg *wasn't* completely loyal. Like many of Germany's scientists, he did not believe in the Nazi cause and purposefully failed to pass along everything he was learning about atomic fission. He fled to Switzerland, and thanks to information provided by Berg, he was picked up in the Bavarian Alps on May 3, 1945. Five days later, Germany surrendered.

After the war, the OSS was disbanded. Berg did some work with the CIA and returned to his hometown of Newark, New Jersey, to live with his brother.

Making the world safe for democracy did not make him a wealthy man. He had earned about $5,000 a year working for the OSS. There was no government pension or baseball pension. A prosperous stationery business he had started in his baseball days had been mismanaged while he was tracking Nazis through Europe. The Internal Revenue Service claimed he owed $60,000 to $80,000 in back taxes. (They settled for $5,000.) He had never made much money as a lawyer, preferring the study of law over its practice.

Berg never cared about money anyway, and he was happiest prowling used-book stores and filling his apartment with the treasures he found there. He never married. The only woman known to be a part of his life was a Scandinavian living in London during the war.

He was chosen to receive the Medal of Merit, the highest honor given to civilians in wartime. He turned it down, calling his contribution to the war effort "modest." He never spoke of his life as a spy and refused to put his accomplishments in writing even when the government requested he do so. Berg was so secretive that even his brother didn't know he was a spy until after the war.

At the end of his life, Berg was persuaded to write his autobiography. A major publishing company offered $35,000 and a meeting was set up at the Algonquin Hotel in New York. The editor shook Berg's hand and said, "It's a pleasure to meet you. I have loved all your pictures."

"Pictures?" Berg asked. "Who do you think I am?"

"Why, aren't you Moe of the Three Stooges?"

Disgusted, Moe got up and walked out. The story of his life would be left to others (Louis Kaufman, Barbara Fitzgerald, and Tom Sewell, who published *Moe Berg: Athlete, Scholar . . . Spy*, from which much of the information in this chapter comes).

Berg died on May 30, 1972, after a fall in his apartment. He was seventy years old and a true, unheralded Renaissance man. If he hadn't actually existed, Moe Berg would have made a wonderful fictional character.

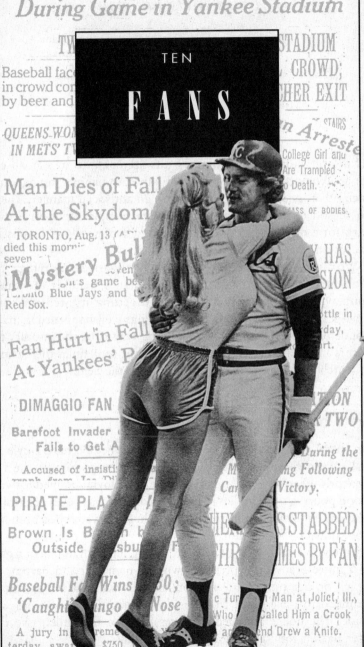

"I'm a Mets fan now."

—Thirty-four-year-old Joann
Barrett, after being shot during
the sixth inning of a game at
Yankee Stadium in 1985

If a large number of laboratory rats are confined in a small cage for an extended period, they'll eventually start fighting, biting, eating each other, and generally behaving in an antisocial manner. There's no reason to assume that fifty thousand people sitting in Fenway Park for a doubleheader would be any different—with the possible exception of the part about cannibalism.

We think of the friendly confines of a ballpark as our refuge from the real world—the world of crime, lunatics roaming the streets, gunplay, and people acting irrationally, getting arrested and sometimes killed. Unfortunately, all those things have happened in major-league ballparks. Baseball is still a long way from the insanity that occurs in the stands at soccer matches, but sometimes there's more to watch in the bleachers than there is on the field.

Shot at the Ballpark

On July 4, 1950, a fifty-six-year-old man named Bernard Doyle had just turned to say something to the fan next to him at the Polo Grounds when a bullet hit him in the head. Doyle slumped forward, blood pouring from his left temple, and died. It was never determined where the bullet came from, though police believed it had been fired from outside the stadium.

Thirty-five years to the day later, during the sixth inning of a game in Yankee Stadium, a pregnant woman named Joann Barrett was struck on her right hand by a bullet. This time the bullet was determined to have come from *inside* the stadium. No arrests were made. The police searched unsuccessfully for the bullet; two days later Barrett found it inside her pocketbook.

We've yet to reach the point where shootouts occur regularly in the stands, but there has been one. In 1917 in Los Angeles, a semipro game between a white and a black team was in progress when two men who were betting on the outcome got into a gun battle. Five people were caught in the crossfire, but none was fatally wounded.

The most unusual ballpark fatality occurred at a game in Morristown, Ohio, in 1902. A fan named Stanton Walker was keeping score. He asked the man next to him if he could borrow a knife to sharpen his pencil. As he was taking the knife a foul ball hit him in the hand and drove the blade into his chest.

Fell off the Stadium

Considering how often it has happened, baseball has made surprisingly little effort to prevent fans from falling, jumping, or being pushed off stadiums. In 1982, a woman leaped headfirst from the upper deck of Riverfront Stadium in Cincinnati during a game between the Reds and Pittsburgh Pirates. She had been drinking and a container of liquor had been left behind at the railing. She was dead on arrival at General Hospital.

The following year a man fell or jumped from the mezzanine of Yankee Stadium onto a concrete ramp near the left-field bullpen. In two separate incidents in 1991, people fell about seven stories from the Skydome in Toronto. One lived, the other didn't. Both had been playing a game in which they leaped from one elevated ramp to another.

They Died for Television

Other fans have died while enjoying the game in the comfort of their own homes. In 1969, while the Miracle Mets were creating their miracle, a Queens woman named Margaret Graddock told her husband, Frank, she wanted to watch the TV soap opera *Dark Shadows*. Frank wanted to watch the Mets-Cubs game. They argued the point, and Frank beat his wife about the head and body with a clenched fist. She went to sleep and never woke up. He was charged with homicide.

In 1972, eighteen-year-old Sheila Stodghill and her younger

brother Ronald were arguing over whether the family radio would be tuned to the World Series between Oakland and Cincinnati. Sheila ended up stabbing Ronald in the chest and killing him. She was charged with first-degree manslaughter, but charges were dropped when she convinced a grand jury that her brother ran into the knife after she picked it up to defend herself.

Two hours after the killing, the game was postponed because of rain.

When Henry Aaron was going for his 715th home run in 1974, a Jacksonville, Florida, cab driver named Clarence Weatherspoon came home early in hopes of seeing the historic moment on television. His wife, Annie, told him to get back in his cab and earn some money. An argument followed and Clarence shot Annie twice. With bullet holes in her hand and ear, she ran from the apartment. Clarence then shot himself in the head and didn't live to see Aaron break the record.

Cheering and Jeering

The right to boo and shout insults is a time-honored baseball tradition. Most players accept even the rudest obscenities from the stands as part of the game, but sometimes emotions take over. Hotheads like Ty Cobb (see chapter 8) and Babe Ruth would charge into the stands and go after abusive fans.

In 1991, Cleveland outfielder and recovering alcoholic Albert Belle threw a ball at a fan who had sarcastically invited him to a keg party. The same season, Jose Canseco tried to attack a fan who taunted him after Canseco was seen early one morning leaving the apartment of the pop star Madonna.

Connie Mack, a more refined gentleman, would never stoop to physical force in such situations. In 1927, he had a fan named Harry Donnelly *arrested* for heckling the Athletics at Philadelphia's Shibe Park. Mack actually showed up at Donnelly's hearing and accused the twenty-six-year-old fan of causing outfielder Zack Wheat and infielder Sammy Hale to make errors that cost the Athletics ballgames. Donnelly was so cruel to "Bustin' Bill Lamar," claimed Mack, that the outfielder had become useless to the team and had to be released.

Donnelly was held on $500 bail for disturbing the peace. Lamar never played again.

The immortal Bill Klem claimed to be the first umpire to throw a fan out of a game. Klem recalled a 1911 game in Philadelphia when Mordecai Brown was mowing down the Phillies for Chicago and a fan kept up a steady flow of abuse. Klem marched over to the man and said, "Sir, you did not buy that seat to insult ball-players."

"Go ump the game, you big fathead," answered the fan.

"You are gone now, my friend," said Klem. "Officer, throw this man out."

Running onto the Field

One sure way to get thrown out of a ballpark is to run onto the field, a practice that has become so commonplace that it's lost much of its shock value. In 1949, Joe DiMaggio was pestered on several occasions by fans who dashed into center field in the middle of games and demanded his autograph. They didn't have "card shows" back then.

Long before Morganna the Kissing Bandit and Toppsy Curvey, there was Kitty Burke, a nightclub dancer in Cincinnati. In the eighth inning of a 1935 game, Paul "Daffy" Dean was on the mound for St. Louis when Burke ran out on the field, grabbed a bat, and stepped up to the plate. Dean lobbed her a fat one, and she bounced back to the box.

The most elaborate and dramatic attempt to take the field occurred when an actor named Michael Sergio parachuted into Shea Stadium in the first inning of the sixth game of the 1986 World Series. Sergio had heard that the Mets were disappointed in the support they were getting from New York fans, so he swooped in with a "LET'S GO METS" banner trailing behind him.

After a graceful landing, he managed to slap hands with pitcher Ron Darling before being handcuffed and led to a police van. He refused to tell the Federal Aviation Administration who flew the plane, and he pleaded guilty to criminal trespassing and reckless endangerment.

The Mets won the game, one of the most exciting in World Series history, and beat the Red Sox the next day to win the Championship.

The fear is, presumably, that a fan on the field might harm a player. It's a distinct possibility. On several occasions, major-league players have been attacked. After Buck Herzog of the Cubs was accused of offering money to Rube Benton to throw a game in 1919, he was attacked in his car by a fan. "You're one of those crooked Chicago ball players," the fan shouted. "When are you going to confess?"

Herzog jumped out of the car and fought with the fan. After the two rolled into a ditch, a friend of the fan ran over with a knife and stabbed Herzog three times. He recovered, but never played ball again.

Johnny Beazley, a rookie pitcher with the Cardinals in 1942, was knifed by a man in Philadelphia's Penn Station when Beazley refused to let the man carry his suitcase. Pittsburgh Pirates third baseman Jimmy Brown was jumped and beaten in 1946 by four men as he was putting his equipment into the trunk of his car after a game at Forbes Field. In 1924, American League umpire Ducky Holmes was attacked in his car by two St. Louis fans who were unhappy with his calls.

Throwing Stuff on the Field

In recent years, however, most fans have been content to hurl projectiles from afar. Batteries and bullets were thrown at Dave Parker. Wally Joyner was grazed by a knife thrown from the stands in Yankee Stadium. Hank Aaron was hit in the head with an orange. A Boston fan lobbed a cherry bomb into the Minnesota Twins' dugout. An arrow pierced the ground next to Dave Winfield. Dick Allen made history, of sorts, by taking his position in the field with a batting helmet on to protect him from unidentified flying objects.

Dennis Martinez was hit in the head with a beer bottle as he stood by the bat rack in Comiskey Park. The police arrested a guy named Perry Galanos, who spent twenty-six weekends in jail for the crime. In 1929, American League umpire Emmett Ormsby was knocked unconscious by a barrage of bottles thrown by Cleveland fans after a decision against the home team. Philadelphia shortstop Joe Boley and coach Kid Gleason were also hit in the downpour of bottles.

The most pathetic display was put on by fans in the left-field stands at Cincinnati in 1974. Houston outfielder Bob Watson had crashed into the wall trying to catch a drive off the bat of Merv Rettenmund. The lenses of his sunglasses were shattered and his face was bleeding from the cuts. As he lay dazed in the warning track, Reds fans showed their concern by dumping beer, ice cubes, and paper cups on his head.

Celebrations That Got Out of Hand

When the St. Louis Cardinals won their first World Series in 1926, the fans were dancing in the streets. Unfortunately, cars were also driving in the streets. Thirty people were injured, and two teenage boys died after being hit by cars.

Sometimes you're just so happy your team won that you have to go out and kill somebody. In 1984, when the Detroit Tigers won their first World Series in sixteen years, downtown Detroit erupted into a full-scale riot. A crowd of about forty people surrounded a police car and torched it, all the while shouting "We're number one!" Two other cop cars were ripped apart.

Cops took to the streets in riot gear. The street was covered with broken glass and illegal fireworks. Thirty-two adults and two juveniles were arrested for disorderly conduct. Somebody had jumped off the scoreboard and broken both wrists. Southwest General Hospital was filled with people who had been hit in the head with flying beer bottles.

One fan was enjoying his last celebration. Raymond Dobryzynski, twenty-seven, was found dead in the street less than a mile from Detroit Stadium. He had been shot in the back.

Everyone has his own way of celebrating. In 1977, a journal called *Diseases of the Colon and Rectum* published a paper about a homosexual man who had celebrated the World Series victory of the Oakland A's by having his partner shove a baseball where the sun most certainly does not shine. The ball was removed and the patient recovered.

Caught in Natural Disasters

Game 3 of the 1989 World Series had not yet begun at 5:04 on October 17 when San Francisco was rocked by its biggest earthquake since 1906. There were no casualties in the stadium, but dozens of people died when a section of the Nimitz Freeway fell apart.

Actually, baseball *saved* lives in this situation. Many people had left work early to go to the game or watch it on TV, so there were fewer cars than usual on the freeway.

Baseball's worst natural disaster occurred at Yankee Stadium on May 19, 1929. In the fifth inning, just as Lou Gehrig came out of the dugout to step up to the plate, an unexpected deluge of rain poured down. "The sky suddenly opened up and a solid sheet of water, so dense as to obscure from sight objects only a few score feet away, roared down," reported the *New York Times*.

Fans in the bleachers instantly got up and stampeded for the exits. Thousands of people converged on one small opening. A few people at the front fell and were trampled by the panicked crowd. Two of them, a Hunter College sophomore and a sixty-year-old truck driver, were killed. Sixty-two others were hurt, laid out in rows on the ground. Thirty-two fans sued the Yankees.

Fans Who Sue

Anybody can go buy a baseball in a store for a few bucks, but catching a foul in the ballpark is one of the great joys of fandom.* On the back of every ticket to a major-league game, there's a message in fine print. It says, basically, that if you get hit by a ball at the ballpark, you can't sue. If a foul ball knocks you senseless, tough luck.

But that disclaimer hasn't stopped people from trying. In 1982, a fourteen-year-old girl in the box seats at Shea Stadium in New York was glancing at the scoreboard when she was hit by a line drive off the bat of Mets left fielder Steve Henderson. The ball struck her face with such force that the stitches left an impression. She was

---

* Before the 1920s, fans were expected to return foul balls that landed in the stands. In 1916, the *New York Times* reported that three men had been arrested for petty larceny in the grandstand at the Polo Grounds when they refused to surrender baseballs.

blinded in her left eye and left with a concussion and a shattered cheekbone. Her family sued the City of New York for $2.75 million, but a jury ruled against her.

Sometimes the fans win. In 1939, Julius Schwab was waiting for a game between the Giants and Cubs to start at the Polo Grounds when he was hit in the nose with a ball that had been fungoed out during fielding practice. He sued and a jury awarded him $750. Schwab's case hinged on the fact that he was able to convince the jury that he had *not* tried to catch the ball. If he had made the effort, it was determined, he would not be entitled to any damages.

In 1986, Cleveland outfielder Cory Snyder threw his bat into the stands. Two fans were injured, one with a broken nose. They collected $50,000. Snyder testified that pine tar had made the bat stick to his hands and fly away wildly.

At least one fan has been killed by a flying object while watching a baseball game. In 1904, a twelve-year-old boy was attending a game in Chicago when a foul ball hit him in the temple. He died three minutes later. There is no record of any lawsuit filed by his family.

ELEVEN

THE BASEBALL ESTABLISHMENT

> *"Baseball must be a great game*
> *to survive the fools who*
> *run it."*

—Hall of Famer Bill Terry,
New York Giants player and
manager

Scandals involving the baseball establishment rarely get as much attention as ones involving ballplayers. The men who play the game are infinitely more interesting than the men who run it. However, baseball authorities wield an enormous amount of power, and their frequently stupid, unfair, and illegal decisions are the equivalent to white-collar crime in the "real" world.

Before the commissioner system began in 1920, the game was governed by men like Harry Pulliam, Albert Spaulding, and Ban Johnson. Pulliam, the National League president, suffered a nervous breakdown and shot himself in the head. Spaulding, a lifelong power junkie, used unscrupulous tactics to drive competing baseball leagues out of business and did everything he could to see that the sport conformed to his standards. Johnson made every effort to sweep scandals—such as the Ty Cobb/Tris Speaker affair of 1919—under the rug. He too would have psychological problems before being forced out of office.

The Commissioner of Baseball is popularly portrayed as an omnipotent, all-knowing Solomon who issues decrees that are fair to all and punishes those who need it. The truth is, the Commissioner of Baseball is a man (and always a man) handpicked by the club owners to serve one function—to act in their best interests. In most cases, this means keeping the cash flowing.

When the Black Sox Scandal threatened to destroy the game, it was in the owners' interest to select a tyrannical "czar" who would rule baseball with an iron fist and restore its respectability. Federal Judge Kenesaw Mountain Landis got the job. He had more power over his domain than the President of the United States had over his.

The owners quickly realized they had made the commissioner's office *too* powerful, but it was too late—Landis had been appointed commissioner for life. When he finally died in 1944 (and it took his death for black players to be allowed in the majors), the owners appointed a series of weaker figurehead commissioners who would "play ball" with them. As soon as the commissioner did something that displeased the owners, he was bounced out of office. General William Eckert lasted just three years. "Happy" Chandler tossed Brooklyn Dodgers manager Leo Durocher out of baseball for the 1947 season and refused to explain why. Four years later, the owners tossed Chandler out.

Baseball commissioners have not evolved into a higher life form over the years. Peter Ueberroth and A. Bartlett Giamatti turned their heads while the owners were involved in a collusion scandal that would keep hundreds of millions of dollars in their pockets and out of the pockets of their players. The owners eventually were forced to pay back more than $200 million.

After he was voted out of office, Bowie Kuhn's law firm collapsed with liabilities of $11 million. He packed up his New Jersey home for a quick move to Florida, where there is better legal protection for bankruptcy victims. Florida deputy sheriffs searched for him to serve him with papers from New York creditors. For a time, nobody knew where Kuhn was.

These are the men who make the decisions about what is in "the best interests of baseball."

The one-man commissioner system is on the road to extinction. The Players Association has become powerful. Players and owners, with their savvy agents and lawyers, are no longer willing to allow a single individual to be their accuser, judge, and jury in disciplinary cases.

In 1920, Commissioner Landis threw the Black Sox out of the game for life after a jury had acquitted them of wrongdoing. There was little outcry. It didn't even occur to the players that they should have lawyers.

Nowadays, everybody sues. When Cincinnati Reds manager Lou

Piniella said umpire Gary Darling had a bias against his team in 1991, Darling didn't walk away, like umpires used to. He slapped a lawsuit on Piniella that demanded $5 million in compensatory and punitive damages. When Pete Rose and George Steinbrenner got into trouble, their lawyers cut intricate deals with the commissioner, negotiating every word of their "agreements."

It's inevitable that someday a player, manager, or owner will take baseball and the baseball commissioner all the way to the Supreme Court—and win. When that happens, the commissioner's office will become a ceremonial position, somewhat like that of the Queen of England.

THE DOUBLEDAY MYTH
How Albert Spaulding Rewrote History

It seems fitting that baseball's first scandal occurred with the game's origin. Credit for the preposterous story that Abner Doubleday invented baseball belongs to one man—Albert Goodwill Spaulding.

Spaulding was one of the game's first great pitchers. He went 57–5 in 1875 and was pretty good with the bat too, hitting .318. When the National League was formed the next year, he helped write its constitution. The following season he retired as an active player and set aside $800 to start the sporting goods company that bears his name. In a short time he became baseball's first multimillionaire. While building his fortune, he was also president of the Chicago White Stockings, and worked tirelessly to promote baseball around the world.

Spaulding was opinionated and ruthless. He treated players like slaves, used unscrupulous tactics to drive competing baseball leagues out of business, and worked to ruin his business competitors. The 1884 edition of *Spaulding's Guide* claims that another company's catcher's mask was "liable to disfigure a player for life."

Up until the turn of the century, there had been little concern about the origin of baseball. In 1903, pioneer baseball writer (and inventor of the box score) Henry Chadwick wrote an article that explained what most people already assumed to be true—that the game of baseball had evolved from the English game rounders.

Spaulding believed baseball had been born and developed exclusively in America. To Spaulding, baseball was more than a game; it had played a part in shaping the American character and symbolized American values. He argued that baseball had evolved from a colonial American game called "one old cat." The object of that game was to hit a ball with a stick, club, or wagon-wheel spoke and run to a base. Fielders would make outs by hitting the runner with the ball.

In the 1905 issue of *Spaulding's Guide*, Spaulding wrote: "Having read the writings of Mr. Chadwick that our American game of Base Ball originated from rounders, and having been taunted with this statement around the world, generally spoken in derision of our game, I am now convinced that Base Ball did not originate from rounders, any more than Cricket originated from that asinine pastime."

To settle the issue, Spaulding called for a national committee and handpicked a group of baseball experts to carry out a long-term investigation into the birth of baseball. Former National League president A. G. Mills was appointed the committee's chairman.

In July 1907 a letter arrived from "a reputable gentleman" named Abner Graves, a seventy-one-year-old mining engineer from Denver.* According to Graves, "the present game of Baseball was designed and named by Abner Doubleday of Cooperstown, New York, in 1839."

Graves, who had been brought up in Cooperstown, recalled a day in his youth when some boys were playing marbles behind a tailor shop and Abner Doubleday drew a diamond-shaped diagram with a stick in the dirt. According to Graves, Doubleday explained the game and instituted the rule that made tagging the runner or touching the base a "put out." Doubleday also named the game "baseball," claimed Graves.

Abner Doubleday, who had died fourteen years before Graves

---

* The letter from Abner Graves and all the other evidence gathered by the Mills Commission were lost in a fire in 1911.

sent his letter to the Mills Commission, was a well-known general with the U.S. Army. He was second in command at Fort Sumter in 1861, and fired the shot that set off the Civil War. Later he commanded troops at the battle of Gettysburg. (He was also the great-great-uncle of New York Mets owner Nelson Doubleday.)

Albert Spaulding was thrilled with the discovery of the Doubleday story, and urged the Mills Commission to give it "serious consideration."

"It certainly appeals to an American's pride," he wrote, "to have had the great national game of Baseball created and named by a Major-General in the United States Army."

The Mills Commission report was released on December 30, 1907, with the claim that "the first scheme for playing Baseball, according to the best evidence obtainable to date, was devised by Abner Doubleday at Cooperstown, NY in 1839." The report added that the game of baseball "has no traceable connection whatever with 'Rounders,' or any other foreign game."

The Mills Commission bought the Graves story hook, line, and sinkerball, choosing to overlook the overwhelming evidence that proved Doubleday had *not* invented baseball. For starters, Doubleday's family moved from Cooperstown in 1837, two years before the inaugural game Graves claimed he witnessed. Doubleday was a twenty-year-old cadet at West Point when he was supposed to be playing marbles in Cooperstown, and Abner Graves was just five years old at the time.

If Doubleday *had* invented baseball, he never told anyone. After retiring from the Army in 1873, he wrote many magazine articles on topics of his own choosing, and didn't mention the game once. When he died in 1893, he left behind sixty-seven diaries, none of which mentioned baseball. He died seventeen years after the National League had been founded, so he was well aware that baseball had bloomed into a popular sport and had plenty of opportunity to claim credit. There is no mention of the game in his obituary.

Most remarkably, A. G. Mills was a personal friend of Abner Doubleday for twenty-five years, but was not aware that the man had invented baseball until Graves said so in a letter fourteen years after Doubleday's death.

———

Today the Doubleday story has been totally discredited, and it has often been said that Abner Doubleday didn't invent baseball; baseball invented Abner Doubleday.

Nevertheless, the Mills Report was accepted as truth in 1907. The myth was solidified twenty-seven years later when a dust-covered attic trunk belonging to Abner Graves was found in a farmhouse in Fly Creek, New York—three miles from Cooperstown. Inside the trunk was a torn-up, battered baseball.

The ball was purchased for $5 by Stephen C. Clark, a Cooperstown resident who had made a fortune through his association with the Singer Sewing Machine Company. Clark put the ball on display in Cooperstown's Village Club, and its popularity sparked the idea of creating a museum devoted to baseball.

The Baseball Hall of Fame opened in Cooperstown in 1939—the 100th anniversary of the game's mythical invention. Albert Spaulding, who had died in 1915, was one of the Hall's charter members.

Today, half a million people a year visit the Hall of Fame, where the ball found in Abner Graves's trunk is displayed proudly and identified as "the Abner Doubleday baseball." After an explanation of the Abner Doubleday story, a caption on the wall reads, "Only cynics would need to know more."

As for Abner Graves, he turned out to be not such a "reputable gentleman" after all. In 1924, when he was ninety years old, he asked his wife, Minnie (who was forty-eight), to bring him a cup of coffee. When she did, he accused her of putting poison in it. Then he pulled out a gun and shot her four times at point-blank range.

"Tell Abner I forgive him," Minnie said before lapsing into a coma.

"I hope she dies," said Abner Graves.

She did. A jury found him mentally unbalanced, and he spent the last two years of his life in a Pueblo, Colorado, institution for the criminally insane.

So Who *Did* Invent Baseball?

Every year, it seems, somebody unearths proof that baseball is older than previously believed. In 1991, Baseball Hall of Fame librarian

Tom Heitz discovered a clipping from the July 13, 1825, issue of the Delhi, New York, *Gazette* that reads:

A CHALLENGE
The undersigned challenge an equal number of persons of any town in the county of Delaware to meet them at any time at the house of Edward B. Chace to play the game of BASS-BALL, for the sum of one dollar each per game.

The notice is followed by nine names.

THE CAMPANIS DEBACLE
Baseball and Discrimination

Ted Koppel nearly fell off his chair. He had just asked Al Campanis if prejudice was the reason that there were so few black managers, coaches, and executives in major-league baseball.

"No, I don't believe it's prejudice," Campanis said. "I truly believe that they may not have some of the necessities to be, let's say, a field manager, or perhaps a general manager."

The April 6, 1987, edition of *Nightline* was supposed to be commemorating the anniversary of Jackie Robinson's first game with the Brooklyn Dodgers. The last thing Ted Koppel expected was to hear a blatantly racist statement from the vice-president and general manager of the team that had courageously broken the color barrier forty years earlier.

KOPPEL: Do you really believe that?

CAMPANIS: Well, I don't say that all of them, but they certainly are short. How many quarterbacks do you have, how many pitchers do you have, that are black?

KOPPEL: Yeah, but I got to tell you, that sounds like the same kind of garbage we were hearing forty years ago about players.

CAMPANIS: No, it's not garbage, Mr. Koppel, because I played on a college team, and the center fielder was black, and in the backfield at NYU with a fullback who was black. Never knew the difference whether he was black or white.

We were teammates. So it might just be, why are black men, or black people, not good swimmers? Because they don't have the buoyancy.*

Millions of Americans got up to adjust their sets, call their friends, or call in complaints to ABC. It couldn't be true. Campanis must have been drunk or senile. He couldn't be that racist. And even if he really believed what he was saying, he couldn't be stupid enough to say it in front of a national television audience.

After all, Al Campanis had been a friend and teammate of Jackie Robinson in the minors.** He had discovered Roberto Clemente. He spoke Spanish, French, and Greek (okay, so he was born in Greece).

"I must say I'm flabbergasted," Koppel said when he came back from a commercial break. "I'd like to give you another chance to dig yourself out."

> CAMPANIS: I have never said that blacks are not intelligent. I think many of them are highly intelligent, but they may not have the desire to be in the front office. . . . They're outstanding athletes, very God-gifted, and they're very wonderful people, and that's all I can tell you about them. . . . They are gifted with great musculature and various other things, they're fleet of foot, and this is why there are a lot of black major-league baseball players. Now, as far as having the background to become club presidents, or presidents of a bank, I don't know."

Campanis was fired two days later, his forty-four-year career in baseball wiped out in five minutes. "I feel that this is the saddest moment of my entire career," he said in a public apology. Dodgers manager Tommy Lasorda broke down in tears three times while talking to reporters about the incident.

Ironically, Al Campanis probably did more to advance the progress of blacks in sport than all the speeches, protests, and articles

---

* Actually, Campanis was right. A study by John C. Phillips published in the *International Review of Sport Sociology*, titled "Toward an Explanation of Racial Variations in Top-Level Sports Participation," found that "blacks were considerably less buoyant than whites."

** Campanis played in the majors—seven games at second base for the Dodgers in 1943. He got two singles in twenty at-bats.

on the subject combined. His appearance on *Nightline* generated so much publicity that the entire nation became aware that prejudice was alive and well long after Jackie Robinson had been ceremoniously allowed to play baseball with white men.

At the time of the Campanis incident, there were no black managers or general managers in baseball. There was just one third-base coach. The only black man in a front-office position was all-time home run leader Hank Aaron. A *USA Today* survey showed that only 17 of 879 top administrative jobs in baseball were held by blacks. That's 1.9 percent. The next year—post-Campanis—that number became 9 percent. The year after that it was 15 percent.

As serious as the Black Sox, Pete Rose, Ty Cobb/Tris Speaker, and Jimmy O'Connell/Cozy Dolan affairs may have been, baseball's most disgraceful scandal was the total exclusion of a group of players for sixty years simply because of the color of their skin. The conspiracy to keep blacks out of baseball extended all the way to the commissioner's office.

A few black men, most notably Moses Fleetwood Walker and his brother Welday, played in the majors in the 1880s. It was Chicago White Stockings manager Cap Anson who was largely responsible for their banishment.

Anson hated blacks with a passion. In 1884, he refused to let his team take the field for an exhibition game against Toledo if Moses Walker was the catcher. This happened several more times over the next few years. The influence of Anson, one of the most powerful men in the game and a future Hall of Famer, caused baseball to slam the door on blacks in 1887. Contracts to black players were simply halted. The color barrier was up.

Over the years several attempts were made to get around the ban. In 1901, John McGraw tried to sign a black player named Charles Grant by passing him off as a full-blooded Indian—"Chief Tokohama." In 1943, Bill Veeck wanted to buy the Philadelphia Phillies and stock them with Negro League stars. National League president Ford Frick blocked the sale and saw that the Phillies were purchased by William Cox instead. Less than a year later, Cox was thrown out of baseball for life when he was caught placing bets on games.

Leo Durocher once said he would sign up black players in a minute if the powers that be would let him. He was called on the carpet by

Commissioner Landis for making that statement, and he later denied it. Landis would not even allow major-league teams to play exhibition games against Negro League teams during the off-season.

In 1943 Landis announced, "There is no rule, nor to my knowledge, has there ever been, formal or informal, no understanding, subterranean or sub-anything, against the hiring of Negroes in the major leagues."

It was just *understood* that blacks could not join this exclusive club.

The baseball establishment used various theories to explain why there were no blacks in the big leagues. Ford Frick said the public "has not been educated to the point where they will accept them." He also claimed that "colored people did not have a chance to play during slavery, and so were late in developing proficiency."

Landis died in 1944. Three years later, Jackie Robinson arrived. Landis's replacement, "Happy" Chandler, would later say, "Judge Landis had been in office twenty-four years and never lifted a finger for black players."

Chandler would later try to claim some of the credit for knocking down the color barrier. He may have stepped aside and let it happen, but it would be hard to believe he led the revolution. A year after the color barrier was broken, he embraced the Dixiecrats, a segregationist party led by Strom Thurmond. In 1968, he had aspirations to be presidential candidate George Wallace's running mate.

On April 26, 1945, the major-league owners met in Cleveland and a report on integration in baseball was circulated. Written by league presidents Ford Frick and William Harridge and owners Phil Wrigley, Larry MacPhail, Tom Yawkey, and Sam Breadon, the report stated that "however well intentioned, the use of Negro players would hazard all the physical properties of baseball." After the meeting, all copies of this report were collected and destroyed.

A year later, the owners met at the Waldorf-Astoria in New York to vote on whether or not they should admit black players to the major leagues. The tally was 15 to 1 against. Brooklyn Dodgers president Branch Rickey was the only dissenting vote. He angrily got up and left the room. Shortly after, he signed Jackie Robinson, and the sixty-year-color barrier came down.

Afterward, the other owners denied that any report existed or that any vote had been taken. Branch Rickey was furious, and said,

"I'd like to see the color of the man's eyes who would deny it."

History has made Branch Rickey out to be baseball's Abraham Lincoln, but for all his good intentions, he had more than one ulterior motive for signing Jackie Robinson. He knew the color barrier would inevitably fall, and he wanted to be in position to scoop up the best players when it did.

Two years earlier, Rickey had launched "the United States Negro Baseball League," which was to play games at Ebbets Field when the Dodgers were out of town. He was slammed in the press at the time by Washington Senators owner Clark Griffith, who said Rickey was trying to set himself up as a "dictator" of blacks in baseball. The USNBL was essentially an attempt to develop a black farm system, and Rickey, after all, was the man who had created farm systems in the first place.

Furthermore, black and white New Yorkers were calling for—demanding—an end to the color barrier, and Rickey could secure a place in history by forcing the issue. And it wouldn't hurt the Dodgers' bottom line if thousands of black fans suddenly began to surge through the turnstiles at Ebbets Field.

It should be noted that Rickey—sometimes called "Mahatma"—made little effort to sign blacks to off-field jobs with the Dodgers.

The signing of one black player certainly did not put an end to prejudice and discrimination in baseball. The Washington Senators moved to Minnesota in 1961 because of racist attitudes that came straight from the team's owner. "I'll tell you why we came to Minnesota," Senators owner Calvin Griffith said at a Minneapolis Lions Club luncheon. "It was when I found out you only had fifteen thousand blacks here. Black people don't go to ballgames, but they'll fill up a rasslin' ring and put up such a chant, it'll scare you to death. . . . We came here because you've got good, hardworking white people here." Griffith did not realize a reporter was at the luncheon.

In 1964, San Francisco Giants manager Alvin Dark stirred up a controversy similar to what would later surround the Al Campanis incident. A reporter quoted Dark as saying, "We (the Giants) have trouble because we have so many Negro and Spanish-speaking players on this team. They are just not able to perform up to the white ballplayer when it comes to mental alertness. . . . You can't make most Negroes and Spanish players have the pride in their team that you can get from white players. . . . You couldn't name three colored players in our league who are always mentally alert to take advantage of situations."

Like Campanis, Alvin Dark was not an overt bigot. He had played on integrated teams for eleven years and was commended by the NAACP for making Willie Mays captain of the Giants. He said he was "gravely misquoted," but writer Stan Isaacs stood by his story and other writers agreed that Dark had expressed those opinions. Mays had to talk his teammates—mostly black and Hispanic players—out of revolting against Dark. Dark (whose nickname was "Blackie") was gone in 1965.

Shortly after Bowie Kuhn was elected Commissioner of Baseball in 1969, the American Civil Liberties Union asked him to open the Baseball Hall of Fame equally to players of all races, and admit Negro League players as well as major-leaguers. According to baseball historian John Holway, Kuhn's legal counsel replied that "Cooperstown is a private club that does not come under interstate commerce or the civil rights laws passed by the U.S. Congress."*

As recently as 1966, many hotels and nightclubs were still refusing to serve black players. For many years there was an unwritten rule that no more than two blacks would be signed to any one team. To this day, there is criticism that only black *superstars* get to play in the majors, and even then they are often excluded from the "thinking" positions—catcher, shortstop, and second base.

It is common knowledge that black Americans have rejected baseball as a spectator sport and that the percentage of blacks among fans is minuscule. With the tradition of racism that began in the early days of the game and continues long after Jackie Robinson and Al Campanis, it's easy to see why.

Wops, Kikes, Spics, Chinks, and Whores

While blacks have certainly received the worst of it, baseball has not been particularly discriminating in its discrimination. There has been prejudice against Asian players, Latin Americans, Jews, and Italians. *Life* magazine thought it was complimenting a young Joe

---

* In 1971, Satchel Paige became the first Negro League player inducted into the Hall of Fame.

DiMaggio by writing in a 1939 profile, "Instead of olive oil or smelly bear grease he keeps his hair slick with water. He never reeks of garlic and prefers chicken chow mein to spaghetti."

Native Americans have long been outraged that Cleveland chose to call its team "the Indians" and used a big-toothed, pointy-headed character as its symbol. Russell C. Means, a Sioux and director of the Cleveland American Indian Center, complained in 1972, "How long do you think the stadium would stand if the team were called the Cleveland Negroes with a caricature of Aunt Jemima or Little Black Sambo and every time a ball was hit some guy would come out and do the soft shoe?"

"Women have been making big inroads into sport, but baseball always has been and always will be a man's game," said *Colliers* magazine in a 1928 article. "It's not a woman's sport, and for that reason wherever the ladies intrude they usually cause trouble."

That sentiment has changed little over the years. A woman named Bernice Gera fought legal battles for four years to win the right to umpire in the Class A New York-Pennsylvania League. She was harassed so severely that she quit seven innings into her first game. Pam Postema made it as far as Triple A ball in the 1980's, despite the fact that she was spit on, propositioned, and called a dyke and a whore. She could take it, but she was never promoted to the major leagues, and quit trying in 1989. In 1991, a woman named Teresa Cox filed a lawsuit for the right to umpire.

In 1987, the public relations director for the Atlanta Braves filed a sex discrimination suit against the team when she was refused entry to the clubhouse and team bus—a problem also encountered by female sportswriters. And it took years of legal battles before girls were finally admitted to the Little League in 1974.

The subject of a woman actually *playing* in the majors rarely even comes up. A few women have played in the minor leagues over the years, and an entire league of female players popped up during World War II. Someday a woman is certainly going to come along who has the skill to compete on a major-league level. She will have a difficult battle ahead of her.

THE MOST FAMOUS ASTERISK
IN THE WORLD

Commissioner Ford Frick's Effort to
Keep the Babe Alive

The day before he died, Babe Ruth summoned his old friend and ghostwriter Ford Frick to his bedside at New York's Memorial Hospital. The Babe could barely speak, and Frick only stayed a few minutes. But the fact that Frick was one of the last people to see Ruth alive was an indication of how meaningful their friendship was.

Years later, when Frick ascended to the position of Commissioner of Baseball, he showed that friendship more clearly by making one of the most controversial—and dumb—executive rulings in baseball history.

It happened in 1961, the year the American League expanded to ten teams after being an eight-team league for sixty years. To accommodate the two extra teams, the season was expanded from 154 to 162 games. At the time, nobody thought to ask how this change might effect statistics and records.

By the middle of July, home runs were flying out of American League ballparks at an alarming rate. Yankees outfielder Roger Maris had thirty-four and Mickey Mantle thirty-three. Sluggers Rocky Colavito, Harmon Killebrew, Jim Gentile, and Norm Cash were all hitting the long ball.*

It seemed quite possible that Babe Ruth's long-standing record of sixty home runs in one season might be broken. Maris, in particular, was nineteen games ahead of Ruth's pace.

It wasn't the first time Ruth's record had been threatened. Hack Wilson hit fifty-six home runs in 1930, just three years after Ruth's sixty. Jimmy Foxx and Hank Greenberg came closest, with fifty-eight home runs in 1932 and 1938, respectively. Not much fuss was made about any of them.*

---

* Killebrew and Gentile would end up with forty-six home runs, Colavito forty-five, and Cash forty-one. Mantle hit fifty-four.

* Many people believe that Greenberg would have broken the record, but in the last days of the season pitchers walked him rather than allow a Jew to hit the most home runs in a single season. In 1969 Reggie Jackson hit forty-seven homers and said he was walked at the end of the season in order to prevent a black man from breaking *Maris's* record.

But by the time 1961 rolled around, Ruth's record had taken on a life of its own. When baseball fans thought of the number sixty, they didn't think of the number of seconds in a minute, or minutes in an hour. They thought of Babe Ruth.

Sixty home runs in a season *belonged* to Ruth. Old-timers in particular wanted the record—and their memories of baseball's golden age—to live forever. "A lot of people didn't want me to break Ruth's record," Maris recalled later.

Maris was typically understating the case. He was getting death threats at the time.

On July 17, Commissioner Frick held a press conference and issued this ruling:

> *Any player who may hit more than 60 home runs during his club's first 154 games would be recognized as having established a new record. However, if the player does not hit more than 60 until after his club has played 154 games, there would have to be some distinctive mark in the record books to show that Babe Ruth's record was set under a 154 game schedule and the total of more than 60 was compiled while a 162-game schedule was in effect.*

As much as Babe Ruth was loved, the press and public saw Frick's ruling and the timing of that ruling as an obvious attempt to throw a protective screen around the past.

"That was just damn stupid," Hank Greenberg told sportswriter Maury Allen. "Conditions always change in baseball—day ball to night ball, new towns, new teams, new parks. They don't make rulings every time something like that changes."

Times change, and records fall. It would take Pete Rose longer than Ty Cobb to get all those hits. It would take Hank Aaron longer than Babe Ruth to hit all those home runs. Neither would suffer the indignity of a "distinctive mark" belittling their achievement.

"A season's a season," said Roger Maris bluntly.

The home run hitters of 1961 came under incredible pressure as the countdown to game 154 neared. Maris, then twenty-six, suffered the most. He was leading the home run derby and was not used to the media circus that gathered as he drew closer to Ruth. It was widely reported that he had become so nervous, his hair was falling out in clumps.

Part of the problem was that Roger Maris was not particularly liked by the baseball establishment or the media. There was a general feeling that if *anybody* had to break Ruth's record, it should be Mickey Mantle, Willie Mays, or somebody *heroic*. Maris was a .260 hitter who happened to be having a career year. He was feeding off inferior expansion-team pitching. He wasn't deserving. He was just lucky.

To some members of the press, Maris was boring. He didn't tip his cap to the crowd or go out drinking and tell funny stories. Sportswriters made him out to be cold, paranoid, and jealous of Mantle's popularity. Fans would shout obscenities and throw things at him from the stands.

"I hope he doesn't do it," Babe Ruth's widow, Claire, commented.

At the end of 154 games, Maris had 59 home runs—one less than Ruth. In the additional eight games at the end of the season, he hit numbers 60 and 61. The final home run came on the last day of the season off rookie right hander Tracy Stallard. Few people knew that Maris hit number 60 on his 684th at-bat, while it took Ruth 689.

Maris had hit more home runs in a single season than any other man ever—*but*—he didn't hold the record. Every baseball fan knows there is an asterisk in the record book next to Maris's 61 home runs indicating that he didn't hit all 61 during the old 154-game season.

In truth, Commissioner Frick never said *anything* about an asterisk. He used the term "distinctive mark," and did not explain how it would appear in the record books. At the end of his press conference on July 17, sportswriter Dick Young got up and said, "Maybe you should use an asterisk on the new record."

There never was an asterisk or *any* distinctive mark. The record books published by the Elias Sports Bureau and *The Sporting News* list both records—Ruth for home runs in a 154-game season, and Maris for home runs in a 162-game season. In *The Baseball Encyclopedia*, there is nothing to indicate a difference between Ruth's record and Maris's record. The all-time, single-season record for home runs is listed as follows:

1. Roger Maris, 1961   61
2. Babe Ruth, 1927   60

However, Frick saddled Maris with a *symbolic* asterisk, and it would follow Maris for the rest of his life. He had made history, but the baseball establishment said it didn't really count. The record was tainted. Maris would later say that after he broke Ruth's record, baseball was no fun for him anymore.

"I always had the feeling he was hurt, and hurt badly, by that ruling," said Yankees third baseman Clete Boyer. "It just gave us all, especially Roger, some feeling of emptiness about the final homer, as if it were more of an exhibition kind of thing, like a spring training homer."

Maris died in 1985. He was only fifty-one. An editorial in the *New York Times* that week described the asterisk controversy as "one generation's way to preserve its youth."

It worked, in a way. To this day, the number 60 *still* makes baseball fans think of Babe Ruth. And the word "asterisk" will always make them think of Roger Maris.

Aftermath

In 1991, Commissioner Fay Vincent moved to finally drop Ruth's sixty homers from the record book. "I'm inclined," he said, "to support the single record thesis, and that is Maris hit more home runs in a season than anyone else." On September 4, 1991, baseball's committee on statistical accuracy voted to remove the invisible asterisk.

LEGALIZED SLAVERY?
Curt Flood and the Death of the Reserve System

"A peon remains a peon no matter how much money you give him."

That was the essence of Curt Flood's argument in 1969 when he single-handedly took on the baseball establishment and fought the game all the way to the Supreme Court in a struggle to overturn eighty years of tradition. History may someday place him alongside Babe Ruth and Jackie Robinson as one of the players who most significantly changed the game.

Flood's gripe was with the "reserve clause," a series of agreements that required every player to sign contracts that included an option on the following season. Players were thus bound for life to the team that originally signed them—unless they were traded, released, or sold. At contract time, it was take it or leave it. Unlike a guy in any other job—or in any other sport—a baseball player did not have the right to say "I quit" and seek employment elsewhere within his profession. Baseball had unlimited power to conduct its business, restrict competition, and discipline teams and players.

Flood referred to the reserve clause as "baseball's right to treat human beings like used cars." Others called it legalized slavery.

To the club owners and baseball establishment, the reserve clause prevented players from jumping from team to team and setting off bidding wars. They believed it kept the game running on an even keel.

The reserve clause was instituted back in the 1880s by Albert Spaulding and other early baseball authorities. In a 1922 landmark decision, the Supreme Court voted 9 to 0 to uphold the reserve clause. Justice Oliver Wendell Holmes explained that baseball "is not interstate business in the sense of the Sherman Act," so it was not subject to federal antitrust laws. Baseball was a game, not a business, making it immune to antitrust suits. This decision would be used to keep the reserve clause in place for most of baseball's history.

Curt Flood was not the first person to challenge the system. Danny Gardella filed suit in 1949, Jim Prendergast in 1952, and George Toolson in 1953. But all of them were mediocre players who got little support (Gardella played three years, Prendergast pitched ten games, and Toolson never reached the majors). All settled out of court, leaving the legality of the system in place. Gardella received $60,000 to drop his case.

Flood was a name player. He was signed in 1956 by the Cincinnati Reds, earning a salary of $4,000 his first year. He was traded in 1957 to St. Louis, where he hit .293 over the next twelve years and won seven Gold Gloves for his centerfield play. He appeared in three

All-Star games and three World Series. By 1969 he was one of the highest-paid players in the game, earning $90,000 a year.

After that season, the Cardinals traded him to the Philadelphia Phillies.* "Player trades are commonplace," Flood said later. "The unusual aspect of this one was that I refused to accept it."

During his years in St. Louis, he had established a home and business interests. He didn't want to uproot his life and go from a winning team to what he called "the least cheerful organization in the league." He said he would retire instead.

Thinking it over, Flood decided the problem wasn't Philadelphia. The problem was that he didn't believe any organization should be allowed to own a man and pass him around without his consent. An individual should have control over his destiny.

Flood called Marvin Miller, executive director of the Players Association, and told him he was considering taking baseball to court. Miller gave it to Flood straight—he would very possibly be sacrificing his future baseball career and any managerial or coaching jobs. A lawsuit could take years, and history indicated that Flood would most likely lose.

There was another reason for Flood not to file suit—the Phillies offered him $100,000, and all he had to do was play *baseball* for a year, for heaven's sake.

He went ahead anyway. "Win or lose, the baseball industry would never be the same," Flood said. "I would leave my mark."

The 800-member Players Association voted to support his case, and former U.S. Supreme Court Justice Arthur J. Goldberg agreed to argue it. Flood filed suit against Commissioner Bowie Kuhn, the presidents of both leagues, and the twenty-four team owners, demanding changes in the reserve system and $1.4 million in damages. On December 24, 1969, he sent the following letter to the commissioner:

> Dear Mr. Kuhn,
>   After twelve years in the major leagues, I do not feel that I am a piece of property to be bought and sold irrespective of

---

* For trivia buffs, Flood was traded with Tim McCarver, Joe Hoerner, and Byron Browne for Richie Allen, Cookie Rojas, and Jerry Johnson.

my wishes. I believe that any system which produces that result violates my basic rights as a citizen and is inconsistent with the laws of the United States and of the several States.

It is my desire to play baseball in 1970, and I am capable of playing. I have received a contract offer from the Philadelphia club, but I believe I have the right to consider offers from other clubs before making any decisions. I, therefore, request that you make known to all Major League clubs my feelings on this matter, and advise them of my availability for the 1970 season.

Curt Flood

Kuhn replied:

I certainly agree with you that you, as a human being, are not a piece of property to be bought and sold. This is fundamental in our society and I think obvious. However, I cannot see its applicability to the situation at hand.

The elimination of the reserve clause was a threat to the team owners, who were well aware that salaries would skyrocket if they had to compete with each other for players' services. In public, they explained that the game of baseball would be ruined without the reserve clause.

League presidents Charles Feeney and Joe Cronin issued a joint statement that claimed "chaotic results" would follow if the reserve clause was eliminated, and that "professional baseball would simply cease to exist." Bowie Kuhn said it would be "impossible to maintain the integrity of the game and maintain honesty among clubs and players."

To the baseball establishment—and many fans—Flood was being greedy. What more could a guy want out of life than to make six figures for hitting and throwing a ball?

The trial, which began in May 1970, was a parade of twenty-two witnesses—half of whom contended the reserve clause was evil (Hank Greenberg, Jackie Robinson, Bill Veeck, Pete Rozelle) and half of whom believed it to be the cornerstone of the game (Cronin, Feeney, Joe Garagiola). Not one active ballplayer showed up in court to support Curt Flood.

Interestingly, *Flood v. Kuhn* took place around the same time as

Roe v. Wade—men and women fighting for control over their own bodies.

As the case dragged on, Flood got restless. He had been advised not to play baseball because it would damage his case. His business ventures were failing, but if he were to start new ones it would give the appearance that he expected to lose in court.

He moved out of the country for a year—to Copenhagen. While there, he got a phone call from Bob Short, owner of the Washington Senators. Short had acquired Flood's contract by giving a player to the Phillies. He asked Flood whether he wanted to come home and play again. Short even agreed to give Flood a contract without a reserve clause in it.

Flood missed baseball. His lawyers advised that because he had already sat out a full year, playing again would no longer damage his case. Flood signed a one-year contract with Washington for $110,000. The commissioner insisted the reserve clause be in the contract.

Curt Flood, then thirty-three, returned to baseball. Unfortunately, he no longer had the skills, hitting .200 over thirteen games. Threats against his life and his children became serious. He decided to quit the game for good, moving to the Spanish island of Majorca and buying a tavern.

That's where he was when he got the news on June 6, 1972, that the Supreme Court had voted 5 to 3 against him. Justice Harry A. Blackmun acknowledged that the reserve clause was an "aberration" and an "anomaly," but refused to overturn the previous rulings in its favor. Even the Justices who had voted against Flood criticized the reserve clause, but said it was the responsibility of Congress to correct any injustice.

Flood had lost, but his effort raised the national consciousness on the issue and encouraged others. In the 1970s, the Players Association took a different strategy. Instead of going to court to prove that the reserve system violated antitrust laws, players were encouraged to play out their contracts and an option year (one year beyond the length of a contract), and then file a grievance to claim free agency.

The owners had already agreed that an independent arbiter—Peter

Seitz—would rule on all grievances between players and management. Before that, grievances had been decided by the Commissioner
of Baseball, who was handpicked by the owners.

In 1975, two players "played out their options"—Andy Mes-
sersmith of the Dodgers and Dave McNally, who was playing for
Montreal at the time. On December 23, Seitz ruled in their favor
and declared them free agents. The owners immediately fired Seitz,
but it was too late. The reserve clause, in effect, was dead. Suddenly
players were free to shop their services around.

Curt Flood does not receive credit, as Jackie Robinson did, for his
struggle to change the game of baseball.* He was portrayed as an
angry, ungrateful black man out to destroy the National Pastime—
peanuts, Cracker Jack, and our way of life. He went broke. His
marriage collapsed. He drank too much. He gave up everything he
had achieved to do what he considered was right. The pioneers are
always the ones with arrows in their backs.

Before we give the Nobel Prize to Curt Flood, it should be noted
that he was not a saint. He didn't have that much to lose when he
took on the baseball establishment—he was thirty-two and at the
end of his career anyway. Also, after playing just thirteen games for
Washington in 1970, it would have been honorable to refuse pay-
ment for a full year of work. He chose to keep the money.

The reserve clause died not because of lawsuits and salaries and
arbiters. It died because it was morally wrong, and the nation was
in a mood to correct injustices. The Flood case, which began in
1969, was baseball's small contribution to the Woodstock Generation. Along with blacks, women, and homosexuals, it was only
natural for baseball players to demand fair treatment.

"Change was in the wind," said Bowie Kuhn, the last man you
would expect to combine two Dylan protest songs in one sentence.

It had been said that without the reserve clause, players would
bounce from team to team, sending salaries soaring and alienating

---

* Flood, like Robinson, had to deal with racism. In 1964, a man brandishing a gun
threatened a real estate agent who was in the process of leasing a home to Flood and his
wife in a suburban white neighborhood in Alamo, California.

fans. Teams would go broke. Competition would die off because the best players would be snapped up by the wealthiest teams. The minor leagues would die off.

Some of this has happened. The most obvious change in baseball over the last twenty years has been in players' salaries. The average salary in 1975 was about $45,000. Today, it's around half a million dollars, and stars like Roger Clemens and Darryl Strawberry are pulling down an incredible $5 million a year. In 1991, 223 players made $1 million or more, and 44 made more than $3 million.

Even Curt Flood came to believe that the pendulum had swung too far in the other direction—free agency had gotten out of hand. The huge salaries are at least partly to blame for increased ticket prices, the game's recent drug problems, and the arrogance shown by contemporary baseball players.

More important, free agency has taken a piece of the game away. It's become harder to root, root, root for the home team, because half of the players may very well be on visiting teams next season.

"Baseball fans, of which I am one, want to believe in the myth of the home team," wrote columnist Russell Baker. "The home team is composed of players who year after year fight for the honor of the bleak, decaying city. . . . The home team may, in fact, be one of the few things that help you to continue tolerating this pretty awful hometown."

These illusions have been destroyed. In the past, we naively believed Mickey Mantle *was* New York, Carl Yastrzemski *was* Boston, Walter Johnson *was* Washington. In truth, the reason these players became associated with these towns was that they were bound to the teams there by the reserve clause.

Free agency has proved once and for all that baseball is most definitely a business as much as it is a game. We like to believe that ballplayers play for the love of it, but the sad truth is that playing baseball is a job like any other. Players have become itinerant entertainers who go where the best gigs take them. Fans have been forced to face this reality.

Killing the reserve clause didn't kill baseball. TV revenue, endorsement contracts, salaries, and merchandizing have become enormous, leading analysts to say the game is more popular than it ever was. But now that popularity is measured in dollars, not love.

Aftermath

Essentially blackballed by baseball, Curt Flood has held a number of positions, including guitar teacher, cartoonist, sportscaster, and commissioner of Little League baseball in Oakland, California. He is married to actress Judy Pace and lives in Los Angeles.

COLLUSION
The Big Fix

The collusion scandal of 1985–1987 remains a vague, complicated incident that most fans never understood when it was happening and forgot as soon as it was over. It was so easy to ignore boring newspaper articles on that legal mess when you could read about how the Mets, Dodgers, Cubs or Tony Gwynn did last night.

But according to Marvin Miller, former director of the Major League Baseball Players Association, collusion was "the greatest scandal in baseball history."

With the reserve clause dead and free agency in place in the late 1970s, aggressive owners like George Steinbrenner began doling out huge sums of money to improve their teams. Dave Winfield got $20 million for ten years. Bruce Sutter got $10 million for six years.

Somebody asked Joe DiMaggio what he would say to George Steinbrenner if he was a free agent. Joltin' Joe replied, "George, you and me are about to become partners!"

It became clear to all the owners that it was going to cost a lot more to run a competitive major-league baseball team than ever before. That's a powerfully distressing thought to a man or woman who has millions of dollars and wants millions more. If only there was some way (the owners must have wondered) to live with free agency without having to pay an arm and a leg for free agents.

There was one way to accomplish that. Nobody ever said anybody *had* to bid on free agents. If all the owners were to agree *not* to compete with each other to sign free agents, the players would be forced to sign with their old teams again. Salaries would go down and the owners would regain the control over the game they had before Curt Flood came along and opened his big mouth.

That, of course, would go against the spirit of free enterprise. It is also exactly what happened.

The Random House Dictionary of the English Language defines "collusion" as "a secret understanding between two or more persons prejudicial to another, or a secret understanding to appear as adversaries though in agreement."

Something funny happened to players who filed for free agency in 1985. After slugger Kirk Gibson led the Detroit Tigers to the World Championship with twenty-nine home runs and ninety-seven RBIs, not a single team other than the Tigers made him an offer. And no team wanted Gibson's teammate Jack Morris, who won two games in the World Series and was one of the best pitchers in the game. Phil Niekro received no offers after a 16–12 season. Carlton Fisk expected to get some interest after hitting 37 home runs and driving in 107 runs. He got just one offer, and it was later withdrawn.

Things were even fishier the next season. The game's top stars who tested the free agency waters—Ron Guidry, Tim Raines, Bob Horner, Andre Dawson, Lance Parrish, Rich Gedman, and Bob Boone—did not receive a single competitive offer. These were the best players in the game, and nobody wanted them.

Most of them signed up with their old teams again. Parrish took a $50,000 pay cut. Dawson went to the Cubs for half of what he had been earning with the Expos. Horner went to play in Japan.

It was more of the same in 1987, when salaries for major-league players actually decreased (2 percent) for the first time in years. Suddenly and coincidentally, every single major-league team decided it was no longer interested in signing free agents. Even George Steinbrenner wasn't pulling out his checkbook anymore.

Either it was an incredible coincidence, or the owners had agreed among themselves that they weren't going to bid on each other's free agents. This would be in clear violation of Article 18H of the player/owner labor agreement, which prohibits "concerted action" among teams or free agent players.

"It's just a trend," explained Commissioner Peter Ueberroth. The catch phrase the owners used was that they were exercising "fiscal restraint."

In February 1987, the Major League Baseball Players Association filed a grievance charging that the owners had acted "in concert with one another" to knock back salaries. They commissioned a study that found the players lost between $70 and $90 million due to collusion—and that was just for the free agents of 1985.

Various smoking guns were found, many of them pointing in the direction of Ueberroth. Kirk Gibson's agent said the Altanta Braves were very interested in Gibson on a Monday, but backed off right after Ueberroth met with owner Ted Turner later in the week. At a meeting in December 1986, Ueberroth told general managers to share "information about who was doing what about what players and that sort of thing, what the status of negotiations are . . ." There was a memo dated October 16, 1985, from retiring director of player relations Lee MacPhail that advised clubs against frantic free agent signing. Ueberroth requested that it be given serious consideration. It seemed more than a coincidence that a year after he had become commissoner, all the free agent dollars suddenly dried up.

It was front-page news on September 22, 1987, when arbitrator Thomas T. Roberts ruled that baseball's club owners *had* acted in concert to block the movement of free agents and dilute their bargaining power. The owners, it was revealed, had even used a "data-bank" to compare their negotiations with free agents.

Roberts's ruling was a crushing, humiliating defeat for the owners. They were required to pay $10.5 million to the 1985 free agents. When all the millions had been counted up for 1986 and 1987, the owners agreed to pay $280 million plus interest to players disadvantaged by collusion. That didn't include any penalty—just the money the players would have earned if the owners hadn't conspired against them.

It was also decided that many of the players who signed with their old teams could be free agents again if they wished. A week later Kirk Gibson signed a three-year, $4.5-million contract with the Dodgers. At the press conference introducing him to Los Angeles, he said he had wanted to play for Detroit his entire career, "but if it wasn't for the owners colluding in 1985, changing the market, so to speak, right in my face, I wouldn't be here today."

To most of us, arguments over whether a player deserves to earn $2 million or $3 million a year sound absurd. They're all million-aires! How can they complain when *we're* struggling to put food on the table? The collusion scandal sounded like petty whining among men who were overpaid even before they were colluded against.

But beyond the millions of dollars, collusion was a real scandal in that it damaged the cherished "integrity of the game." By agree-ing not to bid on free agents, the owners had committed sport's most heinous sin—not trying to win.

"Wasn't the Black Sox scandal of 1919 a case of players taking money for playing not to win?" wrote Marvin Miller in *A Whole Different Ball Game: The Sport and Business of Baseball.* "This scandal was not about just eight men on one club over an eight-game series; it involved all the owners, all the general managers, all the club officials, both league presidents, and two baseball commissioners—*over three seasons. . . .* It was undeniably an agree-ment not to field the best team possible, tantamount to fixing, not just games, but entire pennant races, including post-season series."

If there were any doubts about the existence of collusion, they vanished as soon as the scandal was exposed. Caught with their hands in the cookie jar, the owners—who had said they were losing money—once again opened up their wallets and spent wildly, en-abling players like Jose Canseco, Roger Clemens, Dwight Gooden, and Darryl Strawberry to become $5-million-a-year men.

UMPIRE SCANDALS
Nobody's Perfect

Considering that baseball has been played professionally for nearly a century and a half, it's remarkable that only one major-league umpire has been caught taking a bribe to sway the outcome of a game.

That was back in 1882, when William G. Thompson, mayor of Detroit and owner of the local National League team, the Wolver-ines, suspected that umpire Dick Higham was in collusion with gamblers. Detectives were hired to investigate him, and they came up with two letters which implicated the umpire. Higham's code, it was discovered, was to write "buy all the lumber you can" if the game was fixed for Detroit to lose.

Higham claimed that he had never seen the letters before, but the National League had a handwriting expert examine them and it was determined that Higham was the author. He was expelled from baseball for life and, logically, became a bookie. Previously, Higham had been known as the first umpire to wear a face mask.

Some other hanky-panky has taken place through the years. In 1972 federal agents raided the home of a maître d'hôtel at a Baltimore restaurant, on suspicion of bookmaking, lottery, and maintaining a gambling establishment. They found three address books containing the names of eleven major-league umpires. Telephone numbers of two of the umpires were in the book, and addresses for the other nine. Reports quoted the maître d' as saying the umpires were part of "my Christmas card list."

A probe by Commissioner Bowie Kuhn's office found no evidence of wrongdoing on the part of any umpires. The names of the eleven men were never revealed.

The most titillating umpire scandal took place in 1960, when two young Baltimore nightclub dancers set up and attempted to extort money from American League umpires Ed Runge and Bill McKinley.

Runge testified at a magistrate's hearing that he and McKinley went to a motel in the Maryland suburbs of Washington with two women—Mary Jane Spencer, twenty-one, and Helen Ela, twenty-four; Runge and McKinley were fifty and forty-two, respectively. The young women had met the umpires while working in a Baltimore nightclub and had been instructed by their employer to go out with them. What took place in the motel was not reported, but it seems unlikely that the foursome discussed ground-rules.

As it turned out, Spencer was engaged to be married. Her fiancée, Donald E. Anderson, approached the umpires with his business partner Robert Waldron and said that unless each of the umpires paid him $2,000, he would damage their reputations. Two meetings took place in Washington-area restaurants.

The umpires informed the police, who staked out both meetings and arrested Anderson and Waldron at the second one, in Baltimore's Friendship International Airport. Both men were indicted for unlawfully conspiring to extort, as was Mary Jane Spencer.

The umpires went back to work making simpler life decisions, such as "safe" versus "out and "fair" versus "foul."

Another sex scandal came out in 1988, when National League umpire Dave Pallone was investigated in connection with a sex ring involving teenage boys in Saratoga Springs, New York. Pallone was cleared but thrown out of baseball anyway when he publicly admitted his homosexuality (see chapter 1).

But the most unexpected scandal involving an umpire occurred very recently. On April 24, 1990, twenty-four-year National League veteran Bob Engel walked into a store in his hometown of Bakersfield, California. He removed seven boxes of Score baseball cards from a display and walked to a corner of the store. There he pulled a brown paper bag from the waistband of his pants and put the boxes in the bag. As he was walking out of the store, a security guard stopped him. He was arrested for commercial burglary and petty theft. The 4,180 baseball cards in the bag were estimated to be worth $143.98.

When the story hit the papers, the managers of a Costco Warehouse store in California told police that in January, Engel had tried to stuff fifty packs of baseball cards in his pockets in that store. The incident had not been reported to the police at the time.

Engel, fifty-six, pleaded no contest, underwent counseling, and retired from baseball. His sentence was three years on probation and forty hours of community service.

When asked why he stole the cards, Engel told police, sensibly, "To collect and trade."

There have been many more umpire scandals than these, but we never hear about them. In 1991, two umpires were put on probation when they were caught placing small bets on sporting events through a bookie, but the scandal was hushed up and their names never revealed. It is the commissioner's opinion that an umpire's authority would be undercut if disciplinary actions against him were made public.

APPENDIX 1

Hall of Famers

Ty Cobb: Charged, along with Tris Speaker, with arranging a fixed game and betting on it in 1919. He was exonerated, but was fired as manager and never hired again. A terror off the field, he knifed a man on at least one occasion and pistol-whipped another. He has been described by historians as psychotic and paranoid.

Babe Ruth: A nonstop sex machine who patronized prostitutes, was hit with numerous paternity suits, and contracted venereal disease. He also loved to gamble, and would wager as much as $25,000 on a single horse race. He nearly killed himself more than once by driving recklessly and smashing his cars.

Ban Johnson (American League president): He suffered a breakdown after being humiliated by Commissioner Landis in 1926, collapsed, and showed signs of mental problems before being relieved of his duties.

John McGraw: Heavy gambler. Was arrested in 1904 for unlicensed public gambling. Was partners in a Manhattan poolroom with Arnold Rothstein, big-time gambler and money man behind the Black Sox Scandal. McGraw won $400 betting on the 1905 World Series.

Tris Speaker: Charged, with Ty Cobb, of arranging a fixed game and betting on it in 1919. He was exonerated, but was fired as manager and never hired again. Member of the Ku Klux Klan.

Grover Cleveland Alexander: The greatest alcoholic ever to play the game. His wife had to hide her perfume because she was afraid he'd drink it.

Cap Anson: Confirmed bigot who helped kick black players out of baseball and erect the color barrier that would keep them out for fifty years. Once jailed for drunkenness.

Charles Comiskey: Penny-pinching owner of the Chicago White Sox whose ridiculously low salaries contributed to his team's throwing the 1919 World Series.

Albert Spaulding: Driving force behind the myth that Abner Doubleday invented baseball. Ruthless and unscrupulous businessman.

Rogers Hornsby: Compulsive gambler who was sued by a bookie for welshing on $92,000 in losses. He was traded several times and lost at least two managerial positions because of his heavy betting. Member of the Ku Klux Klan.

Ed Delahanty: Drunk as a skunk, he was put off a train in 1903. When he tried to walk across a bridge, he fell over Niagara Falls and was swept to his death.

George Kelly: Named in O'Connell/Dolan gambling scandal in 1924. Cleared of any wrongdoing.

Michael "King" Kelly: Drank himself to death at age thirty-six.

Johnny Evers: Suffered a nervous breakdown, 1911.

Rube Waddell: Arrested for nonsupport, bigamy, and assaulting his father-in-law. Accused of accepting a $17,000 bribe from New York gamblers to sit out the 1905 World Series. The accusation was never investigated.

Ray Shalk: Admitted taking up a pool of money in 1917 to pay Detroit players as a gift for beating the Red Sox.

Eddie Collins: Admitted taking up a pool of money in 1917 to pay Detroit players as a gift for beating the Red Sox.

Frank Frisch: Named in O'Connell/Dolan gambling scandal in 1924. Cleared of any wrongdoing.

Wilbert Robinson: With John McGraw, he introduced a professional gambler to Boston Red Sox catcher Lou Criger. The gambler would later offer Criger $12,000 to throw the first World Series in 1903.

Mickey Cochrane: Suffered a nervous breakdown, 1936.

Jimmy Foxx: Heavy drinker.

Paul Waner: Heavy drinker.

Dizzy Dean: Named as co-conspirator in a 1970 federal probe into illegal gambling.

Rabbit Maranville: Admitted alcohol abuser.

Joe DiMaggio: Associate of fight manager and gambler Joe Gould in the 1940s. Obsessed with ex-wife Marilyn Monroe, in 1954 he broke down what he thought was her apartment door. The terrified woman inside agreed to an out-of-court settlement of $7,500.

Ted Williams: Was fined $5,000 for spitting at fans.

Rube Marquard: Arrested and convicted of scalping tickets to the 1920 World Series.

Whitey Ford: Admitted cheating with spitballs, mudballs, and scuffballs during his career.

Mickey Mantle: Forced to leave baseball when he accepted a job with Del Webb's Claridge Casino Hotel in Atlantic City. Reinstated in 1985. Known for being a heavy drinker.

Larry MacPhail: Longtime friend of handicapper Memphis Engleberg, MacPhail entertained him and casino owner Connie Immerman in his private box in 1947. Leo Durocher complained, and *Durocher* was thrown out of baseball for the year.

Willie Mays: Forced to leave baseball when he accepted a job with Bally's Park Place casino in Atlantic City. Reinstated in 1985. Also accused during the Pittsburgh drug trial of using a liquid amphetamine.

Hack Wilson: Penniless, he drank himself to death in 1948. The National League paid for a coffin so that he would not be buried in a pauper's grave.

Rube Foster: Became mentally imbalanced and was permanently institutionalized in 1926.

Frank Robinson: Was arrested and pleaded guilty to carrying a concealed weapon in 1961.

Juan Marichal: Attacked Los Angeles Dodger John Roseboro in 1965, repeatedly slamming a bat against the catcher's head.

Don Drysdale: Arrested for drunken driving, 1991. Pleaded no contest.

Willie Stargell: Accused in the 1985 Pittsburgh drug trial of distributing amphetamines.

Ferguson Jenkins: Arrested in 1980 for possession of marijuana, hashish, and cocaine. Convicted.

Gaylord Perry: Admitted cheating on the field throughout his career. "I reckon I tried everything on the old apple but salt and pepper and chocolate sauce toppin'," he wrote in his autobiography, *Me and the Spitter.*

APPENDIX 2

Banned for Life

Thirty-one Men Out: The Permanently Ineligible List

Paul Carter: Chicago Cubs pitcher accused of fixing games in 1920.

Hal Chase: Great first baseman and incorrigible gambler. Banished in 1919.

Eddie Cicotte: One of the Chicago White Sox (Black Sox) who threw the 1919 World Series.

William Cox: Phillies owner, made bets on his own team in 1943.

Bill Craver: Involved in the Louisville gambling scandal of 1877.

Jim Devlin: Involved in the Louisville gambling scandal of 1877.

Cozy Dolan: With Jimmy O'Connell, offered $500 to Phillies shortstop Heinie Sand if he would "not bear down" in a 1924 game.

Phil Douglas: Wrote a letter to Les Mann of St. Louis offering to desert the New York Giants for money.

Jean Dubuc: Involved with Hal Chase and Heinie Zimmerman in fixing games. Banned in 1919.

Happy Felsch: One of the Chicago White Sox (Black Sox) who threw the 1919 World Series.

Ray Fisher: Banned for contract jumping in 1921.

Horace Fogel: Phillies owner, banned after accusing National League umpires of fixing the pennant in favor of the New York Giants.

Chick Gandil: One of the Chicago White Sox (Black Sox) who threw the 1919 World Series.

Joe Gedeon: Second baseman for St. Louis and friend of Swede Risberg, involved in the Black Sox Scandal of 1919.

George Hall: Involved in the Louisville gambling scandal of 1877.

Claude Hendrix: As a pitcher for the Cubs, agreed to throw a game in August 1920.

Richard Higham: A National League umpire in 1882 bought off by gamblers.

Joe Jackson: One of the Chicago White Sox (Black Sox) who threw the 1919 World Series.

Benny Kauff: Accused of throwing games, but was thrown out of baseball when he was charged with auto theft and receiving stolen property in 1920.

Dutch Leonard: Dug his own grave by admitting he threw a game in 1919 with Ty Cobb and Tris Speaker. Cobb and Speaker were exonerated.

Lee Magee: Involved with Hal Chase and Heinie Zimmerman in fixing games. Banned in 1919.

Fred McMullin: One of the Chicago White Sox (Black Sox) who threw the 1919 World Series.

Al Nichols: Involved in the Louisville gambling scandal of 1877.

Jimmy O'Connell: With Cozy Dolan, offered $500 to Phillies shortstop Heinie Sand if he would "not bear down" in a 1924 game.

Eugene Paulette: Accepted gifts from St. Louis gamblers in 1919.

Swede Risberg: One of the Chicago White Sox (Black Sox) who threw the 1919 World Series.

Pete Rose: Cincinnati Reds manager and former star, accused of betting on baseball—including the Reds—in 1989.

George Steinbrenner: New York Yankee owner, paid $40,000 to convicted gambler Howard Spira. Banned in 1990.

Buck Weaver: One of the Chicago White Sox (Black Sox) who threw the 1919 World Series.

Claude Williams: One of the Chicago White Sox (Black Sox) who threw the 1919 World Series.

Heinie Zimmerman: Involved with Hal Chase in fixing games. Banned in 1919.

BIBLIOGRAPHY

I didn't make all this stuff up, I wasn't there when it happened, and it didn't come from personal interviews ("Say, Joe, tell me about the time you were brought up on morals charges in 'sixty-eight").

By and large, the information in this book was collected by combing new and old newspaper articles, magazines, and books. I gratefully acknowledge the following.

Periodicals

The *New York Times* and *Sports Illustrated* were invaluable sources, and relevant material was also found in *Time, Newsweek, The Sporting News, Jet, New York, People, Life, The Saturday Evening Post, Collier's, Sport, American Mercury, American Magazine, Literary Digest, Rolling Stone, American Health, Gentlemen's Quarterly, Business Week, Ebony, Mac-Lean's, The New Republic, Ladies' Home Journal, Penthouse, Smithsonian, The New Yorker, The National Pastime, Baseball Research Journal, Esquire, Baseball, Spaulding's Official Baseball Guide, True*, the *Boston Globe*, the *Boston Herald*, the *Philadelphia Inquirer*, the *St. Paul Pioneer Press*, the *Los Angeles Times*, and the *Chicago Tribune*.

Books

Aaron, Hank. *I Had a Hammer* (New York: HarperCollins, 1991).
Alexander, Charles C. *Ty Cobb* (New York: Oxford University Press, 1984).
———. *John McGraw* (New York: Viking Penguin, 1988).
Allen, Maury. *Bo: Pitching and Wooing* (New York: Dial Press, 1973).
———. *Damn Yankee* (New York: Times Books, 1980).
———. *Roger Maris: A Man for All Seasons* (New York: Donald I. Fine, 1986).
Asinof, Eliot. *Eight Men Out* (New York: Holt, Rinehart & Winston, 1963).

Astor, Gerald. *The Baseball Hall of Fame 50th Anniversary Book* (New York: Prentice Hall, 1988).

Boone, Robert S., and Gerald Grunska. *Hack* (Highland Park, IL: Highland Press, 1978).

Bouton, Jim. *Ball Four* (New York: Dell, 1970).

Bowman, John, and Joel Zoss. *Diamonds in the Rough: The Untold History of Baseball* (New York: Macmillan, 1989).

Braine, Tim, and John Stravinsky. *The Not-So-Great Moments in Sports* (New York: William Morrow, 1986).

Cepeda, Orlando, and Robert Markus. *High and Inside: Orlando Cepeda's Story* (New York: Icarus, 1983).

Cobb, Ty. *My Life in Baseball: The True Record* (Garden City, NY: Doubleday, 1961).

Connor, Anthony J. *Voices from Cooperstown* (New York: Macmillan, 1982).

Cosell, Howard. *What's Wrong with Sports* (New York: Simon & Schuster, 1991).

Creamer, Robert. *Babe: The Legend Comes to Life* (New York: Simon & Schuster, 1974).

Dark, Alvin, and John Underwood. *When in Doubt, Fire the Manager* (New York: Dutton, 1980).

Deutsch, Jordan A., Richard M. Cohen, Roland T. Johnson, and David S. Neft. *The Scrapbook History of Baseball* (New York: Bobbs-Merrill, 1975).

Dickson, Paul. *Baseball's Greatest Quotations* (New York: HarperCollins, 1991).

Duren, Ryne. *The Comeback* (Dayton, OH: Lorenz Press, 1978).

Durocher, Leo. *Nice Guys Finish Last* (New York: Simon & Schuster, 1975).

Ford, Whitey. *Slick* (New York: William Morrow, 1987).

Frick, Ford. *Games, Asterisks and People* (New York: Crown, 1973).

Golenbock, Peter. *The Forever Boys* (New York: Carol Publishing, 1991).

Hall, Donald. *Dock Ellis in the Country of Baseball* (New York: Simon & Schuster, 1976).

Hernandez, Keith, and Mike Bryan. *If at First* (New York: Penguin, 1986).

Holway, John B. *Blackball Stars* (Westport, CT: Meckler Books, 1988).

Howe, Steve. *Between the Lines* (Grand Rapids, MI: Masters Press, 1989).

James, Bill. *The Bill James Historical Baseball Abstract* (New York: Villard, 1986).

Kahn, Roger. *Joe and Marilyn* (New York: William Morrow, 1986).

Kaufman, Louis, Barbara Fitzgerald, and Tom Sewell. *Moe Berg: Athlete, Scholar, Spy* (Boston: Little, Brown & Company, 1974).

Kelley, Kitty. *His Way: The Unauthorized Biography of Frank Sinatra* (New York: Bantam, 1986).

Kuhn, Bowie. *Hardball: The Education of a Baseball Commissioner* (New York: Random House, 1987).

LeFlore, Ron. *Breakout: From Prison to the Big Leagues* (New York: Harper & Row, 1978).

Levine, Peter. *A. G. Spaulding and the Rise of Baseball* (New York: Oxford University Press, 1985).

Lieb, Fred. *Baseball As I Have Known It* (New York: Coward, McCann & Geoghegan Inc., 1977).

Mann, Arthur. *Baseball Confidential: Secret History of the War Among Chandler, Durocher, MacPhail and Rickey* (New York: David McKay Company, 1951).

Mantle, Mickey. *The Mick* (New York: Doubleday, 1985).

Martin, Billy, and Peter Golenbock. *Number 1* (New York: Delacorte, 1980).

Mazer, Bill. *Bill Mazer's Amazin' Baseball Book* (New York: Zebra Books, 1990).

McCallum, John. *The Tiger Wore Spikes* (New York: A. S. Barnes & Co., 1956).

McLain, Denny. *Nobody's Perfect* (New York: Dial Press, 1975).

Miller, Marvin. *A Whole Different Ball Game: The Sport and Business of Baseball* (New York: Carol Publishing, 1991).

Nettles, Graig, and Peter Golenbock. *Balls* (New York: Putnam, 1984).

Okrent, Daniel, and Harris Lewine. *The Ultimate Baseball Book* (Boston: Houghton Mifflin, 1979).

Pallone, Dave. *Behind the Mask: My Double Life in Baseball* (New York: Viking, 1990).

Peary, Danny. *Cult Baseball Players* (New York: Simon & Schuster, 1990).

Pepitone, Joe. *Joe, You Coulda Made Us Proud* (Chicago: Playboy Press, 1975).

Peterson, Robert W. *Only the Ball Was White* (Englewood Cliffs, NJ: Prentice Hall, 1970).

Piersall, Jimmy, and Al Hirshberg. *Fear Strikes Out* (Boston: Atlantic Monthly Press, 1955).

Ritter, Lawrence. *The Glory of Their Times* (New York: Random House, 1966).

Rogosin, Donn. *Invisible Men: Life in Baseball's Negro Leagues* (New York: Atheneum, 1983).

Rose, Pete, and Roger Kahn. *Pete Rose: My Story* (New York: Macmillan, 1989).

Rust, Edna, and Art Rust Jr. *Art Rust's Illustrated History of the Black Athlete* (Garden City, NY: Doubleday, 1985).

Ruth, Mrs. Babe. *The Babe and I* (Englewood Cliffs, NJ: Prentice Hall, 1959).

Schoor, Gene. *Joe DiMaggio: A Biography* (New York: Doubleday, 1980).

Seymour, Harold. *Baseball: The Early Years* (New York: Oxford University Press, 1960).

———. *Baseball: The Golden Years* (New York: Oxford University Press, 1971).

Shlain, Bruce. *Oddballs* (New York: Penguin, 1989).

Sifakis, Carl. *The Encyclopedia of Gambling* (New York: Facts on File, 1990).

Smith, Norman Lewis. *The Return of Billy the Kid* (New York: Coward, McCann & Geoghegan, 1977).

Smith, Robert. *Babe Ruth's America* (New York: Thomas Y. Crowell, 1974).

Sokolove, Michael Y. *Hustle: The Myth, Life, and Lies of Pete Rose* (New York: Simon & Schuster, 1990).

Sowell, Mike. *The Pitch That Killed* (New York: Macmillan, 1989).

Summers, Anthony. *Goddess: The Secret Lives of Marilyn Monroe* (New York: Macmillan, 1985).

Thorn, John, and Pete Palmer. *Total Baseball* (New York: Warner Books, 1989).

Voigt, David Quentin. *American Baseball: From Gentleman's Sport to the Commissioner System* (University of Oklahoma Press, 1966).

Vlasich, James A. *A Legend for the Legendary* (Bowling Green, OH: Bowling Green State University Popular Press, 1990).

Wallechinsky, David, and Irving Wallace. *The People's Almanac* (Garden City, NY: Doubleday, 1975).

Winfield, Dave. *Winfield: A Player's Life* (New York: Norton, 1988).

Wolff, Rick. *The Baseball Encyclopedia* (New York: Macmillan, 1990).

INDEX